W9-BZV-194

Journey to the Ice Age

PETER L. STORCK

Journey to the Ice Age:
Discovering an Ancient World

Published by UBC Press
in association with
the Royal Ontario Museum

17 16 15 14 13 12 11 10 09 08 07 06 05   5 4 3 2

Printed in Canada on acid-free paper

National Library of Canada Cataloguing in Publication

Storck, Peter L., 1940-
    Journey to the Ice Age : discovering an ancient world / Peter L. Storck.

Includes bibliographical references and index.
ISBN 0-7748-1028-9

    1. Storck, Peter L., 1940- 2. Royal Ontario Museum. 3. Paleo-Indians – Ontario.
4. Ontario – Antiquities. 5. Archaeologists – Ontario – Biography. 6. Paleontologists – Ontario – Biography. I. Royal Ontario Museum. II. Title.

E78.O5S763 2004   971.3   C2003-907093-X

Canadä

UBC Press gratefully acknowledges the financial support for our publishing program of the Government of Canada through the Book Publishing Industry Development Program (BPIDP), and of the Canada Council for the Arts, and the British Columbia Arts Council.

Published by UBC Press in association with the Royal Ontario Museum.

The Royal Ontario Museum gratefully acknowledges the Louise Hawley Stone Charitable Trust within the ROM Foundation for its generous support of this publication.

Printed and bound in Canada by Friesens
Set in DTL Albertina and MetaPlus
Editor: Camilla Jenkins
Designer: George Vaitkunas
Cartographer: Eric Leinberger
Proofreader: Gail Copeland
Indexer: Patricia Buchanan

UBC Press
The University of British Columbia
2029 West Mall
Vancouver, BC V6T 1Z2
604-822-5959 / Fax: 604-822-6083
www.ubcpress.ca

Contents

Maps, Tables, Illustrations, Photographs

Illustrations

Photographs

ACKNOWLEDGMENTS

THIS BOOK IS TWO THINGS. First, it is the story of my work as an archaeologist and my search for an ancient people. From that personal story the book moves outward to encompass the work of other archaeologists and scientists across North America also involved in the search for the founding peoples who discovered and colonized the New World at the end of the Ice Age. Thus the book flows back and forth between the personal story of one search and the collective story of many searches, the personal story revealing a more intimate glimpse into the search process and the collective story revealing the significance of individual contributions to the whole. Because of this particular approach – the autobiographical combined with more conventional science writing – I believe that perhaps I can be more comprehensive in these acknowledgments than might otherwise be appropriate, and mention individuals who influenced my becoming as well as those who helped me with my work.

I should start at university and with my teachers, for that experience and those people have shaped much of my life. The two teachers who had the greatest influence on me happened to be teaching courses in introductory archaeology and physical anthropology at a time I happened also to be failing courses in pre-commerce, economics, and chemistry. These teachers, Chester S. Chard and William S. Laughlin, introduced me to the human and pre-human past, subjects that I bonded to like a duckling to its mother. For these subjects became a sort of intellectual home for me, first nurturing me at a time of crisis and then preparing me for a life I hadn't previously imagined. Other teachers entered my life: archaeologist David A. Baerreis, cultural anthropologist Homer Barnett, paleoclimatologist Reid Bryson, geographer Karl W. Butzer, Pleistocene geologist Robert F. Black, palynologist Louis Maher, Paleolithic archaeologist Hansjürgen Müller-Beck, zoologist William Reeder, human paleontologist John T. Robinson, botanist Jonathan Sauer, and Maya archaeologist J. Eric Thompson – a remarkable conjunction of scholars who were leaders in their fields, or about to become so. And late in this roster of people came archaeologist James B. Stoltman, a young scholar in his first teaching position and perhaps the first teacher with whom I had any significant reciprocal relationship. For although he was my advisor I also became his first doctoral student, an important milestone in the career of an unproven tenure-track professor. I must also mention one teacher I never met, Loren Eiseley, whose reflections on archaeology, evolution, and the human condition were deeply evocative and inspiring to me at a time of intellectual bonding and whose writing has power over me to this day. Unknowingly, these teachers shaped the person as well as the would-be scholar, for my interests and life work have become inextricably bound up with who I am.

After university I continued to benefit from other teachers. One of the more important was the late A. Douglas Tushingham, chief archaeologist at the Royal Ontario Museum (ROM) and later a member of the board of trustees and an honorary trustee. I would like to acknowledge Doug's key role in the decision to hire me at the ROM and for his support during those early years when I had such difficulty finding a way into the research I wanted to do. I am also grateful for his imagination in establishing in May 1965 the ROM *Archaeological Newsletter,* which he asked all field archaeologists working on ROM projects to write. Doug thought that newsletters should be written from the field, should "have an immediacy, human interest, and an atmosphere of enthusiasm ... [and should] ... make you feel that you are actually present on the excavation." I had not been trained to write this way when I came to the museum fresh from graduate school in 1969. But I soon came to enjoy writing for the public and discovered that having to write in non-technical language often gave me a clearer understanding of what I was doing, or supposed to be doing. Plain writing has a way of cleansing the mind. Over time I came to feel that the newsletters signified benchmarks in my work. I couldn't foresee that they would also help structure this book; indeed, without them I might not have written it. In a sense this book is therefore Doug Tushingham's legacy to me. And, through me, to you the reader.

I would also like to acknowledge my colleague in Ontario archaeology at the ROM, the late Walter Kenyon, who not only supported my work but gracefully listened to what I'm sure were frequently very naïve remarks from a junior scholar and younger, less experienced man.

Gary Sealey and Bob Bowes, staff in the former Ontario Department of Lands and Forests in the 1970s, were wonderfully supportive at a critical time in my work. Gary Sealey arranged for me to work in Killarney Provincial Park during my first field season in Ontario. Somewhat later, Bob Bowes gave me an opportunity to fly over the full length of the Niagara Escarpment in a helicopter and photograph prominent valleys I was considering for archaeological work.

The guidance and assistance I received as a new assistant curator at the ROM and a new field archaeologist in Ontario was just a beginning. Over the next thirty years, I was also to receive much help from a wide variety of colleagues in archaeology and the natural sciences. Many of these people are mentioned in the text and newsletters but I would like to take this opportunity to thank them as a group for agreeing to take part in my work and making it much more significant because of their unique contributions. I would also like to add the names of a few colleagues not mentioned in the text: Robert Ethier, Bob Gray, David Loftus, and Phil Kor of the Ontario Ministry of Natural Resources. Without their support I could not have conducted my field project in the Kolapore uplands in the 1990s. I should like to add to these the name of Paul Karrow of the University of Waterloo, a Pleistocene geologist who helped me immeasurably through his writing, which proved vital in my fieldwork, and through his direct advice. Many others, fellow students, colleagues, administrators, and members of the general public also helped me greatly over the years. I hope they are pleased with the private knowledge that they helped with this book, even though their contributions remain anonymous.

I would like to thank the following individuals for commenting on specific sections of the book, in essence for helping me to keep my facts straight and up to date. While I almost invariably made the changes they suggested, they are not, of course, responsible for the way in which I put the facts together. I hope they approve. They are: archaeologist Daniel Amick, Loyola University; archaeologist Thomas Andrews, Prince of Wales Northern Heritage Centre; Pleistocene geologist Peter Barnett, Ontario Geological Survey; archaeologist Robson Bonnichsen, Center for the Study of the First Americans, Texas A and M University; physical anthropologist Jerome Cybalski, Canadian Museum of Civilization; paleontologist Daniel Fisher, Museum of Paleontology, University of Michigan; archaeologist Jack Hofman, University of Kansas; avocational archaeologists Michael Kirby and Christine Kirby, Ontario Archaeological Society; paleontologist Richard Laub, Buffalo Museum of Science; paleobotanist John H. McAndrews, Royal Ontario Museum; paleoecologist Alan Morgan, University of Waterloo; archaeologist Richard Morlan, Canadian Museum of Civilization; archaeologist David Overstreet, Great Lakes Archaeological Research Center; paleontologist Jeffrey Saunders, Illinois State Museum; archaeologist Arthur Spiess, Maine State Historic Preservation Commission; consulting archaeologist Andrew Stewart, Toronto; physical anthropologist Christy G. Turner II, Arizona State University; geologist Peter H. von Bitter, Royal Ontario Museum; consulting archaeologist Ronald F. Williamson, Archaeological Services Incorporated, Toronto; and two reviewers of the book for the ROM and UBC Press, archaeologist Bradley T. Lepper, Ohio Historical Society, and archaeologist Robert McGhee, Canadian Museum of Civilization.

Other scholars contributed to this book by answering questions or even lending me their books (in one instance, the same book several times): geologist Nick Eyles, University of Toronto; invertebrate paleontologist David Rudkin, Royal Ontario Museum; and geologist Vincent Vertolli, Royal Ontario Museum.

Rosemary Prevec conducted the initial analysis of the Udora animal bone. Surprisingly, Arthur Speiss was able to take some of the identifications a bit further. I am grateful to both for giving a sense of completion to one of the themes in my work and to Arthur specifically for an extra measure of wonder in the arctic fox.

I would like to thank Sharon Hick, former librarian at the Royal Ontario Museum, for helping me to find some published papers I did not have and for doing it in such a joyful way. Heidi Ritscher, through her wonderfully competent work organizing the collections from my last field project at the ROM and then her successful MA thesis on that material, unknowingly helped me make the transition to work as a curator emeritus.

Ken Lister, head of the Department of Anthropology at the ROM, and Mima Kapches, curator, facilitated access to the collections, often with little warning from me, so I could retrieve artifacts for those inevitable photographs I decided I must have. And Angela Raljic was wonderfully helpful in co-ordinating everything.

The studio photographs of artifacts were taken by Bill Robertson, formerly of the ROM (pp. 96, 99, 181, 190, 195, 232), and Brian Boyle, ROM staff photographer (pp. 35, 300). The drawings of hands shown using and making tools (pp. 169-76) were done by John Pemberton for a ROM gallery. The cover illustration of Early Paleo Indians spearing caribou was done by

Ivan Kocsis, also for a ROM gallery. The drawings on pp. 11, 30, 98, 177, 201, and 272 were prepared by Emil Huston. J Hosek, former ROM staff artist, did the drawings on p. 42.

I would like to acknowledge the following crew members and volunteers, 1969-98: Thomas Andrews, Ellen Badone, Anne Barkworth, Bernice Baumgart, Craig Belfry, Marilyn Bettridge, Luc Bouchet-Bert, Patricia Boyer, Judy Buxton, Brian Clarence, Julie Cormack, Gary Coupland, Isabella Czuba, Catherine D'Andrea, April DeLaurier, Susan Duncan, Jane Edward, Peter Fenton, Theresa Ferguson, Shaneli Fernando, Birgit Fischer, Jacqueline Fisher, Angela Flynn, Sheelagh Frame, Lorne Fromer, David Gillespie, David Goldberg, Rita Granda, Alicia Hawkins, Andrew Hinshelwood, Malcolm Horne, Mary Jackes, Lawrence Jackson Sr., Tara Jenkins, Angela Keenlyside, Daniel Kerr, Christine King, John Kolar, Jennifer Kottick, Jonathan Kovacs, Chris Kular, Peter Lambert, Marc Lamontagne, Craig Liddle, Ruby Lindley, Kenneth Lister, Vivian Livojevic, Adam Lord, Eva MacDonald, Wayne McDonald, Paul McEchean, Thomas McGreevy, Jennifer McKee, Mark Mahood, Kathryn Mills, Paul Morris, William Moss, Joseph Muller, William Newhook, David Patterson, Laura Peers, Matthew Peros, Marion and Stewart Press, John Prideaux, Diana Primavesi, Susan Ralph, Jason Reitemeier, David Robertson, Frank Ruddock, Richard Sanders, Shelly Saunders, Stephen Scharbach, Becky Sigmon, Donald Slater, Rhan-Ju Song, Kyla Spence, Patrice Stephens-Bourgeault, Andrew Stewart, Paul Stone, Marianne Stopp, Jeffrey Storck, Lisel Storck, John Switzer, Leonora Talevi, Sandra Taylor, Claire Toner, Susan Tupakka, Lorraine Underell, Catharina van Waarden, Linda Walsh, Christopher Watts, James Weyman, Raven White, John Wood, and Robert von Bitter. The crew supervisors deserve special mention: Gordon Dibb, Lawrence Jackson, Mima Kapches, Ingrid Kritsch, Anne MacLauglin, Heidi Ritscher, Natalie Rogers, Carol Stimmel, and Kathy Yasui.

The owners of principal sites mentioned in the text were: the late Mr and Mrs Edward Banting and Mr and Mrs Reg Fisher, Mr William Hussey, Mr and Mrs Byron Taylor, and Mr and Mrs Ken Thomson. There were, of course, many others whose permission to work on their properties was of equal value, indeed crucial to the work highlighted in this book and to the overall research. I regret that they must remain anonymous in this book, as they are too numerous to mention, but the work conducted on their properties and artifacts recovered are part of the permanent record of my work curated by the Royal Ontario Museum. That record contains the names of all the landowners who were so generous, and all future scholars who work with this record and re-study the collections will learn of my debt, and their own, to these people.

The following bodies have generously supported my work: the federal government, through the Canada Council and the Social Sciences and Humanities Research Council of Canada; the Ontario government, through the Department of Lands and Forests, the Ministry of Natural Resources, the Ontario Heritage Foundation, and the Ontario Youth Secretariat; and the Royal Ontario Museum, through the Department of Museum Volunteers Research and Acquisition Fund, the Jack Freedman Ontario Field Archaeology Fund, the Office of the Chief Archaeologist, and the ROM Foundation, and within that body, the Louise Hawley Stone Charitable Trust, which made this book possible.

I'm especially grateful to Glen Ellis, managing editor of the Publications Department at the ROM, for his support of the book, his help in finding a publishing partner for the ROM (ultimately UBC Press, a very good choice), and his assistance in approaching the ROM Foundation for financial support. I would also like to thank Lisa Golombek, chair, and Chen Shen, committee member, of the Art and Archaeology Editorial Board at the ROM, for their help in shepherding the manuscript through the submission and peer review process.

The first draft of this book was written in Walters Falls between September 1997 and December 1999. The revised manuscript was prepared in Berkeley between January and August 2003.

At UBC Press, I would like to thank R. Peter Milroy, director, and Emily Andrew, acquisitions editor, for their support of the book during the manuscript selection and approval process. Camilla Jenkins, editor and overall co-ordinator of the project, was superb with her editing pen and gentle suggestions and helped me to improve the manuscript immeasurably from an earlier version that I had naïvely thought was completely lucid. I hope we have swept cleanly and thoroughly. Eric Leinberger, cartographer, produced atlas-quality maps. George Vaitkunas, designer, created a wonderful book design, a very appealing cover, and the diagrams on pp. 75 and 109. Finally the proofreader, Gail Copeland, reduced to nil or nearly so the possibility of embarrassing mistakes, and the indexer, Patricia Buchanan, made it possible for myriad things to be found easily in the text.

Finally, I must mention Judith Buxton, who in encouraging me to be me makes other things possible.

I must end by alluding to the anonymous people of the prehistoric past and the more distant pre-humans, whom we wish to know and from whom we have much to learn: to satisfy our curiosity, to understand ourselves better, and in so doing, perhaps to make a brighter world.

This book is dedicated to my teachers.

INTRODUCTION

THIS BOOK STARTS IN A SMALL FIELD. The field is hidden behind a sagging split-rail fence, moss-covered with age, and the thick growth of small trees and brush that have grown up around the posts and rails of that narrow refuge. The field is at the end of a long dirt track, at the very back of a farm in south-central Ontario. At the far end of the field, a flat bench of sandy ground slopes down to a large cedar swamp, a tangled and gloomy place that extends for miles eastward into the next township and beyond. The field is quiet except for the raucous cawing of some crows in the trees along the fence row and the dry rustle of grasshoppers darting from the stubble under the feet of a lone human figure walking across the field. At first glance the field seems quite distant from the modern world, and unaffected by it. Yet the dimly heard rush of cars and trucks on unseen roads is a reminder that the world is not far away. This nearness is also evident in the large tree stumps scattered along the fencerow and in the bits of glass, rusty metal, and brick exposed in the sandy earth thrown up by a farmer's plough. Clearly the world and its turbulence have visited this field and changed it. But after that brief intrusion the field was as quickly abandoned. And the slowly walking figure enjoys the sense of abandonment, and the feeling of suspended time it brings.

Despite its peacefulness, the field is not as empty and unremarkable as it seems. This is an illusion, which the slowly walking figure will realize in just a few short steps. For the field and adjacent cedar swamp are actually a sort of museum. This museum without walls is filled with the bits and pieces of previous times and different worlds. Relics of the past are everywhere – in the rise and fall of the land and the sediments they contain and in the fossils they entomb – and yet are jumbled together and camouflaged by our preoccupations with our own lives and the thin veil of the present. In a moment this veil will disappear briefly for our hiker, interrupting his walk and changing him in a small but important way. He suddenly pauses and looks again at something on the ground that seems out of place. Angular and symmetrical, it stands out from the clump of soil within which it is partly embedded. He pulls at it tentatively, frees it from the earth, and then picks it up. For an instant he is uncertain and then realizes with growing excitement that it may be an Indian relic, possibly even an arrowhead. As he turns it over carefully in his hand, almost unbelievingly, he admires the way in which the stone was shaped. The distinct weight and feel of it immediately stimulate a strong sense of connection with the past and an empathy for another human being, long dead. Who did it belong to, he wonders, and how long ago did the person live? The hiker stands for a long time lost in thought and wonder and then carefully pockets the artifact and turns to go, thinking of the story of discovery he will tell his friends.

But that story is sadly incomplete. Our hiker would be surprised to learn that the artifact was not made within the last few hundred years but over 11,000 years ago. He would also undoubtedly be impressed that what he thought was an arrowhead was actually the tip of a throwing spear used for hunting caribou. And that the person who made this spear point was a member of a small band descended from a group of colonizing people who were the first humans to occupy the land after the retreat of glacial ice at the end of the Ice Age. Finally, our hiker might be astonished to learn, because he wouldn't have imagined the very same place to have once been so different, that the family of the person who made the spear point lived for a short time on that very spot, not on the edge of a cedar bog as today but on the shore of a glacial lake. That lake, larger by far than any of the Great Lakes today, was bordered to the north by the retreating ice sheet. And from the shoreline where our hiker now walks, a vast parkland tundra began. Filled with small clusters of spruce in protected areas and along water courses and large open areas of grasses, mosses, and lichens, this parkland tundra extended far south and beyond the future city where our hiker would be born and live.

The story of the Ice Age people who lived in this place, hidden within the small tool in the hiker's pocket and in widely scattered corners of the modern landscape itself, was written only after a very long search. This book is about that search and the story it revealed.

Both the search and the story recounted here are told from the perspective of my own personal journey in archaeology over almost thirty years, a long career that I am happy to say is not yet over. While autobiographical, this is not my last work but more a progress report. And being autobiographical, it is a personal document rather than a textbook. It is also, as these things must be, a reflection of a particular time, in this case the period from the mid-1960s to the present. Consequently, my story encompasses only a very small part of the total history of archaeology and the centuries-old effort to determine when people first colonized the Americas and how they lived when they arrived. Although I am a latecomer to the long chain of scholars who have worked before me on this problem, I have faced questions – and personal doubts – that I believe are felt by all who wish to learn and to expand knowledge.

The task is difficult and involves asking appropriate and sometimes new questions, obtaining the information relevant to answering those questions, and interpreting the information correctly. All are crucial, influencing the final results of the research, but the first two – asking the appropriate questions and finding the relevant information – are often very difficult to translate into actual fieldwork. This is true, in part, because archaeological sites become more difficult to find as one moves deeper into the archaeological record. And clearly without archaeological sites and the information they contain, nothing further can be done. This problem of finding sites – of knowing where to dig – intrigues people, as do the many challenges of interpreting the archaeological record. These interests, shown time and again by all kinds of audiences after public talks, are what stimulated me to write this book. Although the ultimate objective of my work is to write about an ancient people and the world in which they lived, that story contains within it a parallel one about the actual process of doing archaeological work and the successes and failures along the way. These stories, one scientific and the other more personal, are inextricably bound because as individual scientists our interpretations of the lives of the people we wish to know are shaped by the strengths and weaknesses of our own scholarship. There is an irony in this: that the story of the past can unknowingly be altered, through error and bias, by the very people who wish to discover it. It is therefore comforting to know that the final picture will be drawn by the synthesis of numerous individual accounts such as this. For that purpose, this is my story.

As a student and would-be scholar of the initial peopling of North America, I've had opportunities to visit and work at some very important sites, but since 1970 my fieldwork has been focused in Ontario. While this province is very large and obviously important to the people who live here, it is also clearly a very small place in the western hemisphere as a whole. How and why, you might ask, is the study of the early peopling of Ontario important to those outside Ontario? The answer to that question has to do with the way in which science progresses. It is generally uneven, with advances in knowledge leapfrogging from one place to another. Only a few decades ago archaeological interpretations of the earliest peoples in Ontario, indeed much of eastern North America, were based on discoveries in the southwestern United States, where the earliest discoveries were made, and in the western Plains, where many kill sites had been found with preserved animal bone. Over the past fifteen or twenty years that situation has changed, and today nearly everywhere in North America archaeologists can look to local and regional discoveries for their interpretations. Archaeologists now realize that the earliest peoples in different parts of North America may have led quite different lives under different ecological conditions. This is certainly true for the Great Lakes region and possibly part of the northeastern United States, which may have constituted a single, distinct ecological zone at the end of the last Ice Age, requiring somewhat different kinds of human adaptations than those required in the Plains, the southeastern United States, or the far north. Furthermore, in recent years, archaeological research on the earliest peoples in Ontario has in some respects outpaced that in neighbouring provinces and states. For now, at least, the data from Ontario provide one of the most detailed pictures of the nature of early human occupation in the Great Lakes region as a whole. The data therefore serve both as a framework for interpreting new discoveries and as a target for other archaeologists to challenge. For these reasons, the developing story in Ontario is of widespread interest.

Finally, I had another motive for writing this book. I wish to give something back to the general public for the years of funding that supported my work. Generally speaking, the public hears very little about the results of tax-funded research. Even the academic community frequently sees only fragments of scholarship from larger projects. Final reports, whether technical or written for the general public, are much rarer. There are probably many reasons for this, but judging from my own experience, perhaps one of the most important is that from day to day or even year to year, most scholars are completely preoccupied with the demands of the academic world. And this world places a very high value on productivity and excellence. This is not unreasonable. Considering the freedom in academic research to work when and how you want, these standards are necessary. But there is a drawback. The most common ways in which productivity and excellence are achieved are by publishing short papers (which add up quickly and therefore contribute to productivity) on narrow topics (which can be researched in depth and therefore demonstrate excellence). Inevitably, the average academic will find him- or herself in a kind of closed loop, writing up short papers to establish a track record and simultaneously to obtain future opportunities to improve that record. The danger in this, aside from the risk of never accomplishing anything substantial, is that a person may also become progressively more concerned with beginnings – grant proposals, abstracts of yet unwritten papers to be delivered at conferences, plans for future fieldwork, and so on. This treadmill goes in only one direction – forward – and at one setting – ever faster. And sometimes it turns in on itself and focuses on ever narrower subjects. There is no time left for endings, such as final reports that have been thoroughly and completely researched or books for the general public.

This book is an attempt to change that, at least with respect to my own actions. And thus it is about endings, the results of research.

Technical Note

The Early Paleo-Indian peoples discussed in this book are known primarily from their stone tools. These tools include distinctive types of spear points (such as Clovis and Folsom) that give their names to the total assemblage of objects. These assemblages are often technically referred to as complexes (the Clovis complex, Folsom complex). In this book I have somewhat loosely referred to complexes as cultures. At best this is an oversimplification because the stone tools and other objects that survive in the archaeological record were once just a small, and possibly even unimportant, part of any human group's cultural identity. Nevertheless, for my purpose here I prefer the word culture because it humanizes the story.

Academic opinion is divided over whether the word *mastodon* should end with or without a final "t." The difference of opinion involves questions about evolutionary relationships and the most appropriate names for reflecting those relationships, as well as about the correct way to form vernacular words derived from Greek. As there appears to be no consensus, I have decided to use the term most familiar to the general public, *mastodon,* following the third edition of the *Oxford Dictionary of Current English* and other modern dictionaries.

All radiocarbon dates are expressed in radiocarbon years before present (years BP). By convention the present is regarded as 1950, a time before the ratio of radioactive and non-radioactive carbon atoms in the atmosphere, a property crucial for calculating dates, was affected by nuclear testing. Attempts to correlate radiocarbon years with calendar years, by dating, for example, objects of known calendar age, indicate that radiocarbon dates falling between 10,000 and 11,500 years ago, the age span we are concerned with here, are *younger* than their equivalent calendar dates. Thus, a radiocarbon date of 11,000 years BP, for example, represents a calendar date of approximately 12,950 years ago. The disparity between radiocarbon years and calendar years is not important for the discussion in this book, however, and as there is no universally used correlation scheme uncorrected radiocarbon dates are presented.

Time also has other meanings in this book. The story of my research is written chronologically, as it occurred. I tried to write from the perspective of what I knew, or thought I knew, at particular times and of what was then generally known, or thought to be known, in my discipline. The additional, boxed information, however, represents current knowledge, at least for the period 1997-2003, when I wrote and made final revisions to this book. Thus in the following pages, time flows in several dimensions simultaneously: geological and archaeological time, as measured through radioactive decay; calendar or historic time; and personal time (as I remember it). All flow at vastly different rates yet are part of a single story.

Journey to the Ice Age

1 BEGINNINGS

AT VARIOUS TIMES IN OUR LIVES each one of us will want to know more about ourselves and about the nature of the inner person who determines how we respond to the world, often without our conscious awareness or complete understanding. This question about self is a uniquely human question. As individuals we may never find an answer, but in looking we will all consider our origins. The search for origins begins with parents. From there it moves to grandparents, and beyond them to their parents, and their parents – again and again, in a seemingly infinite regression – embracing ever more family lines with each successive generation into the past, until the whole lineage looks like branches in the veins of a leaf or the tributaries of a great river.

The question of origins also concerns the nature and identity of the larger group of people to whom one belongs, whether friends, an age group, a trade or profession, a group with common interests or beliefs, a community, or a nation-state. The ties to these larger groups are very strong and have much to do with how we live our lives.

The cultures to which we belong also express an interest in origins. Almost universally, ideas about our origins encompass the beginnings of humankind and the relationship between humans and the spiritual world. The question of origins is a fundamental part of organized religion as well as traditional and folk belief systems. In the history of western thought this interest in origins eventually attracted scientific inquiry as well, first in astronomy and later in the evolving fields of biology, geology, human paleontology, and archaeology. Over the past 200 or 300 years knowledge of the physical and cultural development of our own species has increased exponentially and played a key role in the development of a more heritage-conscious world. We cannot know in what directions our knowledge will expand or change, but judging from the past we can be sure there will be many surprises, and some shocks.

Leaving the future for the future, what do we think we know today about human origins? Certainly the most fundamental discoveries affecting the study of human origins were conceptual in nature, changing the way in which people viewed the world. Among the earliest were the concepts of stratigraphy and of prehistoric time, the idea that human history extended much deeper into the past than could be interpreted from biblical genealogy. These as well as later conceptual discoveries were the product of ongoing changes in human thinking that took place gradually in a community of scholars. Although they cannot be said to have been made by individuals, the ideas crystallized most notably in the work of such geologists as William Smith and Charles Lyell in Britain and, in the newly emerging field of archaeology, a number of people in Britain and France. The most widely known of these today is perhaps Boucher de Perthes. These individuals and others shaped the new concepts of stratigraphy and prehistoric time in papers read before various associations of scholars and avocational scientists and in publications dating between roughly the mid-eighteenth and the end of the nineteenth centuries.

Stratigraphy came to be recognized first: the idea that layers of sediments and rocks recording earth's history occurred in the order in which they were deposited (unless later disturbed), with the oldest layer at the base and the youngest at the top of the stratigraphic section.

Prehistoric time was recognized somewhat later by applying the principle of geological stratigraphy to the study of deposits containing both the bones of extinct animals and human artifacts – in effect, a merging of geology and archaeology. This ultimately demonstrated that humans in Britain and western Europe once lived at the same time as animals that had since either become extinct or no longer lived in the region, such as cave bear, mammoth, rhinoceros, aurochs (wild cattle), and reindeer. And with this realization came the concept of prehistoric time; the word itself seems to have been used for the first time by Daniel Wilson in his book *Prehistoric Annals of Scotland,* published in 1863.

Inevitably, the concepts of prehistoric time and geological time beyond that would be combined with Charles Darwin's idea of biological change through time by the process of natural selection: organic evolution.

GEOLOGICAL SUBDIVISIONS OF THE ICE AGE

Episode	Beginning (years BP)	Selected event
Quaternary Period		
Holocene Epoch (or interstadial/ interglacial of the Pleistocene?)	**10,000 to present**	
Pleistocene Epoch (the Ice Age)		
Late Pleistocene Wisconsinan glaciation		Champlain Sea Lake Algonquin
Late	30,000	Lake Iroquois
Middle	60,000	
Early	115,000	
Sangamonian interglacial	135,000	
Middle Pleistocene	790,000	
Illinoian glaciation	190,000	
Early Pleistocene	1.8 million	

Note: Glacial and interglacial episodes during the Middle and Early Pleistocene in North America have not yet been firmly identified or dated.

Sources: Adapted, in part, from Barnett (1991-2) and Fulton and Prest (1987).

Period		Years BP (before present)
European Contact (historical period)		400
Mississippian (soutwestern part of region)		1,000 (and into historic period)
Woodland		3,000 (and into historic period)
Archaic		9,500 to 3,000
Paleo-Indian	Late	10,500 to 9,500
	Early	11,000+ to 10,500
pre-Clovis		unknown

Note: The Woodland and Mississippian periods overlap to some extent chronologically because the terms also refer to different cultural traditions that were, in part, contemporaneous. Dates for all periods are approximate and vary within the region.

Sources: Based on data in Ellis and Ferris (1990) and Birmingham and Elsenberg (2000).

Although Darwin's watershed 1859 work, *On the Origin of Species,* appeared during the same period in which the concept of prehistoric time emerged, the notion that biological evolution applied to humans as much as it did to other animals took longer to find acceptance. Once it did, however, the human fossils that were then coming to light – such as those of the first Neanderthal from a cave in the Neander valley in Westphalia – gradually came to be seen differently. Thus the concepts of stratigraphy, prehistoric time, and organic change, once accepted and interrelated, provided the necessary basis, indeed prerequisite, for studying human origins.

The next century and a half would be noted for advances in excavation methods, the development of methods for absolute dating, and ever more sophisticated methods of analysis. These advances contributed to two major achievements: recognizing the great antiquity and complexity of the hominid lineage, including humans and pre-humans; and uncovering the record of anatomical and behavioural changes (first non-cultural and then cultural) involved in the long process of becoming human. Unfortunately, our ability to describe the fossil and archaeological records has far outpaced our ability to explain and understand them.

Today it is widely believed that one of the most ancient ancestors of our own species – the australopithecine, *Australopithecus afarensis* – developed in southern and eastern Africa around four million years ago. Earlier ancestors have been suggested but to date A. *afarensis* is the earliest *best-known* of the hominid species ancestral to the human line.

We recognize the next stage of hominid evolution in the form of *Homo habilis.* This species may have evolved from A. *afarensis* or another still unknown, advanced form of australopithecine. *Homo habilis* is believed to have made the first stone tools that can be recognized as such in the prehistoric record. These tools are referred to as Oldowan, after Olduvai Gorge in Tanzania, and appear around two and a half million years ago. Some archaeologists believe they signal the presence of learned behaviour, possibly even the beginnings of culture, at least in pre-human form.

Homo habilis or some related form ultimately evolved into *Homo erectus,* possibly the first species in the human line to move out of Africa and into more northern climates. *Homo erectus* colonized much of the Old World from southern and central Europe to central China and into southeast Asia. Wherever it lived, the species is remarkable for its conservative stone tool technology, based, for the most part, on hand-axes and cleavers in the west and on pebble chopping tools in the east. These tool forms persisted almost unchanged for several hundred thousand years.

The place and time of origin of our own species, *Homo sapiens,* is still unclear and strongly debated. Some believe that our species evolved over 100,000 years ago in Africa and then dispersed throughout the world, replacing more archaic species of humans, including the European and West Asian Neanderthals (*Homo sapiens neanderthalensis*). Other paleontologists believe that *Homo sapiens* evolved semi-independently, with significant gene intermixture between evolving groups, in several regions of the Old World from those same archaic populations.

Once evolved the modern species, *Homo sapiens sapiens,* spread rapidly throughout the remainder of the world, except for the Antarctic. Recent research in the southern hemisphere tells us that Australia was colonized by modern humans between 40,000 and 60,000 years ago, and perhaps earlier. In the far reaches of the northern hemisphere colonization was slower, possibly because of the difficult cultural adaptations required of life in cold climates. Human hunters didn't reach the western edge of northeastern Siberia (western Beringia) until perhaps 35,000 years ago.

The Americas are more of a mystery. They were certainly the last of the continents to be colonized by humans. But when, exactly, did that occur? The answer would fill a large book and still be unclear. The fact is, archaeologists don't know.

In the mid-1960s, when I entered the academic scene as a young graduate student, archaeologists were split into two factions on the issue. The majority believed the best evidence indicated that the earliest humans to live in North America were Early Paleo-Indians of the Clovis culture, dated between roughly 11,000 and 12,000 years BP (before present) at sites in the southwestern United States by the still newly developing radiocarbon dating technology. These dates were generally consistent with earlier paleontological evidence indicating that Clovis people hunted at least two forms of mammoth and extinct bison while later groups of Early Paleo-Indians, called Folsom, focused on one or several species of bison, all of which became extinct at the end of the Ice Age. The discovery in the late 1920s and early 1930s, prior to the development of radiocarbon dating, of extinct animals in direct association first with Folsom- and later with Clovis-type projectile points (both probably used on the ends of spears) was the first solid evidence that human occupation had some respectable antiquity in the Americas. The topic had been debated from one extreme position to the opposite for over a century. Archaeologists who believed that Clovis people were the earliest occupants of the New World also argued that their culture was an indigenous North American development, made by the descendants of northeast Asian colonizers who had crossed

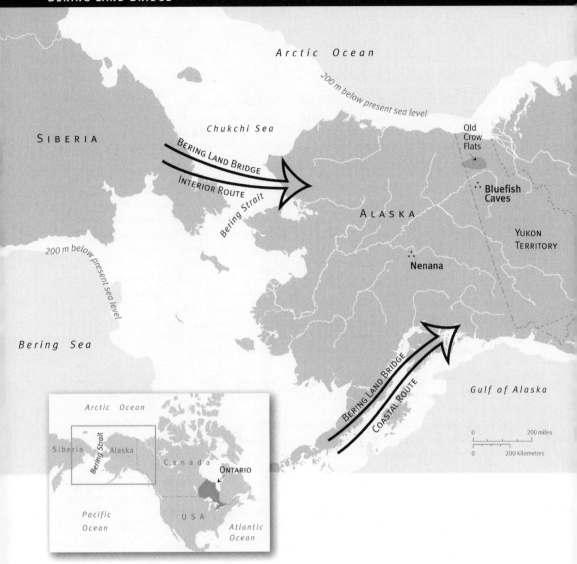

Submerged portion of Beringia between Siberia and Alaska and proposed routes of entry by colonizing peoples into the Americas near the end of the Ice Age. At the height of the last glaciation, roughly 20,000 years ago, sea level was perhaps as much as 125 metres below its present level, exposing as dry land much of the current sea bed between the two hemispheres. The 200 metre contour below modern sea level is shown on the map.

Adapted from Hopkins 1982, 4.

The Ice Age: A Time of Contrasts

It is perhaps fitting, and maybe not entirely coincidental, that our own species – *Homo sapiens* – an animal capable of great extremes of behaviour, has its origins in a time of great contrasts: the Ice Age. This popular term is a synonym for what geologists call the Pleistocene Epoch. With our own age, the Holocene, these two epochs are part of the most recent period in the geological time column – the Quaternary.

The Holocene Epoch encompasses only about 0.5 percent of the Quaternary Period. We live in an instant of the most recent period of geological time. But we have deeper roots, for the human lineage has its physical and cultural origins in the Pleistocene, a time of dramatic climatic fluctuations between glacial and interglacial conditions stretching back perhaps two million years.

The Pleistocene is divided into three parts: Early, Middle, and Late. The Late Pleistocene began with an interglacial, the Sangamonian, dated between approximately 135,000 and 115,000 years BP. This was followed by the last episode of glacial activity, called the Wisconsinan Stage in North America, named after the state where deposits of this age were first described in the late nineteenth century. The Wisconsinan Stage is divided into several episodes of glacial advance, alternating with episodes of ice retreat, called interstadials. The last glacial advance, during Late, or Classical, Wisconsinan time (dating from 30,000 to 10,000 years ago), reached its maximum extent about 20,000 years ago. Shortly thereafter, the final retreat began. It continued past the somewhat arbitrary boundary between the Pleistocene and the Holocene, placed at 10,000 years ago when the seas rose to their modern levels. Yet even then, most of Ontario remained buried beneath glacial ice. Because of its mass and size, the ice was out of phase with the climatic reversal that had initiated glacial retreat several thousand years earlier. And two of the original centres of ice accumulation from which the continental ice sheet grew – one west of Hudson Bay in the Keewatin District and the other in central Quebec – would remain ice covered until as late as 8,000 or 7,000 years ago, well into the Holocene Epoch.

Around 5,000 years ago, the last remnants of the ice sheet in Canada melted back to the present borders of two residual ice caps on Baffin Island, west of Greenland. These two ice caps and some mountain glaciers are all that remain of the former continental ice sheet in one of its original centres of growth.

Although the last ice sheet is gone, a larger question remains. How did the climatic reversal that ended the last glaciation differ from earlier ones during periods of ice retreat within the Wisconsinan Stage, or from that of the preceding Sangamonian interglacial? Has the Ice Age really ended? Or have we simply entered a brief, non-glacial interval (an interstadial of the Wisconsinan perhaps or, alternatively, a longer interglacial)? This question is still unresolved. The Ice Age may not be over.

a land bridge between Siberia and Alaska during the last glaciation at times when sea levels were lower than today.

In opposition to the prevailing opinion in the mid-1960s, a smaller group of archaeologists believed that humans colonized the Americas much earlier than 12,000 years ago, perhaps between 20,000 and 30,000 years ago, if not earlier still. The long list of seeming evidence cited in support of this idea included sites in both North and South America. Aside from their potential antiquity one of the things these sites had in common was that they contained simple tools – or objects thought to be tools – but no projectile points. Since these unnamed people, or perhaps many peoples, were believed to have predated a Paleo-Indian stage of occupation characterized by the use of projectile points, the proposed earlier stage of human occupation was referred to, logically enough, as the Pre-Projectile Point stage.

Folsom-type fluted spear point drawn from a cast of an artifact from the Lindenmeier site in Colorado.
Emil Huston, Artpole Studio.

Clovis-type fluted spear point drawn from a cast of an artifact from the Naco site in Arizona.
Emil Huston, Artpole Studio.

Moving beyond School

This split opinion on the antiquity of the peopling of the Americas was part of the intellectual tool box I carried with me in September 1969 from graduate school at the University of Wisconsin to my first job as a professional archaeologist. In the fall of that year I joined the staff of the Royal Ontario Museum, known more colloquially as the ROM, in Toronto, Canada. I was hired into a section of the museum impressively titled Office of the Chief Archaeologist, headed by Dr A.D. Tushingham, an

The Last Door

Clear archaeological and biological evidence tells us that the Americas were peopled from Asia, across an ancient Ice Age land bridge connecting Siberia and Alaska. Of course, there are contrary views within anthropology and other fields. But while random boatloads of Asians or Polynesians, for example, *might* have drifted onto the South American coastline during the late prehistoric period, they almost surely were not the initial colonizing people. They would have arrived, if at all, much later and would not have made a significant impact on the biological or even cultural heritage of resident New World peoples.

In addition to furnishing evidence that northeast Asia provided the springboard for the colonization of the New World, archaeology tells us that the human occupation of that corner of the world occurred very late in the prehistoric record – indeed, at the very end of human dispersal throughout the Eurasian land mass, including New Guinea and Australia. Thus, in the story of human radiation throughout the world, the far northern corner of the Siberian arctic was the last door.

Only fragments of that doorway exist today. These have been camouflaged by the rise in sea level at the end of the Ice Age, and somewhat later on land by the development of the boreal forest and, north of the treeline, by sedge-tussock and dwarf shrub tundra. This is the modern Arctic. But of course it has not always been this way. At times during the Ice Age, the seas withdrew and became locked into glacial ice. The Chukchi Sea, a southern arm of the Arctic Ocean north of Siberia and Alaska, retreated northward. And the Bering Sea to the south, bordered by the Aleutian Islands, withdrew

into the north Pacific and almost ceased to exist. The result was a new land mass known as Beringia or, more popularly, as the Bering Land Bridge.

It was this new land mass that allowed the interchange of a large number of both plants and animals between the Old and New Worlds. And, in due course, humans as well. During the height of the last glaciation, about 20,000 years ago, Beringia extended over 1,000 kilometres from north to south and roughly 4,000 kilometres from the eastern edge of the Central Siberian Plateau, across northeast Siberia and Alaska, to the margin of the Laurentide Ice Sheet in the western Yukon. Beringia spanned about 95 degrees of longitude, approximately 26 percent of the earth's surface along the Arctic Circle.

Beringia was thus more than just a corridor between two continents. It was large enough to have affected atmospheric circulation and generated its own strongly continental climate in eastern Siberia and western Alaska (in contrast with today's maritime climate). Strangely, perhaps, considering its northern location, Beringia was largely unglaciated except in mountainous areas.

Beringia was also home to a unique assemblage of interrelated communities of plants and animals, referred to collectively as the Mammoth Steppe. This name comes from both its presumed appearance, an essentially treeless and dry steppe, and its largest mammal, the woolly mammoth (*Mammuthus primigenius*), which left thousands of bones, tusks, and the occasional frozen mummy in the permafrost. Other animals were woolly rhino (in Siberia), camel (in the Yukon), horse, bison, reindeer, steppe antelope, mountain archaeologist who had worked for many years on the prehistoric record underlying the city of Jerusalem. As a new assistant curator I was employed specifically to work on the earliest part of the prehistoric record in Ontario, extending from about 8,000 to 12,000 years ago, or as far back as it went. That was for me to determine.

I was shown to my office in the basement of the museum. The office was at one end of a large rectangular space that held a few work tables, a wet lab at the opposite end of the room complete with large sink and fume

sheep, moose, and muskox, to name only a few of the more prominent ungulates. In fact, their presence has given rise to a long-standing and ongoing debate about the "productivity paradox," the name given to the apparent difficulty of reconciling the rich fauna with the sparse vegetation suggested by the paleobotanical record. Clearly, the ecosystems of Beringia were complex, and also without parallel in the modern world.

The last door in the human journey to the modern world opened outward, not to a limitless horizon but to another door, or possibly two. These are the doors south, through or around, the retreating ice sheets. For these thresholds had to be crossed before the Americas could be colonized and populated.

Perhaps the most obvious of the two doors is the so-called Ice-Free Corridor between the Cordilleran Ice Sheet centred in the Rocky Mountains, and the Laurentide Ice Sheet to the east. These two ice masses merged during the maximum advance of the last glaciation but then separated during subsequent ice retreat, creating a corridor between their respective margins. Today there is much ambiguity about whether the corridor was actually open along its entire length – from Alaska and the Yukon to the northern Plains – at the time of the supposed early human migrations during the Late Pleistocene. Another problem is the environment in that corridor. Situated between two ice masses, the corridor would have contained large glacial lakes, forming imposing physical barriers to human movement. It would also have received cold air draining off the Cordilleran Ice Sheet to the west and the Laurentide Ice Sheet to the east. The environment in the corridor could have been very hostile

to both plant and animal – and thus, human – life.

There may have been a second, possibly more important, doorway into the New World. This is proposed by archaeologists who are not satisfied that the Ice-Free Corridor was available during the earliest episodes of human colonization and who also doubt that the earliest peoples were oriented exclusively to terrestrial food resources. This doorway is the Pacific coast of North America from Alaska to northwestern Washington State, between the melting front of the Cordilleran Ice Sheet and the edge of the exposed continental shelf. And it is suggested that the colonizing peoples who used this route may have been adapted to a maritime way of life that originated on the southern margin of Beringia itself.

Unfortunately, no sites occupied by colonizers from Beringia have been found in either corridor – inland or coastal – although archaeologists have been, and still are, looking very hard.

To make the current scene more confusing, the earliest well-documented sites in eastern Beringia (central Alaska, and grouped into an archaeological construct called the Nenana complex) are roughly contemporaneous with, or only slightly earlier than, the earliest Clovis sites in the southwestern United States. The Nenana people don't seem early enough to have been the ancestors of Clovis peoples to the south. And Nenana projectile points are hard to imagine as precursors of Clovis-type spear points. To archaeologists, the connections between the peoples who lived in Beringia and those who inhabited the unglaciated south are as difficult to see as the doors that made those connections possible.

hood, and, along one wall, a floor-to-ceiling bank of glass-fronted storage cabinets containing over a million artifacts from Ontario. This entire space, informally the Ontario division of the Office of the Chief Archaeologist, was referred to as the Long Room.

My office was brand new, built just for me. It was also very small, about three metres square, and not much bigger than the heavily used grey metal desk at the back wall. With a chair in front of the desk for a visitor, the office door barely closed. In the back wall was a large, high window of frosted glass with a deep sill at roughly shoulder height. The glass was heavily reinforced with wire in a diamond pattern. Although the glass was frosted, the dirt that had accumulated on it both inside and outside over the fifty-seven years since the building had been erected would itself have made the window opaque. Little more than a feeble glow of outdoor light passed through. Even on the brightest sunny days my office was in perpetual twilight. At all other times it was positively gloomy.

Immediately adjacent was a much larger office, also newly built, an event I assumed was triggered by my hiring. This office was occupied by Walter Kenyon, a very imposing, indeed overwhelming, senior archaeologist who studied the more recent end of the archaeological time scale. Since he was very senior to me, it was only appropriate and right that his office, desk, and space for visitors – two chairs rather than one, plus knee room – were larger.

Opposite the two offices sat another imposing person, secretary Peta Daniels, who, I later learned, felt very much put out because during the renovations to the Long Room an office had not also been built for her. Instead, her desk had been shoved next to the exterior door to the Long Room and opposite the two curators who, in her opinion, should not have warranted special treatment because her work was no less important. Despite this bad beginning we later became quite good friends, down to the present day. I soon learned that before my arrival she and Walter Kenyon had worked only a few feet apart while facing one another across two desks pushed back to back at one end of the storage space. At least she no longer had to suffer that.

Plunked in my new office, thinking of my new colleague on the other side of the wall, I felt much like a person suddenly thrust onto the upper seat of a see-saw. By working in the early part of the prehistoric record I was supposed to provide some sort of academic counterbalance to the work of Walter Kenyon. Needless to say, I was very green, very naïve, and very much an academic lightweight. I was also, at this early stage in my career, much more serious about things than I probably should have been, much less witty than my senior colleague, definitely retiring if not actually seriously introverted, and, because I was still surrounded by the lingering aura of a student, certainly much less inspiring to the general public. Because of these limitations, I felt that I had to gain academic weight fast. The senior administrators at the ROM assumed and expected that I would bring down my end of the see-saw very soon, as did my colleagues in the archaeological community. And the general public, I thought, would be no less demanding. The question was, how should I start?

During the difficult months of casting about for a research project, I eventually remembered or was reminded that the ROM occurred in the same province as the very well-known, even infamous, Sheguiandah site. In fact, the site was only a five- or six-hour drive from my office in Toronto.

Sheguiandah is located on the northeastern corner of Manitoulin Island, in northern Lake Huron. Sheguiandah became widely known in the North American archaeological community during its excavation in the 1950s because of controversy about its possible age. The site was excavated by the late Thomas Lee, who at the time was a staff member of the National Museum of Canada in Ottawa, today the Canadian Museum of Civilization. The controversy stemmed from Lee's opinion that the lowest occupations at the site were at least 30,000 years old. This put them into the so-called Pre-Projectile Point stage. Indeed, the artifacts were consistent with the definition of that stage since there were no projectile points, and the tools consisted entirely of bifaces, some of which were very roughly made. Bifaces are oval or pointed artifacts with bi-convex sections, shaped by removing flakes from both faces of an object. They contrast with unifaces, which are shaped from only one face. Lee thought that the geology clearly supported his interpretation of the age of this material. He was impatient with those who doubted his interpretations without having visited the site or studied the collections. And he was both stung and frustrated when his views were not supported by those who had seen the deposits, seemingly been receptive to his views, and subsequently either published or voiced contrary opinions – or kept silent altogether.

Several years after the excavations, at a new position at Laval University in Quebec City, Lee claimed that he had been forced out of his employment at the National Museum because of his interpretations. Whatever happened to Lee also effectively mothballed the site. He never returned after the final year of excavation in 1955, nor had anyone else in the fourteen years prior to my employment at the ROM. This lack of activity was curious, not only because of the site's obvious importance but also because several of Lee's senior field assistants, including Walter Kenyon, had since become prominent archaeologists and could have initiated their own work. Perhaps they were cautious because Thomas Lee was still bristling over his experience at Sheguiandah and his perceived treatment by the National Museum. Understandably then, as a newcomer to Canada and the local archaeological community, and a complete neophyte beginning what I hoped would be a long academic career, it was completely unthinkable for me to consider, or even briefly fantasize about, starting up renewed excavations on the site.

At this point, however, I learned something quite by chance that made it possible to imagine something like a sequel to Sheguiandah, an intriguing thought that spawned my first field project in Ontario. I learned that the Department of Lands and Forests, a division of the provincial government responsible for Crown land in Ontario, wanted an archaeological survey of a new park: Killarney Provincial Park. This park was located on the north shore of Georgian Bay, just across a narrow channel of water from Manitoulin Island and Sheguiandah. The crucial connection between the northern part of Manitoulin Island and Killarney Park is that both are underlain by a very hard but brittle rock called quartzite. This material is well suited for making stone tools, as the prehistoric occupants of Sheguiandah clearly knew, since the debris of tool making was scattered all over the site, in some places forming steep slopes several metres thick. Prehistoric peoples were probably initially attracted to the site because of the quartzite and the opportunity to replace lost or damaged tools.

In 1969 there was already archaeological evidence that some of the same people who occupied Sheguiandah, or at least people of the same culture, had also visited the region of Killarney Provincial Park. In the late 1930s and early 1940s an archaeologist from the University of Michigan at Ann Arbor, Emerson Greenman, discovered two sites on former beaches on a ridge overlooking a small inland lake several miles from the modern shoreline of Lake Huron. These beaches were at elevations about 90 metres and 100 metres above Lake Huron. Greenman announced the discoveries and updates of his ongoing work in several letters that appeared between 1941 and 1943 in the prestigious journal *Man,* published in Great Britain.

Greenman called the two sites George Lake 1 and 2, after a large lake of that name in what would later become the southwestern corner of Killarney Park. Curiously, the sites actually occurred near a different and much smaller lake nearby, and Greenman probably selected the name George Lake because it was a more pronounced landmark. George Stanley, a geologist who worked with Greenman, measured the elevations of the relic beaches associated with George Lake 1 and 2 and determined

Sheguiandah and George Lake sites

levation
metres above sea level)
300
4 miles
4 kilometres
Bay of Islands
North
hannel
Little
Current
Sheguiandah
Manitoulin Island
Fraser Bay
La Cloche Mountains
Killarney Provincial Park
Blue Ridge
Killarney Ridge
George Lake
(GL1 and GL2)
Killarney
Georgian Bay
68
637
Sudbury
North
Bay
Killarney
Provincial
Park
Manitoulin
Island
Georgian Bay
Bruce Peninsula
Lake Huron
Ontario
Collingwood
Goderich
Toronto
Lake Ontario
Hamilton
Sarnia
London
Windsor
Lake Erie

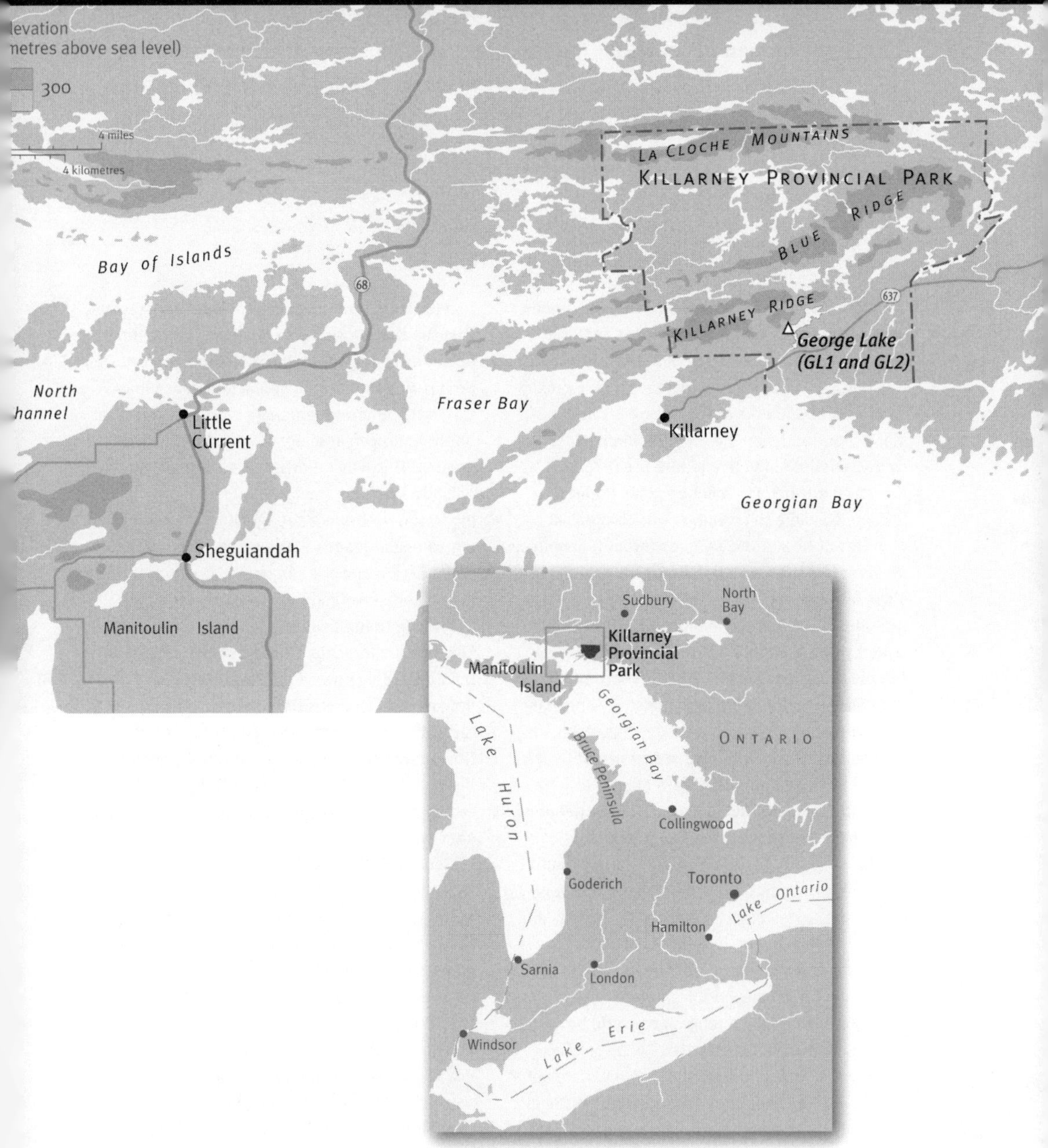

that they were postglacial because they occurred at lower elevations than the former beach of a much earlier lake, glacial Lake Algonquin (at 148 metres). Greenman thought that the occupations were contemporaneous with the relic beaches on which they occurred because a few artifacts at both sites had been smoothed by wave action. Although he and Stanley were clear that the relic beaches were of postglacial age, however, they were uncertain about a more precise chronological age for them and for the human occupations that occurred there. In a published remark after the fieldwork, Greenman stated that George Stanley speculated the site had been occupied perhaps 16,000 years ago. But in the final report on

Who, How Many, Where, and When

Since the early twentieth century there has been little doubt in anthropological circles that the Americas were populated from Asia. This notion was initially suggested by the geographic proximity of Asia and Alaska at the Bering Strait and, more importantly, by the Mongoloid physical characteristics of living and late prehistoric Native Americans. In recent decades it has become possible to investigate the biological affinities of New World peoples through genetics. Most recently, the study of biological relationships between Asian and New World peoples has returned once again to the fossil record, stimulated by new analytical methods and a growing sample of ancient human skeletal material. Outside the realm of biology, the study and classification of New World languages has also contributed to questions of Native American origins.

Biological and linguistic data appear to have implications for nearly all aspects of the peopling of the New World: who, the geographic origins and thus identity of the colonizing population(s); how many, the number of colonizing episodes; where, the routes of entry across the Bering Land Bridge; and when, the time(s) of entry.

In a landmark paper published in 1986, a linguist and two physical anthropologists suggested that New World languages could be classified into three stocks that corresponded roughly with the distribution of three variants of a dental pattern (Sinodont) derived from northeast Asia. The authors argued that this evidence, and

to a lesser extent other genetic data, suggested that the New World was colonized during three episodes of migration. Initial colonization was by people or peoples who spoke languages ancestral to the Amerind language stock, including all South American and most North American languages. This was followed by a colonizing episode involving the ancestors of people belonging to the Na-Dene language stock, encompassing some languages in the greater Northwest Coast region and the subarctic. The final colonizing episode involved the ancestors of people belonging to the Eskimo-Aleut language stock. This three-part scenario has been quite influential and widely quoted, but over time it has also drawn increasing criticism from those who don't recognize the same dental patterns, classify North American languages differently, question the correlations between genetic, linguistic, and archaeological data, or emphasize other kinds of data entirely.

Genetic data indicate very clearly not only an Asian origin for Native Americans but also, because Native Americans are genetically distinctive, a long period of relative isolation. Some geneticists doubt whether genetic data can be used to recognize the residual genetic heritage of specific colonizing groups in modern populations because of presumed genetic change since initial colonization and drastic population reductions after European contact. Estimates of when those founding populations arrived in the New their work, published in 1942, neither Greenman nor Stanley mention that age estimate. Stanley writes only that the former beach at the George Lake 1 site was formed at "the close of the Pleistocene ice age, late in the Wisconsin glacial stage."

Twelve years later, after Lee excavated at Sheguiandah, he and Greenman argued about the relative ages of the occupations at Sheguiandah and George Lake 1 and 2. Lee thought George Lake 1 was equivalent in age to the second youngest of five successive occupations at Sheguiandah: essentially only a couple of thousand years old. Greenman thought George Lake 1 was much older.

World based on genetic mutation rates are also subject to error because they cannot be precisely quantified.

Perhaps the most provocative issue is the question "who," or at least the particular spin placed on this question by recent studies of ancient human skeletons. These studies suggest that early populations are distinctive from modern Native Americans and more closely resemble populations from south Asia and the Pacific Rim. This observation has led some scholars to hypothesize that the New World may have been colonized during two episodes of migration from northeast Asia, the first by people with a generalized morphology that persists in southeast Asians today, and the second by later populations that had evolved the distinctive northeast Asian, or Mongoloid, dental pattern, and to a lesser extent skeletal pattern, and who were ancestral to modern Native Americans. The implication is that the earlier population was genetically absorbed by the later population. This concept became politicized when it was announced that Kennewick Man, the skeleton of an adult male found in Washington State and dating to c. 8,400 years BP, had Caucasoid-like characteristics.

The use of the word Caucasoid in the Kennewick Man study has charged the issue of origins with racial overtones because to the general public the word implies (much too narrowly) European. To some Native Americans, the thought that an earlier Caucasoid population may have

preceded the ancestors of modern Native Americans seems just another attempt to separate Native peoples from their heritage. Use of the term Caucasoid has also been strongly criticized by some physical anthropologists who object to comparisons with modern races (required in forensic, medico-legal studies of isolated human remains that attempt to determine the personal identity of the individual and whether a murder has been committed). The critics would have preferred a comparative study of Kennewick Man with populations of the same geological age. Some also doubt that craniofacial features can reveal much about biological affinity between populations because the data are so strongly affected by age, sex, health, environmental influences, and intrapopulation variation.

It would be unwise to predict how biological or linguistic studies in the future will contribute to the question of origins. There is no doubt of their importance, or that the final answers will be revealed in small fragments, in many different fields of study, and in different groups of data – all pointing in the same direction.

Beginnings, 1970, Killarney
Provincial Park. Assistant
Frank Ruddock is on the
left, the author on the right.

Photograph by Becky Sigmon.

The conflict was never resolved. And like Sheguiandah after Lee's excavations, George Lake 1 and 2 were not reinvestigated by other archaeologists after Greenman's work.

Clearly, there was need for additional work. George Lake 1 and 2 were relatively small and might not have potential for renewed excavations, but their presence strongly suggested that other sites might be found in the surrounding region. I therefore gladly accepted the invitation to work in Killarney Park in 1970. I hoped that any new sites I discovered would provide better opportunities than those offered at Sheguiandah or George Lake 1 and 2 for dating and culturally identifying an early human presence in the region, whether pre-Clovis or Paleo-Indian.

Pretty ambitious!

Since Killarney Provincial Park was classed as a wilderness park in 1970, as it still is, the fieldwork promised to be a novel experience for me. Novel because, although I had gained a fair background in camping through a long field season on the isolated south shore of Kodiak Island, Alaska, I would need a new skill for working in Killarney Park. I would have to learn to get around in a canoe. Strange as it might seem I had never even been in a canoe before, and I certainly didn't know what to look for in buying one. Following the advice of Walter Kenyon, I purchased a durable sixteen-foot aluminum canoe with square stern for a small motor. I wanted the motor for contingencies, although I didn't expect to use it much because most of Killarney Park was off-limits to power boats. I also assembled a mix of other equipment, including a lot of army surplus stuff. This was before the time when you could buy quick-dry clothing and the latest high-tech wilderness gear designed for comfort and backpacking. I loaded it all into a British Land Rover – a type of vehicle I had never seen before, let alone driven – turned the ignition key, and drove out of the ROM parking lot. I must admit feeling very self-conscious and immensely proud as I drove north through an upscale part of the city. My exotic vehicle, I thought, with the canoe strapped on top and the name "Archaeology, Royal Ontario Museum" boldly painted in white on the door, should conjure up a most romantic image to those I passed on the street, whom I thought of as much less fortunate than I because they were not archaeologists. Thus, with one assistant, I headed off. Into the fabled North Woods.

The letter that follows, published by the ROM as part of a series of archaeological newsletters, was written in pencil, intermittently when time permitted and often by the light of a gas lantern on days when it was too stormy for fieldwork. Although the letter is dated August of that summer it was actually written about half way into the three-month-long project. At the time I thought … well, perhaps it's best just to let you read the letter:

BEACHCOMBING INTO THE PAST
AUGUST 1970, KILLARNEY PARK, ONTARIO

Perhaps at first thought there would seem to be no possible connection between archaeology and such a pleasurable pastime as beachcombing. In many ways, however, my assistant and I are, in fact, "beachcombing into the past" as we walk along ancient raised shorelines that were formed over the last several thousand years, looking for the tools and campsites of early man. Hopefully these shorelines will lead us back into the early prehistory of man's occupation of Ontario, perhaps even to the time of his first appearance in the region 10,000 or possibly even 30,000 years ago.

We are working in the extreme northwestern part of the Georgian Bay area in the rugged hilly region of the La Cloche Range. The range extends along the northern shore of the North Channel and Georgian Bay from the mouth of the Spanish River on the west to Killarney Provincial Park on the east, a distance of approximately eighty kilometres. Most of our work to date has been on that part of the range which is within the boundaries of the park. The park takes its name from the nearby village of Killarney, which in the summer is a port-of-call for yachts from all over the Great Lakes and even the Atlantic coast as far south as Florida.

The La Cloche Range is formed of quartzite that was deposited as sediments in shallow seas approximately 2,000 million years ago. It actually consists of three distinct and roughly parallel ridges or smaller ranges; from north to south these are the North Range, the Blue Range, and the Killarney Range. The ruggedness of the land and the high local relief gives the entire range a mountainous character even though the absolute heights are fairly modest; one of the highest peaks has an elevation of 335 metres. The ridges may be flanked by long steep slopes of broken angular rock or by nearly smooth and vertical cliffs several hundred feet high. The quartzite sometimes makes cliffs and bare rock slopes appear snow covered when in the glare of strong sunlight. Numerous lakes occur not only in the valleys between the ridges but at surprisingly high elevations on the ridges themselves. Several times after climbing up talus slopes for a half hour or more we have suddenly come upon small secluded lakes of a few acres in size near the very summits of the ridges, several hundred feet above the valley floors. Numerous long and narrow steep-sided bays occur where the ranges plunge into the waters of Georgian Bay and the coastline must be very much like the fjord-indented coast of Norway.

The La Cloche Range is potentially interesting to the archaeologist for two reasons. First, fine-grained quartzite is a reasonably good material for making stone tools and consequently one might expect to find numerous archaeological sites in the region. Second, the area was deglaciated at a relatively early date and would have been available for occupation by early hunters and gatherers.

During and after the retreat of the continental ice sheet in this region 10,000 to 12,000 years ago, substantial areas of the La Cloche Range were periodically inundated by various lakes occupying the Huron basin. Many of these lake levels were higher than present ones and resulted in the formation of sand and gravel beaches at various elevations on the slopes of the ridges. In a rough, rocky land with little soil, these beaches would have offered relatively flat and well-drained sites for temporary hunting or fishing camps or workshops for the manufacture of stone tools. This, of course, is based on the premise that prehistoric man was here early enough to have been a contemporary of some of these early lake stages. Several sites excavated a number of years ago do, in fact, suggest that this may have been the case. Most notably, these are the two George Lake sites in Killarney Provincial Park, excavated by Emerson Greenman of the University of Michigan, and the well-known Sheguiandah site on Manitoulin Island, excavated by Thomas Lee, then of the National Museum in Ottawa. Unfortunately, because of the complex or ambiguous geological contexts, the dating of these sites has not been clearly established and remains somewhat controversial. Furthermore, the majority of the stone tools are "types" that may be found only in quarry or manufacturing sites. There are too few diagnostic tools that are sufficiently widespread elsewhere to indicate how these people were related to others in the Great Lakes region. These problems can perhaps be resolved only with the excavation of additional sites containing representative samples of stone tools in more readily datable contexts. We are going to try to find such sites and, if successful, return next summer for full-scale excavation.

I have often been asked by people interested in archaeology how I know where to dig. Frequently, archaeological sites are in remote areas or simply out-of-the-way places, and visitors are naturally curious about the circumstances of discovery. It surprises me how often they are visibly shaken when they receive a reply such as "it takes a lot of walking," instead of the clever insight they expected. If I knew the answer to that question, life would be very pleasant indeed. I have asked that question of myself often this summer – daily at least and, sometimes it seems, even hourly. While the process of locating a site is not entirely random, as the preceding discussion of prehistoric beaches has shown, a certain element of chance and luck, both good and bad, is involved.

Our first job when working on the slope of a ridge or some other area for the first time is to locate and determine the extent and number of ancient beaches. This is often not too difficult or time consuming as the beaches are generally well defined and not badly eroded. A few weeks ago, for example, we located a very clear shoreline on the slope of a small bay on Georgian Bay and approximately 61 metres above its surface. A deer trail followed the ancient shore since it is the easiest way to cross the slope. As we walked along the trail we could see very clearly the nature of the shoreline and visualize how it must have looked some hundreds or thousands of years ago.

This ancient shoreline, consisting of short, alternating segments of sand and gravel beaches, cobble beaches, and exposed bedrock, could be found today on any stretch of shoreline of Georgian Bay. In fact, we have spent a good deal of time on the present shoreline in order to be able to better visualize the character of the ancient shoreline we are studying.

In an effort to increase the effectiveness of the survey, we are preferentially selecting for more intensive study those beaches that would seem to have offered the greatest possible attraction for human occupation. These would probably have included beaches located: (1) adjacent to streams draining inland lakes; (2) in protected bays; and (3) at the ends of portages. These various beach locations can be roughly determined by studying a topographic map and darkening a particular contour line that, from field observation, probably represents the water level of a former lake stage. We have also visited the Sheguiandah and George Lake sites to obtain some idea of their location with respect to beaches, stream systems, etc., so that we will not overlook similar geographic situations in our work.

Once we have located a promising beach the real work begins. Most of the beaches are heavily forested, and if they have been logged in the recent past the undergrowth can be quite dense. Several times in the thick brush I have almost felt the panic of claustrophobia as it seemed hundreds of hands were grabbing at my arms and legs. This is where my analogy to beachcombing breaks down. While it is true that we are working on beaches, they are not warmed by the sun or caressed by gently lapping waves or soft humid breezes. Instead of shorebirds and other innocuous forms of life of at the water's edge, these beaches are the dark, tangled, and frequently swampy home of what must surely be the world's largest species of mosquito as well as the infamous black fly, which has the physique of a hyena and is just as ugly. Thinking about anything other than bugs sometimes takes real concentration.

Attempting to find a site on a heavily overgrown beach requires some luck and a lot of digging. My assistant and I generally space ourselves a short distance apart and then walk parallel to the long axis of the beach, systematically turning over the sod with a shovel every fifteen or thirty metres. Those areas of the beach that are more likely to have been occupied, such as the crest and backshore zone, are sampled at shorter intervals. In addition, we also check the numerous "tree-throws" for tools and flakes. These are small mounds formed from soil that has dropped from the roots of fallen trees. Hopefully, if a campsite of any size is present, our digging will intercept it. However, considering the large areas we cover, it would be possible to walk over a site and unknowingly sample only the sterile areas. This possibility is ever present, and the discouraging thought recurs every time we complete the survey of a particularly promising beach with no results.

We have surveyed large parts of Killarney Range and Blue Range during the past eight weeks and have located a small number of sites and several scattered finds of artifacts. One site, located on an ancient beach approximately sixty-eight metres above the level of Georgian Bay, does contain artifacts similar to those found at Sheguiandah and the George Lake sites. Unfortunately, the site is small and, from the exploratory work we have done, there seems to be little chance that the occupation can be accurately dated. We have only just passed the half-way point in our field season so although we have not yet found what we are looking for we still have ample time and more than enough beaches to walk over. Perhaps in the next few weeks, possibly even tomorrow, our "beachcombing" will suddenly lead us back into the life of early man.

Postscript

A postscript is a place for an added thought, and the story of how that summer ended is a proper postscript. It's unfortunate that a postscript couldn't have been added to the bottom of my newsletter or that I didn't make it the subject of a second letter. This is a fine example of a beginning that, as far as the public was concerned, never had an ending. But of course it did have an ending, although not really a very happy one.

As you read in the letter, my assistant, Frank Ruddock, and I did in fact succeed in finding at least one site that might have been what I was looking for. It was situated on a former beach roughly sixty-eight metres above the modern level of Lake Huron and on the edge of a steep hillside of

Lamorandière Bay, an extension of Killarney Bay on Lake Huron just south of the southern border of Killarney Park. Of course the beach hadn't always been at that elevation or isolated from water. It had been uplifted since the end of the Ice Age as the land readjusted to the removal of the tremendous weight of glacial ice. Thus the beach was quite old, and at the time of fieldwork I speculated and hoped that the people who made the tools and flintknapping debris we were excavating had been contemporaneous with the beach.

Later that fall, after detailed study of the geological data and the artifacts, I concluded that the fossil beach was indeed old, dating between 10,000 and 10,500 years ago, but that the artifacts were younger and made by Shield Archaic people, dating to perhaps 8,000 years ago or 8,500 at the earliest. The artifacts indicated that the site had been occupied by people who postdated the beach and lived much later in the prehistoric record than those I was hoping to find. A couple of years later I would publish a short paper in a regional journal on the site and what we found there. But in the fall of 1970 I realized that, insofar as what I wanted to do, my discoveries hadn't led anywhere.

This was also my fear about further work in Killarney Park: that it wouldn't lead anywhere, at least in the time I thought I had available. This is not to say that I decided the park didn't have the potential I initially thought it had. I hadn't changed my views. I continued to think, and do to this day, that other sites comparable to Sheguiandah and the George Lake sites may yet be discovered in the park. Instead, my fear about committing myself to further work in the park arose from a more mundane and practical problem. Trees, and a very small shovel.

The wonderful forests of Killarney Park made it very difficult for me to work where I needed to be. Keep in mind that the work was not being conducted along modern shorelines, stream courses, or portage routes that provided pathways of movement and living places for late prehistoric and modern peoples alike. Instead it was taking me into a fossil landscape, characterized by a completely different system of lakes and rivers and their now relic beaches. In essence, it was a parallel world but one very different from our own environmentally and also far removed in time, persisting today only as fragments in the most remote parts of the park, high up on the quartzite hills of Killarney Ridge, Blue Ridge, and other ranges to the north. The work was thus narrowly focused. This is the archaeological equivalent of putting all your eggs in one basket. If the focus fails, the project fails.

And it was the trees, and also my own limitations, that made the focus fail. Since I was limited to probing here and there with a small shovel in a heavily treed landscape, my chances of finding what I was looking for, except by sheer accident, was in reality probably next to nil. And while tramping about with my small shovel I had lots of time to reflect that a surprisingly large number of important archaeological sites had been found by accident. This is especially true for the earliest sites in the prehistoric record, whether Paleo-Indian ones in North America, Early Paleolithic in Eurasia, or pre-human in East or South Africa, to mention only a few. And they are most often found by people other than archaeologists! This thought became more worrisome as time passed. Eventually I faced the fact that I had taken a chance in 1970 when I decided to work in the fossil landscape at Killarney. And I worked hard to make a good idea work. But then caution took hold of my thinking and I realized I couldn't continue with the risk. Especially with a new job at stake and the beginning of a career.

Reluctantly, I abandoned the work I had begun in Killarney Park and started looking for another path to travel.

2 THE ELUSIVE TRAIL

IT WAS ALMOST INEVITABLE. After I had given a public talk about my latest research, someone in the audience would come up after the program and ask if I could tell them what was known about the area where they lived, often a place very distant from where I had worked. Usually I wasn't able to tell them anything, which I could see was disappointing. To ease that disappointment somewhat I would then explain that, for the most part, archaeological research is very uneven across space and that generalizations about the past are necessarily based on sites quite distant from one another. Large areas between these sites may be totally unknown, and the larger those unknown areas are the weaker the archaeological record and the story it tells.

In the early 1970s Ontario fell into one of these unknown areas, at least with respect to Early Paleo-Indians, who were then the earliest people known to have lived in North America. Evidence for these late Ice Age hunter-gatherers in Ontario was pretty meagre. It consisted of a handful of spear points in cabinets at the ROM and perhaps a couple of other institutions in the province. The ROM held a total of eleven Early Paleo-Indian spear points when I arrived in 1969. Considering that the museum's entire collection of prehistoric material from Ontario contained perhaps a million individually catalogued specimens, the ratio of later artifacts to Early Paleo-Indian spear points indicated the odds of finding additional pieces made by Ontario's earliest people were roughly 90,000 to one.

Interestingly, one of the eleven specimens had been described and illustrated in the eighteenth annual archaeological report for Ontario,

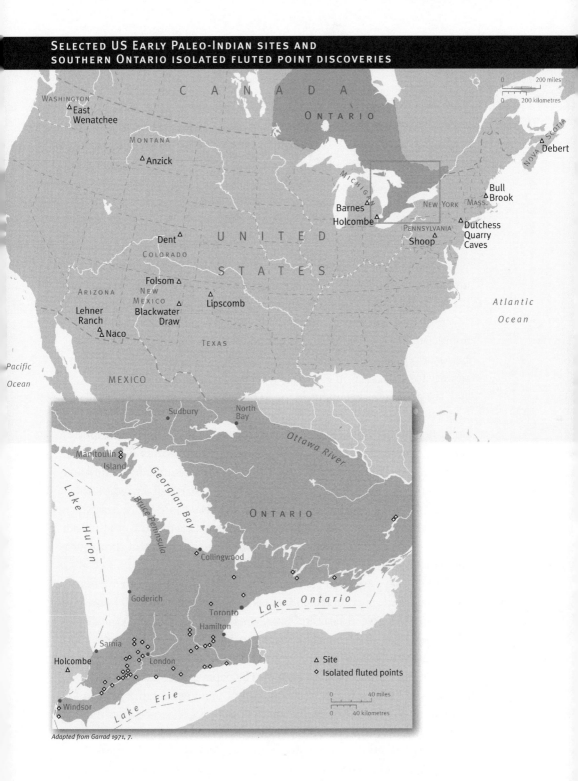

CANADA

ONTARIO

0 200 miles
0 200 kilometres

WASHINGTON
△East
 Wenatchee

MONTANA

△Anzick

MICHIGAN

NOVA SCOTIA
△Debert

Barnes △
Holcombe △

NEW YORK MASS.

Bull
△Brook

PENNSYLVANIA

△Dutchess
 Quarry
 Caves

Dent △

UNITED

Shoop △

COLORADO

STATES

Atlantic
Ocean

ARIZONA
Folsom △

NEW
MEXICO

△Lipscomb

Lehner
Ranch

Blackwater
Draw

△
△Naco

TEXAS

Pacific
Ocean

MEXICO

Sudbury

North
Bay

Ottawa River

Manitoulin
Island

Georgian Bay

Bruce Peninsula

ONTARIO

Lake
Huron

Collingwood

Goderich

Toronto

Lake Ontario

Hamilton

Sarnia

Holcombe
△

London

△ Site
◇ Isolated fluted points

Lake Erie

Windsor

0 40 miles
0 40 kilometres

Adapted from Garrad 1971, 7.

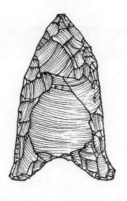

Earliest recorded Early Paleo-Indian fluted spear point find in Ontario. First published in 1906 by David Boyle, curator-archaeologist at the former Ontario Provincial Museum in Toronto.

Emil Huston, Artpole Studio.

published in 1906 by David Boyle, the first curator of the provincial archaeological collection that later formed the basis of the ROM holdings. Boyle recognized the unusual qualities of the artifact, describing it as "peculiar in shape as well as in the way it has been flaked," but he didn't appreciate its significance. Indeed he couldn't because the culture and period it represented wouldn't be recognized by the archaeological community for at least another eighteen years.

The other ten specimens in the ROM collection were noted briefly by Kenneth Kidd in a 1954 paper that appeared in the journal *American Antiquity*, published in the United States. Kidd illustrated eight of the eleven specimens, including the one described by Boyle. The only other information he provided was the locations where they had been found, by county and township if known, the whole paper taking less than half a page. At the time, however, rather than describing the material thoroughly, it was probably more important to make the ROM's material known to the wider North American archaeological community on the chance of stimulating more detailed study or fieldwork in Ontario.

Other than the eleven artifacts at the ROM, only seven other Early Paleo-Indian spear points from Ontario had been documented in the published record between 1907 and 1970, when I started reviewing the data. These specimens, all from the extreme southwestern part of the province, were illustrated in a 1934 paper by Jesse Figgins, then director of the Colorado Museum of Natural History. His paper was concerned with Folsom and Yuma artifacts in North America and was an outgrowth of his work in 1926-7 at a site in northeastern New Mexico, named after the small community of Folsom nearby.

The Folsom site had been discovered in 1908 by a cowboy named George McJunkin, who noticed bison bones exposed in the wall of Wild (or Dead) Horse Arroyo. For unknown reasons the site was not visited until 1926, when it was excavated by the Colorado Museum of Natural History for animal bone for a display. Unexpectedly the paleontologists found human-made artifacts as well. The site became nationally famous the following year when Figgins demonstrated to several colleagues that fossil bison bones were in direct association with the artifacts, firmly establishing that humans had appreciable antiquity in the New World. The artifacts were spear points that would come to be called Folsom. These were beautifully made and skilfully thinned, or fluted, for attaching to a spear. They were also totally unexpected – surprisingly sophisticated compared to what many in the archaeological community expected to find during the decades-long and ultimately unsuccessful search for an American Paleolithic comparable to that in Europe.

After the discovery at Folsom, Figgins and other archaeologists recognized the significance of Folsom-type spear points and other still unnamed types of fluted points found elsewhere in North America. This is how the fluted points from Ontario came to appear in Figgins's 1934 paper. The specimens were drawn to his attention by a geology student at the University of Western Ontario, William J. Patterson. Interestingly, Patterson was to become involved in "Early Man" research again nearly twenty years later when, as the owner and editor of a newspaper on Manitoulin Island, he publicized Thomas Lee's work at the controversial site of Sheguiandah.

Despite Boyle's, Figgins's, and Kidd's tantalizing records of Early Paleo-Indian artifacts from Ontario, it wasn't until 1971 that someone attempted to pull together information on all such artifacts held at major public institutions in the province and by private collectors. This survey, published by Charles Garrad, brought to light nearly three times the number of artifacts previously known. A huge increase. But it was still a very small sample, barely fifty artifacts. This was perhaps less than what a single group of hunter-gatherers would make, and lose, in a year or two, let alone the several centuries that the people of this culture probably lived in the region. These artifacts provided the merest beginning for building a picture of Early Paleo-Indian life in Ontario, a picture that could be developed fully only with knowledge of the complete tool kit, social organization, subsistence activities, and patterns of movement about the landscape, seen in an environmental context. Drab words, but they stand for all the details of life that gave identity and meaning to a once living people and their time.

If someone had asked an archaeologist during this period about Paleo-Indians in Ontario, she or he would have been able to say little more than that they once lived in the area. The fifty or so isolated spear points documented that clearly, but little else. To give a better idea of what these people might have been like, the archaeologist would have been forced to talk about what was known in the United States, particularly the Southwest (New Mexico and Arizona) and the western Plains (Colorado and Wyoming). There, numerous sites had been found containing not only abundant artifacts but also preserved animal bone and material for radiocarbon dating, often buried in stratified deposits and reasonably well protected from later disturbances. As well, because these first discoveries influenced all later thinking about Paleo-Indians (the disadvantage, if not actual tyranny, of precedence), western North America had widely come to be thought of as the classic region of Paleo-Indian culture. Or at least as a reference point for comparing material found in other regions.

Closer to Ontario a few sites were known in Michigan, Pennsylvania, New York, and, more distantly, in Massachusetts, just north of Boston. Farther up the Atlantic coast the Debert site, in Nova Scotia, was the most northerly and Canada's only contribution to the roll call. Curiously it was also the only Paleo-Indian site east of the Plains to have been radiocarbon dated at the time. When I reviewed the situation in 1970 no Early Paleo-Indian sites were known in Ontario. Actually that's not quite true, although I didn't know it at the time. By the mid-1960s some sites had already been discovered in extreme southwestern Ontario but these were not to be fully explored and published for some years yet.

The picture we had in 1970 of Paleo-Indians in Ontario was essentially inferential, drawn from evidence in distant regions but nevertheless provocative. From sites in the western United States, Paleo-Indians first became known to the archaeological community as big game hunters. The first evidence for this was uncovered at Folsom in 1927-8 and five years later at Dent, Colorado, where a heavier type of fluted point was found associated with roughly a dozen mammoth skeletons. In 1936-7 more of these heavier spear points were found at Blackwater Draw Locality No. 1, a site near the town of Clovis, New Mexico. These spear points, later to be called Clovis, were also found embedded in mammoth skeletons. Later discoveries at other sites in western North America indicated that Clovis peoples hunted at least two forms of mammoth, the Columbian and the Imperial, both much larger than the African elephant. Folsom peoples hunted two extinct species of bison (*Bison bison antiquus* and *Bison bison occidentalis*), both also larger than the present-day Plains bison, *Bison bison bison*. The kill sites contain from one to several mammoth or small herds of bison and are impressive records of Early Paleo-Indian hunting abilities. They also reflect highly on the effectiveness of the fluted spear point, certainly one of the most complex stone artifacts ever made, and one that identifies Early Paleo-Indians wherever they occur in North America.

The stratigraphic and temporal relationship between Folsom- and Clovis-type fluted points in western North America was first revealed at Blackwater Draw, where Clovis-type points were found stratigraphically beneath the technologically more sophisticated Folsom-type points. The technological continuity and progression between the two point types indicated that they were part of the same series, and presumably the same culture, while the stratigraphy indicated that Clovis was somewhat older than Folsom, an idea later supported by radiocarbon dating. In the late 1960s Clovis was regarded as dating between 11,500 and 11,000 years BP and Folsom between 11,000 and 10,000 years BP. Archaeologists regarded both types of fluted points as culturally diagnostic of Early Paleo-Indian peoples.

In time the technique of fluting dropped out of use, although some of the other flaking techniques for making Folsom-type points continued to be used, in an ever more controlled manner. Like the earlier evidence of technological continuity between Clovis and Folsom, these changes in the details of projectile point manufacture were thought to reflect cultural continuity between Early Paleo-Indians and their descendants, called Late Paleo-Indians and identified by their long, willow-leaf-shaped points, sometimes with stems for hafting.

Because fluted points are found throughout the continental United States from Alaska to southern Arizona and from the far west to the Atlantic seaboard, when I began my career Early Paleo-Indians were thought to have colonized the entire continent. Radiocarbon dating indicated that this may have taken place within perhaps 1,000 radiocarbon years, extending from roughly 11,500 years ago in the west to perhaps 10,400 years ago in New England and the Canadian maritimes, based on a series of dates from the Debert site in Nova Scotia. Radiocarbon dates from a cave in southern Argentina indicated that the descendants of Early Paleo-Indians may have colonized the entire length of South America as little as 500 years later, by perhaps 10,000 years ago. This evidence of high mobility was reinforced in North America by the fact that Paleo-Indians frequently selected very high-quality stone from which to make tools, particularly the demanding fluted point, and carried this stone sometimes hundreds of kilometres either in a single direction, as if colonizing, or in two or more directions, as if moving within a geographic range.

To explain the successful, indeed explosive, colonization of the Americas by small groups of hunters, archaeologists in the 1960s looked to big game hunting. They argued that Early Paleo-Indians, like the big game they hunted, were able to cross ecological boundaries and live in different regions using the same or a very similar tool kit. Hence the widespread occurrence of the same kinds of artifacts – particularly fluted spear points and one or two other types of tools – across North America. Since mammoth were clearly one of the most archaeologically visible animals hunted in the Southwest and western Plains, archaeologists assumed that these or related animals may have been hunted throughout eastern North America. In Michigan, for example, the nearly identical distribution of isolated Early Paleo-Indian fluted points and mastodon bones seemed to suggest that Paleo-Indians in this region transferred their focus from mammoth, which were perhaps not as abundant as in the west, to mastodon. The mastodon was a browsing, forest- or woodland-dwelling animal physically similar but distantly related to the mammoth and modern elephant and one of the most abundant Pleistocene fossils in Michigan and the mid-continent region generally. In fact, the sharp northward limit in the strikingly coincident distribution of mastodon remains and isolated Early Paleo-Indian spear points in Michigan was commonly referred to – somewhat tongue in cheek, I've always thought – as the Mason-Quimby line, after the two archaeologists who compiled the data, Ronald Mason and George Irving Quimby.

The Early Paleo-Indian Hunting Kit: State-of-the-Art Ice Age Technology

It starts with a special stone, special because, when struck with a stone hammer or pressed very hard with, for example, the tip of an antler, it breaks into thin, conchoidal flakes. Since the size, direction of removal and even shape of these flakes can be predicted and to a certain extent controlled, the removal of a series of flakes from a larger piece can reduce that stone to a desired shape and size, such as a spear point, knife, or scraper. This process is called knapping or, more popularly, flintknapping, and it is analogous to the way in which chiselling, whittling, and sanding wood can produce a piece of sculpture. Unlike wood, of course, the special stone produces very sharp flakes or, if shaped itself, a knife-like edge. The flake may be as sharp as a razor blade or even a surgical knife, while the shaped edge is as

effective a cutting tool as a serrated or scalloped-edge steel kitchen knife.

For stone to cut like this it must have several qualities. It must either be amorphous, lacking a crystalline structure, or have a microscopic structure that does not interfere with the pattern of conchoidal breakage. It must also be homogeneous in internal structure. And for it to be amenable to knapping and useful for cutting, the stone must be both brittle and hard. Not many stones have these qualities. Obsidian, otherwise known as volcanic glass, is both amorphous and also quite brittle. Some rhyolites and basalts, which are also fine-grained igneous rocks, can make good toolstones, although they are less brittle than obsidian and therefore much harder to work.

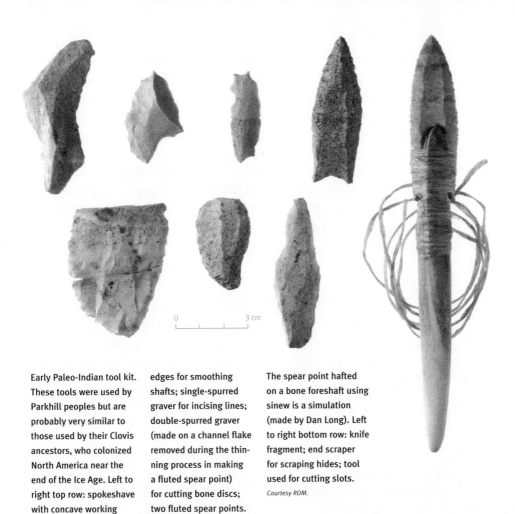

Early Paleo-Indian tool kit. These tools were used by Parkhill peoples but are probably very similar to those used by their Clovis ancestors, who colonized North America near the end of the Ice Age. Left to right top row: spokeshave with concave working edges for smoothing shafts; single-spurred graver for incising lines; double-spurred graver (made on a channel flake removed during the thinning process in making a fluted spear point) for cutting bone discs; two fluted spear points. The spear point hafted on a bone foreshaft using sinew is a simulation (made by Dan Long). Left to right bottom row: knife fragment; end scraper for scraping hides; tool used for cutting slots.

Courtesy ROM.

Sedimentary rocks, which are composed of particles (derived from weathering, the remains or products of plants or animals, or chemical action) may also make good toolstones. Perhaps the one most widely known to the general public is flint. Technically, flint is a form of quartz. Quartz is quite hard, somewhere between the hardness of a steel file and a diamond. Within the category of quartz, flint is identified as a chalcedony, a classification that includes agate, moss agate, jasper, chert, and fossil wood. Of these minerals, flint and chert were perhaps the most widely used for prehistoric tools. Although rarely found large enough to be made into tools, rock crystal and smoky quartz were also occasionally knapped by prehistoric people and may have been especially valued for their rarity,

clarity, or colour and the great skill needed for successful knapping.

The last group of excellent toolstones are heat-altered, or metamorphosed, sedimentary rocks, such as metaquartzites (derived from quartz sandstones) and argillites (which may have little or no quartz). Both rock types are useful as toolstone because their crystalline structures have been interlocked at high temperatures and pressures deep below the surface of the earth. It is this interlocked structure that fosters the shell-shaped, conchoidal fracturing.

These special rocks – obsidian and some fine-grained igneous rocks, various forms of quartz and, finally, both silica-enriched and heat-altered sedimentary rocks – were vital for toolmaking and all the life-giving things those tools provided. For

This picture of Paleo-Indians was enriched in the mid- and late 1960s by the discovery of a few fragments of caribou bone from two sites: the open-air Holcombe site in Michigan, and Dutchess Quarry Cave 1 in extreme southeastern New York State. Some doubted that the Michigan site was Paleo-Indian or that the caribou toe bone found there was from a barren-ground caribou, as the faunal analyst declared. Critics stated that the original size of the bone (the distal end of the first digit on the foot) had been too distorted by burning to distinguish between a smaller, tundra-dwelling animal and a larger, forest-dwelling one. Archaeologists also voiced uncertainty whether the caribou bones from strata 1 and 2 in Dutchess Quarry Cave were truly associated with the fluted point found in

The Early Paleo-Indian Hunting Kit *continued*

Stone Age humans, these special stones can be thought of figuratively as the very source of life.

Early Paleo-Indians used a wide variety of obsidian, chalcedonies and other materials for toolmaking and were quite good at finding the best materials to work. Although we know much about their search for toolstone and the tools they made, nobody knows what an Early Paleo-Indian hunting kit looked like. The stone components of the hunting kit have been dispersed. The spear points that killed or wounded were left behind in carcasses, otherwise lost in the field or, if broken but still tightly bound to the spear shaft, discarded at camp when the spear was rearmed. Worn-out tools were left at a multitude of sites as the band moved about the landscape. The organic parts of the hunting kit, which may have been considerable and vital for the proper functioning of the weapons and tools, have long since decomposed. Nevertheless, archaeologists could probably recreate a hunting kit, or at least a pretty good facsimile of one, from a couple of reasonable and conservative assumptions, miscellaneous bits of information, and several important discoveries: a cluster of grave goods from the Anzick site, a rockshelter in Montana; and a cache of objects from the East Wenatchee site, under an apple orchard in Washington State.

The centrepiece of this kit would have been the fluted spear point, named after the scar or groove, sometimes several, located in the centre of one or both faces and along the long axis of the weapon. The flute scar or scars were created by a thinning process directed at the base of the point; they often extend from a third to two-thirds or more the total length of the point.

Judging from the animals it was used to kill and the tremendous geographic area over which it was used, the fluted spear point was certainly a very effective weapon. Modern experiments on elephants in southern Africa have provided an opportunity for archaeologists to test replicas of Clovis-type fluted points, attached to foreshafts, fitted to longer lances, and propelled either by hand or with the use of a throwing stick, or atlatl. Game managers killed elephants by rifle fire during a culling process to provide a balance between population and range carrying capacity. Archaeologists then tested Clovis weapons on the carcasses to see whether they could pierce the thick hide and penetrate the body cavity. They did. Clearly, Early Paleo-Indian hunters had the technology to kill mammoth and other large animals.

In addition to being a lethal weapon, the Early Paleo-Indian fluted point is also a splendid example of the impressive complexity sometimes involved in the manufacture of prehistoric stone tools, belying the sense of the primitive that lurks in the popular conception of stone tools and the Stone Age. The ultimate goal of many modern flintknappers is to make an exact replica of the Clovis or Folsom fluted spear point. Although they disagree on the exact number of distinct steps the lower portion of stratum 2. Nevertheless, many archaeologists took these discoveries as evidence that Paleo-Indians in eastern North America hunted caribou along the tundra fringing the retreating ice sheet and in open environments farther south. A focus on this animal would help explain how Paleo-Indians could have maintained their big game hunting and highly mobile way of life in the east. In a sense caribou was seen by archaeologists as a replacement for the mammoth and bison so prominent in western Paleo-Indian sites.

In the early 1970s the handful of Early Paleo-Indian fluted spear points from Ontario added little to the continental picture of these people. The fifty or so specimens could do little more than reflect the then current

involved, or whether there actually are any distinct steps, they all agree the manufacturing process demands that a large number of milestones be reached in a specific sequence. Many of these involve manufacturing specific technical attributes. These concern the pattern of flake scars on the surface of the blank, the lateral and longitudinal curvature of the blank, and the location and preparation of the spot on the base that receives the force required to detach the thinning flake and create the distinctive flute scar on the finished spear point. Other factors to be considered include any temporary adjustments needed to fit the blank into a vise or grip, such as a forked stick, or to strengthen it to withstand the forces involved in fluting.

Modern flintknapping experiments show that some of the physical characteristics of the finished point can be produced with different techniques. For this reason, we may never know whether the methods of making modern replicas are exactly the same as those used by Clovis or Folsom knappers. But we know enough of the sequence to realize that a great deal of skill is required and that Clovis or Folsom points are among the highest achievements in flintknapping in the entire prehistoric world.

The Early Paleo-Indian hunting kit probably contained several fluted points as well as blanks for others, both made from two or more types of knappable stone and reflecting the travels of the hunter about the landscape. The blanks probably also served as sources of flakes from which other tools were made. The finished points were probably hafted on short foreshafts made of bone, antler, or ivory, using a glue made from a mixture of blood or animal fat, tree resin, and grit, and then tightly bound with sinew. The butt end of the foreshaft may have been tied directly to the lance or fitted into a socket so that it would detach easily from the lance if the point lodged in the wound of a struck animal. This would prevent the lance from being carried off if the animal was not immediately killed, allowing the hunter to re-arm it quickly with another stone-tipped foreshaft.

Finally, the Paleo-Indian hunting kit probably contained several tools for maintaining the equipment. These might include a spokeshave, a scraper with a concave edge for smoothing and shaping cylindrical objects such as foreshafts and lances; a stout cutting tool, shaped like a bird's beak, for reaming sockets or cutting slots; a stone wedge for splitting wood or bone; perhaps a few small hammer stones and abrading stones; several wooden or antler batons for use as hammers in flintknapping and the tips of antlers for use as pressure flakers for final retouching, or for resharpening broken points and dulled drilling or cutting tools; and, of course, a stone knife for butchering the day's take.

With these few items in a leather bag, a people occupied an entire continent.

interpretation of Early Paleo-Indian life drawn primarily from western North America and the northeastern United States and adjacent Canada. The problem with this picture for Ontario was that it was not based on local data. And this is what created my predicament. Without somewhere to start, how could I develop a program of Early Paleo-Indian research in Ontario? Unlike my work in Killarney Park, there didn't seem to be a logical geographic focus for the work. I could, of course, examine the discovery location of each of the isolated fluted points that had been recorded in the literature and attempt to see what, if anything, they had in common, to find some geographic pattern that would make it possible for me to direct my fieldwork in a logical, systematic way. I made a start in that direction but then, in the midst of my travels to local museums and the homes of avocational archaeologists, decided to look at the problem another way.

Instead of building an hypothesis from the individual items of data – the discovery location of each fluted point – I decided to work from the opposite direction: to predict Paleo-Indian land use from their presumed hunting activities and then use that prediction as a way of focusing fieldwork geographically. In the world of hard science such as physics or chemistry this would be analogous to building a hypothesis and then testing it in the laboratory. Archaeology is not usually thought of in this fashion either by the general public or by some of my colleagues but it can be done that way. The two key elements I chose for building this hypothesis were, first, the somewhat dubious evidence for caribou hunting in eastern North America and, second, the Niagara Escarpment, which was not dubious at all but a solid, hard fact.

My hypothesis, and the early results of my work, are described in the following newsletter, the third of a total of fourteen in my career. Although it isn't my favourite piece of writing, I include it because it shows how I was taking opportunities to find alternative research directions if I couldn't develop something in Paleo-Indian studies. It also shows how vulnerable I was at the beginning of the hardest period in my career, when a small push by my seniors or higher level administrators could have sent me anywhere, including out the door.

RECOLLECTIONS OF A BUSY SUMMER
OCTOBER 1972

As I wrote in a previous *Archaeological Newsletter* this year ... many interesting artifacts and archaeological sites are brought to our attention by cottage owners, teachers, farmers, school children, and others throughout the

The Niagara Escarpment

The Niagara Escarpment is one of southern Ontario's most prominent and beautiful geographic features. Located less than an hour's drive west of Toronto, the escarpment appears as either a dramatic cliff or, where covered by glacial deposits, a line of steep hills that stretch northwest from the Niagara River to the top of the Bruce Peninsula, a distance of over 350 kilometres as the crow flies. From the brow of the escarpment, the ground surface and underlying rocks slope gently downward in a southwesterly direction toward Lake Huron, and Michigan beyond, forming what is referred to geologically as a cuesta, an inclined plane bordered by a steep cliff. And it is this cliff, whether exposed to view or buried, that separates southwestern Ontario from the central and eastern portions of the province.

The rocks of the Niagara Escarpment were deposited in a large basin centred roughly under the state of Michigan, with the eastern and northern rim passing through southern Ontario, Manitoulin Island, Upper Peninsula Michigan, and Wisconsin. During the early history of the North American continent, between about 420 and 445 million years ago, this basin was intermittently covered by warm Paleozoic seas, rimmed with coral reefs. On its eastern perimeter, the basin occasionally received the drainage of rivers originating in mountain ranges on the eastern edge of the continent that predated the Appalachians. As sediments from the Paleozoic seas and distant eastern mountains accumulated in the Michigan basin, great pressures resulting from deep burial and other processes slowly changed the silts, clays, and sands to rock. Several hundred million years later, the rock became exposed to weathering. And then the cycle – from sediment to rock

and back to sediment – repeats. Endlessly. The configuration of the Niagara Escarpment we see today is part of that infinitely repeating cycle of geological change; the exposed limestones, dolostones, shales, and sandstones telling of earlier periods beginning at the bottom of ancient seas and the tops of even more ancient mountains.

The Niagara Escarpment is a formidable barrier throughout its length, whether as sheer cliffs hundreds of metres high or as steep hills. At over thirty places along its length in southern Ontario, however, the escarpment is cut by steep-sided, V-shaped valleys, such as the Forks of the Credit River at Belfountain and the Pine River valley near Mansfield, or by broad, U-shaped valleys, such as the Dundas valley through and under Hamilton, Bronte Creek near Milton, and the Beaver valley south of Thornbury on Georgian Bay. These and other river cuts appear to have been eroded initially by preglacial rivers. Some were then further sculpted and enlarged by glacial ice and meltwater. Finally, most were partially buried by glacial debris – some almost completely. Together, these valleys provided corridors for the roads and railroads of European settlement, and they are no less important today for transportation, most notably the multilane, high-speed highways such as 403 through the Hamilton area and 401 through the Milton area. Perhaps these corridors were Ice Age game trails, attracting both caribou and Early Paleo-Indian hunters who might have attempted to intercept migrating herds of these animals as they moved east-west across the province.

province. This can keep us quite busy and, in fact, this last summer I spent most of my field season surface collecting and testing sites that were reported to us the preceding winter. Our work took us to Flesherton at the head of the Beaver valley, southwest of Collingwood, to Maple just outside of Metro Toronto, the Niagara Escarpment near Milton, Vineland in the Niagara Peninsula, then east to Charleston Lake north of Kingston, and, at the end of the summer (and the end of the "bug season" – at least for the most part), north to Kabinakagami and Wabatonguishi lakes east of White River in the Algoma District of northern Ontario.

Our summer began at Flesherton where, because of the discovery of a large Late Paleo-Indian quartzite spearhead ... we were hoping to find a campsite, or at least other traces of some of the earliest people to move into the province at the end of the Ice Age – probably between 6,000 and 8,000 years ago. Unfortunately, we were unsuccessful in this. At Maple we tested two of several sites where large numbers of artifacts had been collected ... At least one possible Archaic site, occupied some time prior to 1000 BC, warrants extensive testing if this can be arranged with the landowner in the future. We also tested several possible Archaic sites near Vineland, which were reported to us by a student, Neil Ryckman. North of Milton we made an extensive surface collection on a large, possibly early historic site reported by a farmer, Mr W. Wilson, who had first noticed artifacts and large dark stains in the soil while ploughing. At Charleston Lake north of Kingston, we tested a rich habitation site occupied by Iroquoian peoples ... At the end of the summer we went up north to the area where one of my field assistants (Craig Liddle) had previously found some large tools of very high-quality chert. We spent our time on two large lakes testing several sites and surveying for others.

All in all it was quite a varied (and I might say harried) summer, what with all our moving around plus the fact that in July, after nine and a fraction months of anticipation, my wife and I were visited by my avian namesake. The artifacts that were recovered from all of these sites are going to keep me occupied for much of the winter but I am afraid the July visitation is a much longer project.

In addition to the above work I also continued the search for Paleo-Indian sites along the Niagara Escarpment. This summer our survey was limited to the Bronte Creek and Highway 401 gaps that cut through the escarpment west of Milton.

... Perhaps I should explain why I am looking for Paleo-Indian sites along the Niagara Escarpment. This involves a consideration of both geography and what Early Man may have hunted. First, throughout much of its length, from the Niagara River in the south to Tobermory at the tip of the Bruce Peninsula, the Niagara Escarpment forms vertical cliffs or, where covered with sands and gravels deposited by glacial ice, steep hills as much as ninety metres or more in height. Consequently, in many areas the easiest if not the only routes across the escarpment are through the major gaps such as the Bronte Creek gap and the one through which Highway 401 passes. Secondly, relatively recent finds at two sites in Michigan and New York State indicate that early Paleo-Indians may have hunted barren-ground caribou. If caribou were also present in Ontario, they would probably have passed through the major gaps in the escarpment during any seasonal east-west movements ... between the tundra near the ice sheet and the more forested regions to the southwest. The major gaps would have been ideal places to intercept these herds and are therefore areas where I think we might effectively concentrate our search for Early Man sites.

This summer I decided to work mostly in the Bronte Creek gap. For the first few days we drove down all the roads in the gap plotting the location of the ploughed fields on our maps and asking permission to walk over them. Then the leg work began. My two assistants, Craig Liddle and Andrew Stewart, and I walked down every twentieth furrow or so of all of the ploughed fields we could find looking for chert flakes, animal bones, and, of course, the arrowheads that might indicate the presence of a site.

Only three days after beginning our work we found our first trace of Early Man – a small lanceolate spearhead we picked up on a ploughed field almost in the shadow of Mt Nemo, the southern boundary of the gap at its entrance. The spearhead is approximately five centimetres long but was originally probably longer since it appears to have been resharpened. As is typical of such points, the base and the lateral edges on the lower half were ground smooth, presumably to prevent the lashings that held the point to the spear shaft from being cut. We found several flakes within thirty metres of the point and I was excited at the possibility that we might actually have found a campsite. This hope died hard several days later after our test excavations produced only a few flakes and fragments of two arrowheads that were made much later than the lanceolate spearhead. Apparently the Late Paleo-Indian point was lost by a passing hunter and became mixed, through ploughing and other disturbances, with material from later peoples who also visited the area. Later, I learned from a nearby farmer that the top of the hill had been graded to fill in a nearby ravine so that any sites that did exist must be almost totally destroyed. We were extremely fortunate to find the point, considering the amount of past disturbance, and we were none too soon either since a few days later grading operations were begun to make over the area where the point was found into a tee for the fifth green of a new golf course.

About a week later, and two days before we were going to have to stop this project for the summer, we found a second Paleo-Indian point – this one located about a mile from Rattlesnake Point on the north side of the entrance to the gap. This is a so-called "fluted" point, named after the large flake scar or "flute" in the centre of the point at the base, and it may have been made between 9,000 and 12,000 years ago. Nothing else was found near the point and, like the other specimen, it was probably an isolated loss.

0   3 cm

Early Paleo-Indian fluted spear point, also found in the Bronte Creek gap in the Niagara Escarpment.
J. Hosek, ROM.

Late Paleo-Indian spear point found during archaeological survey work in 1972 in the Bronte Creek gap in the Niagara Escarpment, a short distance west of Milton.
J. Hosek, ROM.

These two Paleo-Indian points do not, of course, necessarily indicate that my thinking about where to look for Early Man sites is correct. It may be, but it will take much more evidence than this to demonstrate it. The points do, however, indicate that Early Man was in the area and that future work in the Bronte Creek gap and perhaps other gaps would certainly be worthwhile. Perhaps next summer we will be even more successful and I will be able to report in my next *Archaeological Newsletter* about the discovery and excavation of a Paleo-Indian campsite.

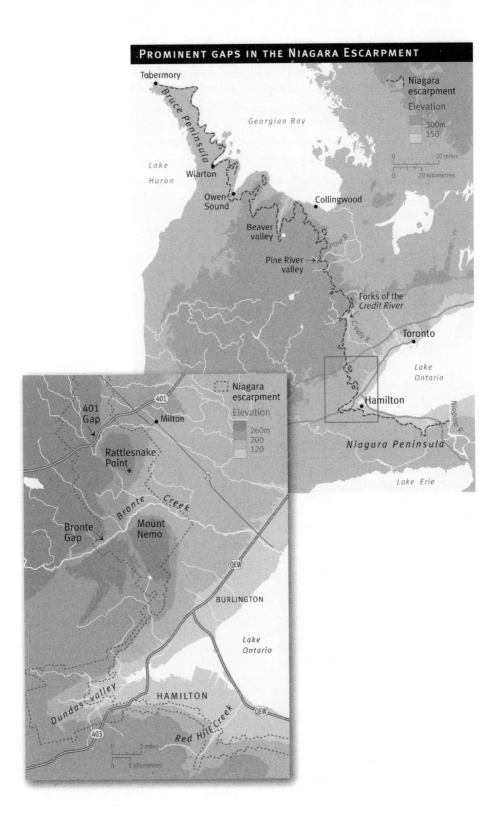

PROMINENT GAPS IN THE NIAGARA ESCARPMENT

Tobermory

Bruce Peninsula

Georgian Bay

```
- - -  Niagara
       escarpment
       Elevation
       300m
       150
0          20 miles
0          20 kilometres
```

Lake Huron

Wiarton

Owen Sound

Collingwood

Beaver valley

Pine River valley

Pine R

Forks of the *Credit River*

Credit R.

Toronto

Lake Ontario

Hamilton

Niagara R.

Niagara Peninsula

Lake Erie

(inset map)

```
- - -  Niagara
       escarpment
       Elevation
       260m
       200
       120
```

401

401 Gap

Milton

Rattlesnake Point

25

Bronte Creek

Bronte Gap

Mount Nemo

QEW

BURLINGTON

Lake Ontario

Dundas valley

HAMILTON

QEW

403

Red Hill Creek

```
0          2 miles
0          2 kilometres
```

Postscript

As you can see from my story I was indeed ... busy. (I wonder to this day why I couldn't have chosen a word other than "busy" to describe something I hoped was much more academic.) It was during this period in the early 1970s that I developed the pattern of working in the pastoral landscape of southern Ontario during the spring and early summer out of trucks and tent camps and then, in the late summer, working in the forest and lake country of northern Ontario out of boats and tent camps. Except for the tents, a forced necessity, I thought this intraseasonal wandering was very clever since I could take advantage of the freshly ploughed fields in the south during the early part of the season to search more easily for archaeological sites and during the later summer, benefit from working in the north during the hottest weather in southern Ontario and also avoid my greatest northern discomfort – bugs! – which, if not totally absent by August and early September, at least had passed their peak.

During this period of hustling between southern and northern Ontario or commuting daily to the museum, my personal life was not

New Discovery on the Niagara Escarpment

In 1997, twenty-four years after I stopped looking for Early Paleo-Indian sites associated with Ice Age game trails through the Niagara Escarpment, I unexpectedly became involved with a newly discovered site in just such a situation. The archaeological site, called Mt Albion West, was discovered by a colleague on the edge of the Redhill Creek Valley, just within the city of Hamilton. At the location of the site, the valley is very deep and broad. Thus, it fits the image of a corridor, and potentially an Ice Age game trail, since it would have facilitated the movement of animals travelling between the top of the Niagara Escarpment and the Lake Ontario basin to the east.

Caribou may have used this corridor. In 1986 I found several burnt caribou bones in a former firepit at a Gainey site near Udora in south-central Ontario, so we know that caribou lived in Ontario at the end of the Ice Age and that Gainey people hunted them. The Redhill Creek Valley corridor may also have been used by mammoth and mastodon. Mammoth bones have been reported in the city of Hamilton from Lake Iroquois beach deposits dating to around 12,000 years ago and at other, undated locations in the region. Although the remains from Lake Iroquois deposits are perhaps 1,000 years older than the Gainey colonization of the region, mammoth may have lived in southern Ontario until the end of the Ice Age, 10,000 years ago. This is certainly true of mastodon, which became extinct at roughly the same time. Thus, both species overlapped early human occupation and may have been actively hunted or scavenged as opportunity allowed. Mastodon remains have been found in the general area of the Mt Albion site, in both the Ontario basin and the southern part of the Niagara Peninsula at Wellandport, Welland, and other locations. Muskox and bison might have lived in the area as well.

Mt Albion West has not yet been completely excavated. The relatively small size of the site and the few tools and tool fragments suggest that it was occupied by a small group of people. The presence of both hunting weapons and a handful of hide-dressing tools implies that this small group contained both sexes, possibly belonging to an extended family or several families of a exactly calm either. My wife, a physical anthropologist, had her own seasonal pattern of teaching during the year and writing in the summer (sometimes in tent camps with me) or doing fieldwork in Africa. And although we were obviously preoccupied with our work and the problems of co-ordinating our comings and goings, our lives were gradually being influenced by our urban environment and our still unfamiliar paycheques, shifting to a somewhat more "normal" existence from the almost monastic life of graduate school. Thus, in 1972, we bought a house, which I thought we would never finish paying for, and had our first child: a girl. She complicated our comings and goings enormously but also softened our lives. We also bought something we had never owned before, an eleven-inch black and white television set. My life was turning upside down.

The same couldn't be said of my fieldwork in the early 1970s. Far from turning me or the world upside down with excitement, the survey work along the Niagara Escarpment had turned into a hard grind. We did have our moments, but the brief excitement of finding the isolated artifacts described in the newsletter threw me into an even darker state of mind as

small band. Most of the tools are made of exotic toolstone: Onondaga chert from the northeastern edge of the Erie basin, approximately forty kilometres south of the site, and Fossil Hill chert from the Kolapore/Blue Mountain uplands in the southern Georgian Bay region, approximately 160 kilometres northwest. If the proportion of these two toolstones reflects the most recent history of band movements, then the group that camped at Mt Albion West had just spent time in the north after an earlier visit to the source of Onondaga chert southwest of the site. Thus, when they stopped at Mt Albion they appear to have been on the southern leg of some sort of north-south cyclical movement, perhaps a seasonal subsistence round.

But were they at the end of their travels before returning north again? This question was raised by a surprising discovery, one challenging my previous assumption that the site was strategically located astride a game corridor for the purpose of intercept hunting. The site is situated on top of an abundant supply of toolstone – called Lockport chert – which appears to have been used for making tool blanks and possibly even fluted spear points. Perhaps the band was retooling. But why here?

The answer may lie in the Ontario basin. Eleven thousand years ago, early Lake Ontario was much smaller than it is today, exposing as dry land large areas of former lake bed. Perhaps Mt Albion was selected to give hunters an opportunity to replenish their tool kit before descending into the Ontario basin, drawn perhaps by overwintering animals. This demands quite an intellectual switch, from thinking of Mt Albion West as a strategic hunting location to regarding it as a possible staging area from which a group of hunters or an entire band could strike out to exploit a completely different ecological setting, possibly during the winter part of their seasonal subsistence round.

These ideas are all very tentative. The trick now will be to find ways to explore and document them to our satisfaction, or to replace them with new ideas.

we continued to walk daily across seemingly endless cornfields, which proved again and again to be archaeologically sterile. To distract myself and keep up my faith in what I still thought was a worthwhile project, I fantasized about great discoveries I might make at any step or in the very next field. I also enjoyed the odd things we found, such as the overgrown wreck of an airplane, shoved up against a fencerow along an out-of-the-way field. And strange as it might seem, I started a golf ball collection. We seemed to find golf balls almost everywhere we went, even in the most remote fields far from any houses or roads. I couldn't imagine where they came from. I wondered if farmers practised swings from their tractors and hay wagons, or from their back yards into the barn yard, where the balls were swallowed by cattle and then scattered over the fields by wandering animals or mechanical manure spreaders. Such are the musings of an archaeological mind with too little archaeology to think about.

The hope expressed in the last line of the newsletter, that I might be able to report on the discovery and excavation of a Paleo-Indian site in my next newsletter, didn't materialize from my escarpment work. That would happen another way and would set me on a different course altogether. But I wasn't to know that for a while.

3 | AN UNEXPECTED TURN

IN ARCHAEOLOGICAL FIELDWORK, indeed any research, new beginnings can happen at any time. They happen when unexpected discoveries change the way of looking at something, or looking for it.

The clue to what would become a new way of looking *for* something – Early Paleo-Indian sites – came into my life just prior to the start of my third year of work along the Niagara Escarpment. The clue was hard to miss, but I can't say that I found it through my own hard work or even by accident. It was handed to me by an avocational archaeologist named Charles Garrad. Charles, or Charlie, as he prefers to be called, came to Canada from England, settled in Ontario to work as an appraiser, and then became interested in the local archaeology. Eventually he was to become totally absorbed by it. Charlie developed a special interest in the Petun people, a distinct tribe or tribes of the Ontario Iroquois who, during the seventeenth century, lived in the Blue Mountain region south of the modern city of Collingwood on southern Georgian Bay. Charlie also became heavily involved with the Ontario Archaeological Society (OAS), an organization for the general public as well as for avocational and professional archaeologists. The OAS gives people at all levels of interest an opportunity to learn about the prehistory of Ontario through its sponsorship of public lectures and workshops, annual symposia, and hands-on experience in archaeological excavation. The society also publishes several newsletters and a scholarly journal. Charlie became president of the organization in 1974 and later served for a long period as administrator.

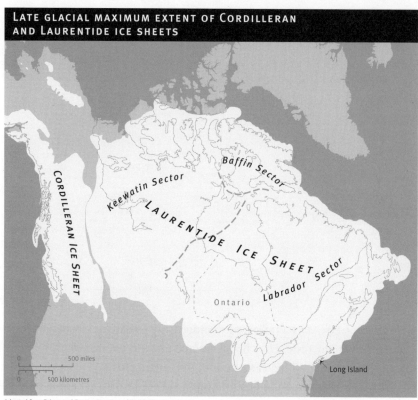

LATE GLACIAL MAXIMUM EXTENT OF CORDILLERAN AND LAURENTIDE ICE SHEETS

CORDILLERAN ICE SHEET

Keewatin Sector

Baffin Sector

LAURENTIDE ICE SHEET

Labrador Sector

Ontario

500 miles

500 kilometres

Long Island

Adapted from Fulton and Prest 1987, 182 and Occhietti 1987, 303.

We first met shortly after I came to the ROM. Charlie was aware of my attempts to start something in Paleo-Indian research and was interested in Paleo-Indians as well. In the late 1960s he had directed a research project for the OAS in commemoration of Canada's 1967 centennial. Appropriately enough the project selected to celebrate Canada's birth as a confederation was designed to celebrate another beginning, at least 100 centuries earlier: the colonization of Ontario, and Canada, by Early Paleo-Indians. For the occasion the OAS decided to do a survey of all the Early Paleo-Indian fluted spear points that could be routed out in a province-wide survey.

In 1971 Charlie published a short paper on the results of that provincial survey in the journal of the OAS, *Ontario Archaeology*. In it he provided information on all the isolated Early Paleo-Indian fluted points from Ontario that were held privately or in institutional collections and that he could personally examine. Some of these artifacts had been published on before, such as those at the ROM, but most had not and were therefore totally unknown except to the institution or individual who held them. Charlie

Again, the Question Who

When the first humans passed through the final door that led from eastern Beringia to the unoccupied North and South American continents beyond, they also became separated from the remainder of the world. For with the final flooding of the central part of the Beringian land mass in the area between Siberia and Alaska at the end of the Ice Age, those colonizing peoples who penetrated deeply into the Americas lost contact with their Asian relatives. And the descendants of those initial colonizing peoples, through several millennia of distinctive cultural development, were unknown to peoples in Africa, Eurasia, and the Pacific. This separateness was far more extreme than that between different regions of the Old World. The peoples of Europe, North Africa, the Near East, and Asia, for example, have a long history of interconnections that became ever more profound after the emergence of agricultural societies and later urban civilizations. Roughly parallel cultural developments evolved in North, Central, and South America, but largely separate from one another and, of course, from the Old World. Thus, when European explorers reached the Caribbean and the Atlantic shores of the western hemisphere in the fifteenth century, the circle closed. The collective human experience, which had fragmented with the disappearance of Beringia, now became global.

The Europeans initiated this new era with a case of mistaken identity, calling the Caribbean Natives "Indians" in the erroneous belief that this "new land" was East India. The Norse had not made the same mistake 500 years earlier when they made intermittent contact with Dorset people (Paleo-Eskimos) and Thule people (Inuit), both in the eastern Canadian arctic, and with Native peoples in Labrador, Newfoundland, and possibly northern New England. But the Norse contact, spanning perhaps a couple of centuries beginning around AD 1000, ceased when Greenland was abandoned during a period of climatic deterioration between roughly AD 1200 and 1450. Somewhat later, beginning perhaps coincidentally during a period of brief climatic improvement, sixteenth-century Europeans began a long period of exploration and soon established permanent settlements.

The Europeans encountered a great variety of peoples in the northeast. These included, to mention but a few, the Iroquoians (the Mohawk, Oneida, Onondaga, Cayuga, and Seneca of New York State and the St Lawrence Iroquois, Huron, Petun, and Neutral of Ontario and Quebec), and the Algonkians of the Maritimes and northern New England (the Beothuk, Mi'kmaq, Maliseet-Passamaquoddy, and Abenaki) and the northern forests (the Cree, Ojibwa, Algonquin, and Ottawa). Unfortunately, these historically known people can be traced only a short distance back in time. This is not because they weren't present earlier but because the slender threads that lead from the sixteenth or fifteenth centuries back into the past are soon obscured in the archaeological record by much broader cultural patterns. And it is these patterns that form the basis for a chronology that marks archaeological time.

In the Great Lakes region, various subdivisions of this chronology are named after the largest river and the dominant vegetation: the Mississippian period, beginning around 1,000 years ago; and the Woodland period, beginning around 3,000 years ago. Before that is the Archaic period, beginning around 9,500 years ago, and a still more remote time, the Paleo-Indian period (literally "old" Indian), which began some time prior to 11,000 years ago.

This descriptive chronology, and the broad cultural patterns it reveals, suggests cultural and biological continuity from the beginning of the archaeological record to the present day. But the broad patterns in the archaeological record were created by many peoples with many identities, most of which will remain unknown. This is the averaging effect of time, large amounts of time. But the question – Who were the first peoples of the New World? – persists and has become more urgent.

ICE LOBES IN SOUTHERN ONTARIO
Adapted from Tovell 1992, 110.

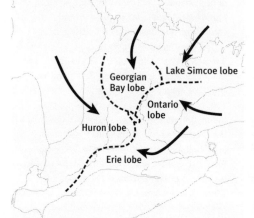

LAURENTIDE ICE SHEET

Georgian Bay lobe

Lake Simcoe lobe

Ontario lobe

Huron lobe

Erie lobe

EMERGENCE OF ONTARIO ISLAND DURING ICE RETREAT
Adapted from Chapman and Putnam 1984, 331.

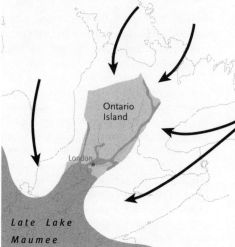

LAURENTIDE ICE SHEET

Ontario Island

London

Late Lake Maumee

EARLY STAGE IN LOWER GREAT LAKES FORMATION, APPROXIMATELY 12,000 YEARS BP
Adapted from Barnett 1991-2, 1052.

LAURENTIDE ICE SHEET

Early Lake Algonquin phase

Glacial Lake Iroquois

Rome outlet

Early Lake Erie

Scale for first three plates

0   50 miles

0   50 kilometres

EARLY POSTGLACIAL LOW-WATER STAGE
IN LOWER GREAT LAKES,
APPROXIMATELY 10,000 YEARS BP
Adapted from Barnett 1991-2, 1073.

(Hudson Bay)

LAURENTIDE ICE SHEET

(James Bay)

Land
Glacial lake
Glacial sea
Ice sheet

0   100 miles
0   100 kilometres

Glacial Lake Agassiz

Thunder Bay

(Lake Superior)

ONTARIO

Sault Ste Marie

Sudbury

Champlain Sea

Ottawa River

Ottawa

Lake Stanley

Lake Hough

(Georgian Bay)

Lake Chippewa

WISCONSIN

(Lake Michigan)

(Lake Huron)

Toronto

Early Lake Ontario

(Lake Ontario)

MICHIGAN

NEW YORK

GLACIAL LAKE ALGONQUIN
AT THE END OF THE
ICE AGE, BETWEEN 11,300
AND 10,400 YEARS BP
Adapted from Freeman 1979 and Hansel et al., 1985, 45.

Early Lake Erie

(Lake Erie)

PENNSYLVANIA

OHIO

Ice margin   North Bay

Lake Algonquin

Toronto

London

Early Lake Erie

thought, correctly, that archaeological research would benefit from bringing together in one publication information on all of these artifacts. After his paper was published the widespread and carefully built network of contacts that Charlie and the OAS had established with farmers, historians, local museum curators, and others didn't just disappear. It continued to function and produced something Charlie thought would interest me.

He was right.

In the spring of 1973 Charlie telephoned to tell me that he had recently visited a farmer in south-central Ontario who had found two Early Paleo-Indian fluted spear points. Two! This was very unusual since finding even one was an extremely rare event. Although the artifacts had been found nearly a decade apart, one in the early 1960s and the other in 1971, the farmer had recorded where he picked them up. One had been found on top of a sandy hill and the second near its base. The farm on which the hill stood was located just outside the modern community of Alliston, a drive of about an hour and a half northwest of Toronto.

Charlie thought the discovery of two fluted points in the same general area might indicate the presence of an archaeological site nearby and graciously invited me to investigate. I drove up to the farm and, even before turning into the laneway, saw hints in the surrounding terrain that told me where the fluted points had most likely come from. These hints formed a very powerful mental image, like that seen the first instant after closing the eyes to a brightly lit object such as a window. And that image is still strong, not only because of its visual impact but also because it provided the clue to a new direction in my fieldwork.

A few moments earlier I had been travelling on a straight gravel road between vast agricultural fields that were completely and utterly flat in all directions, much like the surface of a pool table. I knew immediately that I was driving on an old lake bed that had been planed by the action of shallow waves. Then in the distance, off to the west behind farm buildings at the end of a laneway that I suspected must be the entrance to the farm I was seeking, I saw a low, isolated hill that looked much like a beached whale. The hill itself was actually a drumlin, the geological term for an elongated hill deposited and shaped by moving glacial ice. I turned to the person next to me in the passenger seat of the truck, pointed out the window to my left with excitement and said something like, "That's where they came from, I'll bet! That island! Over there!"

This was not the first time in my life, or the last, that I was to speak about something from the past – a fragment of an earlier landscape – as if it existed today. And I'm sure I often give the impression that I don't always

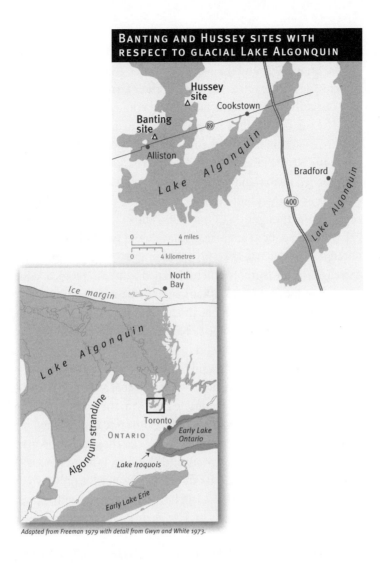

Adapted from Freeman 1979 with detail from Gwyn and White 1973.

live in the present. It's true, I often catch glimpses of the past through a fence line, behind a barn, in a road cut, across a valley. But the person in the car needn't worry; I stop when I need to hold that image, to see it just a bit more clearly. As I did then, looking at that island, seeing it first sculpted by slowly moving glacial ice and then washed by the waters of a large, shallow lake. I had to grab my camera.

The farm was owned by Mr and Mrs Edward Banting. I was surprised to learn that Edward Banting, a slightly built and quiet man, was a nephew of Frederick Banting, one of the co-discoverers of insulin in 1921-3. Because of Edward's relationship with his uncle, a celebrated scientist and Nobel laureate, and a deep interest in things historical, he and his wife, Louise, valued knowledge and the work of science and readily gave me permission to excavate on the hill at the back of their farm. We were all interested to find out if the fluted points had indeed come from an archaeological site.

The top of the hill was planted in grain and wouldn't be harvested until August, so I filled in the first part of my 1973 field season with work along the Niagara Escarpment. During that period, as the excavation date approached nearer and nearer, the sandy hill on the Banting farm loomed ever larger in my mind, eventually eclipsing everything else. And I replayed the thought that I might, for the first time, actually have a site to excavate and data to analyze. Although the two fluted points were reason enough to be excited, their portent for an even more significant discovery increased immeasurably when I learned from a geological colleague the identity of the former lake that made the Bantings' sandy hill an island: glacial Lake Algonquin. Since the history of glacial Lake Algonquin over-lapped the known age range of Early Paleo-Indians in North America as a whole, there was every reason to believe that Paleo-Indians may very well have lived on the former island behind the Bantings' house.

August came and the field was harvested, although a couple of weeks later than expected. After a phone call from the Bantings, I drove to the site in a frantic mood and even before the crew had finished putting up the tent camp I had almost everyone laying out the excavation grid and preparing for excavation. Eating and sleeping, I thought, would just have to take care of themselves. By then I had money for only two more weeks of work that field season, the late harvest having roughly halved my avail-able time at the Bantings' farm. I needed, and very badly wanted, to find something quickly.

I decided to focus on a large area of dark soil on the eastern end of the former island. The almost black soil contained fragments of charcoal, fire-cracked rock, and a few small flakes of chert, probably from tool resharp-ening. It looked to me as though the plough had disturbed some buried firepits. This would be a discovery indeed since firepits often contain some of the most valuable things an archaeologist can find: charcoal for radio-carbon dating and plant identification (to reconstruct the environment); animal bone from food refuse (to determine what prehistoric people hunted or trapped); and broken or worn-out discarded tools (to determine the cultural identity of the people who built the fire).

Within less than a week, my dream of excavating very ancient firepits faded as completely as morning mist in the midday sun. After very careful and time-consuming hand excavation with trowels and spoons and brushes, following the blackened soil as it twisted and turned through the subsoil – meanwhile doing all the other obligatory archaeological things such as note taking, horizontal and vertical mapping, photography, and soil and charcoal sampling – I was left with an impressive microlandscape of moon-like craters and interconnecting channels. This was very suspicious because prehistoric firepits could be expected to be much more regular in shape. But then, who could say that I hadn't found an exception, perhaps an area that had been both intensively and repeatedly used from one visit to the next?

Then came the moment of truth. While kneeling low over one of the small craters and looking through a hand-held magnifying glass at a small piece of charcoal, I saw wood fibres and suddenly learned what we had so painstakingly excavated: the remains of burnt tree stumps! The wood fibres could not possibly have survived more than a few years' exposure to weathering and decomposition, let alone the 10,000 or 11,000 years since the dying of a Paleo-Indian campfire. The partially burned wood was essentially modern and came either from a natural fire or from one deliberately set by a farmer to clear land for cultivation.

As I stood up from my close examination of the charcoal fragment, the disappointment over what I had just discovered was like a physical blow. I realized then that the small chert flakes from prehistoric tool resharpening must have been incidentally mixed in with this historical fire, falsely suggesting that the two events were related. This was not the last time I would unintentionally excavate tree burns using the finest archaeological techniques I knew. After it's all over, you tell yourself time after time that you were right to have done what you did. After all, the tree burn *might* have been a prehistoric firepit. And once you're done, it's too late to go back if you haven't recorded what you found along the way because the very act of excavation systematically destroys what it uncovers. Painstaking excavation and record keeping are fundamental to archaeology and probably also the thing about fieldwork that so impresses the general public. Our crater-like excavation was certainly impressive, both as a hand-crafted hole in the ground and for the investment of time it represented. But it was also profoundly disappointing. I felt as if I had been chasing ghosts.

But I noticed an interesting thing about myself during that short period: a pattern of behaviour that I was to repeat many times and one that may be common among archaeologists generally. First, I focus very strongly on a small piece of ground if I think it may produce something archaeological. If later it seems that it may not, only then do I then cast

Excavations at the Banting site in 1973, which were based on a grid of ten-foot squares. Hoped-for Early Paleo-Indian firepits turned out to be modern tree burns related to forest clearance for cultivation.

Photograph by Peter Storck.

about in all directions, sometimes frantically, for other places to work, as if noticing my surroundings for the first time. I fight this tendency to focus on what's directly beneath my feet because geologists have taught me the value of looking at things with a larger perspective. Still, I'm not sure to this day whether the urge to focus narrowly is part of my personality or whether an excavation grid and a strong commitment to a small, carefully defined space foster the kind of insularity one might associate with homesteading in the wilderness.

In any event, as soon as it occurred to me that I was not digging Early Paleo-Indian firepits I started looking about for other places on the Banting hill. With only a few days left to go on the project, I excavated some trenches on another part of the hill where we had earlier found some flakes and several artifact fragments on the surface of the ground. By great good fortune, we found more material in the plough zone, the soil turned over by cultivation. Possibly *this* was the campsite I had been looking for.

The 1973 season closed with a promise, not only at the Banting hill but for my research generally, since the discovery of Early Paleo-Indian artifacts on a former island of a glacial lake gave me a new sense of direction for my work.

The following newsletter, written after the second season of excavation on the Bantings' farm, describes what we found there in 1974 and on our first attempts at beachcombing on the fossil shoreline of glacial Lake Algonquin:

ANCIENT BEACHES AND THE TRAIL OF EARLY MAN IN ONTARIO
DECEMBER 1974

In an *Archaeological Newsletter* written a few years ago, I drew an analogy between the survey work I was doing in Killarney Provincial Park and beachcombing. Since I was looking for archaeological sites on ancient raised shorelines of postglacial lakes that had drained several thousand years ago, I thought the analogy was appropriate. Understandably it was not the kind of beachcombing that will attract many winter-weary people to the Caribbean this winter, but it was exciting and sometimes pleasurable nevertheless.

This last summer I took up "beachcombing" again, but this time in an area less than an hour's drive north of Toronto, on the former beach of a Late Pleistocene lake – glacial Lake Algonquin – which existed between approximately 10,400 and 11,500 years ago. I first became interested in this lake from an archaeological viewpoint a couple of years ago when I learned that two spear points made by Early Paleo-Indians had been found on a former island of the lake. These people were nomadic hunters and gatherers who probably moved into southern Ontario from the south shortly after the final retreat of the continental ice sheet. The actual date of Early Man's arrival is not known and, in fact, until a few years ago his very presence here was indicated only by a small number of isolated and widely scattered spear points. No campsites were known. Consequently, the report of two spear points ... not only raised the possibility of finding an occupation site for the first time but also suggested that if the shoreline of that lake were walked over carefully other sites might be found.

Lake Algonquin was the largest of the proglacial lakes in this region. It occupied the basins of present-day lakes Michigan and Huron and Georgian Bay, covered the Bruce Peninsula, and inundated the lowlands south of Georgian Bay, creating a number of "finger lakes" that extended as far south as Holland Landing and Schomberg. The continental ice sheet formed the northern border of the lake, and as it retreated northward during deglaciation Lake Algonquin grew progressively larger, ultimately covering all of Manitoulin Island except for the highest ridges, which formed a number of small islands. In the east, the lake drained ... through an outlet near Kirkfield ... [and then through a drainage system that later became] ... the Trent waterway and ultimately into Lake Iroquois, the predecessor of Lake Ontario. The history of Lake Algonquin came to an end after the ice retreated to the area of North Bay and uncovered ... new outlets to the east.

Because of the location of the two projectile points near Alliston and other indications elsewhere that Early Paleo-Indian peoples may have lived on the shores of Lake Algonquin, I decided to try to use a knowledge of the location of the beach as a means of finding other sites. Fortunately, several geological maps showing the location of the Algonquin shoreline and other glacial features in the Lake Simcoe region, and particularly in the Alliston area, were published between 1972 and 1974 so I had a very good idea where the beach was located and could try to "second guess" the kinds of areas Early Man may have selected for occupation. This task was made a little easier with the knowledge that Early Man in this region may have hunted barren-ground caribou. Consequently, I planned to concentrate my search for campsites on higher terrain overlooking possible fording places where caribou might have crossed narrow bodies of water and at the southern ends of the major arms of the lake where caribou might have passed if they had been deflected in their movements by broad expanses of water and forced to follow the shoreline around the lake.

I decided to begin the survey in an area roughly forty kilometres wide and twenty-nine kilometres long, centred on the Banting site near Alliston. Here, in an area 1,160 kilometres square were located two major arms of Lake

Algonquin that formed the southern limits of the lake along its eastern margin. I estimated that this part of the lake contained over 300 kilometres of shoreline, and before the survey was over we were to drive nearly 5,000 kilometres and walk tens of kilometres in an effort to cover the entire area.

At 2:35 p.m. on Thursday, May 30th, after several weeks of having found only a thin scatter of Late Archaic and Woodland artifacts, we finally discovered a Paleo-Indian site [later to be called the Hussey site]! Walking on the top of a former peninsula on the eastern shore of Lake Algonquin, one of the crew picked up a large fragment of an Early Paleo-Indian spear point. All through the morning we had been expecting to find something definitive since the location was excellent (jokingly referred to as "perfect location number 1,001") and we had been picking up numerous but non-diagnostic flakes and broken tools indicating that the area had been occupied prehistorically. Consequently, when it finally came, this discovery climaxed several hours of work, becoming increasingly frustrating because of the strong feeling of anticipation. Although the point could have been an isolated loss unrelated to the other artifacts, the likelihood that we had actually found a campsite was confirmed several weeks later when we re-walked the field and found the basal fragment of another Early Paleo-Indian point.

At the end of the second surface collection, the total sample of artifacts [from the Hussey site] included, in addition to the points, a spurred end scraper (a type of scraping and engraving tool frequently found at Early Paleo-Indian sites), several complete knives, one or two possible blanks for spear points, numerous scraping and cutting tools, and unworked flakes. The artifacts occurred in three loose concentrations, possibly representing different activity areas or even different campsites, and I hope to be able to test part of the site next summer to determine if any material occurs below the zone disturbed by ploughing.

In August I returned to the Banting site with the intention of completing the excavations started the previous summer. In 1973 I had opened up a few test squares near the centre of the site area and this produced evidence of occupation, which I wanted to investigate further. This past summer we excavated an additional 176 square metres and recovered a number of gravers, several blanks possibly intended for spear points, flake scrapers, and a couple of hundred waste flakes produced by repairing and manufacturing tools. While we didn't find a fluted point in this area, we did find part of a channel flake produced in the manufacture of a fluted point. The occupation area is roughly twelve metres in diameter and represents either a small Early Paleo-Indian camp or one of several activity areas occupied simultaneously by individual families or larger kin groups in a band.

On the last day of the dig, we turned up evidence of yet another Early Paleo-Indian occupation area, and after nearly completing the excavation of two trenches one of the crew found a complete fluted point. With only one hour to go, our work could not have ended on a happier note!

Out of the Ice Age:
The Deglaciation of Ontario

Roughly 20,000 years ago, at the greatest extent of the continental ice sheet, Ontario was deeply buried beneath ice. Indeed, almost all of Canada was ice covered. The ice sheet had formed several tens of thousands of years earlier by the coalescence of several ice masses on the Canadian Shield, the two largest occurring in the Keewatin district in the Northwest Territories and in central Quebec-Labrador. Together, these ice masses formed the Laurentide Ice Sheet. In western Canada, the Laurentide Ice Sheet merged with another ice mass called the Cordilleran Ice Sheet formed by the merging of glaciers in the Rocky Mountains. Ironically, perhaps, the northwestern corner of Yukon Territory was the only ice-free part of Canada.

In eastern Canada, the Laurentide Ice Sheet flowed south over Ontario and Quebec to an irregular margin thousands of kilometres distant. That margin, sloping rapidly upward to a thickness of perhaps 500 metres, twisted across the midwestern United States where, in central Ohio and Indiana, it reached approximately 40 degrees latitude. Farther east, the ice margin ran along the northern edge of Long Island in New York State and then extended out onto the continental shelf before curving north into the Gulf of Maine and then northeast to Nova Scotia.

This was the farthest advance of the final glaciation in the mid-continental region and the northeast. Following a climatic reversal around 20,000 years ago, or perhaps earlier, the edge of the still-flowing ice sheet began melting more quickly than it advanced, and the long retreat began. As the ice thinned over southern Ontario, the underlying flow patterns of the ice sheet became more apparent and eventually took the form of distinct lobes controlled by the internal dynamics of the ice mass itself and by the land surface over which it moved. These lobes are named after the modern lake basins in which they were centred and partially formed: the Huron, Georgian Bay, Lake Simcoe, Erie, and Ontario lobes. Temporary halts of the ice lobes formed recessional moraines: ribbons of rough terrain composed of steep hills separated by deep depressions. These were deposited in concentric zones fringing the emerging lake basins that were being vacated by the melting ice.

Farther east, in central Ontario, the major moraines cross the province in an east-west direction. The largest of these is the Oak Ridges Moraine north of Toronto, extending from the Niagara Escarpment in the west to beyond Peterborough and Rice Lake in the east, a distance of over 150 kilometres. This moraine was deposited along the length of several ice lobes, the Georgian Bay and Lake Simcoe lobes flowing from northern Ontario and the Ontario Lobe flowing through the Ontario basin. Today, the Oak Ridges Moraine is a watershed between drainage flowing south to the Ontario basin and flowing north into Georgian Bay. The Dummer Moraine, which also runs east-west but is smaller and farther north, is located in the Kawartha Lakes district and runs east to Madoc and Tweed.

The first part of Ontario to become ice free was the high ground west of the Niagara Escarpment in south-central Ontario, a region geologists call Ontario Island. This area may have emerged from the ice 14,000 years ago, 6,000 years after the beginning of ice marginal retreat from the midwestern United States.

As glacial ice continued to retreat from Ontario Island, meltwater pooled in the southern part of the Huron and Erie basins, forming a succession

Postscript

One of my fondest memories of the 1974 field season is of receiving a working group of visitors from China. The Chinese had come to Toronto with an exhibition of archaeological objects from the People's Republic of China. This stunning exhibition, which attracted visitors from all parts of Canada, the United States, and even Europe, included many objects that

of glacial lakes, such as Maumee and Whittlesey, and in the western end of the Ontario basin, glacial Lake Peel and then Lake Iroquois. It was during the later part of this period, roughly 12,000 years ago, that glacial Lake Algonquin started forming in the southern part of the Huron basin. Over the next 2,000 years, this lake expanded steadily as the ice front retreated north, eventually filling the Michigan, Huron, and Georgian Bay basins, spilling over into the lowlands of central Ontario and engulfing what would later become Lake Simcoe, then extending still farther south in long, finger-like embayments reaching almost to Toronto. The flat agricultural fields surrounding Alliston and the large, commercial vegetable gardens in the deep black soil of Holland Marsh are two of the most prominent remnants of those glacial lake embayments. Throughout the period of its expansion, Lake Algonquin was bordered all along its northern margin by glacial ice. This ice, and the silt it contained from ground-up rock (called rock flour), must have made for a very cold and dirty lake, choked with icebergs.

In eastern Ontario ice retreat from the east end of the Ontario basin created a large proglacial lake, Lake Iroquois, which at first drained through New York State and the Hudson River valley to the Atlantic. Later, lower lake levels in the Ontario basin drained into the marine waters of the Champlain Sea, which invaded the recently deglaciated St Lawrence River valley from the Atlantic. At that time, the valley was still depressed below sea level due to the weight of the former ice sheet. This allowed the sea to reach far inland to the modern cities of Brockville and Perth in eastern Ontario, and some distance up the Ottawa River valley to beyond Petawawa, north of Pembroke. With the sea came fish and

molluscs and at least three species of seals and five of whales, some species of both extending as far west as the Ottawa region. Harp and bearded seals in the Ottawa area probably lived on pack ice and ringed seals on land-fast ice. Farther east in more saline waters fossils of walrus have been found. Eventually the late phase of this marine embayment in eastern Ontario would also receive the meltwaters of Lake Algonquin after it expanded to its most northerly outlets in the North Bay area. From these outlets Lake Algonquin drained east down the Mattawa River valley and into several tributaries of the Ottawa River.

This was the changing world encountered by bands of Early Paleo-Indian hunter-gatherers when they colonized southern Ontario, possibly from Michigan, Ohio, or New York State, sometime after 11,000 years ago. The waters of the emergent Great Lakes and the land itself would be reshaped many times before appearing in their modern form only a couple of thousand years ago.

had never before been seen outside China. I remember in particular the graceful Flying Horse of Kansu, dating from the second century AD, and the burial suit of Princess Tou Wan, composed of over 2,000 plates of cut jade and joined together by gold and silk-wound wire. The Chinese delegation that accompanied the exhibition during its three-month presence at the ROM were entertained and hosted widely in the Toronto area. In due course, someone thought that the delegation might enjoy visiting an archaeological site in Canada. Of course, being in the field, I was unaware of this and totally surprised when I received a call asking if the group could visit our work. How could I say no?

In preparation for the site visit we set up several folding tables under large umbrellas off to one side of our excavations. Ever the gracious host, Mrs Banting provided tea and cookies. The whole scene must have presented quite a sight, with us in our finest dig clothing and best behaviour and the correct Chinese in their blue Mao suits, drinking tea and eating cookies together under gaily coloured beach umbrellas on the edge of a former glacial lake, high above fields stretching to the four horizons. Later, I was told, the Chinese commented politely on the archaeological work but expressed amazement at the huge amount of land owned by Mr and Mrs Banting and their neighbours. Who can predict what will impress?

Aside from the 1974 newsletter, the only thing I published for the general public on my work at Banting was an article that same year for the ROM magazine, *Rotunda*. I published nothing for the public on the 1975 work at Banting, or even on our work at the newly discovered Hussey site, on the western end of a small peninsula in Lake Algonquin, which I mentioned only briefly in the 1974 newsletter and then not by name.

As with my work in Killarney Park and later along the Niagara Escarpment, the public knew only about beginnings, not about endings – how it all came out or what it meant. The work at Banting and the new site, which I called Hussey after the landowner, Mr William Hussey, was both promising and disappointing. The promising part was that I had a new and almost immediately successful approach for looking for Paleo-Indian sites. The disappointing part was that neither Banting nor Hussey were very productive sites, as they contained very little archaeological material: only a few Early Paleo-Indian tools and some stone waste from tool resharpening. Nothing organic survived. Furthermore, the few stone artifacts and debris that had been left behind were all mixed together in the plough zone. Prior to that, the meagre traces of Paleo-Indian occupation had been moved about over a period of 10,000 or 11,000 years by tree growth and decay, rodent burrowing, and who knows what other kinds of disturbances. And any firepits that might have contained charcoal and burnt animal bone (which is not consumed by micro-organisms) had been destroyed, the contents broken up by frost, trampling, or other mechanical agencies and then dispersed. Any spatial patterns of discarded artifact material, firepits, or postholes left by shelters – all crucial bits of evidence that might have revealed how people worked together on the site – no longer existed. Time is not forgiving, especially long periods of time. Thus the only information available for interpreting what Paleo-Indian people might have done on the Banting and Hussey sites was whatever could be inferred from the amount and density of material we found, the range of tool types and their presumed functions, and the general locations of the sites in the landscape.

We determined that there were at least four areas of prehistoric activity on the Banting site. The first we encountered was the burned area that had been disturbed historically by a natural fire or tree removal and burning in preparation for cultivation. This area produced only one Paleo-Indian tool (not identifiable as either Early or Late) and a few widely scattered flakes and unidentifiable tool fragments. A second area also produced just a scatter of material, enough to indicate some kind of prehistoric activity but not enough to locate it firmly. The two remaining areas of the site were more informative. The larger was located just below the crest of the hill, possibly chosen for its southern, warmer and drier exposure or because it reduced the possibility of being seen against the skyline in an open environment by the animals that the Paleo-Indians were watching for. This area produced two Early Paleo-Indian spear points, several other Paleo-Indian tools, and fifty-seven non-culturally diagnostic tools over an area about twelve metres across. The area had the appearance of a small campsite. The fourth area of the site, also located just below the crest of the hill and on the south side, produced several Paleo-Indian tools and evidence for the manufacture of an Early Paleo-Indian spear point. But we also found there two points made by later peoples, indicating that the area had been used by more than a single group.

The Hussey site presented much the same kind of archaeological record. Like Banting, it contained four areas of prehistoric activity, two of which simply recorded the presence of Paleo-Indian people and possibly others as well. A much larger area produced two different types of Early Paleo-Indian spear points, made by different groups of people. There we also found a spear point made by Late Paleo-Indians, descendants of Early Paleo-Indians who, unlike their ancestors, lived in the early part of our time – the Holocene, or Recent, geological epoch – and probably hunted modern fauna such as deer, elk, and moose. We also excavated a few non-culturally diagnostic Paleo-Indian tools and a point made by later Archaic peoples. The artifacts were widely scattered, tantalizing for the range of people represented but not enough evidence to locate firmly a specific occupation by a specific group of people. The fourth area was different. In it we found a complete Late Paleo-Indian point and the bases of three others, as well as two other Paleo-Indian tools and a few other tool fragments, perhaps left by a Late Paleo-Indian hunter who had stopped briefly to repair some tools. We also found nearby a spear point of beaten copper made at a much later time, indicating that the area had been reoccupied.

The nature of the archaeological record at Banting and Hussey suggests that both sites were occupied very briefly by Early and Late Paleo-Indian peoples, and possibly others, during hunting forays in the area, or alternatively by people simply passing through the region.

If contemporary with glacial Lake Algonquin, Banting, located on a small island perhaps a kilometre off shore, would have been accessible only by crossing water or ice. The Hussey site could have been approached on dry land. Both sites might have attracted Early Paleo-Indians if the nearby shorelines provided lichen-rich habitats for caribou. Alternatively, in winter, when protected areas of Lake Algonquin froze, the sites may have provided overlooks and access to large open areas of the frozen lake favoured by congregating caribou watching the behaviour of wolves. The small, and therefore most likely brief, Late Paleo-Indian occupation on the Hussey site is more difficult to interpret because it probably postdated the draining of Lake Algonquin at the end of the Ice Age. At that time, the former peninsula at Hussey may have attracted people who were interested in exploiting food resources in wetland habitats on the recently drained Algonquin lake bed.

The Banting and Hussey sites revealed only the barest trace of Early Paleo-Indian peoples. Much of that was inferential and, frankly, subjective. This was certainly disappointing, but the sites also revealed a new approach to fieldwork and a new interest for me: glacial Lake Algonquin. Perhaps this was the most important thing the two sites were telling me. If I were a believer in fate (which I am not, I think), I might also have thought that it was my destiny to work on Lake Algonquin because in 1973, the year I visited the Banting site for the first time, a preliminary geological map was published showing the location of the former Algonquin beachline in the Alliston area. And a year later another preliminary map was published showing the location of the Algonquin beachline immediately to the north of the Alliston area, just when I was ready to pick up the trail and follow it north. With these maps I could walk behind the geologists, almost step by step. At times I felt like a scavenger, gleaning bits of archaeological information from the leavings of geologists who, like the carnivores of Africa, had brought my meal to earth. As things turned out, I remained a beachcomber of Ice Age lakes well into the 1980s.

My early work along the Niagara Escarpment and in the Alliston area of glacial Lake Algonquin also defined my future in other important ways. I met some people who were to stay in my academic life for a long time. I met Andrew Stewart for the first time when he volunteered to work with me along the escarpment. At the time, he was an impressionable sixteen-year-old high school student who was shocked when I explained to a mixed crew that a raccoon baculum, which someone had picked up from a field we were then walking, was a penis bone. What else was I to do? No one had heard the term baculum before. Since that embarrassing moment Andrew has moved in and out of my life, first as an undergraduate at Trent University in Ontario, later as a graduate student at Cambridge, England, and then the University of California at Santa Barbara, and finally as I write, as a self-employed consulting archaeologist working in the Canadian Arctic and occasionally in Ontario. Andrew was to play an important role in this story by participating in the research and write-up of a monograph on a site I was to discover in 1975, during my third and final season of work at Banting.

During the Banting years I met another person who was to be involved in the same future project as Andrew Stewart. This was Hugh Gwyn, a geologist I first encountered at a restaurant in Alliston. My crew and I had just sat down at a table for lunch when a huge, scruffy, bearded man in shorts and heavy boots sitting with a group of other scruffy people got up from his table, walked over to me and asked, fortunately with a smile on his face, what we were doing in the area. I reluctantly stood up and explained my work as vaguely as possible, wanting only to get back to my lunch. After my brief remarks Hugh explained his work. As I listened I soon began feeling very, very small. Not only had I been rude but I had acted against my own self-interest, for the animated man standing before me was a Pleistocene geologist who was mapping the glacial Lake Algonquin shoreline and other features of the Ice Age landscape – the very landscape on which I was working. I was actually using a preliminary geological map he had published that year as a guide for my own work. Fortunately I don't think that Hugh, being very positive and outgoing, noticed my rudeness, only an archaeologist and an opportunity for him to learn from that person about the ancient people who moved across the landscapes he was reconstructing. I loosened up and after a few more words about our respective field projects Hugh left the restaurant to return to the geological past, and I hurried through lunch to get back to the human past. But we were to meet again several years later when we combined geology and archaeology into a single story, discussed in the following chapters.

I also made some other acquaintances in the early 1970s who were to have an ongoing influence on my work. In 1973 or perhaps earlier, I came to hear about the work of William Roosa, a professor at the University of Waterloo in southwestern Ontario. Roosa had come to Ontario from the University of Michigan, Ann Arbor, where he wrote a doctoral dissertation on the Lucy site, a controversial Early Paleo-Indian site in New Mexico that, some thought, represented an early, pre-fluted-point stage in the development of Paleo-Indians. While in Michigan, Roosa also worked with local Early Paleo-Indian material and published several papers that were to lay the groundwork for much of our current knowledge about the typology of Paleo-Indian points: their size, shape, and method of manufacture. This is particularly important in establishing a framework for interpreting culture history, especially in the absence of radiocarbon dates.

At the University of Waterloo, Roosa was propelled into Ontario Paleo-Indian research by an insistent student, Brian Deller, who was conducting research in extreme southwestern Ontario, where he also worked as a school teacher. Brian took archaeology courses at Waterloo when he could spare the time and repeatedly brought material to the university for Roosa to look at. Out of this sprang a collaborative effort to excavate several sites that Brian had previously documented only from controlled surface collections. In November 1973, a couple of years after he started working with Roosa, Brian wrote to me introducing himself and his work. This letter stimulated an exchange of information about our respective work that we have kept up ever since. I was to receive from Brian many draft manuscripts before they were published, as well as a 444-page PhD dissertation, complete with a full set of duplicate photographs carefully pasted above their respective captions. And on one occasion he lent me some pretty fantastic artifacts; indeed they were and still are unique and therefore irreplaceable. Although I've tried, I don't feel I have been able to match these kindnesses with equally impressive collections or insights.

I was to benefit greatly by the work of Deller and Roosa, and later by another early student of Roosa's, Christopher Ellis. After degrees at McMaster University in Ontario and Simon Fraser University in British Columbia, Chris Ellis became a professional archaeologist and a professor of anthropology at the University of Western Ontario. Roosa attracted other dedicated students who also, from time to time, entered the stage of Paleo-Indian research. Thus a school or cadre of archaeologists in extreme southwestern Ontario, principally Roosa, Deller, and later, Ellis, worked parallel with me as I developed my research in south-central Ontario. I must admit that I occasionally thought I was in competition with this group though I don't think they shared that feeling, and I was frankly envious of some of their discoveries, though again I don't think they felt the same. But as we maintained cordial relations and freely exchanged information, the competition was stimulating and positive. Inevitably, their names come up from time to time in the following story.

As well as the people I met, some of the assumptions I made and the questions I asked in the mid-1970s also stayed with me for a long time. My working hypothesis for discovering Early Paleo-Indian sites, for example, was based on the assumption that the people hunted caribou. I then used that hypothesis to imagine how caribou and people may have moved about the landscape, in order to create a strategy for focusing my fieldwork geographically. The hypothesis needed to be documented and demonstrated as valid, or replaced with a better one (and accompanying field strategy). This was to guide much of my work for roughly fifteen years when, finally, I was actually able to validate it, at least with reservations.

Something else that stayed with me a long time is a question I raised in a research grant application in 1974, so it must have been in my mind even earlier. I had observed that much of the stone used by Early Paleo-Indians for tool making at Banting was a white material, sometimes with yellow mottling. I was very interested in learning where this unknown material came from as I thought that knowing its geological source might lead to the discovery of Early Paleo-Indian quarry sites where toolstone was obtained. Like the hypothesis about caribou, this question would be answered several years in the future. Once answered it was to provide yet another direction for fieldwork that would guide my research for a further decade and longer.

Looking back I see that the first half of the 1970s set the stage for much of what was to unfold over the next twenty years. Unknowingly having established the broad pattern of my future research, I would from that point be concerned with the details. But how interesting they would prove to be.

4 BREAKTHROUGH

THE YEAR 1975 WAS A WATERSHED FOR ME, dividing the early stage of my work from the much longer road to the present. On one side of the divide was the difficult slope upward from 1970, characterized by a hesitant probing in several directions to find a successful way to discover Early Paleo-Indian sites. On the other side of the divide, marked in 1975 by what for me was a momentous discovery, I finally found the path I had been looking for and a focus that was to carry me onward to a succession of discoveries and other divides. The following newsletter, written after the end of the 1975 field season, announces the breakthrough that created such an important watershed in my work.

A SUMMER AT THE BEACH
SEPTEMBER 1975

Those of you who have been receiving the *Archaeological Newsletter* or *Rotunda* will know that for the last several years I have been spending most of my summers at the beach and this summer was no exception. I am not referring to a modern beach, of course, but to the abandoned beach of an Ice Age lake – glacial Lake Algonquin – which existed between 10,400 and 11,500 years ago during the final retreat of glacial ice from Ontario. Since early hunting peoples may have lived on the shores of this lake, I have been systematically searching the shoreline for their campsites. This last summer, with the support of Canada Council, we surveyed by foot, truck, and airplane an eighty-kilometre stretch of ancient shoreline between Glencairn, a short distance west of Barrie, and Thornbury, on Georgian Bay.

We started the survey on May 12th and after only a few days' work found what looked like quite a promising site. Late one afternoon while walking in a field high above the Algonquin beach I spotted several beach terraces about 500 metres away on the edge of a gravel quarry.

Since a good profile was exposed along the face of the quarry I thought it would be worthwhile to take a quick look on our way back to the truck. I had no more than walked up to the soil cut when I found, of all things, a flake graver – a small piercing or engraving tool of a kind made by Paleo-Indian or Early Archaic peoples. I let out a yell and we all got on our hands and knees and started looking more carefully.

We found several other flakes along the edge of the bulldozer cut, all within a shallow soil horizon which had formed after the deposition of the underlying beach gravels. After the initial excitement was over and I could force myself to stop looking at the ground for artifacts, I took a closer look at the general location of the site. The site occurred on the fourth of five terraces above a small creek named Coates Creek. The fifth and highest terrace I assumed was the main beach, which marked the highest level reached by the lake during its history in this area. The lower terraces, including the one on which the site is located, were formed during recessional stages of the lake while it was draining. Since the artifacts occurred in the soil horizon overlying terrace deposits, the site must have been occupied well after the time of the formation of the terrace when the lake stood at a lower level (perhaps during the formation of one of the lower three terraces) or after it had drained altogether. The exact dating of the site, of course, could only be determined by the radiocarbon (C_{14}) dating of bone or charcoal from firepits and I was very interested in testing the site to determine the size of the occupied area. It was a relief to hear from the quarry foreman, Mr D. Garner, that the area would probably not be disturbed further for several months, but I made plans to start work the following week in order to find out as soon as possible whether a major excavation would be required.

Fortunately, with two trucks and a crew of four (later five) I could test the site and still continue the survey which, after all, had barely begun. I decided to spend one or two days each week working with the survey crew selecting promising fields for them to work during the remainder of the week while I and another person excavated at the new site (which I subsequently named Coates Creek). In this way we were able to run both projects concurrently but of course it meant that I was absent from the survey part of the time. It was on one of these occasions that our most exciting discovery was made.

One day, perhaps a week later, the survey crew returned to camp saying that they had found several bags of chert flakes and the basal fragment of a "possible" Late Paleo-Indian point. Everyone was pretty happy and we hurried through supper to have a look at the material.

I was disappointed. The "possible" Late Paleo-Indian point fragment was in fact part of the middle section of a point with the most important and diagnostic part, the base, missing. The specimen was broken in a curious manner and I thought for a moment that it looked like an Early Paleo-Indian point that had been unsuccessfully "fluted" (thinned by attempting to remove a large flake from the centre) although it was difficult to be sure. I assumed this was the best artifact they had found so I wasn't too interested when they started washing up the material. To everyone's astonishment, they found the basal fragment of an Early Paleo-Indian fluted point in one of the first bags they opened! This was made, perhaps some 10,000 to 12,000 years ago, by the first people to live in Ontario after the last ice retreat and it would be an understatement in the finest British tradition to say that we were excited. Everyone started rushing around for washbasins of water and toothbrushes and anything else that could be used for washing artifacts. By the time we had finished, we had found another fluted point (this one only partly finished), two flakes produced by the fluting or thinning process, a couple of gravers, and several scrapers and other types of tools. There could be no question but that they had discovered an Early Paleo-Indian site – and a manufacturing site at that – where the fluted points and other tools were made. The survey crew had obviously been concentrating so hard on picking up the material and not missing anything that they hadn't particularly noticed what it was they were finding.

The site [which I later called Fisher] actually consists of three partially overlapping concentrations of artifacts located on high ground a short distance behind the Lake Algonquin beach. Curiously, the three fluted point fragments and the channel flakes all occurred on the highest part of the site, suggesting that the hunters manufactured their points there while keeping a watch for game – possibly barren-ground caribou and other tundra and open boreal forest species that lived in southern Ontario during Lake Algonquin times. The fluted points are very similar to some excavated from a site west of London. They are, in fact, so similar that if both sites were not occupied by the same group of people, the inhabitants of the two must have been close relatives.

Since I was already occupied with the Coates Creek site and the survey, I put this site at the top of my list of things to do next year. It promises to be a large and important site and it may answer some questions about the movements of Early Man in Ontario and his way of life.

While we didn't turn up any other Early Paleo-Indian sites, I was very happy with the one we did find [and of course Coates Creek] and considered the survey to have accomplished its purpose. We continued our work at Coates Creek for several weeks and tested widely on terraces 4 and 5. There seemed to be scattered materials almost everywhere we looked but adjacent to the bulldozer cut where we found the first artifacts we uncovered part of a small campsite that may have been occupied by Late Paleo-Indian or Early Archaic peoples some time between perhaps 6,000 and 8,000 years ago. We have a fair quantity of material, which is being washed and labelled for analysis now and hopefully the two charcoal samples we obtained from firepits will be sufficiently large for C14 dating.

After completing the survey and our work at Coates Creek we finished the testing of two Early Paleo-Indian sites in the Alliston area, both of which also occur on the shoreline of Lake Algonquin. But that is a subject for another *Archaeological Newsletter.* While it has yet to be proven that Early Man actually lived in Ontario during Lake Algonquin times, I know of no better way to find his campsites than to search along the old beachlines. Besides, what better way to spend the summer than beachcombing?

Postscript

It's a curious thought that one of the very first sites we discovered in 1975, which I called Coates Creek after a nearby stream, was much like the foreshock of an earthquake. It was a minor tremor, a harbinger of a major shock to come. The Coates Creek site was in a very striking setting, near a wide, sweeping curve at the northern end of the mouth of the Mad River valley, where a succession of storm beaches turned north toward the vast open expanse of great bodies of former lakes, the earliest extending right up to the front of the former ice sheet in northern Ontario. Standing there high above those former beach terraces undulating down into the distance and the distant past, I could easily imagine a large body of water lying to the north, east, and south, much like pictures I had seen of the Chukchi Sea below abandoned beaches on the coast of Alaska, north of the Arctic Circle. Yet the imagined scene of the landscape before me occurred possibly 10,000 years ago in south-central Ontario, less than fifty kilometres west of Barrie and only minutes from the village of Creemore.

I didn't really know what I had at Coates Creek. Our first hint of the site was only a couple of tools and some waste flakes gathered from a bulldozer cut and other disturbances. I thought one or two of the tools looked as if they might be old but I didn't know whether they were made by the Early

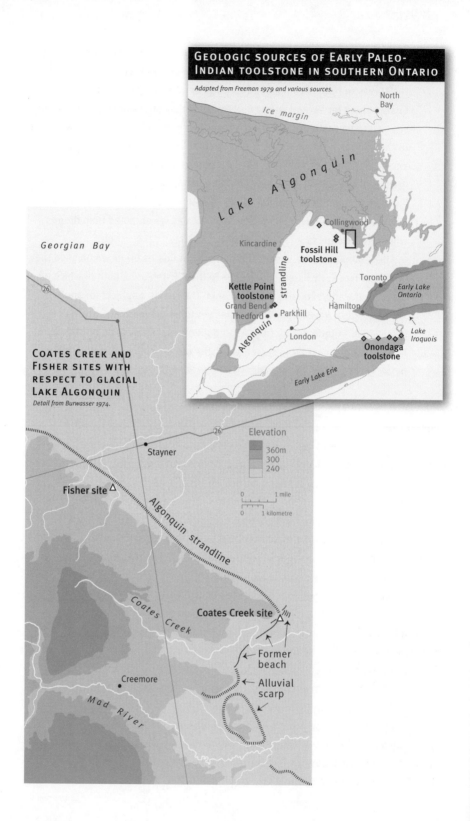

GEOLOGIC SOURCES OF EARLY PALEO-
INDIAN TOOLSTONE IN SOUTHERN ONTARIO

Adapted from Freeman 1979 and various sources.

North
Bay

Ice margin

Lake Algonquin

Georgian Bay

Collingwood

Kincardine

Fossil Hill
toolstone

Toronto

Early Lake
Ontario

Kettle Point
toolstone

Grand Bend
Thedford   Parkhill

Hamilton

Lake
Iroquois

London

Onondaga
toolstone

Early Lake Erie

COATES CREEK AND
FISHER SITES WITH
RESPECT TO GLACIAL
LAKE ALGONQUIN
Detail from Burwasser 1974.

26

Stayner

Elevation

360m
300
240

Fisher site

Algonquin strandline

0   1 mile

0   1 kilometre

Coates Creek

Coates Creek site

Former
beach

Creemore

← Alluvial
scarp

Mad River

Paleo-Indians I was looking for or their later descendants. I was encouraged that the tools and the waste flakes we found were made of that still unidentified white stone I had also found at Banting and Hussey, and that my colleagues in southwestern Ontario believed was associated with Early Paleo-Indian sites. The tools and raw material certainly appeared to be what I was looking for, but Coates Creek clearly needed to be test excavated to find out one way or the other. And this created a problem for me. If I were to test the site, I had to be there personally to plan and monitor what was done, but I couldn't abandon the survey. Coates Creek might not be as early as I hoped. Clearly, I had to excavate Coates Creek *and* continue the survey.

To do both, I reformed the already small crew of eight people into two teams: one to excavate with me and the second to survey. And then I stood aside and let the survey crew get on with the task. That's why I wasn't present on 26 May, the day the major shock occurred and we made our second, and more important, discovery, the site that produced the bags of artifacts mentioned in the newsletter. Strangely, I didn't think to give this second site a name in the 1975 *Archaeological Newsletter,* but I later called it Fisher after the landowner, and the tale in the newsletter, about washing the first few bags of artifacts brought back to our field camp by the survey crew, is only part of its story.

This major find really began at a garbage dump and, earlier still, behind a large hill. Several days before the discovery announced in the newsletter, I had driven the survey crew along the former Algonquin strandline to give them some guidance in selecting fields to investigate. This wasn't an easy matter since the roads didn't always get close enough to allow us see the beachline very clearly, and sections of the beach were sometimes hidden by intervening woodlots or hills. After I'd driven over every road in the area, I tried to think of other ways to see the landscape short of flying, which was my last resort. It was then I noticed the garbage dump.

The dump was located in a large excavation of a former gravel pit. And the gravel pit, I saw from my geological map, had been placed in a former offshore barrier bar of glacial Lake Algonquin. The barrier bar was created by the deposition of sands and gravels carried by strong currents parallel to shore, forming a kind of elongated lagoon behind it, on the landward side. Of course, this evocative picture of 10,500 to 11,000 years ago isn't what my crew members saw. These young adults, part of a generation that was becoming ever more conscious of the nutritional value of the food they ate, the quality of air they breathed, and potential health hazards around them, gazed with some distaste at a large hole in the ground filled with piles of construction debris, old tires, refrigerators and other appliances, and, off to one side, a spreading mound of bulldozed and ripped garbage bags spewing out their contents of paper and plastic, food scraps, and unidentifiable things. All of this was surrounded by a nearly continuous sheet of litter on the ground beneath our feet. A light pall of smoke hung in the air, and through it hundreds of sea gulls wheeled about and screeched at one another in their competition over the scraps of food scattered below. The crew followed very reluctantly at a distance when I walked up to the guard at the entrance. Because I too was in a hurry to leave this place, I wanted to avoid a long explanation of what we were doing and told the guard only that we were interested in the geology

Families, Bands, and Larger Social Groupings in Early Paleo-Indian Society

Early Paleo-Indians were hunter-gatherers. And like most ethnographically known hunter-gatherers, it's fairly safe to assume that Early Paleo-Indian society was based on the family unit and groups of allied families organized into bands. But it's often difficult to identify these social units in the archaeological record. In part, this is because most, if not all, Paleo-Indian sites have been disturbed, sometimes considerably, by the very people who occupied and created them, by later people who occasionally reoccupied them, by a seemingly endless number of natural agencies, and by European settlement and urban expansion. The original patterns of deposition resulting from human behaviour, such as the arrangement of different work and living spaces in a campsite, have thus been severely altered or destroyed altogether. Even if the disturbances have been minimal, or can be eliminated or compensated for statistically, archaeological interpretation is subject to differences of opinion.

Nevertheless, from time to time, we see provocative hints of Paleo-Indian social structure. This is illustrated by two examples, one which is thought to represent an encampment of allied families belonging to the same band and the other a large aggregation of bands.

The first example, a site called Thedford II, was occupied by Parkhill complex people in Ontario and is especially appropriate because these people are part of the central story of this book.

Located in extreme southwestern Ontario, Thedford II was excavated in the early 1980s by Brian Deller and Christopher Ellis, and their findings published in 1992 in a very fine, book-length report.

Deller and Ellis believe that Thedford II was occupied on a single occasion by a group of related families. This is suggested, they argue, by the symmetrical arrangement of five activity areas, consistently two to four metres apart and of similar size (80-100 square metres), around a much larger central area (162 square metres). The peripheral areas each contained a comparable range of tools, suggesting that roughly similar activities were conducted at those locations. In contrast, the range of tools in the central area is much greater and suggests that a somewhat wider range of activities was conducted there. Because of this, and the centrality of the larger area, Deller and Ellis argue that it was used as a communal work area by the several families that occupied the peripheral areas.

The second example, a site called Bull Brook, is located north of Boston, Massachusetts, on the edge of a community called Ipswich. The people at Bull Brook may have been the first Early Paleo-Indians to colonize northeastern North America. The site covers an area of approximately eight hectares and consists of forty-two artifact concentrations, each about seven metres in diameter and ten to fifteen metres apart, distributed in a

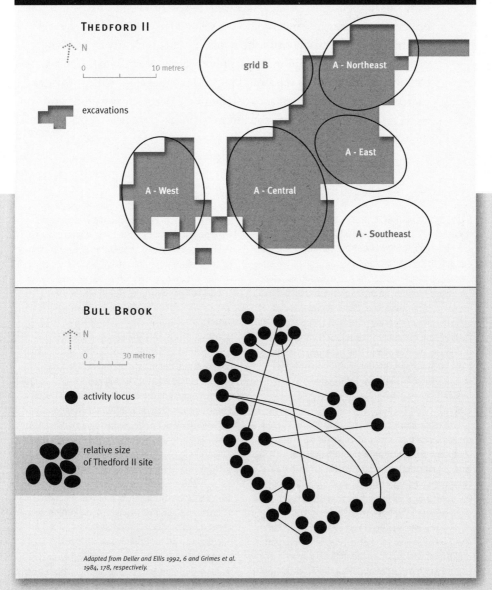

COMPARISON OF SIZE AND STRUCTURE OF THEDFORD II AND BULL BROOK SITES

THEDFORD II

N

0   10 metres

excavations

grid B

A - Northeast

A - East

A - West

A - Central

A - Southeast

BULL BROOK

N

0   30 metres

● activity locus

relative size
of Thedford II site

Adapted from Deller and Ellis 1992, 6 and Grimes et al. 1984, 178, respectively.

circular pattern around the perimeter of a large unoccupied area approximately 100 metres in diameter. Many of the artifact concentrations contained fire-reddened sand and lenses of charcoal, suggesting hearths. The relatively small size of these areas, the range of tools, and the evidence for hearths all suggest that these locations were occupied by groups of allied families, or bands. Furthermore, the fact that pieces of broken artifacts from different areas have been and asked if we could just look around. He probably agreed only because he hadn't been asked this question before.

The view was great! Above the garbage, the remaining edge of the old barrier bar provided an excellent vista of the Algonquin strandline, as if I were out in the former glacial lake itself. It was almost like being in a boat, or perhaps a garbage scow. I could see several large fields off to the west that had not been visible from the roads. The fields clearly crossed the former Algonquin strandline and had only recently been ploughed. Their location with respect to the strandline and condition for survey work were exceptional, and I asked one or two members of the survey crew who had made it this far with me into the dump to make those fields a priority in their work for the next day.

Families, Bands, and Larger Social Groupings *continued*

found to fit together indicates that some of the locations were occupied simultaneously.

The large central area at Bull Brook was apparently deliberately left unoccupied since there are no evident physical barriers to occupation. When first discovered by amateur archaeologists, this area was essentially flat. (The site has since been almost entirely destroyed by a gravel quarry.) Nor is there any reason why vegetation should have prevented occupation in this area. Thus, it may have been defined not by environmental constraints but as a place for informal social activities and possibly even for group ceremonial events.

The remarkable symmetry of Bull Brook, plus the evidence that many of its areas were occupied simultaneously, strongly suggest that the site as a whole was occupied on a single occasion by a very large number of bands – an unusual, possibly unique aggregation. No other sites like it have been found in the New England region.

How was such a large aggregation of hunter-gatherers supported? At the time of occupation, Bull Brook was a fair distance from marine resources. The Gulf of Maine in the Atlantic would have been ten to fifteen kilometres distant because of lowered sea levels, forty to forty-seven metres below present-day mean annual sea level. Terrestrial resources would therefore have been primary. Paleoecological data indicate that the site would have been located in a pine-dominated forest or woodland environment. Caribou was probably the most numerous land mammal but, even if concentrated nearby, the herds probably wouldn't have been large enough to support an aggregation of bands for very long. Thus, the occupation at Bull Brook looks as if it were an unusual event rather than a regular pattern of land use. One archaeologist suggests that Bull Brook was the site of a short-term aggregation of people who were preparing to disperse and colonize a region to the north.

Thedford II and Bull Brook represent, perhaps, opposite ends of the Early Paleo-Indian social spectrum, ranging from allied families to large aggregations of bands. Unfortunately, the interpretations are ambiguous. At Thedford II, they are equivocal because we can't be sure of the origin of the archaeological material, which may come from disturbed and scattered storage pits or dumps, rather than actual living areas, and because the sample size is low, making for unreliable comparisons between different areas. At Bull Brook, the interpretations are ambiguous because the site was not as thoroughly documented during excavation as it might have been and also because the findings have not yet been thoroughly analyzed and published. Despite these problems, Thedford II and Bull Brook illustrate some of the issues archaeologists face when they attempt to see the social world of people in the thin scatter of things in a field.

The story in the newsletter picks up on our activities on the evening of 26 May, when we washed the first few bags of material from the new site hidden in those fields. I remember other details of that night. At the time we were living in a small tent camp, each tent holding only a couple of people, depending on their size and whether they sat quietly. Of course we didn't have electricity either, only gas lanterns. So, the image in the newsletter, of crowded, very excited people cleaning hundreds of small waste flakes and the odd broken tool piece by piece, with toothbrushes in small plastic wash-basins, should be superimposed on another image: small, dimly lit tents with deep shadows and the comings and goings of severely hunched-over people – stepping carefully around other people, bedding, extra clothes, boots, washbasins, hissing gas lanterns, and artifacts drying on wet newspaper – to get fresh water from an outside tap for more washing. These two images merge for an hour or so and then suddenly change as a person – yes, me! – bursts from a tent into the darkness, throws himself into a car, and drives hurriedly away to an isolated phone on the edge of a country road to tell the world of his discovery. Such is science in action. I have seldom been happier.

This discovery couldn't have come at a better time. Since 1973 my colleagues in southwestern Ontario, Brian Deller and William Roosa, had been excavating an Early Paleo-Indian site that Deller had recently discovered and that was proving to be very productive. Their success contrasted starkly with what I had been achieving and I admit that I was green with envy. At their invitation I visited their excavation in 1974 and was quite impressed. The site, which they later called Parkhill, was located about fifty kilometres west of London near an abandoned strandline of a 6,000-year-old lake that had reflooded the basin of glacial Lake Algonquin. The geology was thus somewhat more complex than I had been dealing with in south-central Ontario. But as if in some kind of perverse compensation for that complexity, Deller and Roosa were finding large amounts of archaeological material, including beautifully made fluted points and other tools. And they had more than just quantity and quality. They had a very large site. The artifact material occurred in at least nine concentrations scattered over an area of six hectares. It was the stuff of dreams!

The setting of the Parkhill site was also evocative. Deller speculated that the site, presumably occurring near a right-angle bend of the former Algonquin strandline, had been a gathering place for several bands of Early Paleo-Indian hunters who were intercepting migrating caribou as they drifted along the strandline and turned the corner at Parkhill. So I was not surprised in 1975 when I heard rumours of another productive year of excavation there.

That night of 26 May, as I rushed out of the tent to a phone, I was therefore truly grateful, and relieved, that I had something to shout about. The two or three fluted point fragments we had found in the first bags of material from the new site were clearly similar to those my colleagues were finding at the Parkhill site. They were even made of the same raw material, that unidentified white chert. It looked as if my colleagues and I had encountered, quite coincidentally, the same cultural group of people. Perhaps even the same band.

Understandably, I was desperate to see for myself the new site my survey crew had discovered. So, on 27 May, I took the entire crew to have a look and of course to collect as much additional information as possible. I secretly hoped to find a fluted point myself. We drove down the long lane to the house and there, on a small porch towered over by a huge barn and several even larger silos, I met the landowners for the first time, Mr and Mrs Reg Fisher, after whom I named the site. I was greatly relieved to find that the Fishers were interested in our work and perhaps even more curious about the former glacial lake that had inundated the far end of their farm. Although Mr Fisher didn't know anything about an archaeological site on his land, and doubted there was one since he'd never seen any stone tools, he was happy to let us walk about as we pleased.

We left the vehicle in the farmyard and hiked up the long slope of an enormous cornfield rising to the crest of a hill. And there in the lower distance was the former Algonquin strandline, and farther on the horizon, the offshore barrier bar, marked by a thin plume of light smoke and brief reflections of white from the seagulls soaring over the garbage dump. As I looked about in amazement, one of the people of the survey crew said that we were standing near the first concentration of artifacts they had encountered the day before. And from this location I could see for many kilometres in all directions. In front of me, to the east, was the basin of the former glacial lake stretching off toward the sun and unseen islands north of Barrie over forty kilometres away. To my left and right, the relic strandline twisted north and south into the horizons. And, turning completely around and looking west, I could see far into the interior countryside, behind the former lake, and, on the skyline, the distant ridge of the Niagara Escarpment in the haze. I thought of the many Early Paleo-Indian sites in northeastern North America that had similar commanding views of the surrounding terrain. And I thought also of the archaeological speculation that these overviews reflected the hunter's interest in watching for game animals, principally caribou. And having thought of caribou endlessly during hundreds of hours of walking fossil beaches and, more recently, during my visit to the Parkhill site, it was only natural that I saw the location of the Fisher site in terms of caribou hunting. I was not surprised to find evidence of spearpoint manufacture on the highest part of the site. It confirmed what many archaeologists had assumed about the importance of long-distance visibility to a hunting people. And standing there in the middle of this magnificent 360 degree view, experiencing our new discovery firsthand, I embraced the collective thinking more firmly than ever before. Only much later would I realize that I had entered a kind of mental prison that day, a prison walled with assumptions that could not easily be discarded, even with strong hints of contrary evidence. But that was for the future.

Curiously, after we left that hilltop and trekked back to the vehicles, I didn't see another thing. I was deep in my thoughts, already planning a major excavation for the following year. Indeed, I was already conducting that excavation and imagining the fascinating things we were finding.

I came out of the clouds eventually, although probably not completely. Publicly, I was very controlled, as when I wrote in the 1975 newsletter that "I was very happy with the one [site] we did find and considered the survey to have accomplished its purpose." Privately, I was ecstatic. And I was going to dig, dig, dig!

Excavations at the Fisher site in 1976, showing shovel work in the plough zone and screening for artifacts and debitage. The unit being excavated by the fig- ure in the foreground is one metre square. Left to right: Marc Lamontagne, Gary Coupland, and Lorraine Underell.

Photograph by Peter Storck.

The Missing Years: 1976-7

After the exciting discovery at Fisher in 1975, I didn't write anything for the general public about my work at that site for almost three years, until October 1978, after the second season of excavation. Why? What happened during that time?

Coates Creek

One of the things that kept me from writing about my new project at Fisher was the need to complete the analysis of material from the Coates Creek site.

Although it still took time to prepare I had very little to report. After the first couple of weeks of excavation the rate of artifact recovery dropped off rapidly, and we soon reached the edges of the site only a few metres away from the bulldozer cut that led to the site's discovery. Clearly, our first few excavation squares encompassed nearly the entire site or, more ominously, indicated that the site had been largely destroyed by gravel removal before we discovered it. At the end of the fieldwork, the excavations had produced just one complete spear point and the basal fragment of another, a small number of tools and some flintknapping debris; not very much material to determine who occupied the site, when they lived there, and why. And I wasn't able to get any radiocarbon dates from the charcoal I spoke about at the end of the 1975 newsletter. The only information I had for determining the age of the occupation was the geographical location of the site and the few artifacts it contained.

As I mentioned in the newsletter, the Coates Creek site is on a terrace *below* the level of glacial Lake Algonquin. In fact, the terrace is a remnant of the former Algonquin lake bed, a relatively flat surface, which was later cut into by the waves of a lower-level lake. Thus, if you were to walk across the land surface created by these lakes, you would first walk down a steep slope cut by the waves of Lake Algonquin, then across the relatively flat bottom of that former lake, where the archaeological site occurs, and then once again down a steep slope cut by the waves of a later, and lower-level, lake. Since Lake Algonquin began draining to lower levels roughly 10,400 years ago, the second wave-cut slope – the one cut into the former Algonquin lake bed and below the archaeological site – must have formed some time after that date. And the human occupation above that cut must have occurred later still, after further lowering of water levels removed the threat of flooding by storm waves behind the second wave-cut slope. But how much later the human occupation occurred couldn't be determined by the geology.

The artifacts, however, provided a hint. The basal fragment of one of the spear points found at the site was clearly made by a Late Paleo-Indian flintknapper. The second spear point, a complete artifact, also reflects the skilled workmanship of a Paleo-Indian flintknapper but exhibits something that could be regarded as prophetic of a future time: notches on the sides and near the base, for tying the spear point to a shaft. This technique was to be used widely at a later period in the archaeological record. A notched spear point made using a mixture of Late Paleo-Indian and later manufacturing techniques suggests that the site had been occupied by people who were in the process of making technological innovations to their tool kit. These and other changes – in subsistence, patterns of land use, and other areas of behaviour – had been documented elsewhere at Late Paleo-Indian sites in the Great Lakes region and eastern North America generally. And because of these changes, the descendants of people such as those who lived briefly at Coates Creek, would eventually acquire a new identity, known to archaeologists as Early Archaic. This transition from the Paleo-Indian to the Archaic, which also spanned the transition from the Pleistocene to early Holocene, was a period of profound changes in both the natural world and human society. The single notched spear point from Coates Creek hints at this, and thus gave me the rough estimate I reported in the newsletter for the age of the occupation at that site: between 6,000 and 8,000 years ago. Today, a better estimate would be 8,000 to 9,500 years ago, based on revisions in the dating of the Late Paleo-Indian/Early Archaic transition.

The archaeological record at Coates Creek is very fragmentary: little more than a couple of handfuls of artifacts near a fossil beach. But we might not even have had that if the site had gone undiscovered much longer. It would have been totally consumed by gravel mining. This happens all too often, and Coates Creek is a frightening example of how easily the archaeological record can be erased and the lives of people who came before us lost to time.

A New Gallery for the Museum
During the missing years of 1976 and 1977, when I failed to write anything for the general public about my research, I was actually very much involved with public communication, but not through the printed word. I was heavily involved in the planning and installation of a museum gallery on Ontario prehistory. Planning started in 1974, during my second year at Banting. The exhibits were completed and opened to the public in March 1976, a few months before my first season of excavation at Fisher.

The gallery was located in the basement of the museum, in a single, squarish room crossed by a major public corridor. The gallery was not much larger than a two-car garage but for nearly two years it consumed nearly all my energies. Unfortunately, the gallery was closed and dismantled in about 1980 for the ROM's expansion and renovation. It was open to the public for only about four years, two years longer than it took to plan and build, but a gallery guide describing the exhibits survives, as does a later reprint. On the front cover is a painting of an Early Paleo-Indian hunter dressed in untailored caribou hides and spearing a caribou. And inside the booklet is a photograph of a mannikin intended to represent an Early Paleo-Indian, also dressed in caribou furs, this time tailored. This individual is shown in a reconstructed life scene, or diorama, building a fire to melt tree resin for use as an adhesive to attach a fluted spear point to a foreshaft or lance. The booklet, like a time capsule, preserves my early preoccupation with caribou.

I have carried weighty evidence of that preoccupation down through the years to this very day. A substantial portion of my library of scholarly, coffee table, and popular books – all very heavy – is about caribou behaviour, ecology, anatomy, and taxonomy, and I have detailed studies of the paleontological record of this species and its archaeological occurrence around the world. I lifted and packed and carried and reshelved these books many, many times during household and office moves, each more difficult than the last because of new additions to my library. And gradually I came to feel that the books and the hypothesis they represented, that Early Paleo-Indians actually hunted caribou, were equivalent to the chain of sins carried by Jacob Marley's ghost in Charles Dickens's tale *A Christmas Carol*. My chain, a nearly uncontrollably growing library, was formed by the academic sin of working with only a single hypothesis. And I also carried with me through the years a symbol of this chain: the split half of a modern caribou leg bone, sharpened and polished to serve as a letter opener. I kept this on my desk as a good-luck charm, for opening letters from granting agencies and calling forward the discovery I hoped one day to make.

Brush with the Future
Important events often begin with small things, seemingly quite routine and unimportant. This was the case for me in October 1976, when I received a phone call about some artifacts that had been found in a field in Grimsby, a community located between the Niagara Escarpment and the shoreline of Lake Ontario a few kilometres south of the city of Hamilton.

From the description of the artifacts, the discovery sounded to me like an historic period site, something my departmental colleague, Walter Kenyon, would be more able to evaluate than I. But since he was out of the office for a few days, and the person who called was concerned about the site, I agreed to visit it the next day.

The site was in a large barren field about to be developed into a housing subdivision. The person who had phoned took me to a location where I saw a few unidentifiable bone fragments, small pieces of pottery, and metal fragments on the surface of the ground. Later he showed me several artifacts that he had dug up before he began feeling uneasy about what he was doing and decided to call the ROM. He agreed to let me take the artifacts back to the museum for identification and I returned to Toronto and put them in the lab where Walter Kenyon would be sure to see them: fragments of a copper kettle, some pottery, and several metal axe heads.

The next morning I went to the office early and waited impatiently for Walter to arrive. When I heard him come in a few minutes after nine I decided I couldn't wait for him to discover the artifacts for himself. Instead, I met him as he was saying good morning to the secretary, reversed his direction and took him into the lab without giving him a chance to take off his coat. After a brief glance at the artifacts Walter became very excited and said he thought they probably came from a seventeenth-century Neutral site. This intrigued him since the early historic Neutral, a confederacy of the Ontario Iroquois, was one of the lesser known Iroquoian groups. Walter immediately made arrangements to visit the site. He wasn't to return from that visit for a very long time.

Soon after he saw the site Walter realized that it would have to be excavated. The site appeared to be a mass burial with a large number of grave offerings. Because this was perhaps the first largely undisturbed Neutral burial site to be discovered, all others having been looted by relic collectors, Walter considered that he had a unique opportunity to learn about the culture and lives of early historic Neutral people. He was also aware that he had to move quickly since construction activities for the housing development were due to begin soon. Equally worrying, if left alone too long before excavation began the site might be looted. This is why Walter booked a room in a motel after that very first visit and began organizing the excavation by long-distance telephone.

The first few days and then weeks were exciting for Walter and his hurriedly assembled crew, and for those who remained in Toronto and vicariously enjoyed hearing of the discoveries being made in the field.

Although distant from the work we felt part of it because of our role in helping to hire additional crew members and sending needed supplies to the excavation.

Then, in early November, the larger world suddenly intruded. I received a phone call from Doug Tushingham, chief archaeologist, who asked me to come up to his office in the main building. Doug wanted to talk with me about the work at Grimsby before he met some people who were going to visit him in protest over the excavation of human remains. I hurried up to the main building from our temporary offices in another part of the city (prepared for us in advance of the ROM's major renovation project), and Doug and I started talking about the impending visit. Within minutes he received a call from the receptionist at the main entrance to the building telling him that some people had just come in and asked to see him. Holding the phone, Doug glanced at me in silent question and, guessing what he had in mind, I nodded agreement. He then told the receptionist that he would send someone out to meet the visitors and show them the way to his office. I left Doug's office with a feeling of foreboding.

I identified the visitors as soon as I rounded the corner from the main exhibition hall to the central rotunda just inside the main doors. They were hard to miss: a group of six or eight people off to one side, the men in long braids with bright red bands tied around their heads. While asking their names I shook hands with those who were willing and then led them to Doug's office in the very back of the building. Doug stood up to greet the visitors when they entered his office and offered them seats, while Lucille Hoskins, Doug's long-standing secretary and a gracious, gentle women, offered them tea. They accepted stiffly but clearly hadn't come for polite talk. The spokesman explained that they were representatives of AIM, the American Indian Movement. I had heard of AIM, but little more than that it was an organization of Native activists with a history of protest in the United States, some of it violent. He said that they wanted the excavations at Grimsby to stop because they believed the work to be a desecration of the dead and an insult to Native peoples. They also wanted to see any bones that had been returned to the museum because they were concerned for the spiritual well-being of the dead and the safety of the remains.

From this point too many things happened simultaneously for me to keep track and time seemed to speed up until, finally, everything blurred together. As soon as Doug heard what the activists wanted he began calling various people in the building – the director, security, the technicians who handled artifacts, and so on – to inform them of the protest and the demands. These phone calls triggered other calls and soon Doug was both making and receiving calls. At one time during that frenzy of phone conversations it was clear that Doug was speaking with people in the provincial government about the protest and the excavation at Grimsby. The possible political implications weren't lost on the activists. It didn't take long for Doug to get caught in an impossible situation: trying to answer the questions of an ever-growing number of people outside his office while meeting the demands of those within it. I could see the spokesman and others in the group becoming restless over all this phoning and no apparent action. And then tensely impatient. Being slightly removed from the centre of things, I realized that we were very near some sort of a turning point. Just as the security staff had arranged for the activists to see some of the bones from Grimsby in another location, Doug received one call too many. Suddenly, the mood changed, and while Doug attempted to answer the call and I sat there helplessly wishing I could control the situation by stopping the clock or even pushing it back a few minutes, the activists talked among themselves briefly. After Doug hung up the phone, the spokesman announced that until they achieved their demands they would hold a sit-in. Right there.

I had sensed it coming, yet I hadn't actually formed the thought in my mind. And for a moment I couldn't react. I was frozen in a sudden flashback to nearly ten years earlier when I had seen other sit-ins and their aftermath. This was during the anti-Vietnam protests at the University of Wisconsin in the late 1960s. I had seen the use of threat and intimidation, and violence to people and things. I had been frightened by and attempted to avoid those confrontations, and I was worried now about the potential of this sit-in though I realized this was an entirely different situation. But my earlier experience with confrontation didn't help me deal with it any better; if anything, the experience made this situation even more difficult. I had been marked.

Doug realized that neither he or the ROM should oppose the sit-in. He immediately began making arrangements for security checks, food for the protesters, and numerous other details to help ensure that it was peaceful and contained. He also suggested that I return to my office elsewhere in the city to ensure the security of the Grimsby artifacts that had already been taken to our lab for cleaning and cataloguing. I would thus be available if Walter Kenyon called and needed something for the field. Doug said he would phone the next day if I could be of any help during the sit-in.

He didn't call. The sit-in was resolved the next morning, without violence. A few days later, in part because of legal actions initiated by the

Union of Ontario Indians, Walter Kenyon was arrested over technicalities surrounding his licence to excavate and then released pending a court hearing. Some time during this period the provincial government halted further work at Grimsby. Two months later Walter was permitted to continue the excavation under the terms of a complex agreement between the ROM, the Ontario Ministry of Culture and Recreation, the Ministry of Consumer and Commercial Relations, the Ontario Heritage Foundation, the Six Nations Reserve, the Town of Grimsby, and the owner of the property. The agreement provided for a division of the artifacts between the Six Nations Reserve (near Brantford, roughly a two-hour drive west of Toronto and home to Iroquoian peoples distantly related to the people buried at Grimsby) and the ROM (representing the government's interest in sharing responsibility for curating the material). The agreement also stipulated that after a period of study the bones would be turned over to the Six Nations Reserve for reburial.

With the agreement in place the excavations continued throughout the winter of 1976-7, the frozen ground making it necessary to use propane gas heaters to thaw the earth a few feet at a time in front of the work. Finally, on 4 April 1977, the excavation was completed and Walter Kenyon returned to his office, nearly six months after a visit he had expected would take only a few hours.

Shortly after the site was excavated it was engulfed by a subdivision, paved over under the circular Peachwood Crescent (later changed to Sunrise Crescent) and surrounded by houses. That summer the human bones were reburied at another location. Some time later, a metal plaque would be erected in Centennial Park, immediately south and adjacent to the subdivision, to commemorate the people who had been buried less than a hundred metres away. And on 23 April 1982, five years and nineteen days after he completed work at the site, Walter Kenyon would publish a final report on the excavations in a ROM scholarly publication series and thus also commemorate the people buried there, not by a marker but through greater knowledge of their lives and time.

The excavations at Grimsby revealed much about mid-seventeenth-century Neutral people in Ontario. Surprisingly perhaps, because archaeology is thought of as a science of the past, the excavations also revealed much about Native people living today. And this is what preoccupied me during the early aftermath of Grimsby. Knowing that many Native people opposed not only the excavation of human remains but also the curation of human osteological collections in museums, I began consolidating and reorganizing the ROM collections from Ontario that had formerly been housed at the University of Toronto. The arrangement with the university had made sense in previous years because there had been no physical anthropologists at the ROM, and those at the University at Toronto could make use of the material for research and teaching. After Grimsby, however, because the material had potentially greater public interest, I thought it necessary to bring the collections back to the ROM, where they could be more directly managed. I felt an even greater sense of personal responsibility in this regard when, in October 1977, I was appointed "In-Charge" of the newly formed Department of New World Archaeology. During this period I was also involved in developing recommendations for ROM policy on the repatriation of all human remains from Ontario, which had been requested by one Native organization, and attended meetings between archaeologists and Native peoples on this and related issues.

Since Grimsby I had certainly become more sensitive to Native concerns, but this didn't cause me to change my views about the excavation of human remains or their value in research. If anything I became even more aggressively defensive about these issues. Archaeologists, I knew, had no intention of desecrating the dead when they excavated burials and were doing that work with the best of intentions, for greater knowledge of the past. And I knew that the study of prehistoric human remains had provided great insights and sometimes unexpected knowledge about the history of certain diseases and genetically inherited medical conditions, knowledge that had the potential to alleviate suffering in the living. I knew also that archaeology and physical anthropology provided the only means of learning about the long history of human biological and cultural evolution, and I believed that greater knowledge of the past could lead to a greater understanding of ourselves and respect for our differences. Because of this I was angry that the freedom to do research, as I had been taught to do it and which I took for granted, was being questioned. While all of these views are easily defensible, I would eventually see in hindsight that I was also naïve. For these views are only one side of a very complex issue that would take years to be fully understood. But if I was naïve, so also were the majority of my colleagues. Nearly twenty-five years later the social and political environment in which North American archaeology would be conducted would be very different from what I had known in 1976. I could have avoided much anguish if only I had known and understood then, when I had a brush with the future, the changes that were coming. And if this had been more widely appreciated in the archaeological community, the future itself might have been different.

Archaeology in Conflict

In the 1960s Native American activists gained prominence with demands that archaeologists stop excavating human burials, an activity they regarded as desecration of the dead. Activists also called for the return, for reburial, of human remains and associated grave goods held in museum collections. These demands reflected the opinion of many Native people that the excavation and museum curation of human remains and associated artifacts indicated a lack of respect for Native beliefs, was racist (because in their view the collections comprised primarily Native remains), and symbolized colonial domination and attempted cultural assimilation.

Conflict between Native peoples and archaeologists continued sporadically through the 1970s and 1980s. Local resolutions often provided for the reburial of human remains that had been accidentally discovered or excavated under threat of destruction during urban development. Increasingly, these resolutions also afforded greater protection to Native burials by encouraging avoidance and non-excavation in the course of urban development or, if that wasn't possible, requiring consultation with Native tribes and organizations to resolve problems and avoid confrontation. Many archaeologists, museologists, and members of government – as well as segments of the general public – became more sympathetic to Native concerns. Change was occurring, although slowly and case by case.

In the United States the pace of change intensified in October 1990, when Congress passed the Native American Grave Protection and Repatriation Act (NAGPRA). NAGPRA offers increased protection for Native human remains and cultural objects found on federal and tribal lands. It also provides a basis for determining who has control and responsibility for those remains and objects. In addition, the legislation requires all federal agencies and museums that receive federal funding to inventory their Native American collections of human remains, funeral objects, sacred objects, and items of cultural patrimony. And after those inventories are completed, to inform appropriate tribes of those holdings and, when requested, to return human remains and objects to lineal descendants or prior owners, or to tribes that demonstrate close cultural affiliation to the prehistoric people or culture in question.

NAGPRA legislation has had far-reaching consequences and affects even the earliest part of the prehistoric record. Perhaps the most widely publicized example is the case of Kennewick Man, the skeleton of a forty- to forty-five-year-old male found accidentally in 1996 on the bank of the Columbia River near Kennewick, Washington, and radiocarbon dated at 8,410 years BP. Before analysis could be completed, the skeleton was seized by the US Army Corps of Engineers for repatriation to local tribes for reburial. Legal action by several archaeologists and physical anthropologists, who believed that the skeleton should be more thoroughly studied and preserved for future generations, prevented the skeleton from being immediately repatriated. A federal court decision, in August 2002, nearly six years after the case began, mandated additional study. The judge also decided that Kennewick Man does not fall under NAGPRA because there is insufficient evidence to determine exactly how the ancient skeleton may relate to present-day American Indians.

Two other examples illustrate some of the indirect effects of NAGPRA legislation. In 1992 a fifteen-year moratorium was put in place to prevent further archaeological investigations until 2007 of an Early Paleo-Indian (Clovis) site accidentally discovered near East Wenatchee, Washington. Up to the time excavations were stopped, sixty-one stone and bone tools had been recovered from a small area, possibly a former pit. The presence of several Clovis-type spear points suggests that the assemblage dates between 11,000 and 11,500 years ago. No human remains were found so it is not known whether the tools were part of a burial offering or a cache intended for later retrieval and use. The moratorium was put in place by state government because of protests by local Native organizations that thought inadequate consideration had been given to their objections to archaeological work at the site.

The second example concerns archaeological excavations at the site of Mammoth Meadow II in Montana. The site was threatened with closure in 1995 after human hair was recovered from levels below those containing Late Paleo-Indian artifacts dating between 8,200 and 9,400 years BP. The human hair is therefore potentially older. The site is not a mortuary or burial but a quarry from which toolstone was obtained and shaped into tools. The conflict was resolved after changes to NAGPRA regulations were adopted stating that naturally shed human hair in a non-burial context did not constitute human remains subject to repatriation. But, in deference to Native concerns about the human hair and the belief that Mammoth Meadow II is a sacred site, the Bureau of Land Management, which administers use of the land on which the site occurs, will not allow what some Natives regard as intrusive testing of the hair, such as DNA studies.

These examples illustrate how NAGPRA legislation may affect the growth of future knowledge about the earliest part of the archaeological record, most particularly with respect to human remains. In early 2001 the total sample of skeletal remains from North America dated between 9,000 and 13,000 years ago was represented by only thirty-nine individuals. Of these, most are highly fragmentary. Only eleven are sufficiently complete to be understood as individuals with respect to age, sex, stature and weight, health and injuries during life, and perhaps biological affinities. Kennewick Man is one of the two most complete skeletons available; the other is the Spirit Cave mummy from a site near Reno, Nevada, dated to 10,700 years BP. A court battle preserved Kennewick Man for more detailed study. A request for the repatriation of the Spirit Cave mummy was denied in 2000. But conflict over Kennewick and Spirit Cave is probably not over. And the remains of five other individuals have been reburied. The sample of early material, which ironically increased because of the museum inventories required by NAGPRA, is thus being reduced.

Canada lacks federal legislation comparable to NAGPRA, although archaeological work and the disposition of human remains and artifacts is regulated by provincial, territorial, and Native governments.

Over the past several decades, the way in which archaeology in North America is conducted when Native interests are involved has changed, as has museum curation. A new relationship has emerged and continues to evolve between archaeologists and Native peoples – one of consultation, collaboration, and partnerships. But although this new relationship resolves many issues, it creates another, for many Native people believe that they should have the right to interpret the past in accordance with their own cultural traditions. This is expressed well in a statement by a member of the Navajo Nation objecting to what their children are taught: "We do not want our children to be taught history as you believe it – it will destroy the very fabric of the Navaho people. We must interpret the past from our perspective. The Navajo and non-Navajo views of the past need not be so different but nonnative archaeologists must drop some of their preconceptions and listen to what we have to say to bridge the existing gulf. We will not let non-Navajos write our history or chart our future" (Begay 1997).

This sentiment reveals perhaps the most fundamental sources of stress between Native peoples and archaeologists: the conflict between traditional ways of knowing and the methods of science; and the struggle of Native communities, common to many others in the world, to maintain their own identities in the face of pressures from the larger world. Many archaeologists are worried that the methods of scientific inquiry are being weakened in order to incorporate less objective ways of knowing. The ultimate test is whether any facets of potential knowledge (scientific or not) will be ignored or subverted. Time will tell. Other generations will judge whether we today – Natives and non-Natives alike – are too bound up in our own time to be wise enough for theirs.

Interlude

After the turmoil surrounding the excavations at Grimsby and its aftermath, and the earlier pressures of opening a public gallery on schedule, I enjoyed retreating to the back rooms of the museum during the last few months of those missing years of 1976 and 1977. Returning again to my research was, by comparison to what I had been through, like going on a holiday.

During this period I used the results of my test excavations at Fisher in 1976 to prepare a grant proposal for a much larger excavation there in 1978. For that year I planned a multidisciplinary project that would require the largest excavation crew I had used up to that time. It would also involve the work of several other scholars who had their own separate schedules and budget requirements, all of which had to mesh together during the all-too-short field season. The following *Archaeological Newsletter,* written in the fall of 1978 after the second season of excavation at Fisher, will give you some idea of the planning involved and bring you up to date after those missing years.

AT THE WATER'S EDGE
OCTOBER 1978

... I tested several areas of the site in 1976 and ... we learned that several areas produced different kinds of tools and waste material from tool manufacture. The highest areas of the site produced abundant evidence for the manufacture of projectile points used as tips on thrusting or throwing spears, while the lower areas of the site near the lake margin produced other kinds of tools and abundant evidence for tool manufacture but no points or point fragments. This suggested that the higher areas may have served as lookouts where spears were repaired while watching for game (possibly migrating caribou) while the lower areas may have served as the main living area where other, perhaps more preliminary, kinds of flintknapping activities were carried out. The site also appeared to extend farther south into an area we couldn't investigate at the time because it was planted in grain. For these and other reasons, I decided to return again for a final season of excavation in 1978.

The first year's work at the site raised a number of interesting questions that I wanted to investigate further. First, was Early Man actually contemporaneous with the glacial lake, as the location of the site might at first seem to suggest, or had the site been occupied at some later date after the lake had drained? Second, what was the nature of the vegetation during the possible period of occupation? Third, what was the exact location of the shoreline and its relationship to the site? Although the barrier bar had been mapped previously, the main shoreline had not been identified and a large area between the bar and the site was simply mapped as an area of "moderate relief, partly subdued by lake water or meltwater erosion." Fourth, was the feature mapped as a former pond between the site and the offshore bar actually contemporaneous with the glacial lake, or did it postdate it by a significant amount? Finally, what was the source(s) of the chert used for tool making? Was it locally available in the [Blue Mountain region near] Collingwood [northwest of the site] or did it come from a distant source that might tell us something about the movements of the people?

To answer these questions, I asked a number of people to participate in a multidisciplinary project in 1978. Dr John McAndrews, a paleobotanist at the museum, and his assistant, Donald Slater, took several pollen cores from the former pond in an attempt to determine its age and the nature of the vegetation in the area during its life history. Dr Q.H.J. [Hugh] Gwyn, a Pleistocene geologist at the Université de Sherbrooke in Quebec, and his assistant, André Nolin, conducted a detailed geological study of the site area to determine the location of the shoreline of the glacial lake. Dr Peter von Bitter, an invertebrate paleontologist at the museum, began, with the assistance of Dr Bruce Liberty, a geologist at Brock University, a comparative study of the microfossils in the chert used at the site in an attempt to determine its geological age and possible bedrock source. Finally, lest you think that the archaeology was forgotten, I should add that a crew of eleven university students excavated in several different areas to ensure that we had a thorough understanding of internal variation within the site.

The fieldwork was very successful, and I believe that everyone obtained most, if not all, of the information they were hoping for. The geologists were able to determine that the lowest part of the site was actually a peninsula on the margin of a pond that drained into a lagoon of the glacial lake. Significantly, no artifacts were found below the shoreline, which is good presumptive evidence that the site was occupied during the life of the lake. The pollen data confirm and augment the geological data, show that the former pond was in fact contemporaneous with the lake, and indicate that the vegetation was dominated by spruce. Pollen data from elsewhere indicate that the vegetation may actually have been forest tundra consisting of stands of spruce trees interspersed with treeless areas of herbs and shrubs on the crests of hills and other exposed places. The chert analyses are progressing well, and it looks as if it will be possible to "fingerprint" the archaeological material and determine its source. Finally, the excavations were very productive. Much to my pleasant surprise, we obtained charcoal from a number of possible firepits that may allow us to date the occupation(s). Although I had hoped to find charcoal for dating purposes, I did not in fact really expect to, since in all of eastern North America only three or four sites of this culture have produced C14 dates, our knowledge of the age of this culture coming primarily from sites in the western United States. Although we tried very hard, we couldn't find evidence in the field that these features were the result of historic tree burns or some other natural phenomenon; so, thinking positively and not wanting to take any chances on missing something, I will spend the $175 to $200 per sample that it will cost to submit the charcoal for species identification and C14 dating.

The site was found to be much more extensive than formerly thought and every area produced a surprising amount of material (including a total of nearly 100 fragments of spear points in all stages of manufacture!). This will give us a good deal of information about the "internal structure" of the site and a strong basis for determining whether some of the areas may have been different activity areas within the same occupation, or, alternatively, separate occupations altogether. In this regard, one of the greatest surprises of the summer was the discovery of a spear-point manufacturing area adjacent to the shoreline on the lowest portion of the site. This was completely contrary to my expectations, since, as I explained earlier, I thought that this type of activity had probably been limited to the highest parts of the site and was related to the search for game. Obviously the situation is more complex than this, and while there may be functionally different areas on the site, they are not necessarily related to topography.

The artifacts and other data are just now being washed and labelled and otherwise prepared for analysis, so it will be some time yet before the final results of our work will be known. I am sure the site will tell us a great deal and it will be a pleasure in the coming months to shift my thoughts from a preoccupation with The Search itself and concentrate instead on the fruits of that work and the ultimate objective – a greater understanding of the people themselves.

Postscript

Much of the 1978 newsletter is concerned with questions that I needed to answer to understand what the site could tell us about the Early Paleo-Indian people who lived there. And most of these questions concerned the size of the site and its internal structure, its relationship with glacial Lake Algonquin, and its environmental setting. One question, however, may seem more obscure: the identity of the raw material used for tool making, that white chert I had run into time and again, first along the Niagara

Escarpment, and then at Banting, Hussey, Coates Creek, and now Fisher. This was the same raw material my southwest Ontario colleagues found on Early Paleo-Indian sites south and west of London, over 175 kilometres distant. I hoped that if we discovered the identity of the mysterious white chert we would also gain some insight into the movements of Early Paleo-Indians in Ontario. The underlying reason for this is simple: as people travel they carry or move things around the landscape, in this case toolstone hafted to hunting equipment or in leather bags.

This white chert constitutes most of the toolstone at many Early Paleo-Indian sites in southwestern Ontario. In fact, by frequency of occurrence it makes up 86 percent of the toolstone at Parkhill and 95 percent at Fisher. If the white chert had been acquired by trade – for example, by Parkhill people from Fisher people – one would expect a rapid drop-off in the amount of material from Fisher to Parkhill, with the latter containing only a fraction of that present at Fisher. After all, one wouldn't expect people to acquire all, or even a large percentage, of something as important as toolstone by such a potentially unreliable source as trade. But there is no pronounced drop-off. Instead, the amount of white chert at both sites is very similar, minus a small amount that could be accounted for by wastage through tool manufacture and use. This pattern might be expected if the chert were widely available naturally throughout southern Ontario. In that case it would be surprising only that Early Paleo-Indians made the same choice of stone for their tools, though not deeply surprising if the stone were of especially high quality for tool making. But this can't be the explanation because southern Ontario is underlain by several different bedrock formations of different ages that outcrop in different regions. Since the white chert couldn't be present in several formations, it must have a restricted geographic distribution and therefore have been carried from its source to the Parkhill and Fisher sites, involving the movement of people. So where was the geologic source of this white stone? The southern Huron basin where Parkhill is located? Or the southern Georgian Bay region where Fisher occurs?

The answer has two very different implications with respect to the movement of people. If the material came from a bedrock formation in southwestern Ontario, we could infer only a one-way movement of people and the toolstone they carried, from south to north. This would possibly have been a colonizing movement. But if the material came from a bedrock formation in the Georgian Bay region, not far from the Fisher site, we could infer a *two-way* movement: first from south to north to obtain the material and then south again to Parkhill and other sites where it was ultimately left as waste, or discarded, or lost. The chert could not have been acquired by people moving south from northern Ontario because the north was still ice covered and could not have been occupied. This two-way travel, in turn, implies a seasonal movement, possibly within a restricted geographic range or territory, and thus a pattern of land use comparable to those of early historic hunter-gatherers. Determining the geological source and therefore the identity of the unknown toolstone therefore promised to lead us into a very dynamic realm of human behaviour. Perhaps for many people, the most surprising aspect of this study is that something as cold and inanimate as stone could be so revealing of the lives of the people who used it, and so long – over 410 million years – after the stone had been formed.

In 1978 my southwestern colleagues believed that the unidentified toolstone came from the southern Georgian Bay area. The previous year Peter Sheppard, one of Roosa's students, found large amounts of the material in ploughed fields on top of the Niagara Escarpment, west of the town of Collingwood. And other archaeologists had observed this material as well, believing that it had been "mined" by the ice sheet as it overrode the escarpment from the north and later deposited on the brow of the escarpment as the ice retreated. Consequently, in the archaeological community, the still unidentified white toolstone was informally referred to as Collingwood chert. But no one had yet chipped a piece of this material from "living" rock. And this is precisely what we were determined to do in 1978.

The identity of the toolstone, and the other questions I was asking about human behaviour and the environment, took on a new meaning for me because until the discovery of the Fisher site and the opportunity to work with a team of scholars, I hadn't really had much chance to answer them. But in addition to the new research experience, my work at Fisher introduced other things into my life, one of them creature comfort.

Up to 1978, indeed even as late as our 1976 season at Fisher, I had lived in tent camps. Some of these were quite large, with specially screened tents for cooking and eating and even portable toilets, little rooms easily dismantled by releasing eye hooks, carefully crafted by ROM carpenters and painted the deep royal blue museum colour. And some of these tent camps were in very scenic places, the most memorable the very edge of the Algonquin beach, a steep hillside ten to fifteen metres high. Lying in my tent at night I felt as if I were living on the edge of two worlds, one belonging to the end of the Ice Age and the other to the world of the present.

But as nice as they are, and sometimes romantic, tents are cold and occasionally wet. If you sleep on a mat or mattress rather than in a cot, which I never could manage comfortably, it becomes increasingly difficult with age to get out of bed in the morning. And because you're so close to the ground, it takes a deep knee bend to stand up and put your damp clothes on.

Then there's the matter of hygiene. A tent kitchen is open to everything: people who need to get in and dirt and bugs that can't be kept out. And open-air cooking for a large group of people, by crew members on a rotating basis, is difficult on two-burner camp stoves. Long-term food storage in cardboard boxes and ice coolers is risky. Finally, if you have to carry in all your water from some distance away it's difficult for people to keep clean, especially after hard physical labour in mid-summer. So it was that I decided to try renting a house. It seemed a terribly decadent thing to do, not financially but in terms of lifestyle. Some of the romance of archaeology or any field science is, after all, roughing it. But I was really tired of tents.

The house, with its solid roof and four walls, running water, electric lights, kitchen, bathroom, and basement shower, was positively luxurious compared with my poor tents and plywood outhouses. The comfort was like a spiritual revelation for me in thinking about how to do fieldwork in the future, and I am convinced that it improved the quality of the science we did. The only downside was that my five-year-old daughter didn't like the spiders that were everywhere in the previously uninhabited house and threatened never to visit me again. Nevertheless even without furniture the field house was such a success that I never looked back, and in all my future years of fieldwork never again considered tents. And my daughter visited me anyway.

The Fisher site was a new experience in another way. Abundance. For the first time in my work I was finding a lot of material. It might not have seemed so with each one-metre square we excavated, which produced anywhere from just a few to perhaps twenty or thirty pieces of stone waste flakes and maybe a tool fragment. But after adding a large number of these one-metre squares together, I was obtaining really decent and statistically meaningful samples of from several hundred to a thousand or more items from each excavation grid. Thus, instead of taking the results of my work back to the museum in the proverbial cigar box, I was now taking back entire car loads of material that would take months to clean and catalogue. And the rarest of all artifacts – the small, beautifully made fluted spear point that was the central element of the Early Paleo-Indian hunting kit – was unbelievably abundant.

This was no longer a new phenomenon in Paleo-Indian research, at least to my colleagues Brian Deller and William Roosa in southwestern Ontario. A few years earlier they had found fluted points in great abundance

Artifacts from the Fisher site. Left to right top row: two beaked scrapers, probably used for cutting slots; two single-spurred gravers for incising; end scraper for scraping hides; double-edged spokeshave for smoothing shafts. Left to right bottom row: hammerstone; biface blank probably intended for a spear point; two Barnes-type fluted points; side scraper or knife.

Courtesy ROM.

at the Parkhill site: several dozen in one year of excavation. I had been very, very envious.

But in 1978, when our work at Fisher started producing large numbers of fluted points in all stages of manufacture, I suddenly realized the full impact of what had been hinted at by the first three point fragments we had found in 1975: Fisher was, in part, a point-manufacturing site. It was, therefore, potentially a *source* of fluted points. From that moment, partly in secret competition with Deller and Roosa, I started keeping a tally on the inside cover of my field notebook of how many point fragments we found. And throughout the notebook I jotted down special milestones in that tally and when they occurred. On a page dated 10 June 1978, a warm and sunny day, I recorded that we had found our forty-ninth fluted point. Two days later, at 9:04 a.m. on the first day of our fifth week in the field, crew member Jane Edward found our fiftieth fluted point. With that specimen we surpassed the number of isolated points Charlie Garrad had reported from all of Ontario in 1971 just seven years earlier. Over the next couple of weeks we nearly doubled our sample from Fisher, sometimes finding several point fragments a day. By Wednesday, July 5th, the last day of the excavation, we had found a total of ninety-four fluted points that year! By this measure alone, Fisher was proving to be one of the most productive Early Paleo-Indian sites in all of North America.

The tally of fluted points from the Fisher site was much more, of course, than simply a symbol of archaeological success. Or a boost to my ego. The large sample, which for all years of excavation would eventually reach 156 specimens, meant that we could study how the fluted point was manufactured and also compare it in great detail with other kinds of fluted points and manufacturing sequences in both western and eastern North America. But such a large sample from Fisher also told us very clearly *who* we were dealing with, at least archaeologically speaking.

The fluted points from the Fisher site fall into a group – technically, a point type – called Barnes. It was named by Henry Wright (a University of Michigan faculty member) and William Roosa (a graduate student there) after the site in central Michigan where the points were first recovered in abundance and described in detail. The Barnes site is located a short distance west of the bottom end of Saginaw Bay, a large embayment of Lake Huron that makes southern Michigan resemble a catcher's mitt. Interestingly, like Fisher and other Early Paleo-Indian sites in Ontario and the Great Lakes region generally, the Barnes site is situated on an Ice Age beach, although the shoreline probably predated the Paleo-Indian occupation there by several thousand years.

Secular and Sacred in the Early Paleo-Indian Fluted Spear Point

The Fisher site produced a single artifact that recalls a decades-long debate in Paleo-Indian research. The artifact is a very small – indeed, miniature – spear point made from part of a channel flake taken off a full-sized point during the fluting, or thinning, process in the final stages of manufacture. The miniature artifact is about ten millimetres wide and a little over fifteen millimetres long, the size of a watermelon seed. Was this tiny spear point actually functional? Or was it symbolic? And by extension, what of the full-sized spear point from which the channel flake was taken? Was this artifact, which took considerable flintknapping skills to make and was often beautiful as well, something more than a well-crafted and efficient weapon? Did it also have spiritual or ideational significance that endowed the rare miniature point with meaning as well?

There are hints that it did. Fluting, to thin the basal portion of a spear point, was clearly not a requirement for hafting a spear point onto a foreshaft or directly to a lance, as many other methods were used by Late Paleo-Indian and later peoples in the North American archaeological record who also hunted bison and other large animals. Simple lanceolate-shaped bases, stems, and side or corner notches near the base presumably worked as effectively. Fluting, however, was very demanding, if not actually wasteful, of raw material and time since it often failed, ruining the point. Estimates based on archaeological data and modern flintknapping experiments indicate that the failure rate *might* have been as high as 60 to 70 percent, although this could be substantially reduced depending on the flintknapper's level of skill and the exact method used, about which there is still considerable debate.

What could explain this tolerance for a very difficult and potentially wasteful technique that was technologically unnecessary? Simple cultural conservatism once the technique was invented? Or some more compelling spiritual or ideological reason? Clearly, aesthetic judgments and estimates of the technological demands of fluting reflect our own attitudes, although at some level they might parallel those also held by prehistoric peoples (assuming, not unreasonably, we share certain basic sensibilities). But can we remove ourselves from the issue more completely and find other evidence of prehistoric attitudes and beliefs?

Possibly. Direct evidence that Early Paleo-Indians may have thought of fluted spear points as more than simply functional is the fact that points were occasionally made in two extreme forms: the miniature form, sometimes also fluted or made to look as if it had been fluted; and an upscaled, or giant, form. Several upscaled points were found with the only Clovis burial known to archaeology, at the Anzick site in Montana, and in several caches of cores, tool blanks, and tools in western North America, most notably at the East Wenatchee site in the state of Washington. Clearly, as grave goods, the upscaled spear points were intended to accompany the dead to the afterlife. They may also have been intended, along with cores, tool blanks, and everyday tools, to provide

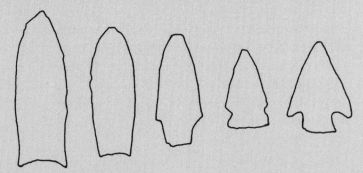

Bases used for hafting projectile points to shafts. Left to right: fluted point (flute scar not shown), unfluted lanceolate, stemmed, side-notched, and corner-notched.

Emil Huston, Artpole Studio.

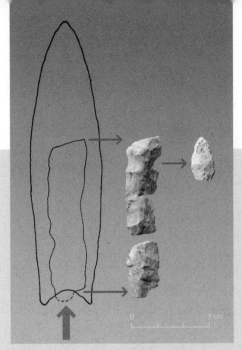

Making a miniature spear point. The miniature point on the far right was made from the fragment of a channel flake, similar to that shown immediately to the right of the outline drawing, produced when thinning (fluting) a point blank from the base during the final stage of manufacturing a full-sized spear point. The arrow indicates the direction of force used to detach the channel flake during manufacture.

Courtesy ROM.

Miniature spear point from the Fisher site.

Courtesy ROM.

the deceased with all the material needed for a complete cycle of tool manufacture and use – from the raw material, through various stages of preforms and freshly made tools, to items that had already been used but still retained the potential for resharpening. Thus, the burial offering at the Anzick site comprised not a random mixture of separate static objects but a dynamic series of interrelated objects promising ongoing usefulness in the deceased's spiritual world.

Miniature points provide another type of evidence that fluted spear points may, indeed, have had spiritual significance. At the Late Paleo-Indian Jones-Miller site in Colorado, for example, a miniature Hell Gap-type point was found near a posthole located in the midst of a 10,000-year-old bison kill, with part of a bone flute and the remains of butchered dog. The archaeologist who excavated the site speculated that the artifacts and the dog, possibly sacrificed, may have been used in a ceremony around a medicine post, perhaps also used as a perch by a shaman, to ensure the success of the hunt. Since people of the Hell Gap culture belonged to the cultural tradition spawned by Clovis some 1,200 or more years earlier, it's possible that a variation of this hunting ceremony extended back to Clovis times. The fact that fundamental spiritual ideas can have great longevity is certainly demonstrated for the period following Hell Gap. For 10,000 years later, historic Plains Indian medicine bundles, which were thought to protect and provide for the well-being of their owner or the people who cared for them, often contained miniature weapons.

There are strong reasons for believing that the fluted spear point was as vital to the ideological and spiritual life of the people it served as it was to their worldly life.

After his work at the Barnes site Roosa continued refining his general classification of fluted points in the Great Lakes region and was therefore well prepared for interpreting the material that he and Deller excavated from the Parkhill site in southwestern Ontario in the mid-1970s. Since the fluted points from Parkhill were identical to those from Barnes in Michigan, it was clear that the Barnes point type had regional significance. In 1977 Roosa used the point type, now also known from northern Ohio and New York State, to define what he called an archaeological complex. And he named it after the Parkhill site. Thus, the Barnes point type – represented by a small, well-fluted point, often with a narrow mid-section and a flaring base that, together, looked much like a fish tail – was regarded as diagnostic of the Parkhill complex.

In the late 1970s the Parkhill complex also seemed to be distinguished from other Early Paleo-Indian complexes in Ontario by the extensive use made of white chert for tool making as well as a tendency for sites to be located on the former Algonquin strandline, presumably for caribou hunting. This interpretation was, of course, conjecture. There was no direct evidence for caribou hunting by Parkhill complex people, only that the Parkhill site and a number of smaller sites in the vicinity seemed strategically located for hunting herd animals.

Now, having defined the Parkhill complex, just what is it in terms of people?

This question can be answered at several levels. At the simplest level the Parkhill complex, or any archaeological complex for that matter, is a consistent grouping of fragments of human behaviour from one site to the next. For this to occur, the ideas or motives behind that behaviour must be transmitted culturally, either by example or by the use of language, or both. Thus the weapon that Deller, Roosa, and I now called the Barnes-type fluted point was the product of people who talked with, or were around one another, on a frequent basis and who passed their ideas from one generation to another. Because the Barnes-type point has a specific size range and appearance, these people clearly held a common vision of what a fluted point should look like and how, in their opinion or experience, it had to be made in order to work effectively. These people also selectively occupied certain places in the landscape such as the Algonquin strandline, possibly because of their hunting requirements. And they also had a strong preference for a particular type of toolstone, possibly because it occurred coincidentally where they otherwise had to be for subsistence reasons.

These are intriguing glimpses into Paleo-Indian behaviour, but they are also somewhat tenuous and terribly fragmentary. The Barnes-type fluted point, for example, was only one of probably many important items in the Early Paleo-Indian tool kit. Yet in the late 1970s we didn't know whether other tool types – such as particular types of drills, scrapers, and knives – might also be diagnostic of the Parkhill complex. But our knowledge of this complex was deficient in even more profound ways as material items reflect only a part of cultural behaviour. Because Early Paleo-Indians were highly mobile hunter-gatherers, they didn't stay at any one place year round but instead lived for short periods at a variety of sites at different seasons of the year, depending on the resources they were exploiting. And they probably ranged widely, harvesting in seasonal succession a wide variety of animals and plants. When they left Parkhill and Fisher, for example, where did they go? We knew that they visited at least one other area, presumably not associated with relic beaches: the source of their toolstone. But where, exactly? And after replenishing their tool kit where else did they go? Did they also visit other regions? If so, how important were those regions in the total annual subsistence cycle and pattern of band movements?

At this point in the narrative, before the story develops a stronger momentum, perhaps I should mention a gender bias. Not a deliberate bias, but one that exists nonetheless. Although I've talked occasionally about bands of people, which, of course, included both sexes, many of the questions I've been posing are presumably related to male activities, although not necessarily exclusively: details of the fluted spear point and how it might have been made; the components of the tool kit used for the manufacture of weapons and other tools; strategies of site selection and land-use patterns related to hunting; and the timing and method of acquiring toolstone. Somewhat later in my work I would discover a cache of tools that reflected the activity of either men or women (see Chapter 5). And later still I would pose additional questions that pertained to the entire band and concerned both male and female activities. But I never developed questions that concerned only female activities, although in the late 1980s I did begin compiling a bibliography of papers on this issue, which was gradually becoming more widely discussed and debated in North American archaeology. I also encouraged the female crew members and assistant supervisors who showed an interest in this topic to develop their own projects, using the data we were excavating. Unfortunately, none did and nor did I. I might have moved more in this direction had I been less focused on the problems of discovering sites, recovering preserved animal bone and plant remains and charcoal for identification and radiocarbon dating, and interpreting technological aspects of stone tool manufacture and use. I'm also tempted to blame the biased nature of the archaeological record, which, when only stone is preserved, seems to reflect so much more readily the male activities of a hunting-gathering way of life. But is this really true? Perhaps part of what I see as bias is actually my own lack of imagination. If I don't succeed in beginning to find a way to correct or reduce that partiality for some future story of Early Paleo-Indians in Ontario, I hope that others will, perhaps even using data I collected but overlooked.

I return again to the late 1970s. The fragmentary patterns that began to define the Early Paleo-Indian Parkhill complex could hardly be seen as anything but a partial image of a once-living group of people. But even if the patterns had been more complete, would they tell us about a specific group of people, or a specific culture? The answer is probably no.

Archaeology is able to deal with a only limited part of cultural behaviour: that which survives the destructive effects of passing time. People, on the other hand, define themselves not only by where and how they live and what they possess, most of which may be perishable, but by kinship and myriad other complex social relationships that determine who is part of the group and who is not. Much of this transcends the meagre remains left for the archaeologist to study and, in fact, may also be partly independent of those remains since a common material culture, especially one that has been severely reduced by selective preservation in the archaeological record, may be shared by many peoples who see themselves as distinct from one another. An archaeological complex may thus be far less than a specific culture and, simultaneously, much more inclusive. Consequently, the Parkhill complex, and other archaeological complexes, or cultures, mentioned in this book probably included several different groups of people who, although broadly related culturally, differentiated among themselves in ways that are archaeologically invisible. Time has evened out all such distinctions and we cannot know the people of prehistory as they recognized themselves.

Despite this problem, knowing that I had Barnes-type points at least gave me an idea of where to look for comparative data when I came to analyze the Fisher material. This is not always an easy thing to know, as I learned from the few and heterogeneous fluted points from Banting and Hussey in the mid-1970s, when we had a much more rudimentary knowledge about Early Paleo-Indians in Ontario.

But the Barnes-type point was significant in another way. It also told me something about the age of the Fisher site, and the Parkhill complex generally, with respect to other Early Paleo-Indian cultures in North America. This clue to relative age concerns the Folsom fluting technique. This was a method of thinning, or fluting, a stone spear point so that it could be more securely attached to a foreshaft or lance, also achieving a less bulky, thinner haft. The thinning, which left a scar, called a flute, almost as wide and nearly as long as the spear point, was probably achieved either by indirect percussion using a stone hammer and a bone or antler punch or hand pressure with a rod-like tool, such as an antler tine. This force was applied to a small, specially made platform, shaped by delicate chipping, on the base of the point. This process of thinning was more precise and sophisticated than that used on the earlier, Clovis-type fluted point.

Since the Barnes point type in the Great Lakes region also exhibits the Folsom fluting technique, my colleagues in southwestern Ontario and I assumed that the Barnes point was made by people who postdated the earliest occupation of the region by Clovis or Clovis-related people who, in the southwestern United States and presumably elsewhere, are known to have predated Folsom. Thus, the occupations at Parkhill and Fisher were not the earliest Paleo-Indian sites in the province. Somewhere, still undiscovered, were even earlier sites occupied by the initial colonizers, either Clovis people themselves or their later descendants.

Although the Barnes-type spear point exhibits the Folsom fluting technique first recognized in the western United States at the Lindenmeier site in Colorado, no one in the Great Lakes region thinks that Barnes is directly related to Folsom. This might be a tempting conclusion, illustrating how first discoveries and names can influence thinking. Unlike Clovis, however, which has a pancontinental distribution, Folsom appears to have been centred in the Plains. Furthermore, in eastern North America, other, very different point types were also manufactured using the Folsom fluting technique, such as the Debert point from a site of that name in Nova Scotia and the Cumberland point in the southeastern United States, not yet associated with an archaeological culture. These point types suggest that the Folsom fluting technique, which is an improvement over Clovis, was independently reinvented several times over a broad area by descendants of the initial Clovis colonizers.

Details!

Well, perhaps. Specialists who study Paleo-Indians have always been accused by their archaeological colleagues, only partly in jest, of being dazzled and preoccupied by fluted spear points. And this may be partly true. Some fluted points are exceedingly beautiful, and all took considerable flintknapping skill to make. But the criticism is unjust because the complex technology is a wonderful way to identify and track people as they moved across the Ice Age landscape of North America.

The 1978 excavation at Fisher revealed a site occupied by the descendants of the initial Early Paleo-Indian colonists who moved into the Great Lakes region at the end of the Ice Age. Although the people at Fisher were not the first, they certainly left a strong imprint of their presence. The question I now had to determine was what it meant. But although I had accomplished a lot during that field season, there was always too little time and too few people to do the work. I hadn't really explored the southern part of the site, which extended onto a neighbouring farm, nor indeed the northern part. Without knowing its full size I couldn't really interpret the site very well and so another at least partial field season was required. I got my chance in 1980.

After the 1980 field season I didn't write anything for the general public on our work at Fisher. In fact I wouldn't write anything at all for the public on our work there for fourteen years, when I finally published an article in *Rotunda* magazine in the summer of 1994 announcing that the final scholarly report on the excavations at Fisher was about to be published.

More than twenty years passed from 26 May 1975, when the site was discovered, to March 1997, when the research monograph was finally published. In that year, my daughter, who had been three years old during the first season of excavation at Fisher, turned twenty-five. Nearly a quarter of a century had passed! It was shocking for me to realize that one of my research projects had taken up nearly the whole of her life.

I tried to describe in that 1994 *Rotunda* article why final publication had taken so long: the difficulties of co-ordinating the work of seven other authors, the lengthy process of peer review and rewriting, other research projects, and the changing technology of computers for both statistical analysis and word processing. I was greatly relieved when the monograph was finally published jointly by the ROM and the Museum of Anthropology at the University of Michigan, Ann Arbor. Neither institution had the resources to do it alone but the financial assistance of the Ontario Heritage Foundation tipped the scale from too expensive to financially possible. But the lengthy monograph is technical and thus largely inaccessible to the general reader. The final word that follows on what we learned should change that.

Fisher: What We Learned

Geological and Environmental Setting
One of the most important objectives of the multidisciplinary work at Fisher was to determine how the site was related to glacial Lake Algonquin. This work was directed by Hugh Gwyn, the geologist I'd first

met on a lunch break during my work at the Banting site on another part of Lake Algonquin. Hugh brought along a graduate student, André Nolin, who was going to use the geological data from Fisher as the basis for a masters thesis.

Hugh and André tramped around all over Fisher and the surrounding region with a shovel and a three-foot-long soil probe, exploring the sediments underlying the cultivated fields and taking samples each about the size of a bread bag for laboratory analysis. Most farmers were quite cooperative and readily allowed access to their fields but I guess one man was overlooked, and when he discovered André digging with a shovel on one of his fields he became quite angry, justifiably so, and (less justifiably) did some shoving. Neither Hugh or I were there but I guess André was able to smooth things out because I didn't hear anything more about the incident and the work continued without further problems. We were lucky. André was more cautious from that point and had a new appreciation for the differences between archaeological fieldwork and class-related geological field trips. Geological explorations are often done along road allowances and in gravel pits, requiring little contact with landowners whose permission has previously been obtained by the university faculty, whereas archaeological work requires lots of time consulting with private landowners. André belatedly discovered that he was in charge of these contacts as well as of the geology.

After the 1978 field season Hugh Gwyn took the sediment samples back to the Université de Sherbrooke, and André eventually followed on his motorcycle. Three years later, in 1981, I received a copy of André's thesis. In French. It might as well have been in some ancient Near Eastern language as I had forgotten nearly all the French I ever learned in graduate school in the United States for one of my language requirements. This was especially embarrassing to me since Canada, of course, is officially a bilingual country. Fortunately, Hugh Gwyn took charge, and he and André produced a shorter English-language version of the thesis, which became a chapter in the Fisher monograph. By the time we finished redrafting and relabelling all the maps and tables showing the distribution of various sediments and their grain sizes, my French had improved, at least with respect to geological terms for sand, gravel, and so forth. Though I would still have difficulty interpreting the label on a can of soup, I could read the contents of a bag of cement.

The detailed geological mapping at Fisher produced a surprise. Although the preliminary geological map I had been using when we discovered the site showed only a single strandline nearby, André and Hugh

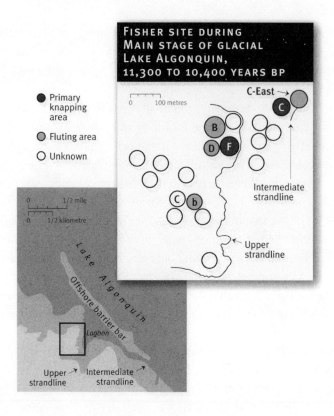

FISHER SITE DURING MAIN STAGE OF GLACIAL LAKE ALGONQUIN, 11,300 TO 10,400 YEARS BP

- ● Primary knapping area
- ◉ Fluting area
- ○ Unknown

0   100 metres

C-East →

Intermediate strandline

Upper strandline

0   1/2 mile
0   1/2 kilometre

Lake Algonquin

Offshore barrier bar

Lagoon

Upper ↗ strandline   Intermediate ↗ strandline

discovered that the site was actually associated with two strandlines. The higher of the two – called the upper-level strandline – bisected the site into an upper portion containing thirteen areas of prehistoric activity and a lower portion containing six areas. The second, intermediate-level strandline occurred about seven metres lower, on the very edge of the lowermost prehistoric activity area, which was also the edge of the site and of the cultivated field. Adjacent to the strandline and slightly below it was a poorly drained area covered with willows and cedars: clearly the former bottom of Lake Algonquin. A third strandline occurred farther east along one of the former offshore barrier bars.

The geological work thus showed that the Fisher site occurred in an area crossed by three different water levels, presumably a succession of falling lakes associated with deglaciation. Had the lakes been rising, the two lower strandlines would have been destroyed by wave erosion, as would the lower portion of the archaeological site itself, leaving only the highest strandline.

How did this falling succession of lakes relate to the Early Paleo-Indian occupation of the site? This question was answered, in part, by a pollen core:

a long column of mud extruded from a small-diameter metal tube that John McAndrews, a paleobotanist at the ROM, had pushed deeply into the bog just east of the site. The mud, actually layers of various combinations of silt, sand, and clay as well as some peat in the upper part of the column, pre-served the remains of tree and other plant pollen, spores, and bits of vege-tation that had accumulated over a long period when the location sampled by the pollen core lay under the water of Lake Algonquin and later, after the lake drained, on the exposed lake bottom. During this period the steady rain of pollen recorded the changing nature of the vegetation in the vicinity of the archaeological site. It also provided a date for the intermediate-level strandline on the lower edge of the archaeological site, and by implication, a limiting date for the Early Paleo-Indian occupation at that location.

The lowermost portion of the pollen record contained high amounts of spruce and pine pollen and lesser amounts of herbs, grasses and sedges, though still high in comparison with today. Spores of another plant were also present, *Selaginella selaginoides,* a small herb with the popular name of spikemoss that today is associated with frost-heaved soil in the zone of continuous permafrost in the high arctic.

The high amounts of spruce, pine, and herb pollen is the signature of a distinctive pollen zone in the Great Lakes region, called the Spruce zone after the dominant tree. Throughout the region this zone is dated from approximately 10,000 (or maybe 10,400) to over 12,000 years BP. The lower, and therefore older, end has not yet been securely dated. Because preserved needles and seed cones of spruce and pine are rare, the large amount of pollen from these conifers – 70 to 80 percent of the total pollen count – is believed to result from both the great abundance of pollen pro-duced by these trees and long-distance wind transport from trees south of the lower Great Lakes. That region had been deglaciated earlier and was therefore at a more advanced stage of reforestation. Trees were probably not all that abundant in southern Ontario, an inference supported by the high amounts of herb pollen, indicating the presence of large open areas.

The distinctive pollen assemblage of the Spruce zone is believed to represent a spruce-parkland habitat, with groves of trees growing in shel-tered locations and in long tendrils along drainage courses. The trees were interspersed with a patchwork of open areas of grasses and sedges in more exposed and drier habitats, such as uplands and west-facing slopes. The northern plant, *Selaginella selaginoides,* indicates that the ranges of some northern flora had earlier been pushed south by the ice sheet as it advanced toward its southernmost limits. Fossil insect data indicate that the mean annual temperature was probably two to three degrees cooler than today. And although the sparse vegetation might have looked much like an area near the treeline in the northern arctic today, warm microhabitats in southern Ontario were home to insects that today live in the boreal forest. The spruce-parkland of southern Ontario during the late Ice Age was not the glacial landscape of popular imagination, except possibly for a narrow treeless zone immediately adjacent to the retreating ice sheet, about 300 kilometres north of the Fisher site. The summers were somewhat cooler and perhaps drier than today, and the winters longer, colder, and snowier, with much larger snowbelts in the modern ski areas on the Niagara Escarpment near Collingwood and on the lee side of Lake Algonquin in the Georgian Bay basin. This climate is like no other major ecological zone in the world today. It was influenced strongly by the high mass of the ice sheet to the north, which altered atmospheric circulation patterns over North America, and by the open vegetation inhabited by mammoth, mastodon, grizzly bear, caribou, giant beaver, California condor, and the mysterious moose-elk, to mention only a few species. The climate, vegetation, and fauna of the Spruce zone were unique.

This paleoecological information helps us to visualize what the landscape around the Fisher site may have been like during the late Ice Age. It also helps date the occupation at the site. As a result of minor fluctuations in the lake margin during the time of the Spruce zone, sediments from the bottom of Lake Algonquin adjacent to the site were interstratified, much like playing cards in a deck, with layers of sand and gravel in the intermediate-level strandline. Artifacts were not found in this interstratified zone, suggesting that the Early Paleo-Indians at Fisher did not venture below the lower edge of the beach. In fact, the geologists working with us believed that they lived no closer than a few metres from the water's edge. Had artifacts extended below that level we would have interpreted the Paleo-Indian occupation as postdating the beach, but with the archaeological material occurring well above the former waterline we could safely assume that the Paleo-Indian occupation was contemporaneous with the beach at the time it was forming. After all, no one wants to camp on wet ground.

That Early Paleo-Indians at Fisher lived on the intermediate-level strandline provides some geologically limiting dates for the age of the occupation there. Hugh Gwyn and André Nolin believe this strandline was formed by what is called the Main stage of Lake Algonquin because of its stratigraphic correlation with the Spruce pollen zone and also because of its elevation at 234 to 236 metres above sea level. This places it roughly on the Main Algonquin uplift curve, originally the horizontal surface of a lake. During the late Ice Age and early Holocene it became distorted into a

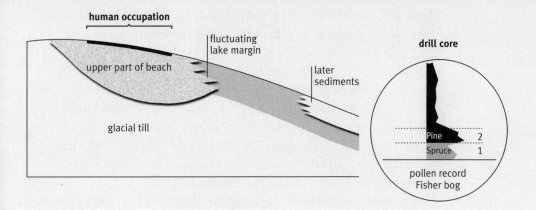

Stratigraphic relationship between the intermediate strandline on which the lowermost Early Paleo-Indian occupation occurred and the Spruce pollen zone below the Algonquin lake bed. The interstratification of sediments between the upper part of the beach and the Spruce pollen zone, and the distribution of archaeological material, show that the intermediate-level strandline and the Spruce zone were contemporaneous. They also show that the Early Paleo-Indian occupation of that strandline occurred some time during the same period, believed from radiocarbon-dated pollen and other environmental evidence to date between approximately 11,300 and 10,400 years ago.

gentle curve rising progressively higher from south to north as the upper part of the earth's crust, depressed by the enormous weight of glacial ice, readjusted to the loss of that weight. A succession of later uplift curves for several post-Algonquin lakes in the Huron basin became shallower as the crustal readjustment neared its end.

If the intermediate-level strandline at Fisher is correctly correlated with the Main stage of Lake Algonquin, it would have formed during the final stage in the long history of the lake. At other locations in south-central Ontario, the beginning of this stage has been dated at approximately 11,300 years BP and the end at 10,400 BP. The younger date provides a fairly secure limit for the Early Paleo-Indian occupation on the intermediate-level strandline if people actually lived adjacent to water as the artifact distribution suggests they did. If the occupation was contemporaneous with the Main stage of Lake Algonquin it was not younger than 10,400 years BP.

But the occupation could, of course, be as old as 11,300 years BP and still be contemporaneous with the Main stage. Or even older still if it was totally unrelated to the Main stage. Nevertheless, the younger limiting date, and the less firm older limiting date, are consistent with what is known of the age span of Early Paleo-Indians in North America as a whole, which extends from 10,200 to 11,500 years BP. The younger geological limiting date of 10,400 for the end of the Main stage of Lake Algonquin is most consistent with the age range for Folsom in the western United States, which extends from roughly 10,300 to 10,900 years BP. I thought this comparison very comforting since the Barnes-type point at Fisher was fluted in the same way as Folsom and therefore the two archaeological cultures should be of comparable age.

But what of the upper-level strandline on the Fisher site? Was it also associated with the Early Paleo-Indian occupation? And if so what implications might it have for dating that occupation?

The upper-level strandline occurs at an elevation of 241 to 244 metres, seven metres higher than the intermediate-level strandline associated with the Main stage of Lake Algonquin. Thus, since the strandlines in the site area represent falling rather than rising lake levels (or the lower two strandlines would have been destroyed), the upper-level strandline must be older than the intermediate-level one. Hugh Gwyn and André Nolin believed that this strandline might be correlated with an Early Algonquin water level dating over 11,500 years BP. Since over half of the archaeological site occurs above this higher level, the geologists suggested that the Early Paleo-Indian occupation may have occurred intermittently over a lengthy period and been synchronous with gradually falling lake levels as they dropped the roughly seven metres between the upper- and intermediate-level strandlines.

I must admit I was dubious. I had no doubt that the Fisher site was occupied several times over a lengthy period. Perhaps it was visited for a few weeks every year or at less predictable times over a period of a decade. Or maybe two decades. But a thousand years or so? From at least 11,500 years BP, the potential age of the upper-level strandline, to 10,400 BP, the end of Lake Algonquin? Not likely, I thought. I couldn't imagine a single cultural group of hunter-gatherers and thirty or so generations having such a stable pattern of land use over such a long period at the end of the Ice Age, a time of great change. Furthermore, if the geologists were right about an early occupation at Fisher contemporaneous with the upper-level strandline at 11,500 BP or earlier, that occupation would predate Folsom. The time slope should go the other way. If the Early Paleo-Indian colonization of North America, south of the ice sheet, proceeded from west to east as radiocarbon dating suggests, then the Folsom fluting technique, which evolved from the earlier Clovis method carried by the initial colonizers, should be younger in the east than in the west.

There was another problem with the suggestion that Early Paleo-Indian occupations at Fisher were synchronous with falling water levels from an Early Algonquin to the Main Algonquin strandline. Geologists, like archaeologists, don't always agree with one another, and in this case they disagree about the history of glacial Lake Algonquin and more specifically with the uplift curve I spoke of earlier. The debate concerns the rate of deglaciation and the dates at which various outlets of the lake were active. Some geologists, but by no means all, think that Lake Algonquin is much older than is currently thought and that the strandline identified with the Main stage of the lake in southern Ontario was actually formed by a post-Algonquin lake. This alternative interpretation doesn't affect the age of the intermediate-level strandline at Fisher, which is dated by correlation with the Spruce pollen zone, but it does affect the *identity* of the lake associated with that strandline and the lower portion of the archaeological site. It would also strongly influence our thinking about the upper-level strandline and the identity of the lake associated with it. And since I didn't have an alternative geological interpretation for the identity and age of the lake associated with the upper-level strandline, I was, to make a bad pun, stranded. There wasn't far I could go with this ambiguity. The upper-level strandline was older than the one below it – the two strandlines on the site representing falling, rather than rising, water levels or the lower would have been eroded away – but how much older I couldn't say.

This is why I wasn't enthusiastic about Hugh Gwyn's and André Nolin's hypothesis that the Early Paleo-Indians at Fisher may have lived intermittently alongside falling lake levels. I *should* have been happier to hear this hypothesis because geologists and paleoecologists have long recognized that the late Ice Age was a period of rapid, even catastrophic, environmental change. Some of this occurred not over millennia or even centuries but perhaps over just decades, a few years, or even hours. Many dramatic changes are reflected or hinted at in the geological and paleontological record: local extinctions, bursting ice dams and sudden floods, and regional temperature and vegetation reversals. These last were due to the release of large volumes of cold meltwater into the Great Lakes from changing drainage patterns of proglacial lakes along the retreating ice sheet thousands of kilometres distant. The Ice Age world was a dangerous place. But there are few archaeological opportunities to see how these and other changes may have affected Early Paleo-Indians.

To my knowledge the Fisher site is unique in this regard in the Great Lakes region. It is at a location where tremendous change occurred, not just in the near vicinity but right across the site itself. For this reason

I should have seen the hypothesis raised by Hugh Gwyn and André Nolin as an opportunity. But I'm afraid I didn't because I wasn't sure I could come up with an answer. Since we hadn't found any charcoal or animal bone for radiocarbon dating, I needed to find other, less certain, ways of dating the span of occupation. And a first step in that direction was to determine the structure of occupation at the Fisher site: how the people organized their activities and whether these were at all related to the two glacial lake strandlines that crossed the site.

The Structure of Human Occupation at Fisher

On the day the Fisher site was discovered the survey crew found three con-centrations of artifact material, one on the highest part of the site and two on the lowest, not far from the former Algonquin lake bottom. These con-centrations wouldn't have impressed a silent observer as each consisted of a dozen or so objects scattered widely about over areas ranging from ten to thirty or more metres in diameter. The artifacts were primarily small chunks of toolstone, waste flakes the size of a fingernail from tool manu-facture or resharpening and possibly the fragment of a broken tool. Only very rarely did we find a relatively undamaged tool. To find this material the survey crew walked very slowly, often hunched over nearly double in order to see the small objects. Sometimes they actually crouched to look more carefully, or got on hands and knees to peer at things before they were touched. I offered a liquid reward for a fluted spear point left untouched on a clod of dirt or under a corn plant that I could photograph for public lecturing. The three artifact concentrations to emerge from this first walkabout were widely separated from one another. The highest was nearly 180 metres from the lower two and those two were 81 metres apart.

After several visits to the site we learned, not surprisingly, that the dis-covery crew had essentially simply encountered the first three artifact con-centrations. They did this in the sense that, while intending to walk a straight line from the highest to the lowest parts of the site, whenever they found an object they stopped and focused on the area around it, walking in ever-widening but eccentric circles. And they did this three times until time ran out. This was perfectly fine on the first visit to a field we hadn't investigated before but of course it told us only what was in the three areas that had been looked at. The rest of the field – perhaps 90 percent of it – was unknown. Consequently, after the discovery of the first three concen-trations, our investigations were more systematic. We came to know Mr Fisher's cornfields, and those of his neighbour to the south, very well indeed. Footstep by footstep and, literally, inch by inch.

At the end of four years of work we learned that the Fisher site contained not three but nineteen artifact concentrations distributed over an area of approximately 22 hectares. They ranged from only a few square metres to 40 or 50 metres in diameter and were separated by anywhere from 24 to 132 metres. Six concentrations occurred on the lower portion of the site, either on or slightly above the intermediate-level strandline (the Main stage) of Lake Algonquin. The other thirteen concentrations occurred on the upper part of the site, above the highest strandline. A total of seven of the nineteen concentrations were excavated, two on the lower part of the site and five on the upper part.

But what did they mean, these clusters of tools and waste material? Were these nineteen artifact concentrations the result of separate occupations produced by short-term but repeated visits to the site by the same or different bands? Or were some of the concentrations part of more complex occupations where different activities had been spatially separated between two or more locations used simultaneously, in a pattern repeated many times?

We knew that the site had been occupied only by Early Paleo-Indian people of the Parkhill complex. No later artifacts were found. This indicates that, unlike Banting and Hussey, the site had not been visited by other prehistoric groups or even by other Early Paleo-Indian peoples of different cultures. This lack of intermixing was fortunate because it meant we didn't have to worry about trying to differentiate the material of separate cultures on a site that had been disturbed over a period of a least 10,000 years by vegetation growth and decay, burrowing animals, erosion, and finally, cultivation. Yet we still had to deal with the fact that the site had been disturbed. I thought the underlying pattern of human behaviour that had produced the nineteen artifact concentrations might still be detectable. The large spaces between the artifact concentrations argued against material from one artifact concentration having been intermixed with another. But disturbances to the site had probably destroyed evidence of the patterning of human behaviour *within* each concentration. Thus I decided to focus on an *inter area* analysis: comparing the artifact concentrations to see how, and if, they differed with respect to tool making and other occupational activities. And it made sense to focus on the seven concentrations we knew best, the excavated areas.

But first the data needed to be computerized. And this is when I first learned how the technological advances in our society can be a hindrance as well as a blessing. At first we recorded data by hand, using a soft-lead pencil on computer cards that were machine-read by a mainframe computer at York University and stored on large spools of magnetic tape. The print-outs for proofreading, stapled together in thick books nearly a foot wide and twice as long, covered an entire shelf the length of my office. Finally, when we were at last able to ask questions of the data and expected to enter the world of nanoseconds, we were jolted back into the real world, as we experienced long delays waiting for very expensive time on the main-frame computer, which, of course, everybody wanted to use. Later, when desktop computers came out, we transferred the data first to 5.25-inch discs and eventually to 3.5-inch discs. But the programs for reading and analyzing these magnetic records, and the power of computers for doing the work, changed almost faster than we could cope intellectually and financially. This is another reason why those unfinished manuscripts stay unfinished for so long, sadly sometimes forever.

Eventually it was done, and the raw data – the individual locations of 1,500 tools and more than 30,000 pieces of waste – were magnetically encoded in zeros and ones on fewer than half a dozen 3.5-inch discs. The complex job of statistically analyzing and interpreting the millions of bytes of data was ultimately done by Andrew Stewart, who as a high school student had volunteered to work with me in the early 1970s along the Niagara Escarpment. Andrew also worked for me in 1978 at Fisher, but the following year went off to England and later California to work on postgraduate degrees. While in California, Andrew wrote asking if he could use the computerized data from Fisher for a short paper he was writing for a course on statistical analysis. I happily agreed and sent him the computer discs. Several months later Andrew sent me his finished paper, thinking, I suppose, that was the end of it.

This paper was only the beginning. It would reproduce offspring time and again, somewhat like mating rabbits: rewrites and re-analyses, one after the other, until it seemed we were stuck in an endless loop of re-doing things, perhaps until time itself ended. The next small step in that nearly fatal direction took place when I decided to write up the spatial dis-tribution of the material for a chapter in the anticipated monograph, using some of Andrew's data and interpretations and other material of my own. Andrew and I talked back and forth about this, and eventually I produced a draft that he edited and I revised. I think at that point both our names were on the title page of the chapter but mine was listed first as primary author. Several months later, or perhaps it was a couple of years, Andrew asked if he could rework his original analysis using some statistical pro-grams that had recently been updated and improved by the person who originally developed them, one of Andrew's academic advisors. I readily agreed since I wasn't very happy with what I had done earlier. And this is how a third draft of the now infamous chapter came to be written. This time Andrew was the sole author because he had done all of the statistical analysis and writing and along the way deleted much of what I had done. Eventually, Andrew's chapter went off for peer review, along with the draft manuscript of the completed monograph. Several months later, and nearly fifteen years after his first short paper for a course in statistics, Andrew rewrote the paper once again – perhaps recast would be a better word since the data and ideas were rearranged rather than substantially changed – this time in response to some criticisms raised by the reviewers. It was nearly too late to ask such a thing of Andrew because he hadn't much of himself left to give to the project, and I was worried for him. But after a couple of weeks of very long rewriting sessions, it was done. And then, a couple of years later, published. A cloud lifted and the dark history of this chapter receded. I recount that memory here because it explains why the road to publication is often so long. Everything would be much easier if the writing, and analysis, could be done only once.

When Andrew's analysis was finished it told us that there were at least two types of artifact concentrations on the Fisher site. The first Andrew called "fluting areas," in part because they contained abundant evidence of spear-point manufacture, identified by rare examples of whole but not yet finished spear points and by the much more abundant debris resulting from failed attempts at thinning and fluting. I had of course recognized these areas in the field during the course of excavation but Andrew's analysis revealed some other less obvious patterns. The fluting areas also contained a large proportion of other kinds of shaped tools – tools made to a basic pattern – that were probably hafted onto handles and therefore carried from one site to the next. To use a modern term, these tools had been "curated": saved and used over a long period. There were many differ-ent types of these tools and the functions of some, along with the materi-als they worked, were determined by another co-author of the monograph, John Tomenchuk. John looked at the tools under a microscope to study the scratches, nicks, scars left by microchips, polishes, and other telltale signs of use-wear along the functional edges. Some of this damage helps to identify the material worked: hard wood or antler, soft wood, dry or green hide, muscle tissue, fish. He identified the function and use of sev-eral kinds of curated tools: scrapers for working animal hide and wood; and tools with narrow bits for cutting slots in wood, bone, or antler. Another highly versatile tool, made with various combinations of small, needle-like tips, had several different functions: slicing, such as to remove the sinew bindings holding spear points to their foreshafts; piercing holes, perhaps in leather; scribing circles, perhaps as decorative elements on tool handles; cutting thin bone discs for use in clothing or perhaps as jewellery; and cutting sockets for joining the wood or bone parts of composite tools. Other, more casually shaped tools were also present. These had been trimmed and sharpened to a minimal extent, presumably only for temporary use. Finally, the fluting areas were characterized by low densities of waste material from the flintknapping process. Unsurprisingly, the material consisted primarily of debris from the final stages of spear-point manufacture and other toolmaking or maintenance activities. These generalized patterns were found in three fluting areas, two on the higher portion of the site, above the upper strandline, and a third on the intermediate strandline on the lower portion of the site.

Andrew Stewart called the second type of artifact concentration "primary knapping areas." Compared to the fluting areas, they contained proportionally higher amounts of blocks of toolmaking material, or cores, early stage tool blanks, unmodified flakes that had been used as tools, and waste material characteristic of the primary stages of flintknapping. Some of the cores were used to manufacture early stage blanks that were later to become knives and spear points. The number of blanks varied considerably among the primary knapping areas so the amount of effort involved in blank production apparently also varied. In addition to this heavy work, other cores were used as sources of flakes, which themselves were used as tools. Sometimes referred to as "spontaneous" tools, these flakes were used for a short period for some specific task without any modification whatsoever and then discarded. John Tomenchuk determined that many of these tools were probably used for cutting, scraping, or shredding organic materials. These patterns were found at four of the seven artifact concentrations we excavated, three on the upper part of the site and the fourth on the lower part less than eighty metres from the single fluting area.

Were the activities in the two different types of artifact concentrations related? And if so how? We didn't find broken tools with matching fragments from the two different types of artifacts concentrations so we couldn't track human activities across the site in this manner. My colleagues in southwestern Ontario, Brian Deller and William Roosa, were much more fortunate. At the Parkhill site, occupied by people closely related to those at Fisher, two channel flakes – pieces removed during the fluting process – from one area were refitted onto two spear points from another area. These refits indicate that the points were made in one place, then used on a short hunting foray from the site when they broke, and finally, returned to Parkhill, probably still hafted to the foreshaft or spear, where they were removed and replaced with new spear points in a different area from the one in which they were made. This evidence indicates clearly that two areas of the site were used either simultaneously or in close succession. The time difference couldn't have been greater because the longer it was, the more likely the two points would have been discarded in the field or at another site altogether. Although we didn't find similar matches at Fisher, I don't think we spent enough time looking, and this is one of those inevitable loose ends that accumulate after every research project. Perhaps someone else can pick it up during a re-analysis of the collection.

A second way to approach the problem of determining how the two different types of artifact concentrations might have been related is by considering their role in the entire toolmaking process. Significantly, the primary knapping areas were used partly for rough flintknapping, such as for manufacture of early stage blanks, while the fluting areas were used for finer work, such as spear-point manufacture from late stage blanks. This suggests that the two areas were part of a continuum in the toolmaking process. The idea is supported by the fact that primary knapping and fluting areas tend to occur in pairs. One pair occurs on the lower part of the site, while a second pair, or perhaps a triad involving a somewhat different separation of tasks, occurs on the upper part. This pair, or triad, is somewhat less convincing because the contrasting patterns of early versus late stage flintknapping are somewhat weaker. But the lowermost pair is fairly convincing and I think represents the spatial separation of two different aspects of tool manufacture, and perhaps other contrasting activities, conducted at the same time by different members of the same group of people. For this reason I believe that many of the nineteen artifact concentrations were the locations of activity areas that were part of larger occupations, not independent campsites in their own right.

Andrew Stewart is a little more conservative in this regard than I. He agrees with me that the lower pair of primary knapping and fluting areas may have been part of the same occupation but believes the other contrasting areas on the upper part of the site may represent a succession of separate occupations that, in terms of human activities, were more narrowly focused and possibly even visited at different times of the year. Considering the complexities involved in interpreting the material, it is not surprising that there are differences of opinion.

The true picture is probably much more complex than we have been able to discover, in part because of the ambiguities in our research results but also because we had time to excavate only seven of the nineteen arti-fact concentrations in the three years we worked at the site. These seven concentrations appeared to me to be the most informative but they consti-tuted less than half the total number of concentrations we identified. Excavating the entire site was not practical. Thus, as is true for almost all research, we had to be satisfied with a sample.

I think it's fairly safe to say that Fisher is probably a mix of different types of occupations over a lengthy period, some occurring at a single location and others involving a spatially separated and perhaps broader range of activities occurring simultaneously at two or more locations. Perhaps these two types of occupations reflected the size of the bands that visited the site, the smaller occupations indicating a smaller number of people. This must remain speculative because it's impossible to estimate the number of people present at any particular occupation from the amount of archaeological debris they leave behind. Though Fisher is one of the largest Early Paleo-Indian sites in North America in terms of both its size and the number of artifacts, it is actually a complex mix of small sites. These small sites occur together because of some advantage the gen-eral locale offered, perhaps for subsistence, that drew people back time and again. But why?

Somewhat surprisingly, Andrew Stewart's analysis of the patterning of archaeological material across the site suggests an answer: glacial Lake Algonquin. It also raises again Hugh Gwyn's and André Nolin's hypothesis that the occupations on the site were synchronous with falling lake levels.

The distribution of primary knapping and fluting areas identified by Andrew Stewart shows a kind of symmetry because pairs or groups of the two different types of areas are associated, physically at least, with both the upper- and intermediate-level strandlines. Had the activities in these areas been independent of the two water levels, we might expect them to have a more random distribution on the site, with the paired areas occur-ring in one part of the site or split between the two areas. The pattern we see suggests otherwise, that paired areas were positioned adjacent to the lake margin during a period of falling levels, first along the upper-level strandline and then along the intermediate.

To establish the plausibility of this idea, I needed to show that the occupations on the upper part of the site were older than those on the lower part. Without radiocarbon dating this can be done only through rel-ative dating. But how?

A possible answer was unknowingly suggested by my colleague in southwestern Ontario, Brian Deller, when he wrote that Fisher may be younger than Parkhill because it contained a specific toolstone, absent at Parkhill, that became accessible only with the draining of Lake Algonquin. This material is called Kettle Point chert and is known from outcrops on the shore of Lake Huron south of the city of Grand Bend. Deller reasoned that Parkhill, lacking the material, must therefore be the older of the two sites. Furthermore, since the fluted spear points at Parkhill are larger than those at Fisher, Deller suggested that over time the Barnes-type spear point was made in smaller sizes. If true, this trend might provide the method of relative dating I was looking for. I speculated that if Fisher had been occupied over a period of falling lake levels, spear points made on the upper strandline might be larger than those made on the lower, intermediate-level strandline.

There are some difficulties with these arguments. First, in the final report on Parkhill, updating all earlier statements on the site, Chris Ellis and Brian Deller indicate that a few tool fragments and some debitage of Kettle Point chert were in fact found. Although none of the tools is culturally diagnostic, Ellis and Deller accept the possibility that they were made by Early Paleo-Indians, rather than later people who reused the site. The chert appears to have been obtained from glacial deposits rather than a bedrock source, but the fact that it was available at all eliminates this chert type as a possible way of dating the Parkhill site relative to Fisher. This leaves us with the size difference in Barnes-type fluted points, with those at Parkhill being larger than those at Fisher. Because of the large number of points from both sites, this difference appears to be genuine rather than a spurious effect of low sample size.

What caused this? Strangely perhaps, it's easier to answer the opposite question: what didn't cause it? Not distance from raw material source. Fisher is only about 30 kilometres from the stone source while Parkhill is over 175 kilometres distant. If distance from the stone source was the cause of the size difference between the two sites, Parkhill points, rather than those from Fisher, should be smaller.

The size difference could be the result of changes in the way spear points were propelled, perhaps reflecting a shift from thrusting or throwing spears to airborne darts propelled by a throwing stick, or atlatl. The change from a larger, heavier spear point to a smaller, lighter dart point could have been stimulated simply by technological innovation or by a change in the species of animal hunted. A shift from caribou to deer, for example, coincident with faunal changes at the end of the Ice Age, might have required different technology or hunting tactics. Deer hunting would perhaps require a weapon effective at longer distances than that for caribou hunting. It is at least conceivable that the size difference has temporal significance. If so, we are left with a crucial question. Can any change in size be detected over the span of time that people occupied Fisher?

The short answer is no. At first this might seem illogical; the Fisher site produced a very large sample of 156 fluted points. The problem is that only a fraction of this sample is relevant to the study of size – only finished examples, unaltered by later retouch – and this subsample is reduced further when divided between the upper- and intermediate-level strandlines. The samples from the upper strandline are not bad, although perhaps not meaningful statistically. The number of specimens ranges from ten to nineteen, depending on the particular measurement in which one is interested. The three samples from the intermediate strandline are totally inadequate, ranging from one to three specimens. We can't therefore say whether the presumed trend toward a smaller spear point actually occurred during the span of occupation at Fisher. And thus we can't date the relative age of the occupations on the upper and intermediate strandlines. It also means we can't say whether those occupations were synchronous with falling lake levels.

This final episode in a complex discussion that meanders around seemingly unrelated topics – uplift curves, the scatter of broken tools and flintknapping debris across a twenty-two hectare field, and the size range of spear points – might appear to have led nowhere. In one sense, that's true: the trail led to a door that couldn't, in the end, be opened. Much research is like this. But along the way, we learned that during one part of its occupational history, the site was situated on the edge of a lagoon on a glacial lake. And further, that the site occurred in a spruce-parkland environment, a patchwork of trees and large open areas of grasses and sedges. Finally, we learned that the site was occupied intermittently by bands of people who sometimes lived at a single location on the site where they focused on one aspect of the toolmaking process and subsistence activities involving either spontaneous tools or formal, curated tools. Conceivably, these occupations were brief preparations for hunting or gathering forays into the surrounding countryside. At other times the people occupied two or more areas on the site simultaneously, where they were involved in the entire toolmaking process and a larger range of subsistence activities. These occupations may have been in preparation for longer absences from the site, perhaps from one year to the next.

But why did people come to Fisher? What was the attraction that caused the site to be reoccupied?

Between the Mountains and the Inland Sea

When I first started work at Fisher I had visions of caribou in my head. These noble animals, I thought, followed the twists and turns of the Algonquin shoreline to the vicinity of Fisher, where they were found or intercepted by Early Paleo-Indians. Several millennia later, in a different geological age, I too tracked the vanished caribou along that same shoreline and found the Paleo-Indians. Thus I was prepared to see the physical attractions of the Fisher site in terms of caribou hunting.

With such a commanding view of the surrounding countryside, it was also easy to believe that the site had been positioned for the advantages it offered as a game lookout, both to the north and south along the shoreline and west into the interior countryside. In a spruce-parkland environment Fisher might have offered much the same visibility of the surrounding countryside as it does today, overlooking a rural landscape of grain fields, orchards, and woodlots. I was so attracted by this thought that I set up a mapping table on top of the site, taped a contour map and aerial photograph to its upper surface, and scanned the surrounding countryside with a pair of binoculars through 360 degrees, marking off the areas that could be easily seen from that vantage point and those that could not. I was looking for some pattern that would tell me the directions that Paleo-Indians might have been most interested in and their distances from the site.

I discovered ambiguity. The site provided excellent views in all directions. No single sight corridor stood out.

If, however, the Paleo-Indians were more interested in *not* being seen, presumably by moving animals, then the view *from* the north was most important since there were more terrain-blocked views in that direction. This strategy might conceivably have been important if Paleo-Indians were camped at Fisher in anticipation of caribou movements through the site area from the north. That Fisher would have been downwind from those moving animals might also have been an important consideration.

As interesting and logical as this may be, it is also speculative and therefore vaguely unsatisfying. At the time I excavated Fisher there was no evidence from anywhere in Ontario, or the Great Lakes region generally, that Early Paleo-Indians actually hunted caribou. And without preserved animal bone we couldn't base our interpretations on anything other than site location and presumed hunting strategies. So my painstaking work with the binoculars proved little except to my crew. Sweating at the end of long-handled shovels in the hot dust of a cornfield while I stood majestically silhouetted against the skyline, scanning the distant hills under the shade of a beach umbrella, they probably thought I looked more than a little eccentric.

While looking for ghostly herds of caribou on that hilltop I was also newly aware that Fisher may have been attractive to Paleo-Indians not only for the organic necessities of life but also for the inorganic. Just prior to the last season of excavation at Fisher, my geological colleague and good friend at the ROM, Peter von Bitter, finally succeeded in tracking down the identity of the unknown white toolstone: the material that Paleo-Indians at Fisher, Parkhill and numerous other sites in southern Ontario used almost exclusively for their tools. On 7 November 1979, Peter von Bitter, alone and wet in the cold of early winter, chipped a piece of that white stone off living rock. With the swing of a hammer he answered a question that had been worrying me for four years. Of equal, or perhaps even greater importance, he opened up an entirely new way of looking for Early Paleo-Indian sites. I would no longer depend on fossil beaches as my only way of investigating the lifeway of Paleo-Indians. And because I could now track them off the beaches, I would be able to see how they used a totally different part of the landscape. Truly, no hammer ever struck with greater effect.

Peter had suspected that the white toolstone came from a bedrock formation in the southern Georgian Bay region. Ploughed fields on the top of the Niagara Escarpment southwest of the city of Collingwood were littered with angular blocks of it, suggesting that the material had been plucked from the earth as glacial ice flowed up the escarpment from the north. When the ice stalled and started to melt back on the upper surface of the escarpment, the blocks of chert were deposited, along with tons of sand and gravel, in the recessional moraines, ribbons of interconnected hills, and deep depressions (called kettles) that mark temporary halts of the retreating ice. With the knowledge that the material had been transported by glacial ice it seemed a simple matter to walk upstream against the flow of the glacier to the bedrock source of the white chert somewhere to the north.

Peter had an advantage over archaeologists who had tried this approach as he was better prepared to use the geological literature for a systematic search in the field. He was also better able to decipher the scattered exposures of bedrock that geologists use to interpret regional stratigraphy.

Peter called on the help of one of his colleagues who had mapped the Niagara Escarpment along its entire length in southern Ontario, the late Bruce Liberty, then at Brock University in the Niagara Peninsula. Peter and Bruce Liberty did what all bedrock geologists do. They searched out and stopped at endless roadside exposures of bedrock. While people drove hurriedly by, wondering what could be so interesting in a roadside ditch the two geologists, together yet wandering separately about, looked intently at the rock through small magnifying glasses. Occasionally they would break off pieces with their hammers to look at fresh surfaces and squirt them with a mild acid to see if they fizzed, a simple way to differentiate limestone from dolostone, a magnesium-rich rock. They also visited bedrock quarries, river cuts, and scenic waterfalls.

Nothing! The missing chert – and its host rock formation – stayed missing. At this point Peter thought the chert might very well be from a "ghost" deposit: that word I have used before with respect to people at the Banting site and, more recently, animals at Fisher. Peter's ghost was the remains of a bedrock formation that had long since eroded away, leaving only the more resistant chert. Peter suspected the ghost was the so-called Guelph Formation, which is present today only as small remnants on the uppermost part of the Niagara Escarpment. But the Guelph Formation held its secrets beneath a mantle of glacial deposits and was not that forthcoming.

The impasse was broken by a piece of fossil coral that had grown in a tropical reef in a warm sea over 410 million years ago. Peter picked up this fragment of the middle Paleozoic era – a time much older than the Mesozoic, the age of dinosaurs – from a field that was almost covered with chert fragments and had been shown to him by Bill Fox, then an archaeologist with the Ontario government. The coral was a well-known fossil in the Silurian-age Fossil Hill Formation. This bedrock unit underlies the caprock of the Niagara Escarpment, the Amabel Formation, which is in turn below the remnants of the higher, and therefore younger, Guelph Formation. Peter immediately wondered if the chert was associated with the coral and therefore came from the Fossil Hill rather than the Guelph Formation.

After returning to Toronto with this piece of fossil coral, Peter contacted another of his colleagues, Peter Telford, who worked with the Ontario Geological Survey and had mapped the region. Obtaining a copy of Telford's most recent map, Peter von Bitter returned to the field a week or so later and started systematically checking bedrock exposures of the Fossil Hill Formation, regardless of where and how big they were. I helped occasionally and realized then that geologists did more than drive comfortably from one roadside exposure to another like bees from flower to flower. They also clawed through dense bush, crossed wide open fields sometimes filled with danger such as a solitary bull in a distant corner, and descended into stream cuts so deep and overgrown that the sun barely penetrated. Peter did this and more with a doggedness and single-minded intensity that was often no less interesting and amazing to me than what we were jointly looking for.

It was on one of those cross-country walks, from which I apologetically excused myself because of other pressing business, secretly with few regrets, that Peter made his discovery. Actually three discoveries. After the first one, the other two happened fast, one upon the other: *three* bedrock outcrops of the Fossil Hill Formation that contained white chert, *in place*. Or, as Peter would have said, *in situ*.

Looking back, it's easy to understand why the chert stayed missing so long. The fossil coral was the key and it would probably have been recognized as such only by a geologist. The coral led to a layer of bedrock that, because it was relatively thin, was sometimes mapped by geologists and sometimes not. In the latter case it was simply included with the overlying Amabel Formation, but if it was mapped, the chert, which seldom interests geologists, was either noted only briefly or not at all. It was thus well hidden, accessible only through the fossil coral as an obscure key to unlock the door to the hidden room beyond and an understanding of the vagaries of geological mapping to pass through that door. It would have been surprising if anyone other than a geologist had been able to find the chert.

The day after his discovery, Peter von Bitter sent a CNCP telegram to Big Bird at the Royal Ontario Museum. It was signed The Baron. Not knowing how to deliver a telegram addressed to Big Bird, I imagine CNCP called the museum and the call was probably bounced around a bit. In due course it was transferred to the secretary of the board of trustees, Frank Dunbar. I can't even begin to think what Mr Dunbar must have thought of its strange address. The only way he could have guessed for whom it was intended was that the telegram was directed to the Department of New World Archaeology at 299 Queen Street West, our temporary home during a massive, museum-wide expansion and renovation project. And I was the head of New World Archaeology.

Mr Dunbar called and asked me if I knew anyone called Big Bird. I paused, suddenly remembering that Peter von Bitter sometimes called me Big Bird because I reminded him in some convoluted way of the yellow character on *Sesame Street*. Peter did this in response to my calling him The Baron because of the *von* in his name and because, despite his Canadian upbringing, he sometimes behaved in ways I thought very, very German.

I remembered Mr Dunbar was on the phone and answered hesitantly that, yes, I was Big Bird, hoping he wouldn't ask why. He went right on as if the silly name weren't silly at all and said I had received a telegram with the message "FFCB." Did I know, he asked, what it meant? My heart stopped! I remembered my joking request to Peter that if he ever found the missing chert to send me a telegram. And I remembered the code we had decided on: FFCB. It meant "Found fucking chert bed." But it never occurred to me that Peter, a sometimes very correct person, would actually send such a telegram or that it would be read to me by someone from such a lofty height in the museum's administration.

Yes, I said, I understood the message. Without a pause, Mr Dunbar crisply thanked me for receiving it, said that he would send me the copy of the telegram, and wished me a good day. And then he was gone. I suddenly understood in his discretion one of the reasons why he was such a good choice for his post. I also saw for the first time the mischievous side of my geology friend. He clearly needed to be watched.

Peter's discovery that the missing chert came from the Fossil Hill Formation was just the first step in documenting the geologic origin and distribution of that important Early Paleo-Indian toolstone. He later determined it had a very restricted distribution, extending from the general area of a small hamlet called Banks on the top of the Niagara Escarpment southwest of Collingwood and west to the eastern edge of the Beaver valley, a distance of about ten kilometres. So far as he could tell no chert was present on the other side of the Beaver valley or farther west until it occurred again in the vicinity of a small hamlet called Walters Falls, twenty kilometres to the west and not too distant from the Bighead River valley, which leads to the town of Meaford on Georgian Bay. The chert, which Peter and I now called Fossil Hill after the bedrock formation, was therefore restricted to a small upland area in the southern Georgian Bay region of Ontario.

This answered one of the questions we had asked before starting work at the Fisher site in 1978. Was the toolstone so widely used by Early Paleo-Indians in southern Ontario carried north from a geologic source in southwestern Ontario, or south from a source in the southern Georgian Bay region? Clearly, it had been carried south. Early Paleo-Indians in southwestern Ontario who used Fossil Hill chert first travelled north to obtain the material from the southern Georgian Bay region and then carried it south again to use it at the Parkhill site west of London and at other sites in the general area. This two-way movement between the southern Huron basin and the southern Georgian Bay region strongly suggested that Early Paleo-Indians moved within a defined geographic range, or territory. This contrasted with the presumed earlier behaviour of the first Paleo-Indians to inhabit Ontario, whom archaeologists thought had moved freely about the landscape as both explorers and colonizers. It was their descendants, such as the Parkhill complex people at the Parkhill and Fisher sites, who settled in and developed a pattern of movements within specific geographic ranges.

The location of the geologic source area of the toolstone also suggested that the Early Paleo-Indians who used the toolstone moved across the landscape following some sort of seasonal rhythm. The uplands of southern Georgian Bay occur today in a prominent snowbelt, caused by northerly and westerly winds that first cross northern Lake Huron and Georgian Bay, where they pick up moisture, and then rise above the uplands, where they cool and drop their moisture as snow. It is this combined lake and topographic effect that creates the snowbelt that today is a major attraction for downhill skiers on the slopes of the Niagara Escarpment near Collingwood and in the Beaver valley. During the late Ice Age, 10,000 to 11,000 years ago, the snowbelt must have been truly impressive. At that time the mean annual temperature was two to three degrees centigrade lower than today, while the mean January temperature may have been as much as five degrees lower. Lake Algonquin would also have provided a much larger source of moisture than modern Lake Huron and Georgian Bay in part because the Bruce Peninsula would also have been submerged. The combination of lower temperatures and a larger source of moisture would presumably have created a larger snowbelt, beginning earlier in the year and persisting longer. And while snow covered the ground, Fossil Hill chert would of course have been inaccessible. Early Paleo-Indians must have obtained it during the snow-free seasons, and probably lived in southwestern Ontario during the other months.

The Fisher site must have played a role in these seasonal movements. The site is located on the western edge of the central Ontario lowlands, not far from the southern Georgian Bay uplands and about thirty kilometres east of the chert source area. Located on the shore of a glacial lake, the site may very well have been strategically positioned to take advantage of lake-margin food resources and to provide a base camp from which people could travel to the uplands to collect toolstone. I was intrigued what we would find up there. But in the winter of 1979, just after Peter von Bitter's discovery and only a few months before our final season of work at Fisher, that question would have to wait for the future.

After considering caribou and toolstone as possible attractions for occupying Fisher, what others were left? What else could we learn from the site location and the stone tool fragments and debris of flintknapping? The answer was unexpected. It came from detailed study of the microscopic damage that forms on stone tools during use. As I mentioned earlier, I had asked John Tomenchuk to join the project in the hope that he could tell how some of the tools were used and what substances they were used to work. I was especially interested in learning whether this approach would help us to understand what Paleo-Indians did in the two different types of artifact concentrations on the site, and in particular whether the activities were totally independent or somehow integrated. Consequently, I asked John to study samples of tools from the single fluting and primary knapping areas on the lowest part of the site, adjacent to the glacial lake shoreline. Being the only artifact concentrations in this portion of the site, they certainly looked as though they might have been functionally integrated as part of a single campsite in which different activities had been spatially segregated. Andrew Stewart was busily exploring this possibility through a comparison of toolmaking activities in the two areas but I wanted other kinds of data as well.

John did his thing with the microscope and long, complex mathematical equations. I followed along far behind, trying to understand what he was doing and what it all meant. I concluded that if his interpretations were correct John was probably an unrecognized genius. The analytical approach he invented, which is described in a four-volume doctoral dissertation, the longest I've ever heard of, seems closer to magic than science. From a stone tool no larger than a Canadian one- or two-dollar coin, for example, John could tell me the strength of the person who used it, whether he or she was right- or lefthanded, how the tool was held and used (whether in a pushing or pulling motion or by twisting), the general category of material it was used to work, and, if that category was wood, its hardness and possibly even identity to the species level. All from a few microscopic nicks and scratches and polishes, including finger polish if the tool had been hand held. I often jokingly asked him why he stopped there and didn't go on to tell me what the person said while using the tool, what time of the day it was, and what the weather was like. I also concluded that John wrote up his results in a unique kind of English. With its long sentences, laden with archaic words and technical terms and broken up by numerous and sometimes lengthy qualifying clauses, the writing was nearly opaque. Sometimes, after getting to the end of a fifty-word sentence, I had absolutely no idea what I had just read. I often kidded John about this, and once, late at night after a long day and several additional hours with John working on a particularly difficult part of his draft chapter for the Fisher monograph, I wanted to throw him out the window. But John tolerated my jokes and sometimes thinly veiled impatience with exceptionally good grace, and we are still happily working together to this day. We discovered that we make a good team: he employs his genius and then helps me to understand what he just did. And then I help him express it for the rest of us.

Everything went well for a time, and then even John was stumped. A handful of flake tools from one of the two areas he was studying on the lower portion of the site, the primary knapping area, exhibited a complex polish that John couldn't interpret. It was like wood but, then again, it wasn't. For a long time John worried about this. Eventually, he started referring to the tools collectively as the "enigmatic cluster."

One evening while eating dinner John suddenly paused and stared down at his plate in a puzzled way, looking with new interest at the fish he had been cutting apart. In that instant, he imagined a stone tool in place of his metal knife and it suddenly occurred to him that the tools might have been used in filleting fish! Could the combination of small, hard bones and very soft flesh, he wondered, explain the complex polish?

With this possibility in mind John visited the local fish market the next day and then came into the laboratory and made a few experimental flakes from some Fossil Hill chert I had saved for flintknapping. After a few minutes he cleared a table and then proceeded to butcher the fish, first removing the heads and then the flesh. He gave the tools a good workout, just to be sure the experiment was long enough to register any use-wear that occurred. Finally, he put the tools under the microscope and carefully adjusted the light and focus. And there it was, that same complex polish. The enigmatic tools were enigmatic no longer.

As I've said, like many archaeologists I had been preoccupied with caribou and the big game hunting aspect of Early Paleo-Indian subsistence. When John told me this unexpected news my first thought was how ironic that we should have evidence of fishing from the Fisher site. My second was how confusing this might be to my colleagues, who would think I named the site in reference to fishing, though of course I had not.

Frankly, I was dubious. It wasn't that I doubted Early Paleo-Indians might have fished. After all, a few charred fish bones had turned up at Shawnee-Minisink, an Early Paleo-Indian site in eastern Pennsylvania, and was the cause of much comment in the archaeological community when the bones were first reported. The real problem was that no fish fossils had ever been reported from glacial Lake Algonquin, and in fact, some geologists doubted whether the lake provided a suitable habitat for fish. Though the cold water might not have been a detriment in itself, it was also probably heavy with rock flour, a very fine sediment produced by the grinding action of ice and carried within it. Fronted along its entire northern margin by the retreating ice sheet, Lake Algonquin must have contained a lot of sediment, which because it was fine would be carried a long way, possibly even to the beaches and the lagoon off the Fisher site. This dismal picture is contradicted somewhat by the presence of molluscs in Algonquin lake deposits, and especially by one species that today lives for the embryonic part of its life cycle in the gut of fish. The molluscs argue for the presence of fish, despite the fact that fish bones are seldom preserved.

John was not dismayed by the lack of paleontological evidence for fish. Instead, he read widely in the literature dealing with the re-establishment of fish populations in the early Great Lakes at the end of the Ice Age, from refugia in the Mississippi drainage area and the Atlantic. I remained sceptical, in part because of the lack of fossil evidence but also because I was very much aware that, for most of my archaeological colleagues use-wear evidence is indirect evidence – second best to the actual recovery of faunal remains. But I had confidence in John's work and was therefore drawn to the interpretation that Early Paleo-Indians exploited fish, at least seasonally, and possibly at the Fisher site.

Fish, the third possible resource that may have attracted people to the Fisher site, adds another habitat to those that Early Paleo-Indian people may have exploited: the waters of a glacial lake large enough to constitute an inland sea. With this combination of resources – fish in the lagoon east of the site, caribou or some other terrestrial mammal along the lakeshore or inland a short distance, and toolstone in the uplands to the west – the Fisher site was truly between the mountains and the inland sea. Ultimately it is this intermediate location and vertical mix of resources within a short distance that may have been the fundamental attraction to human occupation. To learn more I needed to do what I hadn't done before, climb the mountain to the source of that toolstone. But I also had to continue my work on those wonderful beaches because they were so informative about Early Paleo-Indian life there. Opposite ends of the topographic spectrum. But a complete picture of Early Paleo-Indian life, if it could be pieced together at all, would be found in many different places.

5 | Back to Beachcombing

Success is addictive. I wanted to experience Fisher all over again, at some other site of course. But before I could repeat anything I had to solve a problem.

In 1979, after my third year at Fisher, I had no other sites in hand on which to focus my energy and enthusiasm. And I had no money. The ROM had an ongoing item called Field Archaeology in the annual budget, an account used to support the fieldwork of over a dozen staff archaeologists and one or two cultural historians. These people worked in Canada, Central and South America, England, and sometimes France, Spain, Italy, and Greece, the Middle East (primarily Egypt and Iran), and occasionally China. To a lesser extent it also supported the work of a varying number of university-based and independent scholars who held honorary appointments at the museum. These people also worked in Canada and around the world in places such as Peru, Botswana, and the eastern Mediterranean. With all the demands placed on the Field Archaeology budget there wasn't much available for each project, so like everyone else I regarded the funds available to me as seed money to raise additional funding from sources outside the ROM.

The additional money might be as much as 70 percent of the amount required for a particular project. My colleagues who managed the Field Archaeology account often argued with higher level administrators that if the museum were to continue referring to the work of its staff as ROM projects, it should contribute at least 50 percent of the funding. I agreed with this logic but still felt incredibly privileged to have any internal funds at all, unlike my university colleagues, and to be working in an institution so supportive of field archaeology. Much of the credit for this goes to the person who hired me and many of other staff senior to me, A.D. Tushingham, chief archaeologist and manager of the Field Archaeology account when I first came to the ROM.

After Tushingham's retirement in 1979 the Office of the Chief Archaeologist was discontinued and the field funds were allocated by a committee with an elected chair. Formed by the archaeologists and cultural historians on staff, the Committee for Field Archaeology was quite large but, quite unintentionally (and somewhat amusingly, I think), made less unwieldy by the fact that many people were often absent doing fieldwork when meetings had to be called. Of course, we tried to represent their interests as best we could. The committee structure continued until the mid-1990s, when the funds were transferred to the office of Associate Director-Curatorial and dispersed according to an internal peer-review adjudication process that involved deadlines, formal written proposals, a ranking system and a chain of approvals through senior management. Currently, and through a similar process, the ROM Foundation disperses research funds to all of the disciplines represented at the museum and wide-ranging curatorial activities, as well as funds for artifact acquisition and publication. What one person used to do through one-on-one discussions, and later, a collegial group of academics did through group discussions and consensus, is now done in a highly structured and formal way by a large, multi-disciplinary peer review committee. This illustrates something inevitable about institutions: with time they become ever more complex. Ironically, this process intensifies during periods of declining resources when fewer things are possible and life might be expected to be simpler. Simpler it's not!

But back to 1979. Though I could count on at least some ROM money for fieldwork, it would clearly not be enough for any really substantial project. Several years earlier I had developed a method for raising money by first using ROM funds to make promising discoveries and then using those as a form of leverage in requesting federal grants. The initial discoveries gave me some clearly defined goals and ways of achieving them when I applied for federal money, making my proposals much more competitive than they might otherwise have been. I had used this approach for the first time after the initial excavation at Banting to fund my first survey work along the former strandline of Lake Algonquin, again after the discovery of Fisher for test excavations there in 1976, and during full-scale excavations at that site in 1978. I would continue that pattern and manage to obtain external funds every third or fourth year on average during my nearly three decades with the ROM.

In 1979 I had some seed money and a proven strategy for obtaining additional funds. The next question was how to make the seed money work; more practically, this meant deciding where to work next. Which area had the greatest potential for producing early promising results that would attract more money? This was *the* crucial question and one that would stay with me for an entire academic career. It is also pretty much the same question the general public asks most frequently. How do you know where to dig?

Clearly after Fisher the answer wasn't all that difficult: the former shoreline of glacial Lake Algonquin. But where exactly?

During the years leading up to Fisher I had worked steadily northward along the former shoreline of Lake Algonquin from the Alliston region, not far north of Toronto, to southern Georgian Bay. At that point the shore of Lake Algonquin turned west, cutting across the base of the Bruce Peninsula, which had been depressed by the weight of the ice sheet and later inundated by Lake Algonquin. It then turned south, parallelling the modern shoreline of Lake Huron. I had been attracted to this last stretch of Algonquin strandline in the mid-1970s when two colleagues – Paul Karrow, a geologist at the University of Waterloo, and one of his students, Thane Anderson, a paleobiologist at the Geological Survey of Canada in Ottawa – reported on some work they had done in a former lagoon of the glacial lake in the vicinity of the town of Kincardine on Lake Huron. Following up on their work, which I thought might lead to Early Paleo-Indian sites, I did some experimental survey work along the borders of that lagoon in 1976, the same year I test excavated Fisher. The most promising parts for human occupation around the lagoon had unfortunately been built over by the town of Kincardine, but on one of the ploughed fields on the landward side of the lagoon I did succeed in finding some evidence that humans may have been contemporaneous with an early post-Algonquin lake. This evidence was a single chert flake from tool manufacture that had been rolled and polished by wave action. Although tantalizing, the artifact reminded me of the pitifully small clues that had motivated me in my early years. At this point in my work a small discovery – no matter how evocative of a former lake and a human who had walked along its shore – wasn't enough to keep me in Kincardine.

Instead I decided to look east: all the way across the central Ontario lowlands to the other side of Lake Algonquin, a short distance east of modern Lake Simcoe. This region had been studied in the late 1940s by a geologist at the Geological Survey of Canada, R.E. Deane. I first became aware of Deane's work quite by accident during a chance meeting in a museum hallway one day with Walter Tovell, a geologist and director of the ROM from 1972 until 1975. I happened to mention that I was working at the Banting site on Lake Algonquin, which I had identified through Hugh Gwyn's recent geological mapping. Walter thought my work was an excellent idea and long overdue, and he suggested I look at the 1950 report by Deane. Tovell's comment was very timely for my early work at Banting and my simultaneous shift to beachcombing because Deane's regional maps gave me a much larger perspective of Lake Algonquin.

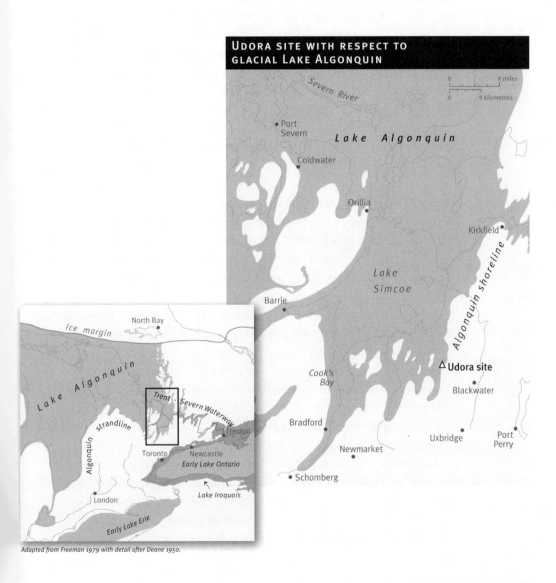

Adapted from Freeman 1979 with detail after Deane 1950.

In my 1979 planning Deane's publication would again be a signpost to the future. His report contains some wonderful maps showing the Algonquin strandline extending east from the town of Midland on Georgian Bay to the city of Orillia at the north end of Lake Simcoe, then around Lake Simcoe, first southwest and then north again, to a small town called Kirkfield, located about twenty kilometres from the northeastern corner of Lake Simcoe. Kirkfield is perhaps best known today because it is the location of lock no. 36 on the Trent-Severn Waterway. This 386-kilometre-long waterway, named after the Trent River draining into Lake Ontario and the Severn River draining into Georgian Bay, allows pleasure boats to cruise through a chain of interconnecting lakes and rivers from Trenton on the Bay of Quinte in Lake Ontario to Port Severn on Georgian Bay.

But Kirkfield is also well known for quite a different reason and to a much smaller group of people. To Pleistocene geologists and those tag-along archaeologists like me who use the results of Pleistocene studies for their own purposes, Kirkfield is much more interesting for its geology than its lock, although the two are actually related.

Kirkfield is the location of one of the outlets of glacial Lake Algonquin. This outlet allowed water to spill down the ancestral Trent River system into a glacial lake in the Ontario basin, Lake Iroquois, and, from there, through the Rome outlet (named after a community in New York State) into the Mohawk and Hudson River valleys and, ultimately, to the Atlantic. Out of curiosity one day I visited the Kirkfield lock and watched the summer crowd in their pleasure boats pass through. They soon became nearly oblivious to me as I stood there trance-like, thinking about the flow of time from one age to another and of water from an inland sea to another sea.

Deane's maps were of too small a scale to be useful for archaeological survey work but they did plot the elevations of the Algonquin shoreline, rising from south to north along two uplift curves. These curves show how the formerly horizontal Algonquin water level has been distorted by what geologists call isostatic uplift: the readjustment of the earth's crust after the removal of the weight of the former ice sheet. With these elevations I could plot the approximate location of the Algonquin shoreline on larger scale topographic maps and add even greater detail by studying air photos that sometimes showed the former shoreline as a low, erosional bluff.

Examination of maps and aerial photos, and a few car trips into the area, indicated that the former Algonquin shoreline on the west side of Lake Simcoe between Orillia and Barrie was highly urbanized. And farther south, along Cook's Bay, the former shoreline, which is now a high bluff just west of the modern shoreline of the bay, was in places crowded with cottages. Clearly, this long stretch of Algonquin shoreline should have been investigated archaeologically a long time ago, perhaps shortly after Deane did his work.

Farther east and several kilometres south of present-day Lake Simcoe, the former Algonquin shoreline was more interesting. In this area the glacial lake created several large offshore islands and, south of the main shoreline, extended in long, narrow, finger-like embayments stretching south toward Toronto. One day while driving through the region, I unexpectedly encountered the small village of Blackwater. The name instantly conjured up images of Blackwater Draw in eastern New Mexico, the type site of the Early Paleo-Indian Clovis culture, and my experiences excavating there in 1963 while still an undergraduate.

After seeing the road sign for Blackwater, Ontario, I stopped the car abruptly, backed up to a point in front of the sign, and reached for my camera. As I took picture after picture, trying to look inconspicuous, I longed to find a site nearby and become known as the archaeologist who found a *second* Blackwater. Alas, the dense spruce forest shrouded the land completely and if Early Paleo-Indians ever lived in the area their sites would be found only by pure luck.

After driving widely throughout the area south and east of Lake Simcoe, I thought the most attractive stretch of Algonquin shoreline for the purposes of archaeological survey was between the small community of Udora, about ten kilometres from the southeast corner of Lake Simcoe, and Kirkfield to the north. This forty-kilometre stretch appealed to me because the land was intensively farmed, and the many ploughed fields would make it possible to look for the broken stone tools and flintknapping debris that would indicate the presence of an archaeological site. This is how I came to choose the area for my next major project.

Having made that decision I had a conflict to overcome. I had also decided to go back to school, and classes were to be held at precisely the best time to do archaeological survey work: in June, before the corn and other crops get too high and obscure the ground. I decided to hire a small survey crew from my seed money to do the work in my absence. I'd done this before, in a sense, when I split my archaeological crew into two parts in 1975, one to excavate along with me at Coates Creek and the other to conduct survey work. That's when we – or rather, my crew – found the Fisher site.

So in 1979 I hired a student to run the survey, Lawrence Jackson. He had worked briefly at Fisher in 1978 and, later that year and the next, in the laboratory washing and cataloguing the material. He had also just finished his masters degree at Trent University with a thesis on Early Paleo-Indians.

I had sat on his thesis defence as an external examiner. With my agreement Lawrence in turn hired a young woman who had also worked at Fisher in 1978, Jane Edward. She had been the one to find our fiftieth fluted point at the site. Lawrence also hired two people he knew from Trent University who had visited us briefly at Fisher, Gordon Dibb and Pat Boyer. These two were later to form their own private consulting firm in archaeology, which is still successful to this day. It was a good crew; everyone had experience and the two senior members, Lawrence and Jane, knew how I wanted things done in the field.

Before they got started I drove Lawrence around the survey region, familiarizing him with the maps and aerial photos, as well as the appearance of the Algonquin strandline on the ground, and pointing out wherever possible the fields I wanted him to investigate. But aside from these obvious fields, many others in key locations relative to the strandline were also open for survey because they were cultivated. Consequently he had a great deal of freedom to select other fields he thought were important and to prioritize the work. After returning to the office I set the administration in motion through our departmental secretary to release the seed money and even promised everyone a bonus if they found something important.

And then I made arrangements to go back to school. At the age of thirty-nine I had already spent nearly 60 percent of my life in school. Finally, in 1969, one year short of a full quarter-century in the classroom, I had finished my last graduate courses and exams and was poised to complete my doctorate. In 1972 I had defended my newly written PhD dissertation before a committee of five full professors by answering questions over a three-hour period – a frightening experience. Finally school years were over. But then, only seven years later, just before my fortieth birthday and the onset of the mid-life crisis that we're all told to expect at that age, I felt the need to go back. What, you may ask, was wrong with me?

Success and time. They were my problem. I had achieved one and been overtaken by the other.

The success happened in 1976 and 1978 at Fisher, where I excavated a large sample of fluted spear points representing several stages in a long and complex manufacturing process. As might be expected this complexity required an equally sophisticated analytical approach to unravel. I knew how I wanted to analyze the material because I had read several excellent papers and monographs that I thought could be combined into a single guiding model for my own work. Yet I felt very insecure. I had never before analyzed a collection of fluted point fragments from a manufacturing sequence. And I wasn't sure I could identify all the individual bits of information I needed to take note of based solely on "book knowledge": written descriptions, photographs, and line drawings published by other scholars. As well, except for some idle experimenting on my own I had never really made a stone tool. Without practical experience in flintknapping I lacked a feel for working with stone and confidence in my ability to analyze the Fisher material for the kind of information I wanted to obtain: how Early Paleo-Indians worked stone into tools, particularly fluted spear points.

My previous experience certainly hadn't prepared me for this kind of analysis. During graduate school and the first few years of work at the ROM I had dealt primarily with small collections of tools and flintknapping debris, mostly with finished spear and arrow points, which I had simply tried to classify into previously identified types. I had worked with an even smaller amount of pottery, which I had also tried to classify and didn't like studying all that much, and with animal bone. Actually, I had more experience analyzing animal bone than stone or clay artifacts. Much of my doctoral dissertation was based on the identification and analysis of over 33,000 pieces of animal bone I had obtained in 1968 from excavations in a small cave in southwestern Wisconsin. Curiously – because I was intending to become an archaeologist, not a zoologist or archaeozoologist – I enjoyed working with bone. With a student's need for tangible evidence of progress and discomfort with ambiguity I had felt more confident in my species identifications than in my artifact identifications. Animal bones are, after all, genetically programmed to grow to predetermined shapes and sizes; even variation is controlled genetically. By contrast, artifacts such as stone tools and pottery vessels can contain significant variation depending on how tightly defined they were by the flintknapper or potter. And the prehistoric classification scheme for these objects may not be the same as the one devised by the archaeologist, although this is what archaeologists would like to achieve. The problems of dealing with this discrepancy would shape many careers in archaeology during the two or three decades preceding my graduate work, and I too would be shaped by them.

But I wanted to take a different approach with the analysis of the material from Fisher. This is how the 156 fluted point fragments, 1,400 other tools, and over 30,000 pieces of debris from tool manufacture and resharpening became my success. But while I was busy finishing my graduate studies and then trying to find an approach for discovering Early Paleo-Indian sites, I was outpaced by developments in my own field.

I learned that a specialty study in archaeology had grown tremendously in recent years and was widely recognized as an informative way of studying stone tools: lithic technology, the dynamics, or *process*, of flintknapping and how stone was actually shaped into tools. This new field of interest would ultimately be expanded to include how tools were resharpened during their use-life – and occasionally reshaped into other tools along the way – until they were finally discarded.

The early interest in studying process was approached by making replicas of prehistoric artifacts. True replicas, in the sense that they not only looked like prehistoric tools in shape, size, and appearance but were, if possible, made using the same sequence of steps and the same flintknapping techniques. The making of true replicas required detailed study of prehistoric tools in a way not done before and was very revealing of human behaviour, one of the central purposes of archaeology. And I had no training in this. Although I had finally succeeded in excavating a large collection of Paleo-Indian stone tools, I therefore needed to retool my own academic skills.

And to do this I went right to the top. I wrote a letter to Don Crabtree, widely recognized as one of the most skilled flintknappers in the world and a pioneer of replication as a means of studying human behaviour. (In 1985, Crabtree's life-long work would be honoured by the Society for American Archaeology, which named an achievement award after him.) I first became aware of Crabtree's work through his 1966 publication of a now-classic paper on replicating the Folsom-type fluted spear point, as represented at the site of Lindenmeier in northern Colorado. And since I wished to learn to replicate the fluted points at the Fisher site, after first learning to flintknap, I wrote to Crabtree asking if he would have time to teach me during a sabbatical leave I was planning on taking in the first half of 1980.

Don Crabtree didn't bother to write; he telephoned, immediately. It was only much later that I learned he seldom answered his correspondence but preferred to call. In the middle of a routine day I casually answered the phone and found myself talking with a legend. Crabtree was going to assist in teaching a course on flintknapping in June and July 1979, sponsored by Washington State University in Pullman. The organizer and instructor would be a former student of Crabtree's, J. Jeffrey Flenniken, who was then working on his doctorate. Crabtree invited me to write to Flenniken, the new director of the Laboratory of Lithic Technology at the university, to ask if I could register.

I wrote to Flenniken and he responded that he would be pleased to have me enroll. He liked to see professionals involved, though I would have to register as a graduate student and pay tuition as if I were taking a four-credit course in their postgraduate enrichment program. I found it ironic to be called a professional, especially as I was filling in a gap in my education. I was also amused that with no other degrees left to earn in my field I would be earning another four credits. And this is how I came to be going back to school again.

It was a new kind of school. The four-week intensive course in flint-knapping was to be held outdoors, and we were going to break rocks from early morning to dark, six days a week – seven if you wanted – and then talk about it at night when there wasn't enough light to see.

In the final covering letter to the six students who were going to take the course, Flenniken wrote that we would be sleeping in tents, two people in each; there was a hospital nearby, an ominous point since we were going to be knapping obsidian; no suits were needed; bathing facilities would be provided by a nearby river; no electricity would be available; and, finally, that the school would be a group effort with a sharing of information. This last was an interesting twist, and made me feel uncomfortable, because I had expected the learning to flow one way. How much experience, I wondered, did my fellow students have? At the very end of the letter Flenniken wrote that there would be no exams or papers. This was not surprising; it would be painfully apparent, in the artifacts we made – or didn't make – how much we had or hadn't learned. Reading between the lines I could see that we were going to live, breath, and bleed flintknapping, in a wild place.

With preparations complete all my plans for the spring and summer were in place. On 14 May Lawrence Jackson and his survey crew left for the field. A month later I left for school. The following *Archaeological Newsletter,* published later that fall, tells how it all came out:

BEACHCOMBING AGAIN, AND THEN A SHORT MIDSUMMER'S (K)NAP
NOVEMBER 1979

In some respects this summer was an interlude – a time for starting the long process of research on material obtained from our last major excavation and for rethinking our future research objectives and making plans for the next "big effort." While some of this planning is done in a library or in the solitude of an office, it may also require a significant amount of preparatory fieldwork in its own right and, in fact, we spent almost as much time in the field this summer as we would have if we had been conducting large-scale excavations.

For fieldwork this summer we went back to beachcombing again, so to speak, and continued investigating the former strandline of glacial Lake Algonquin looking for evidence of early human occupation dating back to perhaps

10,000 or 12,000 years ago. This was a continuation of a long-term ROM survey and excavation project along the Algonquin strandline that has led in recent years to important discoveries in both the Alliston and Collingwood areas. This year I was interested in following the strandline farther north and east around the east side of modern-day Lake Simcoe to see how far north Early Man penetrated into the province after the retreat of the continental ice sheet. If early hunting peoples had actually occupied this area I was also interested to determine whether they established large base camps in this region, as they did in the Collingwood area and farther south near Michigan, or, alternatively, whether they occupied only small, temporary hunting stations during brief forays into the area from base camps located elsewhere.

The area of our survey extended along the east side of Lake Simcoe from Udora in the south to Kirkfield in the north, a distance of approximately forty kilometres. The former Algonquin shoreline is recognizable over most of this area as a wave-cut bluff from three to ten metres or so in height. Our first job was to select and rank the fields according to their archaeological potential, and, therefore, priority for investigation. This was determined by their current agricultural use (we could only really effectively survey ploughed fields where we could see the ground surface and, of these, we were pretty much limited to cornfields since most farmers would not allow us to walk over grain or other crops) and by their proximity to the glacial lake shoreline. Once the fields had been selected, the survey work quickly settled into a routine of asking farmers for permission to do the work and then systematically walking along every tenth furrow or so of each field looking for fragments of stone tools and the debris of tool manufacture.

Our work started on a high note the very first day when we found a spear point possibly dating between 9,000 and 10,000 years ago and located very near the Algonquin beach at the northernmost end of our survey area. Very little else was found at this locality and the artifact probably represents an isolated loss by a passing hunter.

After this heartening and yet disappointing discovery, the survey work descended to a spiritually low level of uneventful routine as field after field produced either nothing or only a few scattered flakes and isolated artifacts that were either non-diagnostic or made by later peoples. To break the monotony – and perhaps to relive a few happy moments – we occasionally returned to the spot of the first discovery only to leave more discouraged than ever after repeatedly failing to find anything else. It took a constant effort – indeed vigilance – to keep the survey properly focused on the former lakeshore where we thought Early Man had lived, and not to be distracted by the promise of modern rivers and lakes where we could be more certain of finding archaeological material even if it wasn't pertinent to our current research.

And then it all changed: first at 2:10 pm on Monday, June 11th, and then on June 13th, and again on June 15th, and again on June 19th, June 20th, June 25th, and June 27th – one discovery after another tumbling over each other with a speed that was numbing. Our spirits soared and in the euphoria of the moment one of the collecting localities was named "Bullfrog's Bellow." When the dust finally settled and we had time to absorb what we had found, we learned with a mixture of surprise and almost disbelief that we had discovered not one site but a site complex consisting of almost two dozen collecting localities situated along an eight-kilometre stretch of the former glacial lake shoreline.

Judging from the amount of material recovered in the surface collections, some of the collecting localities probably represent small, temporary campsites while others represent larger, more lengthy occupations. Clearly the area was very attractive to Early Man for occupation – probably because of the presence of game and/or other food resources; and considering the very abundant material we have obtained to date, there are very likely other sites remaining to be discovered in the fields that have not yet been investigated. This preparatory fieldwork was certainly very successful in identifying additional sites with potential for excavation and in pointing the way for future survey work. Over the next several months we'll start the long planning process for the next "big effort" – the 1980 excavations – in an attempt to learn what these discoveries may tell us about the life of Early Man in Ontario.

After the pleasures of beachcombing, I left the glacial beaches of Ontario for a short midsummer's knap. Although pronounced the same way as nap, the knap I was involved in was not a short rest – quite the contrary – it was a total immersion course in learning, through practical experience, some of the principles of working stone and making tools similar to those used by prehistoric peoples ...

By making tools patterned after prehistoric examples and trying to reproduce the same types of wear through experimental use, the lithic technologist attempts to reconstruct the ways in which prehistoric peoples made their tools and the manner of their use(s). This information has considerable potential for indicating which attributes on the tools and the waste products of manufacture are culturally important and therefore have the greatest value for telling us about the behaviour, way of life, and cultural relationships of prehistoric peoples. Without this experimentally derived knowledge of methods of tool manufacture and use archaeologists may find themselves measuring and comparing the wrong kinds of things – wrong in the sense that they actually tell us little, if anything, about the past.

Except for some "undisciplined" backyard knapping, this was my first experience with trying to make stone tools. I had read a fair amount about it, of course, and had also seen a few movies but an intellectual understanding of something is far different from a practical understanding through application. On the first day of the course I was given a chair under a shade tree, a kit of "tools to make tools," some cautionary advice about how to avoid getting cut by the obsidian flakes, and a few basic pointers about how to make a bifacial blank for a tool. And there I was, like an uncertain writer facing a typewriter containing a blank sheet of paper, facing several tons of cobble-sized pieces of obsidian from which I was supposed to make spear points, arrowheads, blades, or whatever else interested me. Ha!

I knew in principle that to shape a piece of stone into the form of a biface for a spear point, for example, you had to knock or press flakes from the opposite surface to the one receiving the force. But I had a devil of a time trying to get this to work in practice and it seemed that all I could do was to make small angular lumps out of big angular lumps. Jeff would shout encouragement and advice from time to time, such as "there's a biface in every rock," "prepare your platforms," "grind to the opposite face," "raise your margins," and other such pithy things, but it seemed to no avail. Every now and then he would see our frustration and, announcing in a cheerful way that it was time to make a "beeeeeeg one," would, apparently without effort, show us several different flintknapping techniques, and in the process make Paleolithic hand-axes, Folsom fluted points, Mesoamerican blades, or Solutrean willow-leaf-shaped points that chimed like fine crystal because of their thinness. At first these demonstrations caused us to gape at our own angular lumps in abject horror, acute embarrassment, and anguish but they did teach us a lot and gradually our own lumps became thinner and more regular in shape. Because obsidian is extremely sharp, this progress was paid for literally in blood, however, and after only a few days I was wearing several Band-Aids, had a dozen or so other minor cuts, a swollen left hand from holding the material so tightly, and several other unidentifiable aches and pains – not to mention a greater appreciation of and respect for the accomplishments of prehistoric peoples.

In the fullness of time we all improved a lot and by the end of the course I was able to make a fairly decent spear point, burin, or a core and blades. In fact, I was even able to make a type of Early Man point – the so-called fluted point. This was not, I should hasten to add, a replica of a fluted point in the sense that it was made in the same way as prehistoric examples, but it was made using some of the same principles of flintknapping as were used prehistorically.

I returned to Toronto full of enthusiasm to gather together my own tool kit and continue flintknapping in our labs. Because of the press of other commitments, however, I may not have all the time I would like for experimental work but I have certainly gained a better understanding of lithic technology and this will undoubtedly allow me to ask more sophisticated questions in my research in the years to come.

Postscript: School in Retrospect

The flintknapping field school was profoundly stimulating. I thoroughly enjoyed the people and the setting and I liked working with my hands. But I was surprised at the great physical effort and intense concentration that flintknapping required. Often after making something I felt completely drained. At other times, and at the opposite end of the physical and emotional spectrum, I felt positively euphoric at finally being able to make something out of "stone." And I also felt a deep sense of accomplishment that came from making something permanent, at least more so than anything else I had ever made through either my leisure work in furniture making and art or my professional work in writing. The wooden objects I had made and papers I had published might outlast me many decades, or a century or two. The stone tools I had made could outlast me by thousands of years, perhaps as long as the prehistoric artifacts I studied or even those from the earliest part of the human record, hundreds of thousands or millions of years ago. For a person trained in an historical science, with a concept of time that embraced the whole of human history, this was a stunning thought. It also gave me a new feeling about the potential consequences of my own existence and a greater connection with the people of the distant past who had unknowingly left a record of their passing on the far, far distant future. Suddenly I had that same power.

The experience was also stimulating in a far more immediate way. After almost three weeks of daily, painful failures I succeeded in making a fluted projectile point. I was so excited I couldn't stand still and had to walk, all through the lunch hour and into the early afternoon. The artifact I was so ecstatic about was made of black volcanic glass. As with so many others, after much struggle I had successfully worked my way through the first few steps of the manufacturing process but then reached the most difficult part, which I had not succeeded at before – the final and crucially important thinning, or fluting, of the base. I decided to attempt this with a "chest crutch," a dowel rod about two centimetres in diameter and 60 centimetres long, with a T-shaped cross-piece at one end for pushing against with the chest and a copper tip at the opposite end for flaking. The nearly completed point blank, prepared for final thinning, was wedged firmly in a vice made of two-by-four studs placed on the ground. I then stood directly over the blank in a nearly doubled-over position, rested my chest on the cross-piece, and carefully placed the copper tip on the edge of the blank at its base. After checking that everything was properly positioned and at the correct angle, which is vital, I started pushing downward on the chest crutch, slowly at first and then more forcefully until the pressure against my chest made it difficult to breath. Straining to exert my last bit of down-ward strength, I also pulled slightly outward at what I hoped was just the right instant. Three things happened simultaneously. I heard a distinct pinging sound, pitched forward suddenly as the chest crutch cleared the artifact, and noticed out of the corner of my eye a blurred movement. After I recovered my balance I saw the thinning flake on the ground and then turned to look at the artifact in the vice. To my surprise I saw that the thinning flake had detached correctly and left a nice scar, or flute, down the middle of the artifact from the base almost to the tip. With a mixture of great relief from having got this far and growing fear that I would yet spoil it, I carefully reshaped the base of the artifact for a second fluting attempt, remounted the still unfinished projectile point in the vice, and tried the same thing on the other side of the artifact. Again, after carefully positioning the chest crutch and exerting all the strength I had, I pitched forward as the stone suddenly fractured, almost falling on my face. But I could tell from the pinging sound at that instant that I had done it again! And as I removed the artifact from the vice with trembling fingers I thought I had just accomplished one of the greatest achievements of my life.

The technique I used for the final basal thinning, or fluting, process on an experimental spear point had been developed by Don Crabtree for another purpose: removing long, thin flakes, called blades, from carefully prepared blocks or cores of stone. This method had probably never been used prehistorically to manufacture fluted spear points but I enjoyed experimenting with it and it did produce a nice-looking fluted point. It was not, however, a replica because I had not used prehistoric methods. After only a few weeks of training I realized that I didn't yet have the skills to attempt replication, but I knew at least some of the more important basics of flintknapping and had carefully examined the debris produced by different flintknapping techniques illustrated by Jeff Flenniken and Don Crabtree. After their demonstrations I carefully swept up and then cata-logued the debris they produced.

In fact I was to go back to Toronto with several dozen paper bags filled with this material. With this reference collection and my new abilities to recognize the byproducts of different flintknapping activities, I felt much more confident about analyzing the large collection of stone artifacts and debris from Fisher. I also had a firm basis for developing my flintknapping skills further and doing experimental work with different techniques to replicate the flaking patterns and other details I would later observe as I studied the prehistoric material.

Later that fall and during my 1982-3 sabbatical I spent many happy hours at the picnic table behind my house in a suburb of Toronto, breaking stone in ever more sophisticated ways and with all kinds of strange devices. My seven-year-old daughter watched me as seven-year-olds do, with distracted attention. And then one day, while she was alone in the garden as I took a short break from my work, she decided to try her own hand. Luckily I saw her from the kitchen window just as she was preparing to strike a block of chert with a stone cobble. Rushing outside and grabbing a box of bandages on the way, I managed to get to her before the hammer she was holding came down on her finger. But I was impressed that she wanted to try, so instead of banishing her from my outdoor laboratory I showed her how to use my stone, bone, and antler knapping tools and eventually helped her to make her own knapping kit, complete with leather pouch. She was the only kid on the block, and probably also the Toronto area, who was encouraged and helped to break things. And I would later introduce my new enthusiasm to my son, born a little over two months after my return from flintknapping field school. Little do they know, these innocent children, what unusual lives they may enter because of the strange interests of their parents.

The 1979 Field Season in Retrospect

After flintknapping school that summer of 1979 I returned to the ROM and two surprises. The first occurred when I opened my office door and looked into a brick broom closet! It was quite a shock, which must have been apparent on my face and in my frozen posture because I soon heard hysterical laughter all about me as my office colleagues gathered around to enjoy the moment fully. In my absence they had made a flimsy, three-sided wooden partition just inside the doorway to my office, covered it with wallpaper in a brick pattern, and placed a few props around: a mop, water pail, pair of shoes, and some clothes on hooks inside the door. It was very good, as might be expected of museum people, who often create illusions for displaying artifacts. The lesson? Never leave your office colleagues for very long. I should also have remembered that broom closets aren't made of brick.

My second surprise was of an academic nature. My plan to have a survey crew explore the strandline of glacial Lake Algonquin southeast of modern Lake Simcoe while I was away at school had succeeded beyond anything I could have imagined. Lawrence Jackson and his crew had found at least ten Paleo-Indian sites consisting of twenty-one artifact concentrations! This was an almost unbelievable concentration of sites, and it was very probably underrepresented because the study area couldn't be fully investigated in only one field season with a crew of four.

My discussion of the survey work in the newsletter may be confusing because I talk about what "we" did in the field and mention specific dates and times of discoveries, although I wasn't there. Actually, I used the royal or editorial "we" in reference to our collective accomplishment, including the conception, planning, and execution of the project, and I relied on Lawrence Jackson's clocking of the discoveries to convey a growing sense of excitement. In hindsight I have come to regret writing about the work in the collective sense and not highlighting the initiative of the survey crew.

A concentration of ten Paleo-Indian sites and twenty-one artifact concentrations along the former shoreline of glacial Lake Algonquin between Udora and Kirkfield in south-central Ontario contrasted sharply with the southern Georgian Bay region where I had just recently worked. There we had found only a single site, Fisher, although it was quite large. An isolated fluted spear point had been reported near Collingwood, an area I hadn't explored yet, and I had not done much work north of Fisher, so I didn't think I knew the full potential of the region. Nevertheless, it appeared as though the Early Paleo-Indian occupation in the southern Georgian Bay region had been very highly focused spatially; whenever these people occupied the region they returned to the same site or, if there were others we hadn't found, at least a very small number of sites. By contrast their occupation of the southeast shore of glacial Lake Algonquin was much more diffuse.

A similarly diffuse pattern of occupation, though over a somewhat larger area, was emerging in extreme southwestern Ontario through the work of my colleague Brian Deller. In a paper published in 1979 Deller reported that he had obtained Paleo-Indian and Early Archaic material from nine sites and thirty-one collecting localities, all within a relatively small geographic area located a short distance west of the city of London, Ontario. All the sites and collecting localities are associated with glacial lake strandlines, possibly Lake Algonquin as well as those of earlier glacial lakes that pre-dated Paleo-Indians. Of the nine sites, six were occupied by Early Paleo-Indians, as were approximately half of the thirty-one collecting localities. A very impressive concentration of Paleo-Indian sites.

The contrasts in the number and density of Early Paleo-Indian sites in these three regions of southern Ontario may be telling us something. Possibly about the distribution of food resources during the season or seasons of the year in which the regions were occupied, or about the structure of the human groups that used those regions, or perhaps a combination of the two. With respect to food resources, whatever drew people to Fisher in the southern Georgian Bay region could be exploited from a particular site. Whatever was exploited in the Udora-Kirkfield region in south-central Ontario and in the extreme southwestern part of the province must have been more widespread or at least fostered a more diffuse settlement pattern.

While working in the southern Georgian Bay region I had not thought about possible regional contrasts in how Paleo-Indians used the landscape. It was only after the new, startling discoveries in south-central Ontario that the regional contrasts stood out, and my research interests took a subtle shift in direction. Up to that time I had focused almost exclusively on the problem of finding sites to excavate and then determining who occupied them and when. In this way I learned that the same Early Paleo-Indian cultural groups Brian Deller had been detecting in southwestern Ontario (Parkhill complex peoples, and both earlier and later groups of Early Paleo-Indians) also occupied the Alliston area at Banting and Hussey. Later, at Fisher, I learned that people of the Parkhill complex also occupied the southern Georgian Bay region. And after multidisciplinary studies at Fisher I learned that these people were contemporary with glacial Lake Algonquin at least 10,400 years ago and lived in a spruce-parkland environment on the shore of a lagoon from which they may have fished to supplement their big game hunting, perhaps of caribou. These were all interpretations derived from the study of particular sites.

After my initial work in the Udora-Kirkfield stretch of Algonquin strandline in south-central Ontario, however, I suddenly became aware of possible regional differences in Paleo-Indian land use. With knowledge of large numbers of sites in different areas of the province it was possible to glimpse various patterns in Paleo-Indian behaviour that could be seen only by looking at the larger world those people occupied. As well as my older questions about dating and subsistence, for example, I started asking new and in some ways more complex questions about regional differences in late glacial environments and how those differences affected Early Paleo-Indian strategies of occupying and moving across the landscape. With more questions and an awareness of the different kinds of data I needed to find answers, the potential of my work to tell us about Early Paleo-Indian life in late glacial Ontario increased immeasurably. The following newsletter tells about the next step in that work:

A "Behind the Scenes" View of Fieldwork, or the Coming of Age of a Research Program
January 1981

We discovered Feature 2 in the middle of a warm spring afternoon on Monday, May 26th. For the first time since I'd started my search eleven years ago for Early Man in Ontario we found what had clearly been a man-made pit on a campsite that had probably been occupied some 10,000 to 12,000 years ago. The former pit was visible as a large circular stain in the undisturbed soil beneath the plough zone and it contained over sixty tools and large chert flakes that were apparently intended to be made later into similar artifacts. The material probably represents a cache of tools and raw material that was placed in the bottom of a storage pit and forgotten when the site was abandoned. I had not before found undisturbed material like this and it was quite exciting to see it coming out of the ground and to speculate about what it might tell us about the person who had forgotten it and the other members of his band who occupied the site. Situated on the former shoreline of glacial Lake Algonquin in the modern-day Lake Simcoe region, the site promises to be quite large. Through good fortune, part of the site may extend into an undisturbed area between farm buildings and I hope to return at a later field season to work in this area.

This discovery is among the high points of a very successful field season concerned with piecing together the way of life of the first people to occupy the province after the final retreat of the glacial ice sheets. During our work in the Lake Simcoe and, later, Collingwood areas we were occasionally visited by local farmers and other interested people who were clearly impressed by seeing what they regarded as a "behind the scenes" view of archaeology. For me, however, fieldwork is actually the culmination, and sometimes even the anticlimax, of a lot of planning and preparation and the true "behind the scenes" view goes much deeper – right back to the time when the idea for the work was first conceived. This newsletter is about the kind of work that leads up to fieldwork and may answer some of those questions about what archaeologists do when they're not in the field.

The 1980 field project was a direct outgrowth of a pilot project sponsored by the museum and conducted in 1979. That year we had found a number of Early Paleo-Indian sites in the Lake Simcoe region, which I wanted to investigate more thoroughly through additional surface collecting and excavation, and I also wanted to complete some final work on the Fisher site in the Collingwood area to define more precisely the limits of the site and variation within it. This would require a large field party and a higher level of funding than could be provided by the Royal Ontario Museum alone and, consequently, it would be necessary to apply for a research grant, in this case from the Social Sciences and Humanities Research Council of Canada (SSHRCC).

Late in August of 1979, then, I started work on a grant application for a project that I proposed to begin the following spring. The application material sent out by the SSHRCC arrived in a thick manila envelope and consisted of a forty-two-page bilingual booklet of information and instructions as well as a sheaf of forms requiring a variety of information, the core of which is a description of the project and a proposed budget. Since the SSHRCC will send the application to anywhere from three to five scholars in the field for review and their recommendations, the proposal itself should be carefully thought out and clearly written, well documented, and, in this day of "fiscal restraint," scrupulously budgeted. An individual's scholarly reputation is based in part on the quality of his or her research applications and as much time may be spent working on an application as in preparing a paper for publication – in fact, parts of grant applications are frequently incorporated into published papers.

At the same time as I was preparing the application for the research grant I was also preparing an application for a licence to do archaeological work in Ontario. Under the recently revised Ontario Heritage Act, which came into force in 1974, all archaeological work, whether surface collecting or full-scale excavation, must be conducted under licence from the Ministry of Culture and Recreation. A fourteen-page form describing all aspects of the project, from the fieldwork to the housing and publication of the material, must be submitted to the Historical Planning and Research Branch. There, the application is evaluated and checked for completeness and then forwarded to the Archaeological Subcommittee of the Heritage Foundation for further review and recommendations before it is finally submitted to the Minister for Culture and Recreation. Both bodies also require written permission from landowners for all work that is to be done on private property and copies of their letters must be submitted with the various applications as well. It's a bit complicated covering all of the bases and making sure that everything has been filed and documented properly but finally, two months after I had started, I put special delivery postage on all of the applications, which together formed a package almost an inch and a half thick, and entrusted them to the Canada Post.

On 10 January 1980, I received archaeological licence 80-F-0370 from the Ontario government and promptly mailed a copy of it to SSHRCC in Ottawa.

My application was now, five months after starting, technically complete in every detail.

The long winter passed slowly as I worked on other matters and wondered occasionally how my research application had been received. The time came and passed when I expected to hear of any criticisms of the proposal if they were to affect the conduct of the fieldwork or the budget. The profound silence suggested either that the reviewers' comments were favourable or that they were so critical that my application would be turned down flatly without any opportunity on my part for rebuttal.

Finally, on 8 April 1980 – eight months after applying and only seven weeks before I had proposed starting fieldwork – SSHRCC telephoned to say that I would be awarded the grant. Not only that, but I would be receiving all of the funds I had requested – my proposed budget was intact!

Now the work really began – with only seven weeks to go there was everything to do: hire the fifteen-member crew, make arrangements for disbursing the funds, rent the field vehicles and the houses in which we were to live, arrange for telephone service in the two houses, and 1,001 other details that had to wait until this moment but now had to be done all at once. Selecting the crew members was one of the most critical things to be done since the skills and qualities of the people involved could make or break the project. Consequently, I interviewed twice as many people as needed, most for at least an hour, to be as sure as I could about the qualifications and attitudes of each person and that they, in turn, knew precisely what they were getting into.

On May 1st, over nine months after starting work on the grant application and only eleven days from the start of the fieldwork, everything was ready. The last person on the crew had been hired two days earlier and the only remaining thing to do was to get into the trucks and turn on the ignition. It had been a long, long haul since August of the preceding year.

In a very real sense, however, the preparation for the 1980 project goes back far beyond August of 1979. In fact, the chain of interrelated events leading up to this project stretches back at least seven years to 1973, when I first started following the trail of Early Man along the former shoreline of Lake Algonquin. The discoveries of that year formed the basis for the 1974 project at the Banting and Hussey sites near Alliston which, in turn, led to the 1975 discovery of the Fisher site near Collingwood and ultimately to the 1979 discoveries in the Lake Simcoe region. The discoveries of each field season pointed the way to the next so that the work seemed to gain its own momentum and sense of direction quite apart, sometimes it seemed, from my guiding hand. The objectives and hopes for the 1980 project, therefore, were actually determined in many important ways by each succeeding field season and the direction the discoveries have encouraged me to follow. It has been very satisfying for me to see this long-term research project develop to the point where it now promises to tell us a great deal about Early Man, not only in Ontario but by implication about related peoples in the Great Lakes region and the Northeast as a whole. It has taken almost a decade to reach this point, and the long years of searching are being rewarded by the excitement of seeing the work gradually bringing to light the events of prehistory.

Postscript: The 1980 Field Season in Retrospect

This newsletter, written in the fall of 1980 after the first season of excavation in the Udora-Kirkfield area, marked publicly a psychological turning point for me with respect to my work. With the cumulative discoveries of the last half of the 1970s, first at Fisher, then in the geological source area of the Fossil Hill chert, and later in the Udora-Kirkfield area, I believed that I had finally succeeded in putting together a research program. I thought of my work as a program because it involved something more than the excavation of a few Paleo-Indian sites on a catch-as-catch-can basis. Instead, I had become committed to a long-term, systematic effort to work on a number of research questions about Paleo-Indian occupation in different topographic regions of Ontario and the environment or environments in which it occurred. These questions embraced a range of archaeological and anthropological concerns as well as issues in several of the "paleo" natural sciences, such as Pleistocene geology, paleoclimatology, and paleo-ecology. They could be addressed at particular sites though they transcended not only the sites but also the province. My questions were of broad concern to other archaeologists interested in Paleo-Indians, wherever they worked.

With this optimism I had begun the 1980 field season. The first part of the season would be devoted to work in the Udora-Kirkfield area and the second part to final excavations at the Fisher site. Since the two areas were over 100 kilometres apart, this involved some complicated logistics and a complete move in mid-season from one field headquarters to another. Although I thought I had prepared thoroughly for this, we did have one mishap during the second, Fisher part of the project, while at our field headquarters in the village of Glen Huron.

Glen Huron is a wonderfully picturesque village near the crest of the Niagara Escarpment, nestled deeply in the valley of the Mad River where it tumbles down the edge of the escarpment. It seems very far away from the larger world. One day Peter von Bitter, whose visit I had expected to conduct a geology field class for the excavation crew, phoned to say that he couldn't find our house. While the road up the Mad River valley was full of turns and numerous forks to small sideroads, I *had* given detailed sketch maps to all visiting scholars to help them find their way. Strange that Peter would get lost.

I asked him where he was calling from.

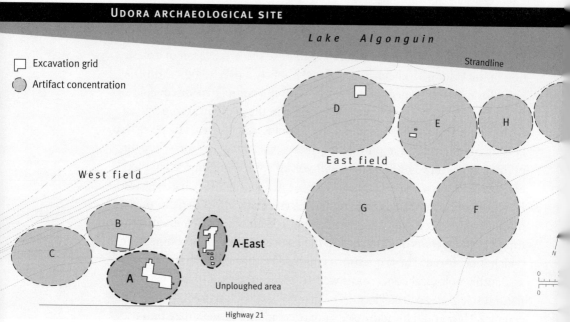

UDORA ARCHAEOLOGICAL SITE

Lake   Algonquin

Strandline

Excavation grid

Artifact concentration

D

E

H

East field

West field

B

A-East

G

F

C

A

Unploughed area

Highway 21

N

Adapted from Storck and Tomenchuk 1990, 49.

He replied that he was in a telephone booth outside a feed mill.

A telephone booth? By a feed mill?

And then suddenly I remembered. Quickly I stood up to lean sideways and look out of the front window of our house. And there he was, across the street.

"Peter, look up and wave hello."

Startled, he looked intently for a moment in my direction and then suddenly waved.

This conversation quickly spread through the house, and when Peter walked in the front door, the crew gathered around for introductions to the esteemed curator of invertebrate paleontology at the Royal Ontario Museum and professor of geology at the University of Toronto, who, after having just got lost across the street from our field house, was going to lead them into the field.

The 1979 survey had given me many sites to choose from for the next stage of my work in the Udora-Kirkfield area. Now I needed to conduct test excavations to determine the research potential of the sites we had discovered and, of course, I also needed to continue the survey work to fill in unexplored areas. With funds from the ROM and the largest federal grant I had received up to that time, I had enough resources to hire a large crew. This was an unfamiliar luxury. I employed the leader of the previous year's survey, Lawrence Jackson, as one of the field supervisors and another member of that field crew, Gordon Dibb, to conduct additional survey work, building on what had been accomplished in 1979. I also employed a graduate student, Mima Kapches, to act as my third field supervisor. She had worked for me several years earlier as a researcher on a bibliography of Paleo-Indian research in North America. To form the excavation crew I hired one secondary school student and eleven undergraduate students from various universities around the province. With a total of fifteen, this was the largest crew I would ever have. To transport everyone I had the use of our departmental vehicle and also rented two station wagons, one to be dedicated to survey work. I arranged for us to live in two houses in succession as we needed one for each part of the project. I did end up in a tent once, when the need to accommodate some visiting scholars temporarily pushed me out of the house, but that was just a brief regression.

In addition to the archaeology crew both Hugh Gwyn and Peter von Bitter, the two geologists who had worked with me on the Fisher project, would be involved in the 1980 Udora-Kirkfield work. Hugh was going to determine the relationship of the archaeological sites to the former Algonquin strandline. Peter was going to investigate potential geological sources of two kinds of toolstone I had not run across before.

I decided to do some test excavations at three of the most productive sites discovered in 1979: Bender and Milwain, both named after landowners; and Udora, named after the small community nearby. The Udora site proved to be the largest, and perhaps most significant, containing a total of nine artifact concentrations. We tested five of these, one of which (Area A) produced the feature discussed in the newsletter.

The term feature is simply a neutral word used in archaeology to describe something in the ground that has to be treated separately from anything else that might also occur in the same excavation unit. A feature may be a firepit, storage or refuse pit, or former posthole of a structure, to name just a few possibilities; in short, any disturbance in the ground, usually marked by a filled-in hole or depression, stain, or concentration of objects. In my work on ploughed fields we looked for features below the zone of cultivation, in the otherwise undisturbed subsoil. Cultivation destroys the upper part of any former disturbance in the ground, but the lower part in the subsoil may remain intact.

As I said in the newsletter, I had never found anything like Feature 2 before, whatever it was. Every other feature I encountered in the preceding decade of fieldwork started out in one of two ways: either as an irregularly shaped black or brown stain flecked with charcoal, which often turned out to be a tree burn; or as an elongated discolouration in the ground that invariably turned out to be a filled-in rodent burrow or some other natural disturbance that happened to incorporate archaeological material nearby. Feature 2, by contrast, consisted of a dense concentration of large flakes distributed in a rough circular pattern. This shape is not usually produced by natural agencies, and for this reason I suspected that the material had been placed in the ground by people. As we continued probing the feature and I saw nothing to indicate that it hadn't been placed there by humans, I became so excited that for several days I felt as though everything was sweet: the weather, despite the reality of a fickle spring; my career, the frequent downs temporarily forgotten; and the world.

I should have had a premonition about Feature 2. For several days the excavation squares in the general area of where we later discovered the feature had produced several unusually large chert flakes. This should have alerted me to the presence of something buried deeper that had been disturbed by the plough. But when I first realized we had come upon a feature it was a surprise nonetheless. Once we saw large flakes embedded in the subsoil, below the level reached by ploughing, we immediately shifted our recording and excavation strategy. We had been excavating by shaving thin peels of soil with broad sweeps of pointed masons' trowels (perhaps the most important tool used by archaeologists) and labelling the artifacts after the one-metre subunit in which they occurred. In the disturbed plough zone greater precision wasn't necessary. Now, digging below the plough zone in the undisturbed subsoil, we started mapping the precise location of each piece and exposing everything *in situ* to determine the shape and internal structure of the feature.

Soon we began finding large chert flakes in direct physical contact with one another and it was no longer possible to excavate without disturbing and removing the material as we dug deeper into the feature. We shifted our excavation strategy once again. After mapping and removing everything exposed we continued digging downward, recording the location of underlying pieces in three dimensions so that we could reconstruct the feature after everything was out of the ground and removing the objects in sequence, assigning each its own field catalogue number and placing it in a separate bag. After nearly a week of this laborious and delicate work with trowels, wooden sticks, and paint brushes we reached the bottom and sides of the feature. What remained was a hole about the size and shape of a bushel basket. Everything that had been in that hole was preserved indefinitely in the detailed measurements we recorded, the complicated maps and profiles we drew, the numerous soil samples we took, and, of course, by the artifacts as well. We collected a lot of information in the field and would get more out of laboratory studies of the soil samples and artifacts. As for the hole in the ground – all that remained of the original shape of the feature – we could even recreate that on paper.

Sitting on the edge of that hole after all the work was done, I thought we had discovered a cache: a collection of objects that had been deposited, presumably by Paleo-Indians, for later retrieval. But a cache of what? I wouldn't know the answer to that question for nearly a decade, after a colleague and I finally completed our analysis of the material. In 1990 we published the results in a technical journal and now, finally, I have an opportunity to tell the general public what we learned.

I think we have good evidence that the feature was a cache of informal tools used for a specific task at the Udora site in the early spring of the year, perhaps 11,000 years ago. The cache was left at the site for re-use in a future year, but for some reason that future never arrived for the people who left the tools, and the cache was forgotten.

But who forgot it? The answer, unfortunately, is somewhat ambiguous. Of the seventy-eight pieces in the cache only six might identify the people who left them there. These six tools are similar to three types of scrapers described in 1988 by my colleagues working in southwestern Ontario, Brian Deller and Chris Ellis. They believed that these scraper types were part of Early Paleo-Indian tool kits.

There are several other hints about who might have left the cache. First, approximately 93 percent by weight of the material in the Udora cache is Fossil Hill chert, a type of toolstone known to have been preferred by Early Paleo-Indian people of the Parkhill complex and perhaps by other groups as well. Second, we found a single Early Paleo-Indian spear point of the Gainey type on the surface of the ground in the same excavation grid (Grid A) that contained the cache. Seven other distinctive Paleo-Indian tools occurred in the same grid, although we couldn't tell with any certainty which culture they were from. Finally, in 1987, I discovered and excavated, perhaps fewer than twenty metres to the east, a small activity area occupied by Gainey peoples. The cultural identification is secure, based on one complete and portions of at least twelve other Gainey-type points.

Fortuitously for interpreting the cache, the presence of this Gainey occupation is additional evidence of intense Early Paleo-Indian activity in this portion of the Udora site. Taken together these observations provide strong circumstantial evidence that the Udora cache was also deposited by Early Paleo-Indian peoples, most likely of the Gainey culture.

The Gainey point type, and cultural complex, is named after a site in Michigan. Both also occur in southern Ontario, where they were first recognized by Brian Deller and Chris Ellis. For technological and other reasons Deller and Ellis believe that the Gainey point is the earliest in a temporal succession of related fluted point types and cultures: Gainey, Barnes (diagnostic of the Parkhill complex, such as represented at Fisher), and Crowfield, the latest. And the fact that Gainey is technologically very similar to the Clovis-type fluted point suggests that Gainey was made by Clovis descendants. And these descendants were very likely the people who colonized Ontario after the retreat of the ice sheet – and left the cache of tools at Udora.

To determine the purpose of the tools in the cache, I asked John Tomenchuk, who had also worked on the Fisher material, to analyze the use-wear damage on the seventy-eight objects we recovered. Of these most were used with a knife-like slicing action to cut the same substance. A minority were used in a scraping motion, and a few in a combination of both slicing and scraping motions. Judging from the nature and distribution of wear polish, the tools were used to cut jack pine or black spruce when the wood was nearly saturated with moisture and thus pliant rather than rigid. The wood that was cut was less than fifteen millimetres in diameter. Both the fresh state of the wood and the size of the object cut suggested tree roots. In fact, some scratches on the tools may have been caused by abrasion from particles of grit – quartz sand – in dirt still adhering to the roots.

John also estimated the force with which the tools were used, based on the size of the microscopic chips that broke off the cutting edges under the pressure exerted during the cutting process. He believed that the tools were used by two people, one stronger than the other. Interestingly, this is indirectly supported by the distribution of the tools in the cache. Statistical study shows that the tools used with different magnitudes of force also tended to occur separately in the cache, although they had since been intermingled somewhat. John considered this evidence that the tools were originally deposited as two separate groups, possibly in skin bags by the two individuals who used them.

As a final part of his analysis John Tomenchuk estimated the amount of wear (edge loss) that had occurred on the cutting edges of the tools, based on experiments using replicated artifacts made of Fossil Hill chert to cut roots of white spruce. From this he determined that the tools in the cache may have been used to cut anywhere from 400 to 1,000 metres of spruce roots, requiring anywhere from 140 to as much as 350 hours of labour (eight to twenty days of work for two people). A substantial amount of effort, but why? What could the roots have been used for?

Historical accounts of subarctic peoples in North America indicate that spruce roots were used for lashing pieces of equipment together and as material for weaving baskets and making nets. Spruce was used because the roots are seven metres long or greater, occur immediately below the surface and are thus accessible, and are small in diameter, requiring little thinning or splitting. The roots were also obtained in the spring and summer when supple and easily worked. Finally, the preparation of spruce roots was not a gender-specific activity but was carried out by whoever needed the material at the time: by men when building canoes, for example, or by women when making baskets.

The use-wear data, combined with ethnohistoric information, suggests not only *what* the tools in the Udora cache may have been used for (preparing material for lashing or weaving) but also *when* they might have been used (early spring). And the cache itself suggests that this activity was intended to be repeated, if it hadn't already been, the next time the site was occupied.

But the cache may have been more than a collection, or two skin bags, of task-specific tools. It may also have represented a considerable source of raw material and thus the potential for making other types of tools if the need arose. Most of the material is Fossil Hill chert from the Kolapore uplands in the southern Georgian Bay region, over 100 kilometres as the crow flies to the northwest. In terms of human travel this source area would have been much farther away during Lake Algonquin times since people would have had to travel far south from the Udora site to skirt the southern margin of the glacial lake before they could head north again and move directly cross-country to the Kolapore uplands. For someone dependent on Fossil Hill chert as a toolstone, the cache of tools at Udora could therefore have represented a substantial bit of security when travelling away from perhaps more familiar country in the western part of the province. Because locally available toolstone was used only minimally at

Udora, central Ontario may have been less familiar to the Gainey people who occupied the site. Peter von Bitter discovered that bedrock sources of local chert occurred north and east of the site, in Ordovician-age rocks of the Bobcaygeon and Gull River formations, which contain several beds of blueish grey and black chert. But these chert types are not present in the Udora cache or even very abundant on the site as a whole. The Udora cache with its exotic stone thus stands out all the more, quite apart from the significance of the tools themselves.

For me, Feature 2 was the highlight of the 1980 field season. It was the only bright spot in the work. In every other respect the season was a disappointment as none of the sites we tested was very productive. As I remarked earlier, this itself was possibly quite meaningful for discerning regional patterns of Early Paleo-Indian land use, but it certainly didn't make digging any easier, especially after all a person had to show from a long day's work was another few excavated holes in the ground and a handful or two of small waste flakes and perhaps one or two broken tools. This happened day after day for each and every day in the five-and-a-half week project.

After a largely disappointing field season I was about to enter an unsettled period in both my personal and my professional life that was to last nearly six years. In succession I would cope with marriage difficulties, the stresses of building a gallery, an unsuccessful grant application, and a research project that started well but was cut off by a landowner who decided not to let me work on his property (more on this later). This was not an easy time. But because the building of a gallery and the false starts in my work are all research related, perhaps I should digress briefly to continue the behind-the-scenes view of archaeology that I initiated in my 1980 newsletter, although certainly not in that same euphoric mood.

A New Gallery for the Museum, Again

One of the activities that gave me the greatest pleasure during the unsettled years of the first half of the 1980s was my involvement in building a gallery, actually my second permanent gallery, probably a rare opportunity in a museum career. I was the only curator in a team of museum people and consultants that eventually included over four dozen people: designers, programmers, carpenters and painters, laboratory technicians, archivists, preparators, artists, sculptors, lighting experts, model makers, a taxidermist, a diorama technician, and a manager. Peter Buerschaper, the head of the art department at the time and a sensitive wildlife artist in his own right, made more people available to the project than I probably had a right to expect. Although I was responsible for writing the outline and much of the content of the story we were to tell, all the people on this very cosmopolitan team helped shape that story officially or unofficially with their advice, questions, and suggestions.

I was also assisted greatly in assembling the intellectual background and material for that story by two quasi-curatorial people. Mima Kapches, then a graduate student specializing in Iroquoian prehistory, took responsibility for that aspect of the gallery. Brian Molyneaux, a field associate at the ROM, developed displays on late-period prehistoric rock art. Later, after she received her doctorate, Mima Kapches was hired through an open, peer-assessed, and Canada-wide competition as an assistant curator in the department, filling the position vacated by Walter Kenyon after his retirement. Brian went on to earn a PhD at the University of Southampton in England. During and immediately following that educational sojourn he wrote and edited numerous books, which surprised all of his friends at the ROM considering how long it used to take him to write four-page archaeological newsletters, a problem I shared. Brian is currently running a program in the United States in cultural resource management, excavating sites threatened with destruction by development or, where possible, shaping that development to avoid sites.

The planning process for the new gallery started in 1980, the year of my exploratory excavations at Udora. By the end of 1981 our gallery concept had been approved at all levels of management and we entered the detailed planning phase. This was completed in December 1983, when a sheaf of detailed construction plans was made available to contractors outside the ROM for competitive bidding. By spring 1984 the rough construction work was finished and we began installing the four dioramas. Finally, over a year later, in June 1985, the Ontario Prehistory Gallery was opened and our work done. It had taken over four years and cost roughly $487,000 – a medium-cost gallery per square foot – but we were also well under budget. I was very pleased with our work and proud that the gallery was highly regarded inside the museum and also praised in the media.

The entrance to the gallery is dominated by a diorama showing three darkly shadowed people preparing to butcher a young woolly mammoth in eastern Beringia. I imagine the scene to have taken place sometime between 25,000 and 40,000 years ago, although it might have occurred earlier or later. Nevertheless, it was definitely a pre-Clovis event, but considering that such occupation had not yet been demonstrated in the New World, how and why, you might ask, did I build a diorama display that, if not actually fictitious, was futuristic in the sense that archaeological documentation, if possible, awaited the future?

The answer to this question has its origins in the mid-1960s, although for the archaeological community generally, a better date might be 1973. In that year an archaeologist at the University of Toronto, William Irving, and a vertebrate paleontologist at the National Museum of Natural Science in Ottawa, Richard Harington, published a paper in the prestigious journal *Science*. They described a remarkable artifact that Harington had found several years earlier in a gravel bar (Locality 14N) of the Old Crow River in the northwest corner of the Yukon Territory. The artifact was made from one of the bones in the lower leg of a caribou, one end of which had been broken, whittled into a spatulate form, and then notched, producing a row of narrowly spaced teeth. Similar tools dating from the late prehistoric period and even recent times had been used in the Old Crow region for scraping moose and caribou skins during the tanning process, but a sacrificed portion of the caribou flesher described by Irving and Harington produced a radiocarbon date of 27,000 years ago.

The flesher was not the only artifact found at Locality 14N. Irving and Harington also reported on two large flakes of bone they believed had been removed by humans from the limb bones of mammoth while the bones were still green, or fresh, and then shaped further by knapping, or flaking, much as stone would be. The two large flakes produced dates of 26,000 and 29,000 years ago.

All three artifacts were stained a dark brown. Furthermore, the staining on the worked and unworked portions of the flesher appeared to be of uniform depth. This suggested that the flesher had not been made recently from old bone, an argument supported by the fact that caribou bone over 1,000 years old is brittle and unsuitable for use. Irving and Harington therefore saw no reason to question the radiocarbon dates. They concluded that the caribou flesher and the mammoth bone flakes – which would have been suitable as tools – had been made by people *well before* the time most archaeologists believed eastern Beringia was colonized by humans. The usual estimate of around 12,000 to 15,000 years ago was based on the earliest dated Clovis sites – at 11,500 years BP – in the American Southwest, with some allowance for the time required to move south into that region from Beringia. This announcement of possibly very early, pre-Clovis occupation in the far north created quite a stir in intellectual circles.

The caribou flesher and its radiocarbon date were certainly dramatic, and in some ways shocking. As well, as Irving and Harington pointed out, Locality 14N was only one of several collecting localities that had produced possibly very old bone artifacts. In 1975 Irving therefore organized a long-term, multidisciplinary project called the Northern Yukon Research Program. One of the objectives was to search for the original deposits that contained the caribou bone flesher and other bone artifacts, possibly an archaeological site or several sites nearby. Irving also intended to conduct work on all aspects of the prehistory and early history of the region.

In 1975 another archaeologist, Richard Morlan, in the Archaeological Survey of Canada at the National Museum of Man in Ottawa, also initiated a long-term research effort in the Yukon. This was called the Yukon Refugium Project, the term refugium referring to the fact that ice-free portions of the Yukon had been a refuge for plants and animals during the Pleistocene. Unlike Irving's research program, which was concerned with all periods, Morlan's project focused specifically on the Pleistocene history of unglaciated areas in the Yukon. Although the projects were defined somewhat differently they overlapped in their concern with the Pleistocene and the Old Crow River valley. Morlan states that he and Irving saw their two projects as complementary rather than directly competitive, although in terms of documenting pre-Clovis occupation there must have been some concern with getting there first.

Both projects continued into the mid-1980s, by which time they had reported the discovery of a human mandible possibly dating between 20,000 and 40,000 years ago, the mandibular fragment of a domestic dog, also possibly of Late Pleistocene age, and over a hundred bones that had apparently been broken, polished, cut or otherwise altered by humans. Most of these were from extinct fauna and therefore dated prior to at least 10,000 years ago. Other items, similarly stained by groundwater and therefore presumably as old, were described with somewhat greater confidence as being artifacts. These included wedges made from antler, possibly used for splitting wood or bone, and an antler baton or billet, which was a rod-shaped hammer possibly used in knapping. Some of the assumed bone artifacts were dated between 11,000 and 12,000 years ago, others between 25,000 and 30,000, and the oldest perhaps more than 50,000 years ago.

Many of the broken bones considered to have been used as tools were from the limb bones of woolly mammoth. In separate papers and monographs published over years, Irving, Morlan, and various colleagues working with them argued that the mammoth bone fragments used as tools could only have been broken from fresh bone and that because of the strength of the bone the only agency that could account for the breakage was human activity. Several natural agencies were considered but discarded as unlikely.

In the late 1970s the fortuitous death of a twenty-three-year-old female elephant named Ginsberg at the Franklin Park Zoo in Boston made it possible to test the hypothesis that fresh elephant bone, and presumably that of mammoth, could be knapped in much the same way as stone. Experiments in butchering Ginsberg, using scraps of bone broken from disarticulated elements of the skeleton, were performed by three archaeologists: Dennis Stanford of the Smithsonian Institution, Robson Bonnichsen of the University of Maine, and Richard Morlan. The results of their work was published in a jointly authored paper in *Science* in 1981. They concluded that elephant bone could indeed be knapped much like stone and, further, that the resulting bone flakes could be used in cutting elephant muscle tissue. Some of the flakes were indistinguishable from, and therefore replications of, many of the assumed mammoth bone tools found along the Old Crow River in the Yukon. Although the bone tools were very effective in butchering, Stanford, Bonnichsen, and Morlan found that stone tools were still required for cutting through the thick hide and, once inside the animal's carcass, through the strong sheaths of thin tissue surrounding the muscles. Nevertheless, the hypothesis that mammoth bone, like stone, could be knapped and used for butchering was validated. This didn't necessarily prove that the presumed mammoth bone tools from the Yukon were actually used as tools but it did mean that they *could* have been used in that way. Still necessary was to discover the tools in an unambiguous archaeological context, and Irving and Morlan intended to continue looking.

This was the stage reached by the Northern Yukon Research Program and the Yukon Refugium Project in the early 1980s when I began planning the Ontario Prehistory Gallery. I needed a strong introduction to the gallery that would merge well with the earliest documented occupation of Ontario by Early Paleo-Indian peoples. I also wanted to talk about the Bering land bridge, the doorway used by early colonizing peoples to reach the Americas, and about the search for pre-Clovis peoples. As well, as a resident of Canada and an employee of a provincially funded museum, I wanted as much Canadian content as possible.

The preliminary results of the two Canadian research programs along the Old Crow River in the Yukon, which together represented an enormous research effort and must have cost several hundred thousand dollars, if not more, seemed an excellent way to introduce the gallery, especially because in 1984, after four years of planning and less than fourteen months from opening, we still thought that the Ontario Prehistory Gallery would introduce an entire cluster of galleries devoted to the Native peoples of Canada. In this much larger context a display concerning the search for pre-Clovis occupation in the Yukon would be even more appropriate since it would precede displays of national scope. I wasn't worried that the Yukon work of Irving and Morlan hadn't yet received wide acceptance. Indeed I didn't know yet what I thought about the data and whether they truly had evidence for pre-Clovis occupations. But I considered the display justified because of the effort that had gone into the search for pre-Clovis occupations in the Yukon and elsewhere in the Americas over the preceding four or five decades and also because of the undeniable fact that the search occupied a firm and significant part of the history of archaeology in the Americas. Besides, I thought, somewhat flippantly, if anyone ever did prove that there had been *no* pre-Clovis occupation – and I couldn't imagine what would constitute definitive proof against an hypothesis that encompassed an entire continent – I could simply put wooden spears tipped with fluted points in the hands of the mannequins surrounding the mammoth and label the display an Early Paleo-Indian mammoth kill. It was very unlikely I would have to do this, even if the Yukon data were not accepted. The search for pre-Clovis would continue into the future and our diorama would then stand symbolically for that search.

This is why I built a display that most curators would probably not have attempted. Unlike the other displays in the gallery, which summarize the state of our knowledge, the mammoth diorama represents a hypothetical stage in the history of human occupation in the Americas that in the 1980s had yet to become knowledge.

Having decided to build a diorama including a young mammoth, we had to be creative. As mammoths became extinct at least 10,000 years ago, no taxidermist could provide us with a stuffed animal. We had to make one. Fortunately, we were able to hire a very good sculptor, Linda Shaw, who made beautiful bronze casts of small but very realistically sculpted modern animals. To help Linda with her work I also obtained for her several publications that provided information about mammoths from frozen carcasses found in Siberia. From these she could determine their size and body shape and other attributes. Their hair was reddish-brown and quite long. Their ears were much smaller than those of modern elephants. Their trunks had more flexible tips, for more precise grasping of sparse tufts of vegetation, and lateral wings, perhaps for carrying snow to the mouth for water. Their tails were shorter than those of modern elephants and totally hair covered. And their feet were much broader. Linda's information was augmented by life studies: mammoths as seen through the eyes of Paleolithic hunter-gatherers who lived between roughly 11,000

Sculptor Linda Shaw positioning an eye in the young woolly
mammoth made for one of
the dioramas in the former
Ontario Prehistory Gallery at
the Royal Ontario Museum.
Courtesy ROM.

and 32,000 years ago and sketched or painted their observations on the walls of caves in western Europe.

With this information, and several thick sheets of styrene, two skins from Scottish Highland cattle, lots and lots of plaster and some insights into how a large-bodied animal would look lying on the ground – curiously humped in the middle as the ground pushed the rib cage of the carcass out of bilateral symmetry – Linda created a most believable woolly mammoth, only a few years old. We had to be satisfied with making a young animal not only to conserve expensive Highland cattle skins but also, and more important, so it would fit in the diorama case. Our mammoth was so lifelike in death that quickly moving and excited children were often stopped dead in their tracks. After staring transfixed for a moment they frequently asked the teachers who breathlessly followed the running herd of children, now clumped about the exhibit in twos and threes, whether we had used real eyes.

To display the working hypothesis that pre-Clovis people in Beringia butchered mammoth with fragments of the animal's own bones, I asked Dick Morlan for the loan of several casts of real artifacts that had been found in the Yukon. I also asked if there were any fragments left of Ginsberg that we could use in the exhibit. He wrote back offering us several wonderful casts, painted and even weighted the same as the originals, and, much to my surprise and delight, one of Ginsberg's tibias. In due course we received Ginsberg's leg bone. It was a very happy occasion as we unwrapped the package and marvelled at the size of the bone. The bone certainly looked fresh, and somewhat bloody, but smelled slightly off, and we realized that in order to prevent insect infestation and perhaps an offensive odour in our gallery we would have to clean the bone thoroughly. We first put it in the ROM's bug room, where carrion-eating beetles consumed whatever flesh remained. And then we attempted to degrease the bone with chemical baths – again and again. Because the bone was so massive we never were able to degrease it totally but eventually we thought it would do. At that point, the bone was a bleached white and we needed to make it look real again, as it was when we received it. Our laboratory technician, Lisa Benoit, worked very hard with plaster, paint, and coloured wax, repairing the damage caused during degreasing and simulating muscle tissue, ligaments, and a little blood. Ginsberg's tibia occupied a prominent place in the front of the exhibit where, placed on two stones, it was just about to be broken by a stone in the uplifted hands of a pre-Clovis man preparing to strike it a heavy blow.

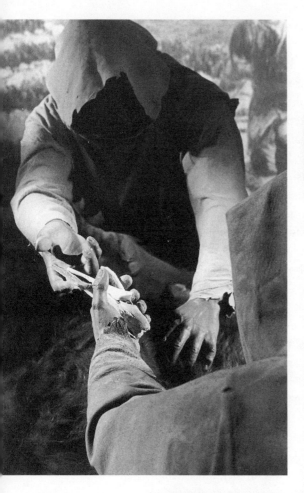

Human figure handing a bone tool to another figure in the pre-Clovis diorama at the entrance to the former Ontario Prehistory Gallery at the Royal Ontario Museum. Their faces are shown in deep shadow to indicate how little we know about the identity of the very first colonizers of the New World, aside from their general northeast Asian origins.

Courtesy ROM.

An Early Paleo-Indian, dressed in tailored clothing made of caribou skins, tying a spear point to a shaft. The figure was part of a diorama in the former Ontario Prehistory Gallery at the Royal Ontario Museum.

Courtesy ROM.

The human figure preparing to break the bone and the two helpers standing on either side of the fallen mammoth were shown wearing hooded parkas of tanned hides from an unidentifiable animal. I used dehaired skins for the clothing as I didn't want to guess what animal species the people might have used for clothing. Certainly mammoth skin would have been too heavy. Similarly, the faces of these unknown people were cast in deep shadows since their racial affiliation, even what species of human they represented, was unknown. If they had lived as long ago as some people thought – whether 30,000 or 50,000 or as even as much as 130,000 years ago, as Irving and colleagues suggested in a paper published in 1981 – they might have pre-dated the modern races or even *Homo sapiens sapiens,* the modern species of humans. With their faces cast in dark shadows the identity of the people in the diorama would be as mysterious to the museum public as it was to archaeologists.

As a postscript to this story it might interest you to know that somewhere along the way, after having made the commitment to create a mammoth diorama, we learned that the proposed cluster of galleries on the Native people of Canada would not be built after all. The dramatic introduction we had planned to an entire floor of displays would stand alone as an introduction to the only gallery on Native people that was then certain. But what a fine introduction it was to be.

Between the building of the gallery and the writing of this book, the case for a very early human presence in the Old Crow region changed dramatically. In 1981 William Irving and colleagues excavated several bone artifacts from a location they thought was near an archaeological site, potentially the first site to be discovered along the Old Crow River and also the oldest there or anywhere else in the New World, dating to perhaps 120,000 years BP or earlier. Unfortunately Irving died prematurely, in November 1986, before that site and its dating could be confirmed.

In 1986 and again in 1990, Richard Morlan reassessed both his and Irving's projects along the Old Crow. Surprisingly the caribou flesher, originally dated at c. 27,000 years BP, was redated at 1,350 years ±150 BP. Three other supposed bone tools were determined to be less than 3,000 years old, but twenty-nine other dates from bones that may have been altered by humans fell into a period extending from 25,000 to 47,000 years BP. Morlan argues that the clustering of dates is as significant as the dates themselves, representing the arrival and persistent occupation of the region by a new agent of bone alteration – humans. If the bones had been altered by natural agencies mimicking human activities, Morlan believes that they would have produced non-clustered, random dates. Unfortunately, the bones are not from demonstrated archaeological sites such as the one Irving thought he had found, and the scientific community remains dubious. And thus our diorama remained futuristic, or symbolic of the hemispheric-wide search for the earliest human occupation in the New World.

The second diorama in our series – and the first dealing specifically with Ontario prehistory – was based on much more firmly established archaeological evidence. This concerned the Early Paleo-Indian occupation of southern Ontario, dating to perhaps 10,500 or 11,000 years ago. The diorama was based on evidence I had found at the Fisher site. In order to avoid using real artifacts in a display that would contain lots of glue and other chemical substances, possibly damaging them in the long term, I made simulated tools from the same stone used by the people at Fisher, Fossil Hill chert. I went to the geological outcrops discovered by Peter von Bitter and dug a large number of blocks of stone out of the bedrock with a crowbar. From this material I made thousands of waste flakes and a few tools that we scattered about the feet of two human figures in the diorama. One large block of chert was also cut, highly polished, and inset into the wall at the entrance to the gallery, with a dedication to the people of prehistory and a greater understanding of the common heritage of our shared, more distant origins.

The figures in the Early Paleo-Indian diorama were shown attaching the fluted spear points they had supposedly just made to wooden foreshafts. And this time, in preparing the human figures, we felt able to show their faces. They were carefully sculpted to represent features of modern Native peoples in an evolutionary sense. But instead of using several life models, we sculpted the facial features after individuals in portrait photographs taken by Edward S. Curtis, a pioneering late-nineteenth- and early-twentieth-century photographer of North American Native peoples. Today I might not use historical Native individuals as models for Early Paleo-Indian figures because of uncertainties over how the earliest and later populations of Amerindians are related. The only other artistic licence we used on the figures was dressing them in caribou furs, made from expensive but quite beautiful skins we purchased in Toronto. At the time there was no evidence that Early Paleo-Indians in the Great Lakes and the larger mid-continent region actually hunted caribou, although it was a reasonable guess given the late glacial environment, paleontological evidence for caribou, and tentative evidence from New England that Early Paleo-Indians may have hunted caribou there. The caribou fur clothing on the human figures in the Early Paleo-Indian diorama was, like the mammoth diorama, a futuristic display.

Beyond the Early Paleo-Indians dressed in caribou furs in the gallery we built two other dioramas from different and progressively later periods in Ontario prehistory: a wild rice harvesting camp on the edge of a lake, dating to perhaps AD 1000; and beyond that, a portion of an Ontario Iroquois stockaded village about 400 years ago.

Across from the dioramas we installed a series of wall cases telling a parallel story with maps; drawings showing people employed in various activities, rendered, most surprisingly but beautifully, with felt-tipped pen; a generous but careful selection of artifacts, some mounted in simulated wooden handles to make their function more apparent; and exquisite drawings of hands showing how the artifacts were used.

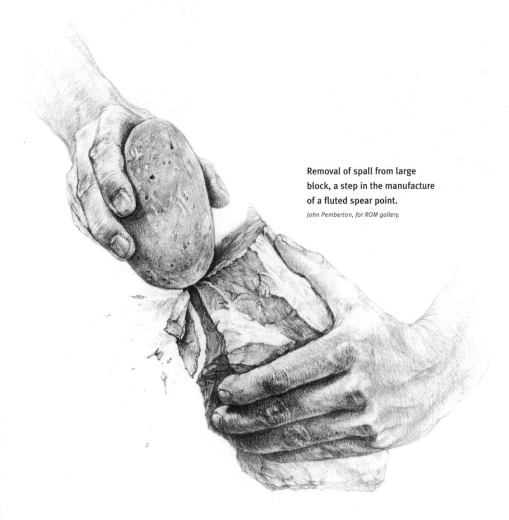

Removal of spall from large block, a step in the manufacture of a fluted spear point.
John Pemberton, for ROM gallery.

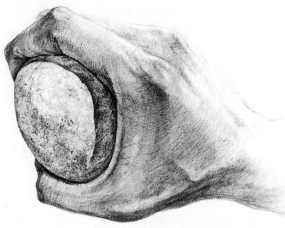

Shaping of preform with stone hammer, a step in the manufacture of a fluted spear point.

John Pemberton, for ROM gallery.

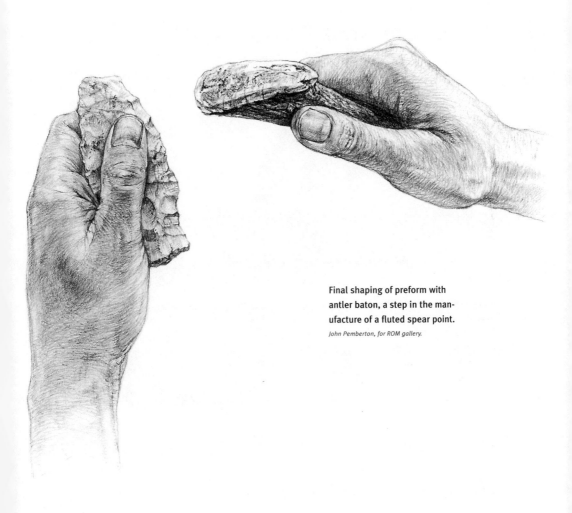

Final shaping of preform with antler baton, a step in the manufacture of a fluted spear point.

John Pemberton, for ROM gallery.

Final trimming of edges with pressure flaker, a step in the manufacture of a fluted spear point.

John Pemberton, for ROM gallery.

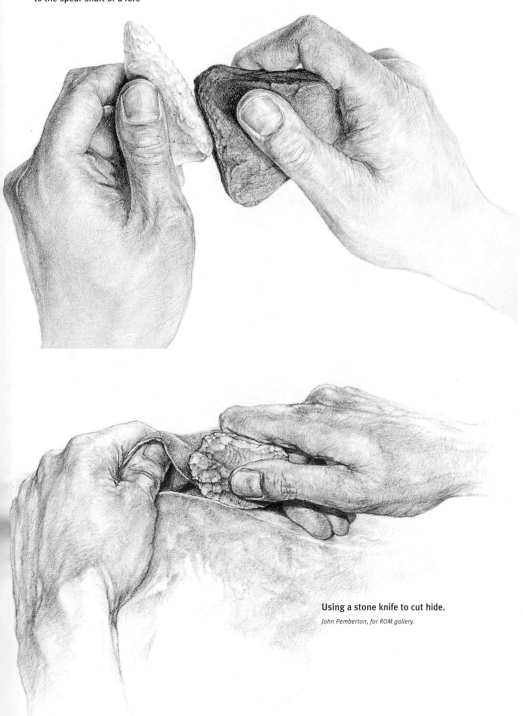

Grinding basal margins of spear point to prevent cutting the lashings that will bind the point to the spear shaft or a fore- shaft, a step in the manufacture of a fluted spear point.

John Pemberton, for ROM gallery.

Using a stone knife to cut hide.

John Pemberton, for ROM gallery.

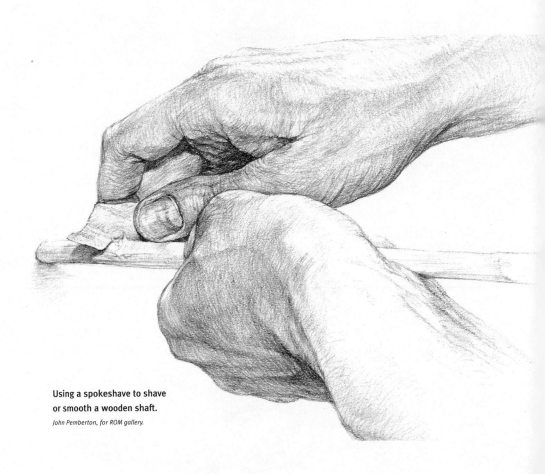

**Using a spokeshave to shave
or smooth a wooden shaft.**

John Pemberton, for ROM gallery.

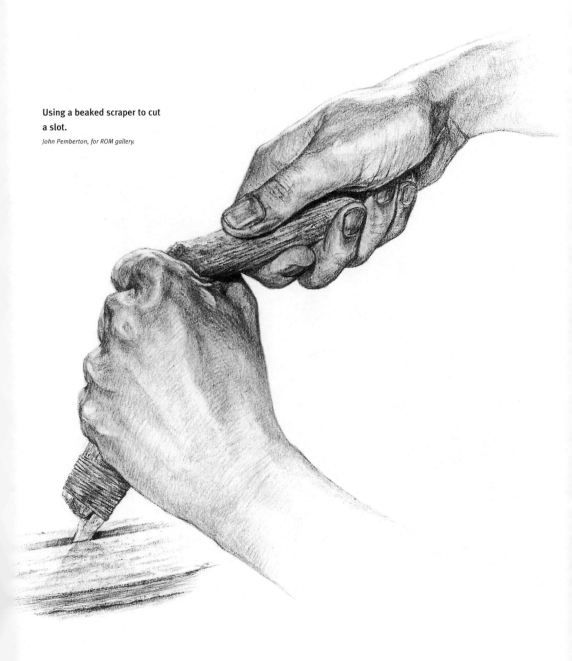

Using a beaked scraper to cut a slot.

John Pemberton, for ROM gallery.

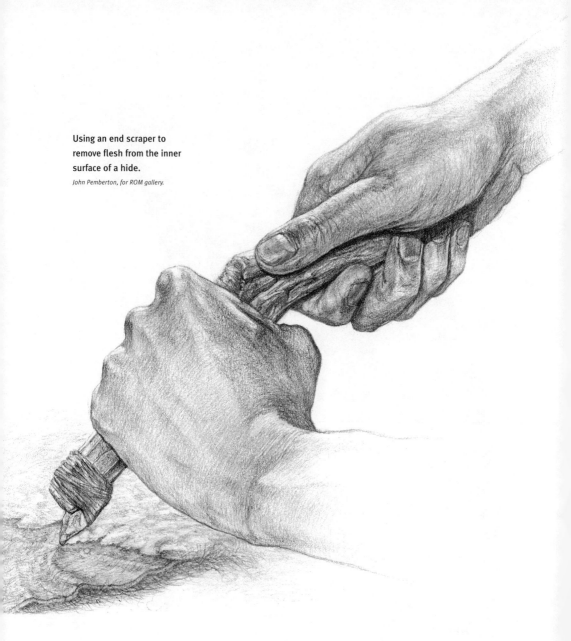

Using an end scraper to
remove flesh from the inner
surface of a hide.

John Pemberton, for ROM gallery.

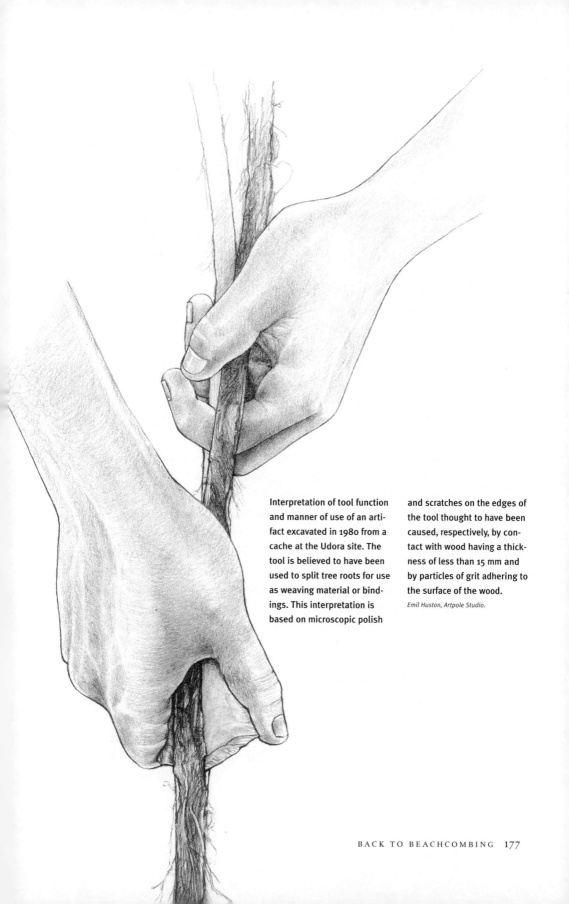

Interpretation of tool function and manner of use of an artifact excavated in 1980 from a cache at the Udora site. The tool is believed to have been used to split tree roots for use as weaving material or bindings. This interpretation is based on microscopic polish and scratches on the edges of the tool thought to have been caused, respectively, by contact with wood having a thickness of less than 15 mm and by particles of grit adhering to the surface of the wood.

Emil Huston, Artpole Studio.

I first saw the use of hand drawings in a museum on the Mediterranean coast near Nice and marvelled at how effective they were in displaying the simplest artifacts, in that instance simply broken cobbles that had been made as early as 380,000 years ago by *Homo erectus*, a species that gave rise to our own. I was stunned to learn that the artifacts had been made almost directly beneath my feet, at a site called Terra Amata that had been excavated in advance of urban development and incorporated into a museum display in the lower floor of the very building that was subsequently constructed there. As I recall, the stratigraphy of the site was preserved off to one side of the back parking lot and could be seen by descending a few steps down a stairway protected by a small shed-like building with a padlocked door.

By themselves the broken cobbles in that museum would only have interested archaeologists, and probably only certain types of archaeologists. But the hand drawings gave the artifacts life and appeal even, I suspected, to the most casual museum visitor. They did this without the need for long labels, or in some cases any labels at all. As well, they were not obtrusive. Photographs of modern hands would have been too contemporary and therefore rather jarring for illustrating the past.

The technique worked just as well for us, possibly even better because of the more complex, varied, and visually interesting artifacts we had available for display. In addition to the satisfaction of introducing this display technique to the ROM I secretly knew that I had strongly imprinted myself on the gallery in an unintended way, for the hand drawings were based on black and white photographs of *my* hands. I hasten to add that this was not vanity on my part. We needed someone's hands as models to help the artist draw one of the most complex and expressive parts of the human body and to illustrate how tools unfamiliar to the artist might have been held and used. And unlike a professional model unfamiliar with archaeology I knew how the artifacts should be held and the effects I wanted to achieve. I was available also whenever photography appointments could be scheduled. For the same reasons my body postures (though not physique) may also be seen in some of the paintings of human figures. Again this wasn't vanity, but through photographs of myself in different postures and holding simulated spears, it was an easy way to show the artist what I wanted in the composition. In addition to strongly influencing the appearance and content of the gallery intellectually through my personal aesthetic judgments, understanding, and interpretation of the archaeological record, my physical person actually became a subtle part of the display.

This process of imprinting, both mental and physical, stimulated a high I had never felt before in an ostensibly intellectual exercise. In my research I had become used to expressing ideas on the printed page but had seldom had an opportunity to manifest them in three-dimensional, physical form. It was a remarkable sensation to see and feel this happen, tremendously stimulating and energizing.

After the gallery was finished I returned one day to the entrance in the quiet of the early morning. Gazing slowly past the young mammoth surrounded by darkened figures and forward through 12,000 years of prehistory to the softly lit granite wall of rock art at the far end of the gallery, glowing dimly with the ochre and black images of a Native belief system, I hoped that the museum visitor would be as drawn and fascinated by the past as I was. I also thought of deeply moving moments in my own past: the first time I walked onto the very top of the Fisher site and visualized a long-vanished people camped on the shores of a glacial lake; and another time, when I sat on the edge of an excavation and wondered about the lives and fate of the two individuals who had never retrieved the tools they had buried for a future day. Remembering these and countless other more fleeting but defining moments, I felt incredibly lucky. I loved what I was doing.

Lost Opportunity

While we were installing the dioramas in our new gallery in fall 1984, I applied to the Social Sciences and Humanities Research Council of Canada (SSHRCC), for a research grant to follow up the excavations I had done at Udora in 1980. The second half of the grant application, written jointly with friend and colleague Arthur Roberts, also requested funds to explore a new site that Arthur had found only a few years before.

We planned to do the work during the 1985 field season. I proposed that the major effort that year – four out of the total six weeks field time – be devoted to a second season of excavation at the Udora site. I hoped to find undisturbed portions of the site between the farm buildings or around the house in the front, side, or rear yards. It was very likely that the site extended into this area since the house and buildings, which were clustered together, occurred in what appeared to be roughly the middle of the site. They were surrounded by three artifact concentrations to the west, including Area A, the closest to the buildings, which had produced Feature 2, and approximately seven concentrations to the north, at least two and possibly several others to the east, and one to the south. It was possible that the area between the buildings had never been ploughed, increasing our chances of finding something undisturbed, possibly even another feature containing charcoal for radiocarbon dating or animal bone to allow us to interpret what Early Paleo-Indians hunted.

The second aspect of the research proposal concerned preliminary investigations at the new site discovered by Arthur Roberts in 1978. Arthur made the discovery – or rather, a crew member of his made the discovery, a sad experience I had had many times – during the course of archaeological survey work for a doctorate in cultural-historical geography at York University in Toronto. Actually, the site wasn't really a site at all. Technically it was a "find spot," the discovery location of a single artifact. But despite being totally isolated, this lone artifact was remarkable for its incredible beauty and very great potential.

The artifact is a very well-made Gainey-type fluted spear point, of crystal quartz. Considering the difficulty of knapping quartz because of its extreme hardness, the artifact was clearly made by a master craftsman. Furthermore, it was made of a material seldom used in North America for fluted spear points, possibly because of the difficulty of finding a large enough crystal without cleavage planes and flaws that would cause breakage. When Arthur Roberts and I wrote the grant proposal, we thought the Newcastle specimen was the only quartz point of its kind in Canada.

The Newcastle spear point contained small bits of bright reddish material in some of the incipient fractures created when cracks had formed during knapping but failed to pass through the material, leaving the partially formed flake that was to be removed still adhering to the specimen. There were also some minute specks of dark reddish-brown material near the base. Analysis of these substances by the Canadian Conservation Institute in Ottawa showed that the bright reddish material was probably haematite, or red ochre. The dark reddish-brown material contained protein, non-hematitic iron (possibly from blood), and unidentified oils. Arthur Roberts thought this substance might be the residue of a hafting cement used to attach the spear point to a foreshaft or lance.

There is other evidence that the Newcastle spear point was actually used. A small but noticeable angle disrupting the otherwise smooth line of convergence of the edges toward the tip, as well as a change in the size, shape, and orientation of flake scars near there, suggest that the tip had at one time been resharpened, presumably to repair an old break. And an impact fracture on the resharpened tip indicates that the spear point had subsequently struck something hard.

The hafting cement residue, evidence of resharpening, and impact fracture all indicate that the spear point had actually been used, despite the considerable effort and skill required in its manufacture and the

Early Paleo-Indian fluted spear point from the vicinity of Newcastle, east of Toronto. The artifact is exceptional because it was made from crystal quartz, which is very difficult to work and rarely used as a toolstone. It is also unusual because it contains traces of red ochre, often used as a pigment, and pinprick-sized spots of dark reddish-brown material near the base. These may be the remains of a glue, composed of blood and plant resins, used to help fix the spear point to a shaft. The large flake scar at the tip, probably caused by impact, and evidence of re-sharpening along the sides indicate that the spear point was actually used. It is shown here at approximately twice natural size.

Courtesy ROM.

unusual material from which it had been made. Or maybe the evidence for use was not what it first seemed; perhaps the spear point had been intended and used solely for a ceremonial activity. Indeed, the use, damage, resharpening, and ceremony might conceivably all have been part of the same event. This possibility is suggested by the presence of red ochre on the specimen, a mineral that was commonly applied to artifacts deposited with burials. And this is what gave the Newcastle spear point its very great research potential. It may have been part of a grave offering.

Arthur Roberts sensed this from the very moment of discovery. And because of the obvious necessity of investigating the site very carefully and, I expect, his awareness of the possible political implications of a burial, he didn't think he could or should do anything further in the field in 1978 when the artifact was discovered. Instead, he concentrated on finishing the field season and later his dissertation. Shortly before he left Toronto for a position on the faculty in the Department of Geography at Simon Fraser University in British Columbia, Arthur left the Newcastle artifact with me at the ROM for long-term, or possibly permanent, curation. We also discussed doing some fieldwork at the Newcastle site in the near future.

The near future arrived in 1984, when Arthur and I jointly prepared our application for a research grant for fieldwork the following year. Because the site might be the location of a burial we were very conscious of the need to proceed cautiously in our field investigations and of our responsibility to recover every bit of information possible. There was no room for mistakes. We felt this way in part because of the great rarity of early skeletal material in North America. Perhaps only a half dozen sites had yielded remains dating between 10,000 and 11,000 years ago, and many of these were fragmentary and not associated with artifacts or well dated. Human remains of known Early Paleo-Indian cultural affiliation were rarer still. In 1984 only one Early Paleo-Indian burial site had been reported for all of North America. This was the Anzick site, located in south-central Montana. The artifacts indicated that the burial had been placed by Clovis people, the oldest Early Paleo-Indian culture known in North America.

The Anzick site was discovered by accident in 1968 during the removal, by heavy equipment, of talus, or slope, debris from the base of a cliff. This exposed a collapsed rockshelter that contained several cranial fragments of two juveniles and more than a hundred stone and bone artifacts, perhaps among the most beautiful and skilfully made that have ever been discovered, anywhere in the world. But the burials and associated artifacts – if, indeed, they all belonged together – were completely disturbed, and the artifacts partially dispersed among the people who discovered the site before archaeologists were notified. As a result it took many years to retrieve all the material, most of which is now housed at the Montana Historical Society in Helena. Sadly, the little archaeological work that could be done in the small amount of deposit remaining after the disturbance doesn't tell us very much about the relationship between the human remains and the artifacts. It is inferred that at least some belong together because both the cranial fragments of one individual and many of the artifacts are covered with red ochre. And the likelihood that all the artifacts are associated as a group is supported by the fact that the more complex artifacts were clearly manufactured with the same flintknapping strategy. Cranial fragments of the second individual were bleached, not ochre covered, a disturbing inconsistency. In the late 1990s further analysis of the skeletal material showed that the ochre-covered remains, those of a one-and-a-half year old, were indeed Clovis age, dating to 10,680 ±50 years BP. The second individual, a seven-year-old, was roughly 2,000 years younger, dating to 8,600 ±90 years BP, and was not part of the Clovis burial.

The artifacts are truly impressive, both for the skill evidenced in their manufacture and for their size. They include at least seven Clovis-type fluted points, one, like the Newcastle specimen, apparently made from crystal quartz. There are also over seventy ovoid and lanceolate bifaces that may have served both as tools and as raw material from which other tools could be made. A miscellany of other smaller tools and utilized flakes, as well as two complete and eleven fragments of cylindrical bone rods with bevelled or tapered ends, probably made from mammoth bone, were also found. Archaeologists Larry Lahren and Robson Bonnichsen, who published an announcement of the discovery in the journal *Science,* interpreted these rods as foreshafts to which Clovis points were hafted. Two kinds of foreshafts were envisioned: one with a bevelled base that was permanently attached to a lance, perhaps used to jab a disabled animal repeatedly; and the second with a tapered base that fitted into a socket at the end of a lance, perhaps allowing the point and foreshaft to remain in the wounded animal and leaving the lance behind for rearming. Unfortunately, any potential association between the cylindrical rods and the Clovis points was destroyed by the heavy earth-moving equipment that disturbed the site. The actual function of the cylindrical rods will thus remain speculative unless or until other rods are discovered in an undisturbed context at another site. We can hope that such a site exists. Similar mammoth bone rods were discovered between 1987 and 1990 as part of a cache of Clovis tools at the East Wenatchee site in the state of Washington, but they were not associated with the fluted spear points in a way that suggested they functioned as foreshafts. Indeed, one of the excavators, Michael Gramly, speculates that they might have served as sled runners.

The Anzick site both fascinated and unnerved me, and perhaps Arthur Roberts as well. It allowed us to speculate on what we *might* find at the Newcastle site and the heavy responsibility this would entail, although Newcastle was unlikely to be a second Anzick. I ranked the chances of what the Newcastle discovery might represent as follows: an isolated find (most likely); a cache of objects somewhat like Feature 2 at Udora (somewhat less likely, but possible); or a burial (very, very unlikely). We decided to play it safe and plan for the least likely but also most complex possibility, politically and scientifically: a burial. Once we knew what we had we could take whatever steps were required, including consulting Native peoples if a burial was found.

Playing safe in archaeology can mean *in situ* preservation, a modern euphemism for leaving it alone – not excavating. But if you intend to do fieldwork, playing safe means using remote sensing as a non-intrusive investigative method. For the first phase of the Newcastle work in 1985 we therefore intended to investigate the discovery location of the quartz spear point by magnetometer, electrical resistivity, and/or ground penetrating radar. These techniques would detect anything buried in the ground that affected the earth's magnetic field, the electrical conductivity of the soil, or the movement of sound waves. We intended to investigate an area of approximately 225 square metres, centred on the discovery spot of the artifact and with some allowance for lateral displacement from its original location by cultivating equipment.

We also wanted to investigate the area by coring, not strictly a remote sensing technique but relatively benign nevertheless. We would use coring to remove soil samples from different depths of the site for chemical and other kinds of analyses. Because of the continental climate of present-day Ontario, with strong seasonal contrasts in temperature and abundant precipitation as snow and rain, we were very much aware that organic materials such as human skeletons and animal bone of Clovis age would probably be preserved only if buried within or beneath a peat bog or other type of permanently wet and thus oxygen-free, or anaerobic, environment. If anything of that age had been buried in the ground at the Newcastle site it was in the worst possible setting for organic preservation: shallowly buried in well-drained soil and thus within the zone of periodic wetting and drying, as well as seasonal freezing and thawing. Anything organic would probably have decomposed long ago. In that case the only evidence that might remain of the object would be high concentrations of the elements it once contained, such as calcium, magnesium, and phosphorous from bone, and perhaps iron (haematite, or red ochre). If so, the vertical and horizontal distribution of those concentrations might be the *only* permanent documentation we would obtain of that object. Knowledge before we started digging of where those concentrations occurred would also help focus excavation quickly and allow us to identify a feature before we cut into it, thus also telling us when to begin the exceedingly careful search for any objects, such as burnt bone in the case of a cremation, or stone grave goods. This job would be the objective of the second field season, which we planned for 1986.

Remote sensing and large numbers of soil analyses are expensive. We estimated that these techniques would cost roughly $16,000, over 75 percent of the $20,800 budgeted for the first field season. And the follow-up excavation, which would be labour intensive, would cost perhaps $22,500. Combined, the two years of fieldwork would cost roughly $43,000. All of this would be spent exploring an area roughly 225 metres square.

We didn't get the money. Our proposal was too expensive for our colleagues who reviewed it for SSHRCC. Perhaps Arthur Roberts and I were too conservative and should have done at least some exploratory testing so that we had some idea of what was there before we requested a grant. Or perhaps we should have budgeted a little less for the remote sensing and soil analyses. Or perhaps it was the people who reviewed our proposal who should have been less conservative. Whatever the case, it was too late for second-guessing and the project died, at least for a time. By erring on the side of safety we inadvertently arranged for *in situ* preservation – non-excavation. And thus the site, if that's what it is, remains for the future.

6 Unfinished Business

In 1986 I tried again. I sent out a second application to SSHRCC for a research grant to excavate at Udora, but this time the site was to be the entire focus of my fieldwork. No other projects would be involved.

The new grant application was a cut-and-paste job, a bit of something old tacked onto something new. From the previous Udora/Newcastle application I took the part of the budget that applied only to the Udora phase and modified it slightly, reducing the crew size from eleven to eight and reducing the total costs by the amount I had available from the ROM. I hoped the new proposal would be better received, in part because of the lower funding request but also because the potential outcome of my proposed work was perhaps more predictable than that of the previous application. The following *Archaeological Newsletter* tells what happened next:

A Question of Time
November 1987

I have just returned from the field and am undergoing the usual painful readjustments to the noise and hustle of urban living. Not the least of my problems is coping with the well-meaning inquisitiveness of my friends and colleagues and the inevitable question that I dread most of all. After first asking how my work on the early human occupation of Ontario and North America went, my questioners utter the fearsome words, "Find any charcoal for radiocarbon dating?" I have answered NO to this question for so many years (fourteen, to be exact) that I have come to dread it. To be honest, I can't even discuss it any more – a fact that has made for some embarrassing lapses in conversation from time to time.

I can now announce to all who have asked me, or would have but hesitated to take the chance, that I may be able to answer that question in the affirmative. If so, I might even have the date printed onto my shirts for all to see so I never have to speak about it.

Perhaps I should start at the beginning instead of at the end of this story and explain that I excavated this summer at the Udora site on the southeastern margin of Lake Simcoe. The site was occupied by Early Paleo-Indian hunters and gatherers during the initial colonization of southern Ontario after the final retreat of the continental ice sheet. Together with other evidence, the strong association of the site with glacial Lake Algonquin suggests that the occupation occurred between 10,000 and 12,000 years ago. The nearest dated site of this culture is more than 550 kilometres away in New Jersey, and we don't know whether the radiocarbon dates from there, or those from more distant regions of North America, can be applied to the Great Lakes region. Without some reliable dates from this area, we cannot place the early occupation of Ontario in a tangible world.

Although we have learned a great deal about Early Paleo-Indian peoples in Ontario over the past fifteen years or so, our success has also been in some ways the cause of our dating problems. We have been forced to depend on survey work in cultivated fields to discover new sites, but the activity of cultivation has apparently destroyed the very thing we need (charcoal or animal bone) for dating purposes. The Udora site seemed to provide a way around this difficulty. Survey and initial excavation in 1979 and 1980 showed that the ten artifact concentrations that make up the site completely surrounded farm buildings and stock corrals. This suggested that an undisturbed portion of the site might have survived adjacent to the buildings or in the laneways and corrals. Basing an excavation project on this possibility was obviously risky, but the potential rewards of success seemed to outweigh the risk. Furthermore, other things I needed to know about the site and the entire region represented a kind of fail-safe position, so that even if I didn't find an undisturbed area the research would still justify the time and money spent. The landowners involved, Mr and Mrs Byron Taylor and Mr and Mrs Ross Stevenson, very kindly allowed us to excavate even though it meant the disruption created by ten people digging in yards, driveways, and a newly sown grain field. Fortunately, I was awarded a grant from the Social Sciences and Humanities Research Council of Canada that, together with my ROM funds, made the project possible. With the receipt of a licence from the Ontario

Ministry of Citizenship and Culture to conduct the work, the hiring of the crew, and rental of a place to live (a closed church!), the arrangements were completed and work started on May 19th.

My field strategy was fairly simple, in theory. Until I had a chance to determine whether an undisturbed portion of the site existed among the farm buildings, the crew would excavate an artifact concentration in a nearby ploughed field. After the two weeks I predicted I would need for my work, the crew could, if I was lucky enough to find something, be transferred to the undisturbed area for the remaining four weeks of the project. This arrangement would provide adequate excavation time in each area. During rainy weather the crew could survey cultivated fields in the region for new sites. We wouldn't lose time because of bad weather, and the project would produce useful data regardless of the productivity (or lack thereof) of any particular aspect of the work. It seemed a good plan, but on one intermittently rainy day we shifted back and forth from excavation to survey work several times, until I finally gave up in exhaustion and frustration at about 3:00 in the afternoon. But aside from that terrible day and a few other trials, things went fairly well.

Because of a chance conversation with a colleague, Patrick Julig, a week before beginning fieldwork, I decided to explore the area around the farm buildings using a motor-driven auger rather than a hand-held posthole digger. I shudder now at my naïveté in even considering doing the work by hand. Had I not opted for the auger, I might still be out there, chipping into the slowly freezing ground.

With the help of Pat Julig and Andrew Stewart, I started augering on the second day of the project. Just after starting the work we brought up a fragment of a hide-scraping tool from an auger hole adjacent to a driveway that led to a fenced-in poultry house and equipment barn. From that moment on I was confident that the auger was giving us a good indication of what was below the surface. I had always thought that the area had excellent potential for containing an occupation, and hence I was delighted to find the artifact. The bad news – there always seems to be some – was that the soil profile showed clearly that the area had been ploughed before the construction of buildings and fences, and wasn't the undisturbed area I was looking for.

We couldn't explore the front yard of the house since the Taylors had recently installed a septic system there, but we augered throughout the backyard, across the gully between the house and other buildings, inside the stock corrals, down the laneways between the buildings and toward the fields and even under the earthen ramp leading up to the main door of the barn. Nothing! Nothing! Nothing! Except for the spot that produced the scraper fragment (as well as tool-making debris from several other auger holes), no evidence of prehistoric occupation turned up. The bottom line was that I had discovered only one activity area and it had been ploughed. With the crew already working in a cultivated field that was producing very little material, I had a difficult decision to make about what to do next.

Since the excavations in the cultivated field were not very productive, I decided to shift the crew to the newly discovered area next to the driveway even though it also had been ploughed, because I thought it might prove to be more productive. This was definitely risky – that inescapable element of chance again – because I was comparing the productivity of a block excavation with that of several auger holes.

I shifted the crew to the new area on Day 14 of the project, and we immediately started recovering artifacts and chipping debris. It was apparent that the new spot, Area A-East, was much more productive than the cultivated field, and we soon detected the presence of two activity areas that yielded abundant evidence of hide processing [see map p. 152]. In addition, we recovered several fragments of spear points of a style characteristic of the so-called Gainey complex, named after a site in Michigan that is currently undergoing excavation. Gainey is thought to be the Great Lakes equivalent of the 11,500-year-old Clovis complex in western North America, the earliest known Early Paleo-Indian "culture." Ours was the first excavation of a Gainey site in Ontario, so we would learn something new no matter what we found.

As the excavation grid was expanded, we continued to define the limits of the two activity areas. The eventual recovery of more than eighty hide scrapers indicated clearly that the areas were used for skin working, and implied that the site served as an important hunting base. We found fewer than a dozen fragments of projectile points, but fortunately they are enough to establish the cultural identity of the occupants. The scrapers also indicate that Area A-East was probably a focus for female activity only, while the men fashioned and repaired weapons on another part or parts of the site.

Despite our failure to find an undisturbed occupation, I would have been entirely satisfied with no more than the results of our work up to this point. However, the site held another surprise for us, one that might eventually remove all lingering traces of disappointment. During excavation of the southern part of Area A-East, we noticed that the plough zone yielded large numbers of stone flakes. The concentration extended below the plough zone, and it was soon apparent that we had found the remains of an ancient pit. Although the pit was not marked by a change in soil colour or texture, it could be delimited by the concentration of flakes, artifact fragments (some

Artifacts from the Udora site. Left to right top row: two end scrapers; narrow-tipped beaked scraper fragment; single-spurred graver; broad-tipped beaked scraper fragment. Left to right bottom row: unfluted spear point; fragments of three Gainey-type fluted points, the first and third of which were heavily resharpened while the middle specimen, a base, probably broke in the haft during use. *Courtesy ROM.*

of which were burnt), and highly fragmented and calcined animal bone. Because the distribution of the material was the only thing that indicated the shape of the pit, we mapped the more than 2,000 artifacts, some no bigger than a sesame seed. All of the pit contents were removed for water screening in the laboratory, to separate out the calcined animal bone and any other material (charcoal, seeds, etc.) that may be present.

The big surprise for us was not only that we had found a pit that had escaped total destruction by ploughing, but also that the pit contained calcined bones that may allow us to date the occupation and identify the animal(s) hunted, perhaps the very species that provided the skins worked by the end scrapers we found. In the end, then, I may actually have found what I was looking for, a feature that produced material for radiocarbon dating, not in an untouched area as I had hoped, but in the very type of disturbed situation I had sought to avoid.

The bone samples will soon be sent off for identification and dating. Before long I may be able to answer that dreaded question about time – and I must say, it's about time!

Postscript

The 1987 discoveries at Udora certainly rewarded my risk taking. The entire experience also marked a great recovery from the low of my 1980 field season. And what a recovery it was! I found a new and unsuspected occupation area on the site and unambiguous evidence that this area had been occupied by people of the Gainey culture, the first Early Paleo-Indians to colonize Ontario and the Great Lakes region generally. And for the first time in seventeen years of fieldwork in Ontario I also found what I despaired to think I might never find: preserved animal bone. At long last I had something organic for radiocarbon dating and might now be able to determine *when* Early Paleo-Indians occupied the region from local material, not from extrapolations based on the dates of archaeological sites in New England or western North America, or even from geological and environmental data such as I had used at Fisher.

There wasn't much more I could have wished for. Well … perhaps a more scenic place to work. I mentioned in the newsletter that we first detected the new area of the site, which I called Area A-East, next to a driveway leading to a barn and other outbuildings. But I didn't mention that our work also slowly extended into a fenced area around a chicken coop. Fortunately there were no resident chickens because the chicken coop is ultimately where we spent most of the field season. By the time we were done we had nearly pedestalled the little house, digging right up to it on two sides, and in the process had removed the remains of a lot of page wire and some split-rail fencing. Around and inside the former enclosure marked by that fencing, highly enriched by chickens and other barnyard animals over who knows how many years, we dug through soil in all its various meanings.

Mixed within this soil, churned up by ploughing and other disturbances, we found the remains of early prehistoric Gainey occupation: broken stone tools and waste from tool resharpening and manufacture. The material was scattered over an area of about 100 square metres in two distinct concentrations, each about six metres across and separated by a much less productive zone about three metres wide. We could tell that the material had been left by Gainey people, as opposed to some other group, by the fluted spear points, the most culturally diagnostic artifact we could have found. Only one was complete – and, oddly, not diagnostic – but

Excavations adjacent to a poultry shed at the Udora site in 1987. The work uncovered two activity areas occupied by Early Paleo-Indian Gainey people and a former firepit that contained fragments of calcined animal bone. The trees in the background are growing on the former lake bottom of glacial Lake Algonquin.

Photograph by Peter Storck.

fourteen fragments of at least twelve other points were clearly of the Gainey type. All had been broken during use and then discarded, some in a fire judging from evidence of heat damage. This sample of twelve fluted projectile points was spectacularly large for such a small area, internally consistent (there being no other fluted point types present), and completely unambiguous (all twelve points being very definitely of the Gainey type). Since the Gainey-type spear points occurred in both concentrations there was no doubt that the two areas had been used by people of the same culture, and most likely during the same occupation. Indeed, probably by members of the same extended family or related families doing somewhat different things in adjacent spaces.

In addition to the satisfyingly large sample of Gainey-type points we recovered a wide range of other tools, among them a drill made from the broken base of a Gainey point, over eighty end scrapers, which are tools often used in dressing skins, and a notched pebble that made me think, possibly incorrectly, of the bolas stones or fishnet weights used by historically known Native peoples. I had never obtained so many end scrapers before from one site, or even from all my years of excavation combined. And I had never heard of a bolas stone or net sinker being recovered from an Early Paleo-Indian site before. Surprisingly, most of the stone tools and debris from tool manufacture and repair were Fossil Hill chert, from geological sources located over 120 kilometres west, allowing for foot travel around glacial Lake Algonquin. A significant amount of another exotic type of toolstone was also present: Onondaga chert from bedrock sources along the northeast shore of the Lake Erie basin, over 190 kilometres southwest, also allowing for foot travel around late glacial lakes in the Ontario basin. These toolstones indicate that the Gainey people who visited Udora had most recently been in the southern Georgian Bay region (represented by the greatest amount of toolstone) and earlier (because of the lesser amount of material), in extreme southern Ontario. Once they reached Udora the Gainey people also explored the local area for toolstone. This is reflected by small amounts of Bobcaygeon and/or Gull River chert on the site, toolstone that would have been obtained either from local bedrock formations a short distance north or from nearby glacial deposits dropped by ice that had overridden those formations.

This revealing picture of the cross-country movements of a pioneering and highly mobile hunting people was just the first indication of what the site might tell us about Gainey people. Their broken tools would also tell us what they did at the site and perhaps why they were there; how they organized their work, from the distribution of tools, and implied activities, across the site; and possibly something of the nature of the social group. This information promised to give us a fairly detailed picture of a short period in the life of an Ice Age people, and it was welcome enough. But the additional discovery of preserved animal bones that, through the alchemy of radiocarbon dating, might fix this picture in time was nearly staggering.

We found the animal bone in a feature at the base of the plough zone. The upper part of the feature, probably a former hearth or trash pit, had been destroyed by cultivation. But the bottom part, below the depth reached by the plough, remained. We couldn't really see the feature because it wasn't marked by a change in soil colour. Rather, it was defined by a noticeable concentration of artifact material in an otherwise uniform expanse of sandy brown subsoil. The concentration consisted of small chert flakes from tool manufacture or resharpening and a small number of tools and tool fragments: a corner of the base, called the ear, of a Gainey-type point; the thinning, or fluting, flake from another spear point that had been made nearby; a spurred end scraper, a diagnostic Paleo-Indian tool with small tips on both corners of a convex scraping edge, presumably used for piercing or incising; and nine other tool fragments.

A feature of any type is a fairly unusual occurrence on Paleo-Indian sites in eastern North America because the sites are so often near the surface and disturbed. And a feature with culturally diagnostic tools, which unambiguously identify the specific group of people who left it, is more unusual still.

This rare discovery was distinguished by something rarer still, the presence of animal bone. At first glance it looked merely like very, very small white or greyish white specks that contrasted with the sandy brown subsoil. But when seen through a hand lens at ten times magnification the fragments were clearly identifiable by a tell-tale groove or pin-sized hole along which, or through, a blood vessel or capillary once flowed; by the hint of a smooth, rounded surface, ridge, or lip that marked an articular end where one bone had once made contact with another; or by bits of a hollow, lattice-like structure adhering to a thin layer of hard material, a chance cross-section through the bone revealing the inner spongy tissue and the outer dense layer, the characteristic structure of mammal bone. All these fragments were chalky white or greyish white because the bone had been thoroughly burnt – calcined – in a fire. Although fire is usually thought of as destructive, this burning was probably the only reason the bone had survived.

I hadn't expected to find a feature, or the calcined bone. As soon as I learned that the new area in which we were working had been ploughed, my hopes of finding something undisturbed completely evaporated. And I was so pleased with the artifact material we were recovering, especially the Gainey-type fluted points and the ever-growing number of end scrapers, that I temporarily forgot the feature we had found seven years earlier in an adjacent ploughed area of the site. I had also forgotten that the proximity of that feature to the area we were digging in 1987 gave us a better-than-average chance of finding another feature.

Even so, I was incredibly lucky to find the second feature, and especially the calcined animal bone. In fact, I was five times lucky. First, located between the farm buildings, Area A-East containing the Gainey occupation had probably been ploughed only for a short period before the barns and other buildings were constructed, and then possibly only by horse-drawn plough, which would not have reached as deeply as modern equipment. Second, the animal bone in the feature had been calcined: burnt so

0   3 cm

Calcined (burnt) bone fragments from a former firepit at the Udora site. The firepit was located within a small campsite known to have been occupied by Gainey people and also contained fragments of Gainey-type fluted spear points, so the bone fragments are closely associated with a specific group of Early Paleo-Indians, the first discovery of its kind in the Great Lakes region. Several of the identified bone fragments are from caribou, hare, and arctic fox.

Courtesy ROM.

thoroughly that the organic contents had been driven off, leaving only the mineralized structure of the bone. Not subject to decomposition or attack by microorganisms, the calcined fragments were only vulnerable to destruction by mechanical breakdown, a threat reduced by that first lucky break, minimal and low-technology ploughing. Third, after a seven-year delay and one failed attempt I managed to return to the site for a second season of excavation, Fourth, I excavated at just the right place. And fifth, I did it just in time. Only a few months after we excavated Area A-East the landowner levelled the area with a bulldozer and laid down a thick bed of gravel as a parking spot for his heavy construction equipment. I hadn't realized at the time that we were, in essence, doing salvage excavation. The federal granting agency would probably not have supported the project had they known about the landowner's plans. Sometimes it's best not to be able to see too far ahead but to leave some things to chance, at least as long as you're at the right place and moment to seize that chance, when and if it suddenly appears.

We took the entire contents of the feature out of the ground and back to the laboratory in several jars and large plastic bags. After we carefully water-screened the soil through very fine mesh sieves, we had accumulated approximately 290 tiny fragments of bone weighing a total of 293 grams. Although a very small sample this was the only animal bone associated with an Early Paleo-Indian occupation between the eastern Plains and New England, and south to Missouri: nearly the whole mid-continent region. It was priceless, as small things often are. And, as I said in the *Archaeological Newsletter,* it promised to tell us how long ago Gainey people lived and what they hunted. The story continues in the following newsletter:

THE OTHER FACE OF TIME
MAY 1990

The *Archaeological Newsletter* is intended to be a news item about the progress of archaeological research as it is actually being conducted – in the field, the laboratory, or the office, wherever discoveries are made. Over the years, the editors of the *Archaeological Newsletter* have urged writers like me to be spontaneous, to shed their protective academic "waffling," and to put down unedited thoughts such as one might in a letter to someone at home or, from the perspective of the field, to a cloistered colleague. As I sit down to write this, I see that the comparison of the *Archaeological Newsletter* to a letter is perhaps more apt than the editors intended. As is often true of letters, mine is grievously late; in fact, I missed my publication deadline.

Not only that, which is dreadful enough, but the last letter I wrote "back home" was sent over two years ago ... The final irony in this long overdue letter is the subject I wrote about – time.

In November 1987 I had just returned from the field with, among other things, just over 300 grams of burnt animal bone ... and a reasonable possibility of [getting a radiocarbon date] ... For those of you who read the newsletter, this is where the story stopped, and you got on with your lives ... [As for me,] I found myself muttering time and time again, in an ever smaller and weaker voice, "No, I still haven't heard about that bone date."

Not long ago I heard from the lab and can now tell you how the story ends, or the first part of it at any rate. In order to do that, however, let me take you back to that time two years ago when I tucked the bone sample into a safe place at the Museum and started looking for someone to date it.

Although I have only a layman's understanding of the complex technology of radiocarbon dating, I knew that so-called "bone dates" are often unreliable. Hence, in order to get the most out of this material I was going to have to ensure that it go not just to an expert in the area of bone dating but to the expert's expert. The question then became, just how does one find such a person?

The answer to this question came to me while I was slumped in a seat at an international symposium, trying to cope with a serious case of "conference fatigue." After vaguely hearing several somewhat turgid papers, I suddenly found my mind cleared and focused by the words of a new speaker as I listened to Dr Tom Stafford describe his success in using tandem accelerator mass spectrometry, or TAMS, to date milligram amounts of individual amino acids in bone. Some of these amino acids, he explained, provided dates that were very close, if not statistically identical, to dates from samples of known ages derived from wood charcoal, the preferred material for dating. His leading research on this new technology seemed to have been designed just to solve my problem, so as soon as the lights came on I jumped out of my seat and cut him off at the coffee urn. After he regained his composure from my sudden, excited appearance, Tom and I discussed the Udora bone and he readily agreed to analyze a small sample as soon as he relocated from the University of Arizona, where he had been working, to a new lab at the University of Colorado in Boulder.

Time – that elusive process of change that I had been trying to measure in order to link a former geological age with our own – slowly passed in our small dimension of the present, and it wasn't until November 1989 that I received a letter postmarked from Boulder. On the way to my desk to grab a letter opener or anything else sharp that happened to be lying around, I held the letter up to a window to see if I could see numbers through the envelope. Nothing but writing. This wasn't a good sign. A quick scan of the letter picked out scattered phrases that had the impact of a truck: "less than 1/1000 of their original protein," "what remains is exogenous and significantly younger than the bone's geological age," "not datable by any existing method," "if you have additional samples now or in the future please send them along."

Well! That seemed to be that. The "mechanism" in the bone that measured the passage of time had broken down, and the "clock" had stopped. I buried the letter and my disappointment in a "dead" research file and turned to other matters. Somewhat later, when I could focus on the Udora bone again without dark thoughts, I sat down and wrote a letter to a colleague in Maine about another problem in studying the material, namely identifying the animals that were represented. I didn't know it at the time but my dead research file was not to stay dead for long.

Before sending samples of the bone to Tom Stafford for dating I had, of course, made sure that I wasn't sacrificing anything that could be identified. Earlier, Rosemary Prevec, a freelance faunal analyst had gone through the 300 grams of bone to identify whatever was possible, preferably to the species level. Tom Stafford received several small pieces of unidentifiable material. I kept the remainder of the material, including several bone fragments that Rosemary had identified, none much larger than an orange seed and many quite a bit smaller. These bones represented rabbit or hare (either eastern cottontail rabbit, snowshoe hare, or arctic hare), fox (either red, grey, or arctic), and a cervid (either white-tailed deer or caribou). With Rosemary's agreement, and on the chance that this material could be identified more precisely or that additional material might be identified, I wrote to Dr Arthur Spiess in Maine to ask if he would be willing to come to Toronto and go through the material. I thought Art was an excellent choice since he had a lot of experience in identifying caribou, which I was most interested in, and if anyone could transform the "lead" in the bone sample into some sort of "gold," he was just the alchemist for the job.

Art arrived in Toronto with a pocketful of modern caribou and deer toe bones [to compare to my unknown material] – this must have given Canada Customs something to ponder – and a great deal of enthusiasm. I got out the archaeological material and we discussed its potential. Later, I introduced Art to Dr Howard Savage, who built up the incomparable University of Toronto faunal collection, and the three of us arranged a time when Art could examine additional comparative material he hadn't been able to bring along in his pocket. We returned to the ROM, and I showed Art the corner of an office where he could work in peace – and left him to it.

Time passed.

Several days later Art burst into my office, thrust my nose into an odd assortment of the most minute bone fragments and proceeded to explain the importance of miscellaneous bumps, grooves, angles, perforations, and other very subtle things for separating one species or group of animals from another. He had succeeded not only in adding to the list of identified material but, for some fragments, in making more precise identifications than had previously been thought possible. As a result, this collection of about 300 grams of broken, burnt bone is, to my knowledge, the largest collection of identified animal bone from an Early Paleo-Indian site in eastern North America (the next largest collection, from New England, has only two species identifications, not three). Our departmental artist is currently photographing and drawing (with much squinting of eyes) the identified fragments. When they have been safely recorded in this way, we will begin the somewhat more risky job (our technician Anne MacLaughlin says, with a steely glint in her eye, that it's *not* risky at all) of casting the fragments so that copies can be taken to other comparative collections to confirm (or, heaven forbid, refute) the identifications.

The new identifications are, as you can imagine, very satisfying. They are also significant in a quite unexpected way. Art Spiess was able to identify at least one species, and possibly two, that today are largely restricted to a particular environment. Since this environment is also known to have been present in southern Ontario at a specific time in the past, I suddenly realized that the bone itself substituted for a radiocarbon date and will, indirectly, tell us the age of the archaeological site. In a curious way, the bone is, in effect, the reverse side of the clock I had tried to read earlier – the other face of time.

The twisting and turning which is part of the process of scientific inquiry led me back to the possible solution to my original question – how old is it? – when I least expected it. I can't reveal the possible age of the animal bone until Art and I have fully worked over all of the data and other implications; the matter is not, alas, quite as simple as I may have made it appear. In the meantime, life is sweet again; I walk with a lighter step and grin like the Cheshire cat whenever asked about those dates. "In due course," I say, "in due course."

Postscript

In due course. Indeed! Over a decade has passed since that 1990 newsletter. What, you might ask with some hint of exasperation, did we find out? What animal species did Arthur Spiess identify and what environment did they occupy? And how might our knowledge of that environment substitute for a radiocarbon date and indicate the age of the Gainey occupation at Udora?

While I told my colleagues the answers to these questions in a technical paper published with Arthur Spiess in 1994, I didn't tell the general public. So, here again is another example of the need for endings: explanations of what all the enthusiasm and hard work accomplished.

Arthur Spiess managed to identify four bone fragments to the taxonomic level of species and three others to the level of genus: (1) two fragments of toe bones (phalanges) from the hoof and one complete bone (a sesamoid) associated with tendons in the lower leg of caribou (*Rangifer tarandus*); (2) fragments of a mandible, lower hind leg, and front foot of either the snowshoe, or varying, hare (*Lepus americanus*) or the arctic hare (*Lepus arcticus*); and (3) one complete bone from the foot of an arctic fox (*Alopex lagopus*). In all cases these identified bones or bone fragments are extremely small. The single complete caribou bone and hoof fragments are about the size of kidney beans. The bone fragments from hare are not much larger than toothpicks. And the single bone from a fox is about the size of a lima bean.

The identification of caribou was particularly welcome because I had been chasing this species, in a figurative sense, for over fifteen years. The pursuit began in 1971 with my first archaeological surveys in supposed caribou migration routes through the Niagara Escarpment. Later I chased ghost herds of caribou along the former strandline of glacial Lake Algonquin, looking for places where their movements might have been channelled or focused by the lake, thus attracting Ice Age hunters. After a decade and a half of beachcombing I finally caught up with caribou in 1987 at Udora. And by 1994 the question whether Early Paleo-Indians in the Great Lakes region actually hunted caribou was finally no longer subject to speculation. At least for Gainey people.

Caribou would have provided just about everything needed for survival, at least seasonally: food; skins for clothing and shelter; and antler, bone, and sinew for tools. The snowshoe or arctic hare would have provided both food and skins. If trapped in winter the arctic fox would have provided a very attractive fur: white or, more rarely, light blue grey.

Although revealing, these three species almost certainly provide only a very narrow glimpse into Gainey hunting and trapping activities. A complete picture of subsistence would probably include several other animal species and perhaps an even longer list of plants. But despite this, and although the six identified animal bones would fit together into a small and very elegant tea cup, the animals that were identified and the environments

Three identified calcined animal bones excavated in 1987 from a former firepit used by Early Paleo-Indian Gainey people at the Udora site.

Emil Huston, ROM.

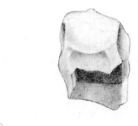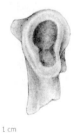

0   1 cm

Distal fragment of a metacarpal from the foot of a hare.

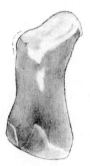

0   1 cm   0   1 cm

Accessory carpal bone from the forepaw of an arctic fox.

Sesamoid bone from the lower leg of a caribou.

in which they live today are familiar to us and thus make the distant past more easily imagined.

These few bones also provide an alternative approach to radiocarbon dating for estimating the age of the Gainey occupation at Udora. We need first to consider the potential of the animals we identified to tell us about the environment and then compare that with what we know from paleo-botanical evidence about the nature and timing of environmental change during late glacial times. Unfortunately, the presence of caribou doesn't tell us very much about the environment. Contrary to the popular image caribou are not exclusively a tundra species. Rather, their ideal habitat is a combination of lichen-bearing forest, where they winter, next to open areas of seasonally luxuriant plant growth, where they give birth in the spring and live in summer. This combination of habitats occurs in the cir-cumpolar taiga, or boreal forest, adjacent to the tundra, in mountainous or hilly regions with alpine tundra or upland grass-sedge meadows sur-rounded by low-lying climax, or long-developed, forest, and in numerous other topographic situations and climates providing a combination of for-est and open habitats. Some herds, or portions of them, may remain in one habitat or another from time to time or, where physically constrained, even live permanently in one habitat, such as on Banks Island in the Canadian arctic archipelago. But the more general pattern involves the seasonal use of both habitats through either long-distance migration such as that between the taiga and the barren grounds in the Northwest Territories or in more localized movements such as in British Columbia and parts of Labrador.

The identification of snowshoe or arctic hare is also not especially helpful for reconstructing the environment since these two species, which belong to the same genus (*Lepus*), have somewhat different ecological tol-erances. The snowshoe hare lives in mid-latitude and subarctic forests, whereas the arctic hare lives in the tundra, although it may also penetrate the boreal forest in winter.

It is the identification of arctic fox that is most significant for recon-structing the environment because this species is more restricted ecologi-cally than either the caribou or the two species of hare belonging to the genus *Lepus*. The arctic fox inhabits the tundra, where it lives on both land and pack ice, although in eastern Canada it lives most commonly in coastal regions. While the southern range of the species coincides with the treeline, isolated individuals may also occasionally drift farther south and penetrate the northern margin of the boreal forest in the winter or spring if in need of food.

Finding arctic fox *with* snowshoe or arctic hare and caribou at the Udora site in southern Ontario indicates that, at the time of occupation by Gainey peoples, the site would have occurred in either a tundra or the northern margin of a boreal forest. Exactly which type of environment depends on the species of hare represented. We would expect to find overlap between arctic fox, caribou, and *arctic hare* in the tundra or near the treeline. Alternatively, if the hare is the *snowshoe hare,* we would expect overlap between all three species at a somewhat more southerly location, in the boreal forest or along its northern edge. These interpretations are based on the assumption that all three species were hunted or trapped within the immediate vicinity of Udora and not brought in from elsewhere.

That's about as far as we can go. It's unfortunate that we can't identify which species of hare is represented or that we didn't recover more animal bone from Udora and identify other species that might provide a less ambiguous picture of the environment. But how quickly we become dissatisfied! After a very long search, I finally had some animal bones to work with. And compared to what I had before – nothing, except for speculation – these few bones represented a huge step forward, regardless of any new limitations they imposed. The somewhat ambiguous environmental picture these animals provide becomes more meaningful when looked at in combination with fossil plant remains, which reflect more directly the late glacial environments in southern Ontario.

As I mentioned earlier, paleobotanists divide the late glacial fossil pollen record in southern Ontario into essentially two zones, and thus units of time. Pollen zone 1, the earlier zone, is referred to as the herb zone and represents an open, treeless environment, essentially a tundra. During this period there is also striking geological evidence of permafrost. This consists of sediment-filled vertical cracks, formerly ice filled, that form interconnecting polygons near the surface of the ground. Some have been found in the vicinity of Kitchener, Ontario, a short distance west of Toronto. Interestingly, the fossil polygons were detected in 1971 by Alan Morgan, a paleoecologist at the University of Waterloo, by deliberate search from a low-flying plane. The polygons became evident late in the growing season because the higher moisture content of the in-filled cracks produced more luxuriant growth in long-rooted cereal crops than did the adjacent undisturbed soil. This differential plant growth revealed the polygonal pattern of the cracks, and their similarity to frost polygons. Judging from climatic conditions in the arctic today where polygons are still actively forming, the fossil polygons in southern Ontario reflect a mean annual temperature of between -3 to -5 degrees centigrade, between 10 and 12 degrees cooler than the present mean annual temperature of 7 degrees centigrade. Morgan suggests that permafrost may have been localized, the result of cold air draining off the ice sheet. The periglacial tundra environment of pollen zone 1, associated with an early period of ice retreat in southern Ontario, ended by perhaps 13,000 years ago.

Pollen zone 2, the Spruce (*Picea*) zone, is characterized by high values for spruce and pine pollen and somewhat lower values – although high by comparison to today – for grasses, sedges, and herbs. Most paleobotanists believe that this pollen assemblage represents a spruce parkland or forest tundra: a sparsely treed environment with large open areas in more exposed habitats, essentially similar, at least in appearance, to the present-day northern edge of the boreal forest near the treeline. This is the type of environment where the arctic fox and the snowshoe or arctic hare identified at Udora would have overlapped, along with caribou. Although there is some disagreement about the lower and upper limiting dates of the Spruce zone, the spruce-parkland environment may have persisted from some time prior to 12,500 years ago to perhaps 10,400 or 10,000 years ago, when it was replaced by a pine-dominated forest with no open areas. Between these dates in central and northern Ontario the margin of the continental ice sheet ice retreated north some 200 kilometres, from the southern Georgian Bay-Lake Simcoe region to north of North Bay on Lake Nipissing and the upper Ottawa River to the east. The zone of ice-induced tundra immediately adjacent to the ice sheet – caused by the proximity of the ice itself, not by the climate – would have moved north as well and thus during the Spruce pollen zone the vegetation in the region of the Udora site would have changed from tundra to spruce parkland. But by the end of the Spruce pollen zone, 10,400 to 10,000 years ago, the Udora region may not have been very distant from the southern margin of the tundra and may therefore have been within range of arctic fox.

This picture of vegetation change during the late glacial period in southern Ontario contains the answer to that frequently asked and dreaded question: How old is it? In the case of the animal bone from Udora, and of course the Early Paleo-Indian occupation there, the answer is more complex than the finite date I had hoped to get from radiocarbon technology. It is an age range extending from the older to the younger limits of the spruce-parkland habitat of pollen zone 2, narrowed slightly by our understanding of the rate of human colonization in North America as a whole. Unexpectedly, this range comes from the ecological preferences of the animals Arthur Spiess identified and from our understanding of vegetational change during the late glacial period.

From this evidence, we can say that Gainey people occupied Udora some time between 12,500 and 10,000 years ago. Allowing for the rate of human colonization in North America known to scholars in 1994, when Arthur Spiess and I started writing our paper, and for uncertainties over the rate of reforestation in southern Ontario, a more conservative range would be from 11,300 to 10,400 years ago. A span of 900 years is certainly very large and not at all like the potential range of a radiocarbon date, which might be as little as 100 years. Unlike a single, finite, and fixed radiocarbon date, however, the paleoecological or faunal age of the Early Paleo-Indian occupation at Udora could be shifted or narrowed and thus made more precise as our understanding improves. Furthermore, the age estimate is based for the most part on local paleoecological data, which is much more appropriate for dating the Paleo-Indian occupation of southern Ontario than are extrapolations from radiocarbon dates in extreme western or eastern North America.

Other Questions

The identification of caribou at Udora raises two other questions: In what season was the site occupied? And how did caribou hunting affect Early Paleo-Indian movements across the province? These are not new questions, of course, but they become more urgent with hard evidence that caribou were indeed hunted by Early Paleo-Indian Gainey people.

The Season of Occupation

Two lines of evidence may indicate which season of the year Gainey people occupied Area A-East at Udora, and both concern caribou.

The first is the co-occurrence of caribou bone and over eighty end scrapers, a tremendous number of tools of this type. Among early historic groups of Native peoples end scrapers were most commonly used for scraping the flesh off the inner surfaces of hides during the tanning process. If the end scrapers were used for this purpose at Udora the activity has several possible implications for season of occupation, depending on how the hides were to be used.

Among historic Inuit, caribou winter pelage – both the hide and the hair covering – was used primarily for tent covers and bedding. The hide was less useful for clothing as it was regarded as too thick for comfort and ease of motion, and the hair sheds easily and abundantly, reducing protection from cold. The summer pelage was less desirable as a raw material because of the numerous holes in the hide caused by infestations of warble fly larvae. After the fly season these wounds healed as the caribou entered peak physical condition during the fall rutting reason and as they gained fat for the long winter. The late fall pelage was thus preferred for clothing, with its relatively thin, unperforated hide and thick undercoat of short hair, yet not too thick covering of outer guard hairs.

If these same seasonal changes in caribou pelage and human preferences prevailed during the late glacial in southern Ontario, then evidence for significant hide-working activity in Area A-East at Udora could indicate either a winter occupation and hide preparation for bedding and tents or a fall occupation and hide preparation for clothing. There is a hint that the skins worked in Area A-East may have come from animals killed in the fall, based on the estimated age of the individual or individuals represented by three caribou bone fragments. Because the three fragments represent roughly the same growth stage and body size, Arthur Spiess believes that the three bones came from a single animal, following the principle that the simplest explanation is also the most likely explanation. They seem to be from a possibly skeletally adolescent between one and two years of age. This would be about the right age for the fall death of an animal born in May or June of the preceding year.

The second line of skeletal evidence for the season of occupation in Area A-East comes from the particular elements in the caribou skeleton: all from the hoof or lower part of the leg. Three other fragments, identifiable only as from a member of the deer family but, again favouring the simplest explanation, probably caribou, also come from the lower leg. Six fragments hardly make for a good sample. Nevertheless, this seeming bias toward the lower leg brings to mind an historic Inuit recipe for a stew or soup made from the feet of animals killed in the late winter and early spring when food stores are low. Feet are desirable because they contain fat and compensate for the leanness of dried meat and the depleted condition of spring-killed caribou. The feet are allowed to accumulate over winter when freezing air temperature preserves them and then used during the first sustained thaws when outdoor work is comfortable. The feet are first skinned and then the toes removed and boiled into a stew along with other bones from the lower leg. After boiling, the discarded bone consists almost entirely of phalanges. Is this the activity that produced the bone at Udora and the accidental burning in a fire? If so, the calcined bone could indicate a late winter and early spring occupation.

Additional evidence for an early spring occupation elsewhere at the Udora site comes from nearby Area A, which produced a cache of tools apparently used to harvest spruce roots for lashing or weaving material. Spruce roots are most pliable in the early spring when the sap starts to run. Although the cache didn't contain unambiguous culturally diagnostic tools, the presence of a Gainey-type spear point a short distance away in the same area suggests that the cache itself may actually have been left by Gainey people. Furthermore, the coincidence of two Gainey occupations in adjacent parts of the site raises the possibility that areas A and A-East were occupied simultaneously.

Thus we have hints of a late winter and early spring occupation and also a fall occupation in Area A-East. These are very weak hints. I would have to come up with strong documentation to convince myself, and my colleagues, that they were both credible and reliable.

To argue for a specific season of occupation based on evidence of hide preparation, for example, I would first have to show from use-wear analysis that the eighty or so end scrapers were actually used to scrape hides rather than some other material. Many Early Paleo-Indian end scrapers from sites in the northeast show wear of a kind thought to result from working a hard substance, such as wood, so the simple identification of a tool as an end scraper does not necessarily indicate the material it was used to work.

To argue for a late winter and early spring occupation from evidence that bone was boiled for food I would have to convince myself that the predominance of bones from the hoof and lower leg of caribou in the feature in Area A-East was the product of *cultural* selection, and not an artificial bias caused by the fact that these particular bones survived because they are denser than many other bones in the skeleton and, also, accidentally found their way into a fire. I would also have to explain why we found no heated and fire-cracked rock with the calcined bone or located reasonably nearby. Large quantities of these rocks would be essential for boiling to extract the grease from the bone, the rocks being heated and dropped into skin bags or skin-lined pits filled with water. But even if I could argue these points successfully, my interpretations might not be fully convincing. This is because ethnographic data, such as the Inuit practice of making stew from caribou toe and lower leg bones, cannot corroborate or prove those interpretations. The ethnographic comparisons are suggestive only, and the burden of proof must be placed on archaeological data and as many independent lines of evidence as possible, all converging on the same interpretation.

Finally, to use information from the tool cache in Area A to support the interpretation of Area A-East, or vice versa, I would have to demonstrate that the two areas were occupied by the same people at the same time. Since there are so few culturally diagnostic tools from Area A, the emphasis would have to be placed on finding evidence for contemporaneity of use. One line of evidence would be matching artifact fragments from both areas. Matches would be expected if broken fragments of individual tools had been taken from one area to the other for reshaping into other tool types or use in spatially separated tasks. Obviously, this analysis would require a painstaking comparison of tool fragments from both areas, involving hundreds, if not thousands, of possible combinations.

I mention these ideas, and some of the ways in which they would have to be explored, because this is the essence of archaeological analysis: imagining possibilities and then coming up with the ways and means of exploring them in both the laboratory and the library. And if you've surmised by now that I'm talking about the present and future, you're absolutely correct. The final analysis of the Udora material has not been completed. This short discussion once again is about beginnings. And for the first time in this book you are on the verge of what is sometimes referred to as the cutting edge. I wouldn't like to apply that somewhat pompous term to my work, although I hope that sometimes I have broken new ground, but it certainly applies well to my personal situation as the work ahead of me at Udora will definitely take me into unfamiliar territory.

Caribou and People: Comings and Goings
The answer to the second question posed earlier, about the effect of caribou seasonal movements in southern Ontario on Early Paleo-Indian Gainey peoples, is unknown because it is bound up in other unanswered questions about the late glacial environment and strategies for finding archaeological and paleontological sites.

Questions about the late glacial environment play a role in this story because caribou behaviour is quite adaptable. The pattern of their seasonal migrations is influenced by many subtly related factors, such as their reproductive cycle, the size of the population, and the carrying capacity of the land, climate and weather, local relief and other aspects of topography, drainage patterns, and, of course, forage. Of all these variables forage is perhaps of central importance because it is the pivotal link between caribou behaviour and the total environment – weather, climate, and landform – within which the animals live.

Caribou forage can be thought of as stratified. At the lowest level it includes terrestrial lichens, fungi, forbs, and shoots of grasses and sedges: all low-growing plants near the ground surface. At the next level of vegetative growth, caribou feed on the shoots and new leafy vegetation of willow and birch. At the highest level of vegetative growth, they eat arboreal lichens: clumps of long, stringy plants that grow suspended from the branches of trees. To the extent that forage influences caribou behaviour, it is the seasonal rhythm of plant growth and the progression of late summer and early fall die-off that affects the pattern of caribou movements. In the spring, as caribou start moving out of the forest and toward calving grounds on the tundra or in open habitats, they feed on growing buds and leaves of willow and new growth of herbaceous plants uncovered by the melting snow. Late in the summer, as this ground cover withers with early frosts, caribou will begin moving in the direction of progressively later plant die-off, toward southern or low-lying spruce forests where, in winter, they eat fungi and the still-green bases of sedges and grasses as long as the plants are accessible through the snow cover. Under conditions of deep snow in mid-winter caribou may feed almost exclusively on arboreal lichens, plants that are best developed in climax spruce forests. Along the edges of frozen lakes and marshes caribou will also feed on water sedges and horsetail (*Equisetum*) protruding through the ice.

Generally this seasonal pattern of plant growth and die-off takes caribou from their winter food range, provided by the forest, to their summer food range, provided by tundra or other open areas. Within these habitats local weather conditions will also determine where caribou will be found. In the tundra the animals seek out areas of early snowmelt that provide access to new plant growth, areas that provide protection from spring storms and freezing rain (which may kill newborn calves), and later in the season windswept areas and residual snowbanks that offer temporary relief from insects. In the forest caribou will seek out areas of light powdery snow that offer access to ground forage, but if this forage is covered by deep snow they will feed on arboreal lichens. During mid-winter thaws caribou may in fact congregate in habitats that provide especially abundant growth of this food.

Feeding patterns and the movements they entail must be taken into account in any reconstruction of the behaviour of prehistoric populations of caribou. At the broadest level this requires knowledge of the pattern of vegetation across the landscape: both the location of and the distance between open areas potentially containing spring and summer forage and woodland or forested areas containing winter forage. How can these vegetation patterns become known?

The basic tool in reconstructing vegetation is, of course, the paleobotanical record. This consists of preserved pollen grains and spores and bits of twigs, seed cones, and other macrofossils held in sediment cores that have been strategically obtained from key areas of the landscape.

Various factors influencing vegetation must also be considered: the pattern of late glacial atmospheric circulation; and the effect on local weather of topography, large bodies of water, and the continental ice sheet itself.

Consider, for example, the effect of water and topography on present-day weather in southern Ontario. Dominant westerly and northerly winds flowing across Lake Huron and Georgian Bay create what is known as a "lake effect": belts of higher precipitation on land downwind of the lakes that in winter form two very prominent snowbelts in southern Ontario. One snowbelt extends north from the Stratford area in the southwestern part of the province to the southern Georgian Bay region between the base of the Bruce Peninsula in the west and Blue Mountain near Collingwood in the east. Here the lake effect is compounded by the presence of an upland region that deflects the air upward, cooling it further and providing even more favourable conditions for the development of snow. This snow-belt is centred over the Dundalk upland, described by two prominent geomorphologists as the "roof" of peninsular Ontario. The upland is formed by the upper surface of the Niagara cuesta – technically, a sloping plain – which rises in an easterly direction from the Huron shoreline at 177 metres above sea level to elevations of over 530 metres, the highest surface in southern Ontario, near the brow of the Niagara Escarpment. In addition to having more snowfall than any other region in southern Ontario, including Algonquin Park, the centre of this snowbelt also has the shortest growing season, perhaps in part because of its elevation.

The second snowbelt, actually part of the first but separated from it by Georgian Bay, is centred over northern Simcoe County, Muskoka District, and the southern portion of Parry Sound District, extending from the Orillia area north to Parry Sound and east to Burks Falls, just west of Algonquin Park.

These present-day snowbelts would probably have been much larger during the late glacial because of the lower mean annual air temperature, two to three degrees centigrade colder than present with possibly a five-degree lower mean January temperature, and the abundant moisture provided by glacial Lake Algonquin in the Huron and Georgian Bay basins. And the snows of winter may have been deeper and persisted longer into spring. What would have been the effect on vegetation? Would these conditions have inhibited vegetation growth and fostered open habitats?

Other questions come to mind. How, for example, would the ice sheet in northern Ontario have affected vegetation? Roughly 11,000 years ago in north-central Ontario the retreating ice front extended from a location north of Sudbury to the upper Ottawa River valley, north of what would

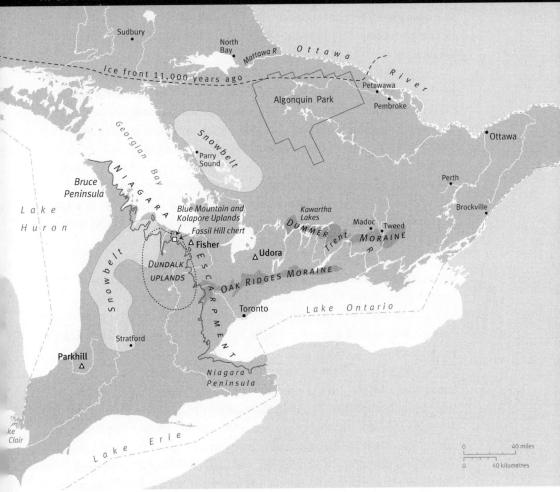

Sudbury

North
Bay

Mattawa R · O t t a w a

Ice front 11,000 years ago

Algonquin Park

Petawawa

Pembroke

R i v e r

Ottawa

Georgian Bay

Snowbelt

Parry
Sound

Perth

Brockville

N I A G A R A

Bruce
Peninsula

Lake
H u r o n

Blue Mountain and
Kolapore Uplands

Fossil Hill chert

△ Fisher

Kawartha
Lakes

D U M M E R

Trent

Madoc

Tweed

M O R A I N E

Trent R

△ Udora

S n o w b e l t

DUNDALK
UPLANDS

E S C A R P M E N T

OAK RIDGES MORAINE

Toronto

L a k e   O n t a r i o

Stratford

Parkhill
△

Niagara
Peninsula

ke
Clair

L a k e   E r i e

| 0 | | 40 miles |
| 0 | | 40 kilometres |

Adapted from Freeman 1979 and various sources.

later become Algonquin Park. The ice front was probably bordered by a narrow zone of raw ground, only recently emerged from beneath the melting ice and not yet re-vegetated. But what lay beyond this zone? A tundra, fostered by the cold, desiccating air that drained off the distant interior of the ice mass? Or did trees grow right up to the ice front, even on the ice itself, on sediments formerly carried within the ice and later exposed on the surface by melting ice, perhaps even burying masses of stagnant ice? Whether tundra or spruce parkland, how wide was this zone before one reached more mature habitats farther south that had been deglaciated decades or centuries earlier?

What about these more mature habitats? Would the Niagara Peninsula have been somewhat milder during the late glacial period, for the same reason it is today, because of its more southerly location in Ontario and the moderating influence of adjacent lakes on air temperature? If so, would this area, one of the earliest to become reforested because of its proximity to plant refugia south of the lakes, have fostered the development of old-growth and therefore lichen-rich spruce forests? Would lichen-rich forests have developed for the same reasons in extreme southwestern Ontario, along the north shore of the Erie basin and around the basin of Lake St Clair between Ontario and Michigan?

Finally, what about south-central Ontario? What would have been the effect on local vegetation and consequent caribou movements of the rugged, hilly country of the Oak Ridges Interlobate Moraine, which stretches across the middle part of the province from the edge of the Niagara Escarpment near Orangeville in the west to beyond Peterborough in the east?

Simply raising these questions forces one to think about southern Ontario as a whole and the effect of regional topographic differences on vegetation. It is clear from a map that during the late glacial period and the life of glacial Lake Algonquin southern Ontario was nearly bisected from north to south. It looked much like the palm side of the upraised left hand, fingers pointing upward. On the left, the base of the thumb represents southwestern Ontario, and the tip, the lower part of the Bruce Peninsula. The remainder of the peninsula would have been inundated by glacial Lake Algonquin, which would also form the gap between the thumb and the fingers. On the right, the palm and fingers represent central Ontario extending from the Ontario basin in the south to the ice sheet in the north.

Could these somewhat separate regions – the thumb of southwestern Ontario and the fingers and palm of the central part of the province – have fostered the development of two patterns of caribou movement?

In western Ontario, seasonal migrations between potential old-growth spruce forests around the southern Huron and Erie basins and, in the north, open areas on the Dundalk uplands would have occurred essentially in a large cul-de-sac, nearly surrounded by lakes, encompassing distances of 100 to 150 kilometres. In central Ontario seasonal migrations between old-growth spruce habitats south of the Oak Ridges Interlobate Moraine, for example, and open habitats or tundra adjacent to the ice sheet in the region of Algonquin Provincial Park would have covered a much larger area and encompassed distances nearly twice as great, upwards of 300 kilometres.

This has important implications for human hunting patterns. Since caribou are in constant motion during periods of migration, no historically known human groups attempted to keep up with moving herds. Rather, the hunting strategy was based on interception of migrating herds. By analogy, in central Ontario, Paleo-Indian hunters may have been limited to intercept hunting during the return of caribou to the southern forests in the late fall. Udora may have occurred in an intercept region. In the cul-de-sac of western Ontario, however, because of the smaller size of the region and the shorter distances between winter and summer caribou habitats, Paleo-Indians may very well have been able to maintain intermittent contact with caribou year round, intercepting herds returning to the southern forests in the late fall and then moving to the northern summering grounds on the Dundalk uplands where caribou could have been hunted as encountered. There would have been the additional attraction of Fossil Hill chert for toolstone in the Kolapore uplands in the southern Georgian Bay region, which may have contained summering herds of caribou. Evidence that Gainey people at Udora, in central Ontario, used Fossil Hill chert suggests that Paleo-Indians moved between southwestern and central Ontario and thus did not develop regionally distinctive patterns of exploiting caribou.

Although these speculations have been expressed as possibilities they are in fact questions, like the environmental questions posed earlier. No one has the answers yet. And a model of late glacial vegetation patterns for Ontario has yet to be developed, although it is an entirely feasible undertaking and has been attempted elsewhere.

In addition to the paleoenvironmental studies, one final category of evidence would be required in any attempt to reconstruct late glacial caribou behaviour in southern Ontario: abundant fossils. Growth patterns in caribou teeth, antler, and parts of the skeleton would provide evidence for the season of death of caribou in different parts of the province.

This would tell us not only *where* caribou were but *when* they were there, crucial information for reconstructing the seasonal pattern of habitat use and the direction and distance of movements between those habitats. We don't even begin to have this information. Why?

To answer this it's interesting to consider another part of the world. Western Germany, like southern Ontario, has a continental climate unfavourable to organic preservation. Beginning perhaps 14,000 years ago, following the retreat of the ice sheet from its last major advance,

Second to None: Early Paleo-Indian Big Game Hunting in Western North America

In the southern Plains of the United States, Early Paleo-Indians hunted both mammoth and forms of bison now extinct. In fact, the kill sites are a substantial, even overwhelming, part of the Early Paleo-Indian archaeological record in western North America. These sites provide a strong contrast with much slimmer evidence in eastern North America that Early Paleo-Indians there may also have hunted mammoth, mastodon, and bison, although in different environments and possibly in quite different ways. It is likely that eastern Early Paleo-Indians more commonly hunted caribou in the tundra and spruce parkland of the greater northeast and white-tailed deer in the forested southeast. But historically, it was big game hunting in the southern Plains that first became known to archaeologists.

Folsom

Folsom, New Mexico, is the type site of the Folsom culture. A type site in archaeology and paleontology is the discovery site that first produces material not seen before and to which subsequent discoveries at other sites are compared. The site is located in Wild (or Dead) Horse Arroyo, about nineteen kilometres west of the town of Folsom. It was discovered in 1908, excavated between 1926 and 1928, and provided the first evidence that humans were both contemporaneous with extinct animals and also had considerable antiquity in the New World. Since the discovery at Folsom, other sites of this culture and isolated artifacts have been found from the Plains of southern Canada to northern Mexico and from the Rocky

Mountains to Missouri, Illinois, and Wisconsin. Ironically, although Folsom was the first Early Paleo-Indian site to be discovered and excavated, both the size and age of the bison kill there were poorly understood until it was reinvestigated in the late 1990s.

Radiocarbon dates obtained within the last decade indicate that the bison kill at Folsom occurred around 10,890 years BP, making this one of the earliest Folsom kill sites known. Reanalysis of the bison bone indicates that the herd consisted of at least thirty-two longhorn bison of an extinct subspecies (*Bison bison antiquus*). The animals were driven up an arroyo, killed, and partially butchered. The tail bones are missing from several animals, suggesting that the hides were removed. At the time of the kill, the hunters were travelling in a northwesterly direction from central Texas. This is indicated by the tools left at the kill and the geological origins of the stone from which they were made: from sources ranging between 230 and 575 kilometres southeast of Folsom.

Other Folsom bison kills in the southern Plains range from just a few animals to small herds. The Lipscomb Bison Quarry in Texas is perhaps the largest Folsom bison kill known, involving at least fifty-two animals. This site consists of a bone bed approximately six metres in an east-west direction and thirty metres long. Some of the skeletons are badly broken and scattered, while others are mainly complete and articulated. In one small area fourteen articulated skeletons partially overlap one another and were oriented in generally the same direction when killed, presumably dur-

Germany and adjacent parts of central Europe were recolonized from refugia in southwest France by big game hunters of Upper Paleolithic cultures. In the region from the Alps to the North Sea, encompassing parts of Switzerland, western Germany, and Denmark, these Paleolithic people moved into a steppe tundra/parkland environment and hunted a wide range of Ice Age and modern species. One of the most important of these was reindeer, the European term for caribou, both being included in the species *Rangifer tarandus*.

ing a stampede, or drive, initiated and directed by a large group of hunters.

In the southern Plains, Folsom bison kills appear to have been made in the late summer and early fall. Unlike late prehistoric and historic bison hunters, Folsom people don't appear to have processed bone for the marrow, an essential element for making pemmican. Instead, recently identified stone filleting tools suggest that they preserved meat solely by drying it in long, thin strips. In the northern Plains, Folsom people appear to have hunted bison in the late fall and early winter and preserved the meat by freezing it in caches.

Unfortunately, except for bison hunting, little else is known about Folsom subsistence. There is some evidence that Folsom peoples also hunted or trapped other big game such as mountain sheep and small game such as cottontail and marmot. Many sites contain bone fragments from a variety of medium-sized and small animals but it's often difficult to determine whether these species were actually hunted or trapped, or simply died natural deaths and became intruded into archaeological sites. Folsom people probably exploited plant foods although there is little evidence for this. Unfortunately, most of our information about subsistence comes from bison bone beds (which may be more readily preserved and discovered than other types of sites) and campsites related to the processing of bison kills. Consequently, other aspects of Folsom subsistence, particularly small game trapping and wild plant harvesting, are too poorly represented for

us to estimate their importance relative to bison and other big game hunting.

Clovis
Blackwater Draw Locality No. 1, New Mexico, discovered in 1932, is the type site for the Clovis culture in North America. In 1936, this site also provided the first stratigraphic evidence that Clovis predated Folsom, a fact later confirmed by radiocarbon dating. At Blackwater Draw, Clovis-type spear points were initially found directly associated with the skeletons of two mammoth (*Mammuthus columbi*). Because of later discoveries of Clovis points with mammoth remains at this and roughly a dozen other sites extending from the northwestern Plains to the desert Southwest, Clovis people have become thought of as big game hunters par excellence. But is this reputation deserved? How did Clovis people kill mammoths? And did they hunt only big game?

Lehner Ranch, Arizona
This site is located in extreme southeastern Arizona, about sixteen kilometres from another Clovis mammoth kill – a single animal – at a site called Naco. The thirteen skeletons at Lehner consist of seven immature animals, ranging from two to fourteen years old, and six mature ones, the oldest being twenty-eight to thirty years old. Jeffrey Saunders, the paleontologist who later restudied the excavated material, believes that the age profile at Lehner is similar to that of family groups of modern African elephants (*Loxodonta africana*) and therefore that the oldest Lehner

animal was a female matriarch and leader of the family. This age structure is the basis of his interpretation that the Lehner mammoths were members of a single family unit killed by Clovis hunters in a single catastrophic event. He also believes that the single animal at the nearby Naco site, whose skeleton contained eight Clovis points, may have been a wounded member of the same family that escaped to die elsewhere.

Using similar evidence, Saunders argues that entire family groups were also killed by Clovis hunters at as many as five other sites in western North America. If so, this suggests that Clovis people confronted herds as part of their subsistence strategy. Nevertheless, they may also have been opportunistic hunters. A total of five other kill sites may represent isolated kills of mature animals or natural deaths that Clovis people opportunistically encountered and scavenged for meat.

Modern experiments with replicas of Clovis-type spear points show that these weapons were capable of piercing elephant hide and penetrating to vital organs. But how could entire herds have been killed? Assuming that mammoth behaviour was comparable to that of modern elephants, Saunders argues that the Clovis hunters could have killed entire family units by beginning with the matriarch. Once the matriarch was down, the rest of the family could be killed as it milled about in confusion, trying to revive the leader. This strategy works well today in Africa, using rifles for culling elephant populations. Clovis hunters may also have attacked the matriarch first. But exactly how the hunters coordinated this first kill and then accomplished the mass kill with spears is unknown, and perhaps unknowable.

The interpretation that Clovis hunters confronted and killed entire herds of mammoths has been questioned by some archaeologists. But it has been most seriously challenged by a biologist and specialist in taphonomy, Gary Haynes. Taphonomy, most broadly defined, is the study of how animal behaviour and geological processes influence the way in which skeletal remains enter the archaeological and geological record. Haynes argues that the age profile of the mammoths at Lehner and other sites is more similar to a die-off due to environmental stress, such as drought, than to the catastrophic death of a complete family group. Using information from modern African elephant kills and ethnographic descriptions of them, the paleontological record, and taphonomic studies, Haynes argues that Clovis people acted not so much like active predators but as spectators at mammoth die-offs around water holes, where they killed the dying and scavenged the recently dead that had been weakened by environmental stresses of the end of the Ice Age, a time of widespread mammalian extinction. The argument is persuasive and also implicates Paleo-Indians in at least some extinctions, although in a minor role and not as a cause.

Clovis people are believed to have hunted forms of now-extinct bison and possibly other large animals. Camel, for example, has been reported at one Clovis site in Wyoming. At that location, a single animal may have become mixed accidentally with a small group of bison that was being driven to a containment area where they and, opportunistically, the camel were then killed.

Almost nothing is known of Clovis use of small animals, birds, or wild plant foods. This disparity and possible bias in the archaeological record, and the highly visible nature of mammoths and bison, may be the reason Clovis people have acquired the reputation of being largely, or even exclusively, big game hunters, although the reputation may be undeserved.

The remains of reindeer and other mammals, birds, and fish that were part of the subsistence of Paleolithic peoples have been found at nearly three dozen sites in western Germany and adjacent regions. One of these sites, near Hamburg in northwestern Germany, produced over 17,000 fragments of reindeer bone and antler, including the better part of an entire skeleton. Despite this, German and other archaeologists working with Paleolithic sites are not satisfied with the faunal record because it is not as complete as they would like. And perhaps they're right. But the contrast with southern Ontario, a region nearly as large as western Germany, is shocking. It has produced only one Early Paleo-Indian site with faunal remains: Udora. This contrast is all the more disturbing when it's extended to all of eastern North America. This huge area has produced perhaps one-third as many late glacial archaeological sites with faunal remains as are known from just a small part of western Europe.

What accounts for this difference? Both regions today have continental climates, and both are underlain over large areas by limestones and dolomites (magnesium-rich limestone), which lead to the formation of alkaline soils favourable to bone preservation. What other than climate and soils might explain the difference between the Early Paleo-Indian archaeological record in eastern North America and the Upper Paleolithic record in western Europe? Perhaps where you look! Many of the archaeological sites in western Europe that have produced faunal remains are caves and rockshelters, much like the Dutchess Quarry Caves in New York State, which produced both Pleistocene-age faunal remains and Early Paleo-Indian fluted points, although they were probably not associated. In Europe, however, preserved faunal remains have also been found in open-air sites, often downslope from artifact concentrations in ploughed fields, buried in glacial lake deposits beneath wet meadows, or beneath postglacial-age peat deposits in bogs. Reading about these sites I have occasionally thought back to my work at Fisher and Udora. These sites, situated on the edge of glacial Lake Algonquin, are adjacent to modern bogs. What would I have found if I had put on a pair of rubber boots, walked into the edge of those bogs with a shovel and water pump, and dug below the wet deposits that have built up over the floor of that glacial lake? Would I have found bones, as the Germans do? And how many Early Paleo-Indian kill sites or even campsites might be found on the edge of other former glacial lakes and wetlands in southern Ontario, extending north across cottage country up to the retreating border of the ice sheet 11,000 years ago, and beyond?

We may never know if discovery is left entirely to archaeologists. There are too few of them, and precious little money. And of equal or possibly greater importance, of those few archaeologists fewer still are in employment that would support such a quest. If archaeological sites are to be found the discoveries will most likely have to be made by a farmer draining a bog for a new field, a bulldozer operator digging a house foundation or a septic system, a cottage owner digging out a bank for a boathouse or pier foundation, a person fishing and glancing at an eroded river bank, or a canoeist, or swimmer, or hiker, or child playing in the water … anyone who happens to notice something in the ground. Whether that something will enter the realm of scientific inquiry – and, later, human knowledge – depends on what the person does next.

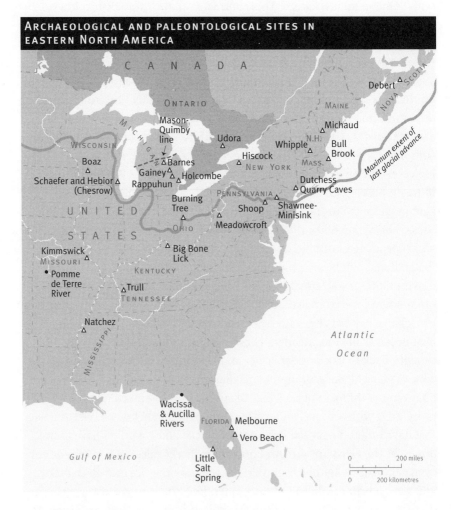

ARCHAEOLOGICAL AND PALEONTOLOGICAL SITES IN EASTERN NORTH AMERICA

The map shows archaeological and paleontological sites, geographic areas, and rivers that have produced evidence of Late Pleistocene human subsistence and adaptations.

Broader Considerations

Outside Ontario caribou remains have been found in Paleo-Indian sites elsewhere in the Great Lakes region and in the northeastern United States. The nearest discovery is from the Holcombe site north of Detroit, which produced a single fragment of a caribou toe bone, a phalange.

This site, situated on a strandline of a small glacial lake that probably drained into glacial Lake Algonquin, was occupied by people who made basally thinned, rather than fluted, points. Because of the association with glacial Lake Algonquin, the excavators argued that Holcombe was occupied by Early Paleo-Indian peoples. Because of the basally thinned points, however, critical reviewers of the excavation report have suggested that Holcombe is a Late Paleo-Indian site.

Caribou bones have also been reported from caves 1, 8, and 9 in the Dutchess Quarry Caves in southeastern New York State. Caves 1 and 8 also contained three complete and two incomplete Early Paleo-Indian fluted points. Several radiocarbon dates from the bone, ranging from 12,720 to 13,840 years BP (roughly 1,200 to 2,300 years older than the earliest dated Clovis site in North America), indicate that the caribou bones predate the Early Paleo-Indian occupation of North America. Caribou probably lived in northeastern North America throughout the last, Wisconsinan, glaciation and possibly earlier, and the bones at Dutchess Quarry Caves were probably carried there by carnivores.

In New England caribou bone has been recovered from two Early Paleo-Indian sites: the southwestern New Hampshire Whipple site, which produced three fragments identified as caribou; and the Bull Brook site north of Boston, which produced a single fragment of caribou bone. Several other fragments from both sites could be identified only as belonging to a cervid, most likely deer or caribou although this taxonomic group also includes elk and moose. Other fragments were identified more generally as from medium-sized or large mammals. Interestingly, Bull Brook also produced a single bone fragment from the modern species of beaver, much smaller than the Pleistocene species.

Finally, the Michaud site in Maine produced a single antler fragment tentatively identified as from a cervid.

That's all. This is the sum total of faunal evidence from eastern North America that Early Paleo-Indians hunted caribou. If we exclude the single identified bone from Holcombe because of the possibility the people there were Late Paleo-Indians and the material from Dutchess Quarry Caves because it predates the Paleo-Indian use of the caves, our evidence for caribou hunting is derived from just three sites: Udora, Whipple, and

Bull Brook. Between them they produced seven bones firmly identified as caribou. Seven!

To this we might add provocative evidence of a different sort: the analysis of blood residues preserved on the cutting edges of Early Paleo-Indian tools. To date blood residues have been reported from two artifacts, an end scraper from the Shoop site in eastern Pennsylvania that may contain blood protein from a cervid, and a fluted spear point from the Debert site in Nova Scotia that is said to contain proteins from caribou. But some archaeologists are doubtful about these results, and about blood-residue analysis generally. If this evidence is discounted we are again left with only the seven identified caribou bones as the sum of our evidence for Early Paleo-Indian caribou hunting. Obviously, we can't tell from the

New Evidence for Mastodon and Mammoth Hunting in the Great Lakes Region

Bones of the American mastodon (*Mammut americanum*), and to a lesser extent mammoth (*Mammuthus primigenius*), are among the most numerous Pleistocene fossils in eastern North America. Mastodon and mammoth bones were often encountered in the late nineteenth century by farmers or construction crews while trenching through bogs and other wetlands to drain them. In fact, bones have been discovered intermittently down to the present day. Unfortunately, they have not always been excavated carefully, and in several cases artifacts possibly associated with mastodon bones have not been well documented. There is still doubt, for example, whether a mastodon discovered by farm boys near Boaz, Wisconsin, in 1897 was actually associated with an Early Paleo-Indian spear point, though hearsay evidence suggests it was.

Unfortunately, the epitaph *possible but not proven* also applies to other, much more recent excavations of mastodon remains in the Great Lakes region. Short field studies, frequently of an emergency nature, and brief announcements of mastodon-human associations have often not been followed up by careful excavation and detailed studies of the bones and the circumstances of their deposition. This lack is critical, for the bogs where mastodon bones are most often found are complex places, subject to many disturbances that can bring objects together that

were never associated. These disturbances can also mimic the effects of human activity.

Fortunately, the long history of neglect, or at least insufficient attention, to mastodon and mammoth sites may be over. Today several long-term studies in the Great Lakes region have produced some surprising discoveries. One such study, initiated in the mid-1980s, is being conducted by paleontologist Daniel Fisher at the University of Michigan's Museum of Paleontology in Ann Arbor. Fisher's work is extraordinary for its ingenuity and comprehensiveness, and because it has produced a framework for conducting research and testing hypotheses that can be applied to the study of any paleontological site where the question of human involvement arises.

Fisher started his work with the excavation of three mastodon sites in southern Michigan and a study of six mastodon collections in the Ann Arbor museum. At each site, Fisher looked for patterns in bone distribution and disarticulation (the separation of skeletal elements) that would indicate whether elements had been pried apart or the carcass cut into units and rearranged in non-anatomical order, presumably from human butchery, transport, and re-deposition. In museum collections, Fisher looked for tool marks and fresh bone breaks. Finally, he determined, when possible, the season of death of the animal, based on the final growth laminations in the tusk.

seven fragments how often caribou were hunted or how important this species was in the diet.

A handful of other bones tell us that in addition to caribou Early Paleo-Indians trapped snowshoe or arctic hare, arctic fox, and beaver, and also fished. And within the last decade several archaeological and paleontological sites have provided clear evidence that Early Paleo-Indians in the Great Lakes and broader mid-continent region occasionally killed or scavenged mastodon and, to a lesser extent, mammoth. We are thus gradually building up the details we need to reconstruct the lives of an Ice Age people. But as hard won and exotic as these details might be, their simple accumulation alone won't add up to a meaningful picture. The details remain just that ... details.

Fisher eventually expanded his study to nineteen sites. These fell into two categories: those where mastodons appeared to have been butchered (ten locations), and those where they had apparently not (nine locations). He then noticed an interesting correlation: animals that showed evidence of human butchery invariably died in the late fall or early winter, whereas those that showed no evidence of human butchery died in the late winter or early spring. He also noticed other patterns. Eight of ten butchered animals were male and most were either relatively young or in their prime. The non-butchered animals were roughly equally divided between males and females, suggesting randomness. From this, Fisher developed the hypothesis that late Ice Age people actively hunted mastodon in the late fall, when the animals were in their prime, and tended to focus on male animals, presumably because they were more solitary and therefore less dangerous to hunt than females, which may have moved about in family herds like modern elephants. The late winter, early spring deaths, Fisher reasoned, were natural events precipitated by weakness or ill-health after a season of stress and selectively preserved at bogs where the sick animals sought water.

Fisher later applied his approach to single skeletons found at the Heisler site in southern Michigan and the Burning Tree site in east-central Ohio. Both yielded evidence that the animals had been butchered by humans. The Heisler mastodon died 11,400 years ago, the Burning Tree mastodon 11,800 years ago (a bit earlier than the earliest dated Clovis site). And both animals died in the late autumn, supporting Fisher's earlier hypothesis of seasonal hunting. In addition, the evidence at both sites suggested that the several piles of butchered remains had been cached in shallow ponds for later use. Most remarkable, Fisher found evidence at the Michigan site of anchors used to hold down the meat caches. These ovoid masses of sand and gravel surrounded by a thin layer of finely chopped plant material were the casts of filled sections of mastodon intestine stuffed with sediment much as a sausage and, fortuitously, lined by what the animals had last eaten. Fisher's experiments with underwater caching of a butchered horse, which remained edible for a long period, demonstrated that this would have been a viable method of food storage. Finally, at both Heisler and Burning Tree, sediments in the area of the intestinal cavity of the animal contained dormant bacteria that had lived in the gut and helped the mastodon digest plant material. Truly, the potential of undisturbed and carefully excavated and studied bone deposits is stunning.

The second research program on mastodons, by Richard Laub, a geologist at the Buffalo Museum of Science, is undoubtedly the longest

But there is another way to use these scraps of information, and everything else we know about the Early Paleo-Indian archaeological record, to develop a coherent picture of how these people may have lived. This approach was taken in the mid-1980s by David Meltzer, a young scholar who tackled the issue for his doctoral dissertation. The central question that concerned him is whether Early Paleo-Indian peoples in eastern North America were specialized big game hunters, an assumption, he pointed out, that was derived from discoveries in the High Plains and the Southwest of Early Paleo-Indian artifacts associated with extinct forms of bison and mammoth.

Meltzer was dubious. He reminded the archaeological community that evidence for big game hunting in eastern North America is limited. In the mid-1980s direct evidence for mastodon hunting or scavenging was

New Evidence for Mastodon and Mammoth Hunting *continued*

excavation of a mastodon paleontological site that has ever been conducted, anywhere: over twenty years at the time of writing. The site, named Hiscock after the landowner, has thus far produced the remains of nine mastodons as well as a rich record of late Ice Age plants and animals, including caribou, stag-moose, California Condor, and giant beaver. The site has also produced five Early Paleo-Indian fluted points, one other stone artifact, a stone bead, thirteen expedient tools of mastodon and cervid bone and ivory, and, most amazing of all, a fragment of a net or textile. None of these artifacts was directly associated with the mastodon bones, but two shaped bone tools, most likely from mastodon, were dated at 10,810 and 10,990 years BP and fall into the period of Early Paleo-Indian occupation. If the mastodons weren't actually killed by humans, their bones were used as raw material for tool manufacture. Two of the nine animals appear to have died in the late winter or middle spring and thus do not fall into the pattern of death and presumed human hunting postulated by Daniel Fisher. Thus, Hiscock appears to be both an archaeological site – since it was at least visited by humans – and a natural death site for mastodons.

The final, and most recent, study emerged from archaeological excavations conducted in advance of urban development. This project, directed by David Overstreet of the Great Lakes

Archaeological Research Center in Milwaukee, Wisconsin, led to the discovery of stone tools in direct association with mammoth bones (possibly woolly mammoth – *Mammuthus primigenius*) at two sites in extreme southeastern Wisconsin. At the Schaefer site, dated at around 10,900 years ago, two, possibly three, artifacts were found directly associated with the bones of a thirty-year-old adult male mammoth. At the Hebior site, dated around 12,500 years ago, three artifacts were found associated with a nearly complete skeleton of another mammoth of undisclosed species, also an adult male. A fourth artifact, a chopper, was found nearby. The artifact associations at both sites are well documented and thus seem unquestionable, but the date for Hebior is surprising since it is roughly 1,000 years older than the oldest dates for Clovis in the west.

The work of Fisher, Laub, and Overstreet seem to resolve one question: whether humans hunted, or at least scavenged, mammoth and mastodon in the Great Lakes region. The answer is a qualified yes for mammoth and a more confident yes for mastodon, at least occasionally. But the work leaves open another question: If some of these sites pre-date the earliest known Clovis, who was it that did the hunting or scavenging? An earlier group of Clovis? People who were ancestral to Clovis? Or people of another identity altogether?

well documented at perhaps only a single site in the mid-continent region: Kimmswick, Missouri, approximately 32 kilometres south of St Louis, where the remains of mastodon were reported in direct association with two Clovis points and other artifacts. Meltzer reviewed other evidence briefly. He noted that in Wisconsin the association of artifacts with the so-called Boaz mastodon was ambiguous. In Michigan the close similarity in the northernmost occurrence of both mastodon remains and isolated fluted spear points discovered in ploughed fields – the so-called Mason-Quimby line – was only circumstantial evidence for association between mastodon and humans. Elsewhere in Michigan evidence of human activity and butchery at the Rappuhun mastodon site was not fully documented. For the remainder of eastern North America, Meltzer thought that there was no acceptable evidence for mastodon-human association despite hundreds of discoveries of mastodon bone from bogs and wetlands. As for other Ice Age fauna the record was little better, coming only from Florida. In that state two sites produced evidence of association between humans and Ice Age fauna: extinct bison and, interestingly, giant land tortoise.

Thus in the mid-1980s the mastodon kill or butchering site at Kimmswick in Missouri, the caribou bone from the Whipple and Bull Brook sites in New England, and two occurrences of human artifacts with extinct fauna in Florida were the only direct evidence for Early Paleo-Indian big game hunting in all of eastern North America. Data from Udora were still ten years in the future. Clearly, the faunal record was too slim to tell us much about Early Paleo-Indian hunting.

But perhaps looking *only* at the faunal record was too narrow an approach. Meltzer suggested that the focus of Early Paleo-Indian subsistence and other adaptations to late Ice Age environments might be apparent in the *structure* of the archaeological record: the contents and arrangement of those contents in space. The idea assumed that different human adaptations (which, in effect, created the archaeological record) produced different and characteristic structures. Meltzer suggested further that by combining our knowledge of late glacial environments in eastern North America with an understanding of ecological opportunities for and constraints to human adaptations it was possible to predict, first, how humans might adapt under particular environmental conditions, and second, how different adaptations would structure the archaeological record. These predictions could then be tested by examining that record.

For the purpose of his study Meltzer divided eastern North America, extending from the Mississippi valley to the Atlantic, into two broad regions: the formerly glaciated north and the unglaciated southeast.

Did They or Didn't They? Big Game Hunting in the Southeastern United States

In the late 1920s and early 1930s, the association of Folsom, and later, Clovis spear points with extinct bison and mammoth in the southwestern United States was an historical precedent. It established that humans did, indeed, have appreciable antiquity in the New World. These discoveries and others that followed soon suggested to many archaeologists that Early Paleo-Indians were big game hunters throughout North America, a notion that persisted for several decades and still echoes today.

In an important review paper in the mid-1980s, David Meltzer reviewed the Early Paleo-Indian record from eastern North America. He concluded that in the southeastern United States, Early Paleo-Indians probably had a generalized subsistence, based on forest resources such as white-tailed deer, a wide range of small to mid-sized mammals, and wild plants. In drawing this conclusion, however, he also downplayed strong hints that the picture is probably more complex.

The complexity begins at the Kimmswick site in eastern Missouri. There, in 1981, Clovis artifacts were reported in association with mastodon bones and two other extinct taxa: giant ground sloth (*Glossotherium harlani*); and long-nosed peccary (*Mylohyus nasutus*), distantly related to Old World pigs. Interestingly, the sloth is represented not by bones from the skeleton but by small bones, called dermal ossicles, which grew in the skin. Of course the skin decomposed long ago but the dermal ossicles suggest that the hide was carried to the site for use, perhaps as a shelter.

But Kimmswick is unusual. Looking east from there into the southeast, the picture of late Ice Age human-animal associations is nearly blank, though not due to the absence of a paleontological record. In fact, there is a surprisingly large record of late glacial and earlier fauna from the region. In a major overview of the North American

paleontological record published in 1980, nearly eighty paleontological sites were described from all eleven states in the southeastern United States. Animal remains are preserved in caves, bedrock fissures, sink holes, swamps, springs, salt domes, river beds, and even unconsolidated sandy deposits. Florida, Missouri, and Tennessee contained the greatest number of paleontological sites and some of the most famous, such as the Vero Beach and Melbourne sites in Florida, and many localities in the Pomme de Terre River valley in west-central Missouri. In the mid-nineteenth century, this region was well known for its fossils and produced the famous reconstructed skeleton of the "Missouri Leviathan" (American mastodon), found by Alfred Koch (1804-67) and on display in the British Museum in London since 1842. Other famous sites include Big Bone Lick in Kentucky, first collected by French soldiers in 1793 (thus becoming the first widely known paleontological site in North America), and the Natchez site located approximately ten kilometres east of that city in southwestern Mississippi. This site became famous in the mid-nineteenth century, when a portion of a human pelvis was reportedly found below the skeletons of three ground sloths (*Megalonyx*). Two other paleontological sites became famous in the first two decades of the twentieth century when they also produced human remains in association with extinct fauna: Melbourne and Vero Beach located in central Florida on the Atlantic coast, approximately 95 and 150 kilometres southeast of Orlando. Today, these human remains are regarded as Holocene burials that intruded into, and are therefore much younger than, the deposits containing extinct ground sloth, mammoth, and horse.

The numerous paleontological sites in the southeast demonstrate that many now extinct animals lived in the region during the last glacial period:

mammoth (*Mammuthus*), American mastodon (*Mammut americanum*), Harlan's ground sloth (*Glossotherium harlani*), and Jefferson's ground sloth (*Megalonyx jeffersonii*, about the size of an ox when full grown), extinct bison (*Bison antiquus*), muskox, horse, and at least two forms of peccaries (*Platygonus compressus*, flat-headed peccary, and *Mylohyus nasutus,* long-nosed peccary). Associated with these animals were such predators as sabre-toothed cat (*Smilodon fatalis*, about the size of a lion but with enormously long, curved canines) and dire wolf (*Canis dirus,* about the size of a grey wolf but heavier in build and with a powerful dentition designed for hyena-like scavenging as well as hunting).

Knowing that these and other species lived during the late glacial period and may have overlapped with human occupation is one thing, but actually demonstrating that humans hunted any of them is quite another problem. Over the past decade or so, however, a growing body of evidence has indicated that Early Paleo-Indian peoples in the southeast actually hunted some of the late glacial fauna. In 1979 in a flooded sinkhole at Little Salt Springs, southwestern Florida, the remains of a giant land tortoise (*Geochelone crassiscutata*) were found pierced with a wooden spear dated at 12,030 years BP. The tortoise had been speared behind the right foreleg between the carapace and the plastron, the hard underside of the body. The animal was then overturned and cooked in place and eaten. In 1984 on the bed of the Wacissa River, northwestern Florida, the partial skull, with horn cores, of an extinct form of bison (*Bison antiquus*) believed to date around 11,000 years ago was found pierced by a stone spear point.

More recently, material from the Aucilla River in northwest Florida and a site in Tennessee has provided evidence of associations between humans and proboscideans: cut marks on bones or tusks; artifacts associated, or near, disarticulated bones; and ivory artifacts made from mastodon or mammoth tusks, possibly used as foreshafts for darts or spears. Of course, the sites producing these provocative discoveries can't tell us whether Paleo-Indians butchered animals that had died natural deaths, scavenged tusks from bone deposits, or actually hunted proboscideans.

The record of associations between Paleo-Indians and the rich Ice Age fauna of the southeastern United States is still very fragmentary. David Meltzer, writing in 1993, stated that in North America as a whole Early Paleo-Indians were probably opportunists with respect to big game hunting and generalists with respect to all other species. Yet the archaeological record from Florida and Tennessee is provocative enough to convince other archaeologists that Early Paleo-Indians in the southeastern United States actively hunted or exploited large fauna as well as medium-sized and small game. And there the debate lies, poised in dynamic tension over the unknown until such time as the balance tips in one direction or the other by the weight of future discoveries.

The formerly glaciated north was defined on its southern margin by the maximum extent of the ice sheet roughly 18,000 years ago and on its northern margin by the border of the still-existing ice sheet between perhaps 10,200 and 11,000 years ago. At that time the margin of the retreating ice sheet occupied a position north of Lake Nipissing and Algonquin Park in Ontario and north of the St Lawrence valley in southern Quebec. Much of eastern Labrador was ice free. Residual ice caps may have existed in the mountains of Maine and New Brunswick 11,000 years ago but had probably disappeared by the end of the Ice Age, 10,000 years ago.

Meltzer suggested that during the period of Early Paleo-Indian occupation the formerly glaciated north consisted of periglacial tundra (though possibly only in Nova Scotia and along the eastern margin of the ice sheet) and open spruce parkland, while the unglaciated southeast as far south as central Georgia and west to Louisiana supported a complex forest containing both boreal and temperate plant and animal species, most notably deer. South of that a moderately wet deciduous forest was developing and already well advanced toward the form it would take in mid-Holocene, or Recent, times.

Meltzer predicted that the tundra and spruce parkland of the glaciated region would have exerted strong selective pressure for the development of a specialized big game hunting adaptation focused on the only gregarious herd species abundant enough to allow humans to survive – caribou. Toward the end of the glacial period mammoth and mastodon would probably not have been reliable prey since they were already well on their way to extinction; if they had not disappeared already their numbers would be few. Meltzer expected that specialized big game hunting would be reflected in the archaeological record by evidence of high mobility, repetitive use of certain parts of the landscape, and flexible social organization. These are all strategies that would apply in an environment where resources such as toolstone and caribou were widely separated but where animal movements were seasonally concentrated and patterned. The separation of resources would require high mobility and flexibility in social organization, ranging from special work parties to extended families, bands, and macrobands. This would result, archaeologically, in a wide range of site types. Seasonally concentrated and patterned animal movements would permit short-term human aggregations at particular sites or in the same general locations from one year to the next. Since these seasonal patterns also contained an element of unpredictability, successful human adaptation would also require widespread social contacts to provide regional knowledge of food resources. These would reduce the possibility that, for example, a particular band would find itself in the wrong place during periods of caribou migration.

By contrast, the forests in the southeast would have provided different opportunities and constraints. Because of the absence of a single, gregarious species such as caribou Meltzer predicted that the late glacial forests would have favoured the development of a more generalized, broad-based subsistence, perhaps centred on white-tailed deer, a species that occurs widely across the landscape. Further, with the exception of toolstone, which was concentrated at specific locations, the more uniform distribution of resources in the forest would encourage a less intensive use of specific areas of the landscape. Meltzer predicted that this would be reflected in the archaeological record by a wide distribution of small sites (because of less spatially concentrated food resources and human processing activities), fewer site types (because of more spatially uniform subsistence activities), and much less evidence of long-distance mobility (because of the greater carrying capacity of smaller areas).

After reviewing the archaeological record Meltzer argued that many of his predictions were met. There did indeed appear to be a dichotomy in the structure of the Early Paleo-Indian archaeological record between the formerly glaciated and unglaciated regions in eastern North America. This dichotomy is reflected in several ways. First, there is a broader range of site types in the formerly glaciated region, possibly reflecting the uneven distribution of resources in a parkland environment as well as the constantly expanding and contracting social units required to exploit those resources. Second, the number of sites and isolated discoveries of fluted spear points show different patterns. The formerly glaciated region has a larger number of sites – nineteen, as opposed to five in the southeast – and a smaller number of isolated discoveries – 556 as opposed to 5,110. The patterns possibly reflect an intensive and repeated use of certain parts of the landscape in the north, resulting in the formation of larger and more easily recognized sites, versus a more diffuse occupation in the southeast. Third, there is evidence of different scales of mobility. Long-distance movement of toolstone in the north, compared with the use of local materials in the southeast, perhaps reflects the greater separation between food resources and toolstone in the north. Fourth, there appear to be regional differences in tool kit contents, with evidence that northern tool kits contained a greater range of different types of tools, presumably designed for specific tasks, while tool kits in the southeast were dominated by simple flake tools, presumably used for a variety of tasks. Fifth, and finally, there appear to be regional differences in tool use, with evidence that fluted points were employed almost exclusively as projectiles in the north, presumably for hunting. This contrasts with the southeast, where fluted points were apparently much more frequently used as all-purpose, hafted knives in many subsistence activities.

Meltzer believed these contrasts indicated that Early Paleo-Indian adaptations in eastern North America were not uniform, as previously supposed, but consisted of two broadly different adaptations: one oriented to specialized, big game hunting of caribou in tundra and boreal parkland environments in the formerly glaciated north; and the other to a more generalized adaptation based on the exploitation of a broad range of plants and animals in mixed boreal-deciduous forests of the southeast.

This is a provocative interpretation. Although Meltzer may have over-generalized to some extent in interpreting the paleoenvironmental and archaeological records, the broad patterns he illuminates seem valid – to a degree. Meltzer's interpretation is certainly a challenge for future research and has shifted archaeological thinking toward a greater concern with the structure of the archaeological record and how that structure might have been created.

Meltzer's study also gives greater impetus to examining the possibility that Early Paleo-Indian subsistence may not have been uniform across North America but instead differently adapted to broad, regionally distinctive environments. By implication this could have occurred in other regions in North America; there may have been many Paleo-Indian adaptations.

I first thought seriously about a distinctive Early Paleo-Indian adaptation to the northeast when Arthur Spiess identified caribou bones from the Udora site. A few years later, in 1995, I invited a paleoecologist and several archaeologists to talk about the issue at a symposium of the Society for American Archaeology. The symposium was stimulating, as such things always are when people who are working in the same subject get together to exchange views and data from the latest discoveries. Not surprisingly, there are many opinions, and the concept of an Early Paleo-Indian greater northeast adaptive zone during the late glacial remains undefined and elusive. But this culminating issue is also a fine example of how research can be both progressively narrowing and simultaneously expanding.

For me, the process began with a glimpse into the new technology of tandem accelerator mass spectrometry (TAMS) radiocarbon dating and the dating of extremely small samples of material, even individual amino acids extracted from animal bone. From there I became involved in the details of identifying animal bone to the genus or species level. This led to a concern with animal ecology and behaviour; late glacial climates and vegetation; the effect of topography, water, and glacial ice on weather and the pattern of vegetation across the landscape; the faunal record from Early Paleo-Indian sites in eastern North America; contrasts between the Early Paleo-Indian record in eastern North American and that of the Upper Paleolithic in western Germany and adjacent areas, leading to questions about whether archaeologists in eastern North America are looking in the right places for sites with faunal remains; general principles governing how humans adapt under different environmental conditions; the structure of the Early Paleo-Indian archaeological record in eastern North America as a whole; and, finally, to the concept of an Early Paleo-Indian greater northeast adaptive zone.

This has been a long and complex intellectual journey. Of course, it is not yet over nor will it be for quite some time. This is why it is so oddly moving and vaguely disquieting to realize how unlikely, unexpectedly, and humbly it all began for me. Outside a chicken coop, with the discovery of a few pieces of bone, pathetically small and hardly seeming worthy of any attention at all.

7 | Back to the Beginning

In the spring of 1990 I received a telephone call from a colleague who wanted to ask me something about a possible future project. Although forward looking, that phone call would also send me back to the past, fifteen years earlier, and even earlier still, to the very beginning of my archaeological career. And also to a much more distant past, possibly the beginning of the North American archaeological record.

The phone call came from Ron Williamson, a founder of one of the largest archaeological consulting firms in Ontario. Ron asked if we could have lunch together one day soon as he had something he wanted to ask me. I asked what it was about but he was vague, so to cover my embarrassment about probing, I talked of my own work and asked about his. Perhaps, I thought, as our conversation continued, he would change his mind and tell me what it was he wanted to talk about, but it soon became clear that he was not going to reveal anything over the phone. Puzzled, I agreed to meet him the following week and from time to time over the next several days I wondered what he had on his mind. The day of our appointment arrived and after we had settled in at the table and talked briefly about one thing and another, Ron paused and looked serious. I knew the moment I had been waiting for all week had arrived. With a mischievous look in his eye he suddenly blurted out the question that brought us to this table: Would I be interested in working with him at Sheguiandah?

I froze! And for a long moment in the crowded and noisy restaurant I saw and heard nothing. I went inward and back into the past, my mind suddenly filled with countless thoughts as I considered the implications of Ron's question. I had first became aware of Sheguiandah in the real world – that is to say, after graduate school – when I arrived in Toronto in 1969 to take on a curatorial position at the ROM and responsibility for studying the earliest part of the prehistoric record. I was soon looking for a research project and belatedly remembered that Sheguiandah was in the same province, located in the northeast corner of Manitoulin Island. I was greatly attracted to Sheguiandah, but also intimidated by it. The site had been the focus of considerable controversy since excavations there by Thomas Lee in the mid-1950s because of his suggestion that it had been occupied 30,000 years ago, a date far older than most archaeologists were willing to accept. In 1969 I was worried by the prospect of working at a high-profile site and by the threat of withering criticism from Thomas Lee, responding to what he might perceive as a challenge from a young, no-name upstart. It had been unthinkable for me to consider, even fleetingly, starting up renewed work at the site so I had decided to work nearby, in Killarney Provincial Park, where I wouldn't have to grapple with Sheguiandah directly in order to reinvestigate issues of human antiquity raised by that site. Now, twenty-one years later, Ron Williamson was asking me to reconsider that decision.

The controversy I was so worried about earlier concerned the age of the lowermost deposits – in Levels III, IV, and V. Level III contained artifacts made by Late Paleo-Indian peoples, perhaps dating between 9,000 and 10,000 years ago. There was nothing unusual about the material or the presumed age. But below that, in Levels IV and V near the base of the site, there was evidence of still earlier occupations. These lower levels lacked projectile points but contained, most prominently, bifacially worked artifacts that Lee thought had probably been used as hand-held chopping and cutting tools. Lee also thought he detected evidence of culture change between the two lower levels because the upper one contained relatively large, thin, and well-made bifaces not dissimilar to Upper Paleolithic tools of the Aurignacian culture in western Europe whereas the lower one contained smaller, more roughly fashioned bifaces, presumably dating from a still earlier period.

The artifacts from Levels IV and V were certainly interesting, but the most important thing about them had little or nothing to do with the artifacts themselves. Rather it concerned the nature of the sediments within which the artifacts were embedded: a mixture of sand, gravel, pebbles, cobbles, and even some boulders, all jumbled together in an unsorted mess. John Sanford, a geologist from Wayne State University in Detroit

Artifacts excavated by Thomas Lee from the Sheguiandah site. Left to right top row: two bases; two complete Late Paleo-Indian spear points. Left to right bottom row: fragment of a large, thin biface; a smaller, more rudely shaped biface. The two artifacts were presumed by Lee to be characteristic of levels IV and V, respectively, and to represent successively older pre-Clovis occupations, predating those by Paleo-Indians in Level III.

Courtesy ROM.

and a colleague of Lee's, thought the unsorted material was till. This was a surprise to both men because till is carried and deposited by glacial ice, and few if any North American archaeologists or geologists expected to see artifacts in such a deposit. It could imply very great antiquity.

Till is formed by glacial ice as it moves across the land, picking up whatever lies in its path. This material is ground and crushed by movement within the ice and then, when melting occurs at the same rate or faster than the ice advances, it is deposited in a variety of forms. Principally it takes the form of a line of hills along the glacier margin, called either a terminal moraine if marking the maximum position of ice advance or a recessional moraine if marking a temporary halt of the ice during retreat. Till may also be deposited in broad sheets as the load embedded in the ice is released. The implication of finding artifacts in till within the zone covered by the continental ice sheet in North America is tremendous. It means that a human occupation site was overridden by the advancing ice sheet. Obviously, it also means that the human occupation pre-dated that ice advance. And this is precisely what Lee and Sanford argued.

But when did that ice advance occur? Lee and Sanford thought the regional geological evidence indicated that Manitoulin Island was never again overridden by ice after the final retreat of the Wisconsinan ice sheet. They thought that the temporary advances, or surges, that punctuated glacial retreat in the Great Lakes region took place farther south, in southern Ontario, and farther west, in the Michigan and Superior basins. Thus, the ice advance that carried artifacts to the Sheguiandah site, or perhaps from one location to another on the site, must have occurred either some time during the Wisconsinan Stage (which contained several retreats and subsequent readvances) or at its beginning. Sanford acknowledged that very little was known about the extent of glacial retreat and readvance within the middle part of the Wisconsinan Stage. In a statement published in 1971, however, he argued that it was "more logical" to assume that the New World had been colonized during times of non-glacial climate and thus that the artifacts in the till deposits at Sheguiandah had been manufactured by people who lived, not during the Wisconsin episode, but during the preceding Sangamon interglacial. In this scenario the artifacts in the till at Sheguiandah would have been deposited by the initial ice advance heralding the onset of the Wisconsinan glacial stage.

The end of the Sangamonian interglacial and the onset of the initial Wisconsinan glaciation was not well dated in the early 1950s when Lee and Sanford worked at Sheguiandah. In a textbook published in 1956 shortly after the excavations at Sheguiandah, Richard Foster Flint, an international authority on Pleistocene geology, stated that radiocarbon dates from wood in the Wisconsinan terminal moraine and related deposits between Iowa and western Pennsylvania dated to around 18,000 years ago. This implied that the Wisconsinan ice sheet advanced over Manitoulin Island much earlier. How much earlier was a subject for educated guesswork.

Lee contacted Ernest Antevs, a highly respected and internationally known geologist, for advice. Although Antevs never visited the site Lee briefed him thoroughly by letter and also made two trips to Antevs' office in Arizona to show him photographs, maps, and other data from the excavations. From these Antevs agreed that the artifacts in the so-called till near the base of the site might very well indicate that humans lived on Manitoulin Island at the end of the Sangamonian interglacial. According to Lee, Antevs cautioned him that few people would accept this interpretation but if Lee wanted to be conservative and appeal to at least a few archaeologists he should, as Lee paraphrased it, "try 30,000 years."

And this is the date Lee used. He and Sanford regarded 30,000 years as a minimum date. Since the age of the Sangamonian was not then known, it was as good a date as any other. In southern Ontario the Sangamonian is represented by the Don Formation: interbedded clays, silts, sands, and gravels deposited at the mouth of a former river flowing into a lake in the Ontario basin. This formation is exposed at the base of the former Don Valley Brickyard in east Toronto, now one of the city's newest public parks. It is sandwiched between two tills and famous for its warm-climate plant and invertebrate fossils, which presumably represent a non-, or interglacial, climate. Today the age of the Sangamonian is estimated to span from approximately 115,000 to 135,000 years ago. One wonders what Thomas Lee, who died at sixty-eight in 1982, would think about these dates. Would he be amused that the estimate of 30,000 years he used for both the end of the Sangamonian and the initial human occupation at Sheguiandah was so conservative? Or irritated that if he was to be damned for his views he hadn't been even bolder?

Lee's minimum date of 30,000 years for the lower two levels at Sheguiandah put Ontario on the map, at least for a small group of North American archaeologists concerned with the peopling of the New World. That date, and the absence of projectile points from the lower deposits, also placed Sheguiandah on the list of so-called Pre-Projectile Point (pre-Clovis) sites. These represented a highly controversial and theoretical stage of human occupation in the New World. A few archaeologists were prepared to accept Lee's interpretations. A somewhat larger number regarded Sheguiandah with reservations, adopting a wait-and-see attitude. But the majority was sceptical or totally unconvinced, and a few, in Lee's view, were hostile. He responded angrily to doubt or scepticism and was also bitter about the silence of numerous geologists who had visited the site during the excavations, seen the deposits at first hand and apparently accepted Lee's interpretations at the time, yet later failed to support his published conclusions. He was no less furious at other colleagues who judged the site without ever having visited it or studied the material.

Over time Lee became ever more angry over the way his work had been received and his alleged forced departure from the National Museum of Canada. He eventually took a position at the Centre d'Études Nordiques at Université Laval in Quebec. And for the remainder of his life, in the *Anthropological Journal of Canada,* which he established and edited, he published bitter rebuttals both of critical remarks about his work and of brief comments about the site that appeared from time to time in scholarly articles, textbooks, and general publications. Lee's anger and frustration took its toll. As he became more vitriolic and sarcastic he gradually reduced the likelihood of convincing people of the validity of his data or the correctness of his interpretations.

During the course of excavation Lee had published several papers on his preliminary discoveries at Sheguiandah in *American Antiquity,* a prestigious journal published in the United States. Two years after the fieldwork he published a very detailed and lengthy overview of his work at the site in a leading national journal, the *Canadian Field-Naturalist.* He subsequently published numerous other shorter papers but these are largely rebuttals to those who didn't accept or seemingly ignored his work and add little new factual information. Shortly before his death in 1982 Lee told Alan Bryan, an archaeologist at the University of Alberta and long-time advocate for the notion of pre-Clovis occupation in the New World, that he had written a final report that had not been published. Lee did not say why, though the implication is that he couldn't find a publisher. He was particularly bitter about this and, having heard rumours from time to time during the preceding years that others would like to reopen excavations at Sheguiandah, thought that no further work should be conducted until his final report was published. He also considered that he should be consulted and involved in any future work at the site.

While this attitude is certainly easy to understand, the archaeological record at Sheguiandah – and Lee and Sanford's interpretation of that record – must be evaluated on the basis of what has actually been published, regardless of whether it is complete. Are the published data enough? Do they provide what's needed for interpreting the site?

For the archaeological community as a whole, the answer is no. Judging by the comments of a few who are unsure about the status of the site and the greater silence of the many who do not mention Sheguiandah when they speak of possible pre-Clovis or Pre-Projectile Point occupation in the New World, other kinds of data are needed. Questions about the age and significance of the lower deposits at Sheguiandah can be resolved only from potentially new information contained in Lee's unpublished final report and, if that is insufficient, from renewed archaeological work.

False Start

In 1975, five years after briefly considering and then dismissing the possibility of reopening investigations at Sheguiandah, I changed my mind. I felt at least a little more daring, partly because I had by then completed my doctorate, in a new, multidisciplinary specialty called environmental archaeology, essential for dealing with problems such as those posed by Sheguiandah, and partly because I was also a bit more confident in my work. But the most important reason for my different attitude toward Sheguiandah in 1975 was my belief that I had found just the right geologist to work with me on the site – Hugh Gwyn.

Hugh is a big, gregarious man whom I liked on first sight. I also immediately sensed that he was probably a very good geologist. And he was certainly interested in the controversy over the dating of the lowermost deposits at Sheguiandah, which he had heard about in geological circles. Intermittently over the course of the 1975 field season and on into the fall of that year Hugh encouraged me time and again to reopen investigations at Sheguiandah. Indeed, his enthusiasm for the project was infectious and stimulated me to re-read the published papers. Clearly, the controversy over the identity and age of the lower levels of the site was a geological, rather than archaeological, problem. The crucial issue, of course, involved the supposed till deposits at the base of the site. Were they really tills? And if so, how old were they?

Only a Pleistocene geologist could say. John Sanford probably had to stretch a bit for his work at Sheguiandah since his training and experience were in bedrock stratigraphy, particularly of Silurian-age rocks, dating between roughly 405 and 425 million years ago. He had also done work in geochemistry and petroleum geology. He was an innovative geologist in his own specialities, however, and therefore obviously capable of expanding into new areas of research. Perhaps a more important limitation of Sanford's work at Sheguiandah, seen most easily in hindsight, has little or nothing to do with his brief foray into Pleistocene geology. Rather, it concerns the history and development of Pleistocene geology itself.

Eon	Era	Period	Epoch	Selected event (eastern North America/ Great Lakes region)	Beginning (years BP)
	Cenozoic[2]	Quaternary[1]	**Holocene (Recent)**		10,000
			Pleistocene		1.8 million
		Tertiary	Pliocene		
			Miocene		
			Oligocene		
			Eocene		
			Paleocene		66 million
	Mesozoic[3]	Cretaceous			
		Jurassic			
		Triassic			245 million
	Paleozoic[4]	Permian			
		Pennsylvanian			
		Mississippian			
		Devonian			
		Silurian			438 million
				Taconic Orogeny[5]	440 million
		Ordovician			505 million
		Cambrian			570 million
Precambrian time					
Proterozoic Eon[6]					2.5 billion
				Grenville Orogeny	1.3 to 1 billion
				Penokean Orogeny[7]	1.9 to 1.6 billion
Archean Eon[8]					3.9 billion
Hadean Eon[9]					4.5 billion

Notes: Periods and events mentioned in the text are highlighted in bold print.
Orogeny is the deformation of the earth's crust (mountain building and rifting),
caused by the collision and separation of crustal plates during continental drift.
1   Origin of humans.
2   Radiation of mammals, origin of primates.
3   Origin and radiation of dinosaurs, origin of mammals.
4   Origin and radiation of vertebrate marine life.
5   Formed the Taconic Mountains along the east coast of North America,
     predating the Appalachians.
6   Origin and radiation of invertebrate marine life.
7   Formed the Penokean-Killarney Mountains, comparable in size to the Himalayas.
     Remnants today are known as the La Cloche Mountains and cross Killarney
     Provincial Park.
8   Origin of life.
9   Origin of earth.

Sources: Based on data in Debicki (1982) and Conde and Sloan (1998).

Sanford did his work at Sheguiandah at a time when the study of tills was in its infancy. Stated somewhat simplistically, tills were regarded as mixed deposits, and if origins other than glacial ice could be excluded that was pretty much all that could be said. Later analytical approaches derived in part from sedimentology – the study of how different types of sediments are deposited and under what environments – would be applied to identify the different kinds of tills and other deposits formed by modern glaciers. In turn these approaches and the knowledge they generated were applied to the study of Pleistocene sediments.

Hugh Gwyn was ideally qualified to use these new analytical tools and knowledge in re-evaluating the supposed tills at Sheguiandah. He had trained during the period when many of the new approaches were being developed and had also acquired long field experience mapping glacial landforms and deposits. He therefore had an extensive working knowledge of the different tills and their stratigraphic relationships in southern Ontario and a thorough understanding of the complex regional chronology of the Pleistocene. In addition to these impressive qualifications Hugh is an intellectually lively, enthusiastic, and warm person, and I thought I would enjoy working with him very much. Thus Hugh – knowingly through his encouragement and unknowingly because of my respect for him as a scholar and a person – provided the impetus I needed to overcome my earlier timidness.

This is how I gathered together my strength over the winter of 1975-6 and began what only a few years earlier had been unthinkable. The first step in preparing to reopen investigations at Sheguiandah was to obtain the permission of the landowner or landowners. Eventually I tracked one down, a ten-year-old boy in Indiana who had just received an inheritance of land from his aunt. Although the title to the land had not been registered when I wrote to the boy's father, I was told that the family had no objection to my excavation and that their lawyer would contact me when the land transfer had been completed. This he did on 7 April 1976, and I was cleared to excavate, at least on that parcel of land. But by April of that year the landowner's permission was irrelevant. I hadn't been able to get a permit from the provincial government to work at the site.

The story of this unexpected complication actually began with Thomas Lee in the early 1950s, shortly after he discovered Sheguiandah. At the time Sheguiandah and all other archaeological sites in Ontario were totally unprotected from urban development or any other form of destruction or disturbance, including digging for relics or simply picking artifacts up from the surface of the ground for private collections. Thomas Lee and others lobbied hard to change this. And they obviously had an effect because in April 1953 the government of Ontario passed An Act for the Protection of Archaeological and Historic Sites. Under a regulation of this act Sheguiandah was one of several sites specifically designated as having heritage value. The term *designated* meant that no one, including a landowner, could alter, excavate, or remove objects from Sheguiandah without a permit from the minister responsible for administering what came to be called the Archaeological and Historic Sites Act.

Although amended several times, a version of this act remained in force for twenty-one years. It was replaced in 1974 by An Act to Provide for the Conservation, Protection and Preservation of the Heritage of Ontario, more simply known as the Ontario Heritage Act. This new legislation continued the designated status of Sheguiandah and other sites that had previously been designated, and permits were still required for alterations to such sites. A parallel system of licensing was also established to govern activities on non-designated archaeological and historic sites. As under earlier legislation, the minister responsible for administering the act would be responsible for issuing permits, and now licences. In so doing, the minister was to be guided by the advice of a newly established agency, the Ontario Heritage Foundation (OHF), governed by a board of directors assisted by government staff. In the case of archaeology, advice to the minister would ultimately come from the archaeology committee of the board.

Under the new legislation any person could apply for a permit or licence to alter an archaeological or historic site. But the minister could refuse to issue one if he or she thought the resource would be damaged by that work. This judgment was based on information obtained from the application, which required a written description of the proposed work and a statement of the individual's qualifications. In this way the archaeology committee of the OHF, and ultimately the minister, attempted to ensure that all people applying for archaeological permits and licences were qualified and capable of doing the work they proposed. I got a very close look at this process between 1984 and 1990 when I was appointed to the OHF board of directors for two consecutive three-year terms. But in 1975-6, when I applied for permission to excavate at Sheguiandah, the Ontario Heritage Act was still relatively new and everyone – the people applying for permits or licences as well as the first members of the new board – was still learning how the system worked, or should work.

I hadn't anticipated any problem receiving a licence to excavate at Sheguiandah. (I naïvely asked for a licence not realizing that since Sheguiandah was designated I really needed a permit.) I was, after all, a qualified archaeologist backed by all the resources of a major museum and had the assistance of an experienced Pleistocene geologist. And we had planned a very small project. At the outset we wanted only to see what Thomas Lee and John Sanford had seen. To do this we proposed excavating one or two small squares in the same area where they had observed the supposed tills near the base of the site. From this we thought we could more effectively plan both the larger excavations and funding we would need over the following year or two and the expertise we would need to resolve the problems and ambiguities raised by the work of Lee and Sanford. My proposal was thus for a test excavation: a small, trial effort to give us the knowledge to focus our work more effectively in a later year when would excavate more extensively. Careful focus would be both necessary and cost efficient to solve the problems facing us, and it would also be a conservation measure in the essentially destructive process of excavation.

I submitted a licence application in the winter of 1975. In early March 1976 I was asked to send a letter to the archaeology committee in reply to a few questions that some of the committee members had about my project. A couple of weeks later I was invited to speak to the committee about my proposal, an unusual occurrence. I explained why I thought test excavations were needed before planning a larger project and answered as best I could a number of questions asked by committee members, all of whom I had known for several years. After a short, friendly visit I was politely thanked for making my presentation and told somewhat formally that I would be informed of the committee's recommendation as soon as possible.

On 22 May I received a letter from the ministry responsible for licensing. Standing beside my desk, I opened the envelope and removed a single sheet of paper. With a small feeling of relief for having reached this stage in the planning I saw that the paper was the long-expected licence for work at Sheguiandah: licence number 76-B-0111. At the top of the certificate someone had typed in my name and the address of the museum. Below that was the name of the site and its location. The rest of the page was completely blank except for a long narrow box at the very bottom which listed the date of issue and expiry date of the licence and, below that on the right, the signature of the minister. At first glance this was all I noticed. And then I saw, just above the box, on the left of the page, a short sentence in small print: "Subject to the conditions on the reverse side." I turned the certificate over and there, in the middle of the page, was the sentence, "This licence is restricted to observational survey only including the surface collection of artifacts. The holder is not licensed to alter or disturb the designated portion of the site through excavation, test-pitting, or any other methods of archaeological sampling which would require breaking the surface of the soil."

I was stunned. I had applied for a licence to excavate and received permission to surface collect, an activity totally irrelevant to the fundamental purpose of my work. Insofar as that was concerned I was told look, but don't touch. And there was absolutely no ambiguity about this. I was expressly forbidden to do anything that would require breaking the surface of the soil. This oddly phrased stipulation about the inviolability of the surface of the ground, a very thin membrane, was certainly all inclusive, covering every conceivable archaeological tool: shovel, trowel, soil probe or any other coring device, even, I suppose, a sharp stick, which all archaeologists use occasionally for excavating delicate objects. The only type of disturbance the licence didn't appear to cover would be that caused by dragging my heels across the site in heavy, hard-soled boots or walking in spiked shoes. But technically speaking, that wouldn't have been an archaeological activity. Only one by an irritated archaeologist.

After reading the ridiculous restriction I didn't even take the time to sit down before telephoning the ministry. Angrily I asked to speak to the staff representative on the archaeology committee. After a short time he came on the line and I told him I had just received a licence to surface collect. "What," I asked, barely keeping from shouting, "is going on?"

It was then I was surprised a second time. There was no mistake. The staff person reaffirmed that the archaeology committee had not supported my request to excavate. Not only that but in a couple of weeks I would be receiving a letter from the minister telling me that he proposed *not* to issue a permit for my work. It was only then that I fully realized I should have asked for a *permit* rather than a licence. But first the minister was acting on the licence application so I guess someone on the committee or in government thought the licence served a useful purpose, and possibly it was designed to salvage something from a bad situation. But probably no one, then or now, could really explain the collective logic underlying this decision. In this way bureaucracies are unique.

The minister's letter arrived a couple of weeks after the look-but-don't-touch licence, saying that the minister proposed to refuse my request for an excavation permit. The minister could have refused me outright, and to this day I don't understand the subtle legal nuance between an outright refusal and a proposal to refuse. Both situations require a hearing before a review board unless waived by the applicant. The letter went on to say that "further disturbance can only be justified by a much more intensive investigation" and that the knowledge gained by "even minimal testing" would be disproportionate to the damage done to the very small portion of the site that remained and was essential to resolving the age of the artifacts in the lowermost deposits. Clearly, the archaeology committee hadn't really heard me when I said, verbally and in writing, that testing was only the first step of a larger project. In addition to being perhaps too conservative by proposing to start with a small test excavation, I had made a procedural error: I had failed to present the government with a plan for a multi-year project, beginning with testing in the first of several field seasons.

To be fair, I could understand their concerns. The archaeological site is indeed fragile and extremely important. It is not, however, as small as the minister's letter implies. At the time the designated area covered over 34 hectares, so the scale of my test excavations involving a few small squares wasn't threatening at all. And despite my stated intent to conduct follow-up work after the testing, I suppose the archaeology committee couldn't be sure that I would actually return to the site for more extensive excavation. Nevertheless I was annoyed that they didn't trust my intentions and mystified by the purpose of the restrictive licence. Thomas Lee's attempt to protect Sheguiandah succeeded in a way that he almost surely hadn't anticipated: the legislation he helped set in motion protected the site twenty-three years later – from renewed archaeological work.

Instead of appealing the minister's proposal to refuse a permit I started planning a much larger project. I explored federal funding possibilities and wrote letters to a variety of geologists and archaeologists whom I hoped would participate in the project, either as co-investigators or as constructive critics of the work. I also drafted a letter to Thomas Lee, informing him of my interest in excavating at Sheguiandah and asking for his support.

I never sent that letter, or finished my planning. Instead I became progressively more involved with the newly discovered Fisher site, which I test excavated in 1976, the year I also hoped to test Sheguiandah. The excavations at Fisher were so productive that I conducted a larger, multidisciplinary project there in 1978 with Hugh Gwyn and several other scholars. After that, I got caught up, as you've seen, in a flintknapping field school (1979), a final year at Fisher (1980), and a new geographic focus for fieldwork in south-central Ontario culminating in two seasons of excavation at Udora in 1980 and 1987. In 1988 I took a study trip to Colorado and Wyoming to study Early Paleo-Indian artifact collections from some of the classic western sites. This might more truthfully be described as a sort of pilgrimage. And finally, in 1989, I considered developing a new research project in the Minesing swamp, astride the Nottawasaga River in Simcoe County, west of Barrie. My attempt to reopen investigations at Sheguiandah receded further and further into the past.

In 1988, twelve years after my failed attempt to excavate at Sheguiandah, the site entered my life once again. I went there for a few days as a host/narrator for a TVOntario film called *Archaeology from the Ground Up*. I appeared in only part of the first program of a five- or six-part series. The series host was Gary Crawford, a colleague at Erindale College at the University of Toronto, who did a very fine imitation of an Indiana Jones-type person in the opening scene, where he was shown running through a cave. My part was much more modest. I first appeared in a hayfield below Sheguiandah, where I talked about the possible significance of the site in the ongoing debate about when people may have first migrated to the New World. Later I appeared on screen again, slowly walking toward the camera across one of the steep slopes on the north face of Sheguiandah. Finally, I was filmed seated and looking at a jumble of artifacts littered about the ground around my feet. The last film clip was of my hands, illustrating how quartzite could be broken and shaped into tools. This scene was actually done off site in a gravel quarry, so as not to pollute the archaeological site. I was proud of this footage, showing a blur of hands, accompanied by the brittle sound of my hammerstone striking the rock in a cloud of dust and spray of small pieces of flying stone.

That last scene was my highest moment. Sad to say, the action sequence with my hands totally eclipsed the screen presence of the whole person. I was embarrassed saying my lines in front of the camera crew, when I could remember them. And when I did get them mostly right I couldn't combine this with being where I was supposed to be; I walked in the wrong direction or stopped in the wrong place. But this experience taught me a valuable lesson: if I had had the choice in my youth between becoming an actor and becoming an archaeologist, I had certainly made the right decision. This mercifully brief foray into the world of film was the only occasion Sheguiandah reappeared in my life between 1975-6 and my lunch with Ron Williamson in the spring of 1990.

Fifteen years after I had planned that ill-fated test excavation the spectre of Sheguiandah appeared again before me. Ron sat, still smiling patiently, but now finishing his second or third coffee after lunch while I, lost in reverie, had hardly started eating.

When it was clear that I had mentally returned to the lunch table, Ron explained that the work at Sheguiandah would be part of a larger study requested by the municipality within which the archaeological site was located, Howland Township, and by two Native communities: the Ojibways of Sucker Creek and the Sheguiandah First Nation. The municipality and the two groups wanted a review of archaeological resources and locations of Native significance in Howland Township and the two Native reserves. They also wanted a reassessment of both the size of the Sheguiandah archaeological site, relative to the designated protected area, and its age and significance. All this information would be part of a master plan used to develop the tourism potential of the area further and also to protect archaeological and Native heritage sites during the course of land development over the next several decades. Ron asked whether I would be willing to serve as a director of the Sheguiandah work and, if so, how I would approach the project and whom I would like to see involved.

I agreed with Ron that Patrick Julig should be a co-director. I had known Patrick for several years and in 1988 served as an external examiner at his PhD defence at the University of Toronto. His dissertation was on Cummins, a Late Paleo-Indian site near Thunder Bay, Ontario, on the north-central shore of Lake Superior. Like Sheguiandah, the Cummins site was a source of toolstone. And because of the great abundance of material, the lack of organic preservation, and a complex geological history involving both glacial lakes and the history of ice retreat, fieldwork and interpretation at Cummins had involved many of the same problems we expected to face at Sheguiandah. For this reason alone Patrick was a good choice but he brought three other advantages to the project. First, he had recently begun re-analyzing some of Lee's artifact collection at the Canadian Museum of Civilization in Ottawa, formerly the National Museum of Man. He thus had first-hand familiarity with artifact material from the site and some of Lee's maps and notes. Second, with William Mahaney, a geographer at York University in Toronto, he had begun tackling the unresolved question of the geological origin and age of the supposed tills in the lower levels of the site by analyzing some of the sediment samples collected by Lee and Sanford. Third, because of his recent appointment to the Department of Anthropology at Laurentian University in Sudbury, only a couple of hours drive from Sheguiandah, Julig was in a good position to provide local support for the project and ongoing involvement in public education, site protection, and follow-up research after the re-excavation had concluded.

After these opening considerations I told Ron that I thought the project should be truly multidisciplinary in scope, involving the geological and environmental sciences. These were essential for interpreting the age of the site. I had three people in mind, though Ron had not worked with the first two I mentioned: Peter Barnett, a Pleistocene geologist with the Ontario Geological Survey; and Thane Anderson, a paleobotanist with the Geological Survey of Canada.

I first met Peter Barnett in 1987 during a pre-conference geological field trip to the Fisher site held in connection with the twelfth congress of the International Union for Quaternary Research (INQUA), held that year in Ottawa. Peter had trained under one of the finest Pleistocene geologists in Canada, Paul Karrow, at the University of Waterloo, and although still relatively young, had impressive field experience. I had no doubt that Peter Barnett, like Hugh Gwyn (who wasn't available for the project), had precisely the skills needed to resolve the geological problem at Sheguiandah, and I knew we would work very well together. Only a couple of months earlier we had worked together briefly on an urgent field project in a former arm of glacial Lake Algonquin near Bradford, a short distance north of Toronto.

What an odd experience that was. In the early spring of 1990 I was asked to investigate the chance discovery of some unidentified animal tissue that had supposedly been brought up from a depth of a little over thirteen metres by a commercial driller coring for a water well. Because the rig vibrated suddenly and quite noticeably at that depth the drill bit was brought back up to the surface for examination. It was then that the animal tissue was discovered, a small squarish lump about 2.2 centimetres long. Shortly after being exposed to air the tissue turned from pink to black, suggesting that burial had delayed the process of decomposition. The drill owner, startled and intrigued by this discovery, placed the tissue in a styrofoam coffee cup, sealed it with tape and aluminum foil and kept it cool in his lunch box until he returned home that night and placed it into the freezing compartment of his refrigerator. Eventually I heard about it and with the discoverer's and landowner's eager agreement, took the mysterious substance back to the ROM for analysis.

I speculated wildly, but privately, about what the tissue could be. I fancied it might be from a very large animal. What else would explain the vibration in the drill rig? The first large animals that came to mind were whale and walrus, known to have lived in the late Pleistocene-age Champlain Sea. At its greatest extent this sea expanded west from the St Lawrence valley into eastern Ontario and up the lower Ottawa valley, where it received the drainage of glacial Lake Algonquin. Hence the possible connection between Lake Algonquin near Bradford in south-central Ontario and whales and walrus in the Champlain Sea. The question is, did sea mammals once live in Lake Algonquin?

Probably not. Although four bones of large whales and two of walrus had been reported from Lower Peninsula Michigan, two of the whale specimens were radiocarbon dated at roughly 720 ±70 years BP and 750 ±60 years BP, and a third at less than 190 years BP. The two walrus specimens appear to have cut marks, and one was apparently used as a club. Paleontologists therefore assume that the fossils were carried to the discovery locations by people in the relatively recent past.

After thinking briefly of whales and walrus I imagined the drill bit striking the carcass of a mammoth or mastodon that, theoretically, could have died naturally or been killed by human hunters on the edge of Lake Algonquin. There was probably a significant population of mastodons living in southern Ontario at the end of the Ice Age. Mammoths were present as well, although they may not have been as numerous as mastodons and probably became extinct earlier. Nevertheless, finding a proboscidean was a distinct possibility, although considering the chances of actually discovering one in a randomly dug water well, quite a remote one. Nevertheless, my imagination soared uncontrolled.

At very short notice Peter Barnett offered to bring another drill rig to the site capable of removing large diameter cores of sediment that, when laid end to end, would record the stratigraphy under the site. One of these cores, we hoped, would produce more organic material, this time in stratigraphic context showing us where the original fragment had come from and also possibly helping to date the material.

I was deeply impressed by Peter's offer. It showed considerable flexibility in the conduct of his own research, which would be delayed several days or longer, and generosity in committing a major piece of equipment and the cost of doing so to what in reality was little more than the proverbial fishing expedition.

But it was the only way to find out what was down there.

Within days of our phone conversation the drill rig arrived and was set up as near as possible to the original well hole. And then we started drilling. This was all done in the traditional snow flurries of early spring and under harsh arc lights that kept the darkness of stormy days and early nights just beyond our work. One after the other the cores came up to the rattling metal work platform surrounding the drill hole and were then carried a short distance to the dark, unfinished warehouse that was being constructed. There we examined the cores excitedly, sometimes under the weak light of flashlights, for a dark layer that might be the remains of an animal or a deeply buried former soil horizon where an animal might have died.

Soon we reached the crucial depth. Nothing. We moved the drill rig a bit closer to the original water well and tried again. Nothing. Thus ended our search. Several months later the original sample of animal tissue was finally identified. It was from a bird!

Our mystery guest was first tentatively identified by the type of muscle tissue it contained: bird rather than mammal. I was greatly disappointed but then wondered if it might be an Ice Age shorebird, or something more exotic – perhaps a California Condor, a possibility that entered my mind only because a few years earlier one had been found in late glacial deposits in New York State, 1,600 kilometres from its modern range.

A little later the bird tissue was more firmly identified by feathers. One day while examining the tissue under a microscope, Cary Gilmour, a ROM technician in what was then called the Laboratory of Analytical Systematics, discovered microscopic fragments of feathers compressed against one of the surfaces of the tissue. These fragments were later identified by Roxie Laybourne, a specialist in bird feather identification affiliated with the Smithsonian Institution. Much of her work involved the identification of feathers caught in damaged or ruined aircraft engines struck by birds. Thus she was used to dealing with very small fragments, often not whole feathers at all, but barbules, the tiny filaments growing from the parallel barbs extending off the shaft of the feather. This is what we had, barbules. Laybourne identified them as belonging to a thrush (family *Turdidae*), the taxonomic group containing, for example, the robin and bluebird.

A robin or bluebird! Imagine the disappointment. Far from the exotic animals I had initially thought, even for a bird. I also soon received the results of the radiocarbon analysis of the small sample of tissue we had sent for dating to a radiocarbon facility. The date? Essentially modern.

In an attempt to explain this Peter Barnett speculated that the body of a modern bird had been carried to the construction site in loads of fill to provide better foundation and drainage for the building. The drill for the water well passed near or through the bird and brought part of it to the surface from a depth much shallower than originally estimated by the drill operator.

The well driller was not convinced, in part because of the rapid colour change of the tissue after exposure to air and also because of the vibration to the drilling rig just before he discovered the tissue. He continued to believe that the tissue must be from an ancient animal.

I wanted it to be from an ancient animal too. But Peter and I couldn't explain away the modern radiocarbon date or that the tissue had come from a bird the size of a robin. We had reached an impasse, and nothing further could be done short of digging up the site with a bulldozer and screening the sediments. Strangely enough this desperate action was discussed and then quickly dismissed as both impractical and too coarse a method for finding anything further. Especially a bird the size of a robin, which, I reluctantly accepted, must be what we had found. Our decision would have been quite different if the tissue had turned out to be from a mastodon or mammoth or whale.

I knew the well driller, and possibly the landowner, wasn't satisfied. Because of that I worried that if they ever made another surprising discovery they might be disinclined to call someone for help. But I thought the newspaper-reading public might have become more sensitive to things in the ground since our work had been covered widely in the local press and generated considerable interest. So, in the area of public relations, although we might have lost something in one direction we probably gained in another.

Two other positive things came out of this project. Much later, Peter Barnett and Thane Anderson, a paleobotanist, discovered that the Bradford cores contained plant remains from a boreal, mid-Wisconsinan forest dating around 39,000 years ago. Because material of this age is not encountered very often, and we had not been deliberately looking for it, this was a totally surprising discovery and perhaps our consolation prize. As for me, I was pleased at the opportunity to work with Peter Barnett. His quiet capability and willingness to take chances with all the resources at his disposal would be needed at Sheguiandah.

Thane Anderson I knew really only by reputation, first through his dissertation on the history of glacial Lake Algonquin and later through his publications. From this I knew he had the expertise we needed to investigate the history of late glacial vegetation recorded in the peat bogs at the top of Sheguiandah. This work might also contribute to an understanding of the age and history of human occupation there.

I thought we also needed a bedrock geologist to collaborate on the project. For that specialty I wanted to invite my colleague at the ROM, Peter von Bitter, who had worked with me looking for the geological source of toolstone used at Fisher and other Early Paleo-Indian sites in southern Ontario. Our third Peter – almost too many to keep track of – could provide us with an interpretation of the geological history of the site prior to the Pleistocene, which covers only a small fraction of all geological time. This would be especially important at Sheguiandah because the site is located on the edge of the Canadian Shield, the oldest part of the North American continent, and the rocks that formed there in the early history of the continent played a very important role in the human occupation of the site.

Finally, I wanted to involve my colleague Andrew Stewart, who at the time was writing a chapter for the Fisher monograph and had by then acquired long experience in archaeological fieldwork. I thought we needed his help in organizing the work and making it run smoothly. And privately I wanted his support on a high-profile project.

Ron and I sketched out other aspects of the project on bits and pieces of paper at the lunch table. Soon, Ron thought he had enough information to write a proposal for submission to Howland Township and the two Native groups who had requested bids for the master plan study. And he had what he needed to submit a permit application to government for archaeological fieldwork on a designated site. By now it was well after two o'clock, a long working lunch, though without martinis. Ron stood up, anxious to get on with his afternoon; unlike me he runs a commercial business as well as his own academic career, so time has other meanings for him. We shook hands and he said he would be in touch.

The events that followed happened so fast I never did write an *Archaeological Newsletter* on our work. In a book concerned with endings for which the beginnings have already been published, this chapter is unique because it contains both. What so often happens to the proverbial traveller, who promises to write but doesn't and tells of the journey only after coming home, also happens to the archaeologist. But perhaps *when* the story is told is less important than that it is told at all.

Better Late Than Never

After meeting Ron I made plans for work at Sheguiandah as if the firm he represented would be awarded the contract for the master plan study. This way I would be fully prepared and nothing but a little time would be lost if the company didn't get it.

I called Thane Anderson in Ottawa and asked if he would be interested in removing a sediment core from a bog on top of the site and interpreting the late glacial vegetation history from whatever pollen and plant material the core contained. Thane, like everyone else I had ever talked with, had heard of Sheguiandah and was intrigued by the possibility of working there. But because of other commitments he couldn't be available for fieldwork in the spring of 1991, when we expected to do the re-excavation. He could, however, make time available in the fall of 1990. I called Patrick Julig and we decided to try to arrange to do the work then. Patrick would organize equipment and obtain the permission of landowners at his end, and I would apply for a permit to work on a designated site. I hoped I wouldn't re-live a part of my own history.

This time there was no problem in receiving the permit. It was very precise, leaving no room for misinterpretation (or any kind of archaeological activity). It provided for "the removal of a pollen core approximately 7-15 cm in diameter from a small bog," but only with the permission of the landowner. Clearly, the ministry continued to take designation very seriously, as indeed it should.

We did our work on 23 November, very, very late in the season. And what a memorable beginning to a memorable project it was, working in the cold of early winter, through a long, rainy afternoon and the darkening shadows of a still rainy early evening, at the bottom of a narrow bedrock crevasse and in the ankle-deep water of a bog under the stark branches of gnarled oaks. We didn't finish until well after dark, the four of us: Patrick, Thane, I, and my better half, who had certainly been on better dates. But what a great evening we had, thawing and drying out in the warmth of a German-Austrian restaurant in a local lodge reminiscent of a European *gasthof*. Our celebration of a fine beginning to fieldwork was fuelled by drink and large plates of schnitzel and red cabbage and, for me, roast duck. In a mood of contentment Thane Anderson looked in my direction and wondered aloud, in his quiet manner, why he hadn't worked with archaeologists before.

During the course of our planning for coring the bog Ron Williamson called to say that the project was on. He had just been informed that his company would receive the contract for the master plan study and anticipated no problem in obtaining the necessary licence for archaeological survey work in the study area and the permit required for re-excavation at Sheguiandah. At long last it was going to happen and we arranged to meet at Sheguiandah on 17 May 1991, forty years after Lee discovered the site.

At Patrick Julig's suggestion we invited Robert Lee, Thomas Lee's son, to visit us in the field. Patrick discussed possibilities with Robert and they agreed that he would visit the site at the beginning of our work to help us identify the locations of his father's excavations and would return later to see what we had discovered. This proved to be an excellent idea. Robert Lee was very helpful in orienting us to the site, which he had visited as a child and young man, and was very tolerant and patient with us, the very people who, while sympathetic to his father's difficulties with the archaeological and geological community because of the supposed extreme age of the site, might very well demonstrate that his father's interpretations had been incorrect. Robert was prepared to play the devil's advocate in defence of his father but, as it turned out, in a non-confrontational way. And we were just as prepared to play the devil's advocate on the opposite side of the argument, should it prove necessary, but also courteously and with respect to his father's memory. Because of these sensitivities the mood on the site was never strained and we enjoyed Robert Lee's visits, and I believe he did as well.

One of our responsibilities at Sheguiandah was to investigate the boundaries of the site with respect to the area that had been designated and protected under the Ontario Heritage Act. Some of the landowners wondered if the designation was too generous and might be narrowed a bit, releasing land from protected status. In addition to re-excavating portions of the site Lee had investigated in the 1950s, we therefore had to explore the entire site to determine the distribution of archaeological material. Because of this I became very familiar with the site, metre by metre.

The site is truly impressive. It covers a large white quartzite hill that juts high above the surrounding fields and glistens brilliantly when sunlight passes through the sparse oaks on its upper ridges and crests. On the north and west faces of the hill the slopes are steep, in places nearly vertical, while the slopes to the east and south are much more gradual, falling gently toward the waters of Sheguiandah Bay on the coastline of Georgian Bay. The only interruption in this slope is the Mystic Ridge, named by John Sanford's son when he was part of Lee's excavation crew. This ridge, one to two metres high and nine to twenty metres wide, runs east along the base of the quartzite hill on its south side and then curves gently north following the contour of the hill until it finally disappears midway along the northeast side of the hill. The ridge was at first mysterious to Lee's crew and then later found to be the remains of an extremely ancient beach. During the course of our work, and somewhat belatedly, we came to realize that this 450-million-year-old beach played a far more crucial role in the formation of the archaeological site, and the supposed till deposits, than Lee or Sanford had suspected.

The very prominent and picturesque hill at Sheguiandah attracted prehistoric peoples for the excellent quality toolstone that the tough quartzite provided. Evidence of quarrying activity and tool manufacture is everywhere. I vividly remember from my first visit to the site in the 1970s the uncomfortable sensation of walking on artifacts, primarily the debris from tool manufacture. It was impossible to avoid. As someone interested in studying the most minute details of stone artifacts I cringed when I walked over the site, hearing the brittle crunch of shifting stone beneath my feet and thinking of the horrible damage I was causing to the very

EARLY POSTGLACIAL LOW-WATER STAGE IN HURON AND GEORGIAN BAY BASINS, APPROXIMATELY 10,000 YEARS BP

North Bay

Sheguiandah

Manitoulin Island

Parry Sound

Lake Stanley

Lake Hough

Georgian Bay

0 — 40 miles
0 — 40 kilometres

Collingwood

Toronto

Adapted from Tovell 1992, 135.

Lake Huron

SHEGUIANDAH ARCHAEOLOGICAL SITE

Adapted from Lee 1954, 102.

Road

Swamp 2

Swamp 3

+ 736

Swamp 4

Swamp 1

Habitation Area

Mystic Ridge

Nipissing strandline

700

650

640

630

620

610

600

0 — 100 feet
0 — 50 metres

Sheguianda

things that most interested me. For a long time I had to remind myself to stop curling my toes inside my boots, an unconscious attempt, I suppose, to make my feet smaller as I walked across the site.

After only a few steps the visitor has a strong impression of walking back into the past. Not only is the debris of tool making everywhere but it often appears to have just been dropped, as if the prehistoric flintknapper left the spot only a few moments ago. Lee expressed this very well in 1951 when he wrote that broken artifacts were found "lying in the midst of little nests of fine chips and flakes, just where they had been made." These little nests – hidden under the moss, barely glimpsed through the branches of shrubs, and distributed around large quartzite boulders that may have been used as work benches – catch the imagination, as the thorns of a bush snag clothing. They inspire more urgent and vivid images of a once-living people than do the large, random scatters of material disturbed by the forces of nature. Perhaps we feel this way because the nests seem to have snagged time itself and stopped it, while the disturbed artifacts remind us that things have changed and time has passed.

Near the top of Sheguiandah the imagination is captured in other ways. There, again in Lee's words, "a truly amazing sight was revealed. Spreading out in a great fan below an Indian quarry and covering about a third of an acre, [stretched] a solid paving of quartzite blocks, chips and worked fragments … [with] no indication of how deep the mass of debris might go!" In 1991, forty years after Lee walked to the edge of this great fan of material, I too was impressed. Never before had I seen anything like it, nor had I expected to outside of fenced enclosures protected by guards. But here in northern Ontario, Sheguiandah survived, in part because of government protection and the protectiveness of local citizens but also because of its still relatively remote location and obscurity. Suddenly I felt nervous about what we were preparing to do. I could only hope that by reopening excavations and writing about our work we wouldn't attract the type of visitation that would ultimately destroy those little nests of chips and flakes and the fragile sense of time, stopped, and the rich story beneath the ground.

Geological Prelude
The story begins not with the human occupation of the site but several eons earlier, deep in geologic time during the early history of the North American continent. In this respect Sheguiandah is unusual for an archaeological site because the geological history of the bedrock on which it occurs is intricately bound up with human occupation 2.5 billion years

later. Peter von Bitter assembled this part of the story for us and showed how dramatically it might influence archaeological interpretations of the age of the earliest human occupation at the site.

The white quartzite toolstone that probably attracted people to Sheguiandah was initially laid down as blankets of sand and mud in a Precambrian sea over 2.5 billion years ago. These sediments were eroded from the then much smaller North American continent to the north and deposited along the continental margin in the region of Sheguiandah. Over time the sands and muds, possibly 2,000 or 3,000 metres thick, were compacted and cemented into sandstones and shales. Some time between 2.5 and 1.6 billion years ago, during a mountain-building cycle called the Penokean Orogeny, the flat-lying sandstones and shales were heated and transformed into quartzites and phyllites, and then folded and uplifted into a great chain of mountains running east-west across the northern Great Lakes region: the Penokean-Killarney Mountain Range.

Over the next 1.5 billion years or so the Penokean-Killarney Range was

Breaking the Clovis Barrier

The discovery in 1926-7 of spear points in direct association with extinct bison at the Folsom site in New Mexico established for the first time that humans had appreciable antiquity in the New World. In 1932 spear points that were similar but differently made, and that later came to be known as Clovis points, were found associated with mammoth remains at a site in Blackwater Draw, also in New Mexico. There they occurred below a layer containing Folsom-type points – the first occurrence of the two points in a stratified site – indicating that Clovis was earlier still. This was later confirmed by radiocarbon dating indicating that Clovis peoples lived between approximately 10,900 and 11,500 years ago. Until recently, no other cultures dated earlier, and most archaeologists took this as evidence that Clovis peoples or their immediate ancestors were the first colonizers of the Americas.

Debate has continued, however, over the possibility that the Americas may have been occupied much earlier than Clovis. Several hundred, possibly even thousands, of papers have been published attempting to document these earlier, pre-Clovis occupations. But few have been very persuasive. This is because of several doubts:

whether the artifacts were made by humans or by natural agencies; whether the artifacts had remained in place since deposition or had been intruded into deeper, and therefore older, deposits or moved into accidental associations; and whether the artifacts were correctly dated. These conditions, or tests, have been difficult to meet and, naturally enough, have refocused attention on Clovis, still the critics' choice as the earliest documented culture.

Thus it has been difficult to break the so-called Clovis barrier, jealously guarded, some have said, by the Clovis police. This term, whispered in the corridors of academe and presumably coined by pre-Clovis advocates, applies to archaeologists who are sceptical or critical of alleged pre-Clovis sites but also seen as heavily involved in Clovis research and thus supposedly biased.

Currently in North America several possible pre-Clovis candidates stand out: an archaeological complex in central Alaska called Nenana after a river valley nearby and dated between 11,000 and 12,000 years BP; the Bluefish Caves in Yukon Territory at the far eastern end of Beringia, the oldest artifact from which is a flaked piece of mammoth bone dated around 24,000 years ago;

gradually eroded down to more or less its present shape, seen so spectacularly in the interior of Killarney Provincial Park and farther west along the north shore of Georgian Bay and the North Channel of Lake Huron.

Roughly 500 million years ago the region was engulfed by a warm, tropical, Ordovician-age sea. As the sea rose against islands of Precambrian quartzite rock such as Sheguiandah Hill, it broke the rock along the shoreline into fragments, rounded and fractured them further, and then concentrated them in rocky beaches that later became cemented into a conglomerate. Many of the quartzite boulders have concussion marks from collisions with other boulders, betraying their origin in a violent surf. Over time the islands were completely inundated, and the Ordovician sea and the marine life within it left thick deposits of calcite and calcium carbonate derived from the shells of micro-organisms. After the seas retreated, the deposits were solidified into limestone enriched with magnesium, called dolostone, a bedrock stratum that geologists have named the Lindsay Formation.

and Meadowcroft Rockshelter in western Pennsylvania, in which the stratigraphically lowest materials are dated between 13,000 and 16,000 years ago. The Nenana complex, proposed in 1989, is still being defined and dated. The Bluefish Caves are currently being prepared for comprehensive publication. And Meadowcroft Rockshelter, already well published, is still being debated. But whatever is ultimately decided about these and other pre-Clovis candidates, none can be the first to break the Clovis barrier. For it may already have been broken in 1989 and again in 1997, with the publication of two large technical reports on a site that had previously received comparatively little attention in the archaeological community.

The reports, written and edited by director of excavations Thomas Dillehay of the University of Kentucky and over seventy other scholars, and published by the Smithsonian Institution, are truly impressive for both the massive amount of documentation and the hefty price (both volumes costing over US$200, roughly Cdn$280). Strangely, the site is not located in Beringia, the presumed gateway to the New World, or even in North America, but in south-central Chile.

The Monte Verde site contains two unrelated episodes of occupation: Monte Verde II, the uppermost occupation, dating roughly 12,600 years ago; and Monte Verde I, in the lower levels of the site, possibly dating to 33,000 years BP. Monte Verde II, the better documented pre-Clovis occupation, concerns us here.

Monte Verde II was a small encampment on the bank of a stream. The site consists of the preserved wooden remains of one separate and twelve contiguous structures. These were constructed of vertical poles set into the ground and secured with horizontal logs, in turn stabilized with stakes driven into the ground along the margins, and covered with hides, probably from mastodon (*Cuvieronius*). These structures were surrounded by several workshop areas where woodworking and food-processing activities were conducted.

The people at Monte Verde II were hunter-gatherers and probably used the site as a base camp for a year or so. During that period, the structures on the site were altered at least once, possibly to accommodate the comings and goings of the twenty to thirty people who lived there, some more or less permanently and others intermittently. Subsistence was based on hunting of

The upper part of the Lindsay Formation consists of shales deposited on the sea bottom. These in turn are covered by shales of a more recent bedrock formation, the Blue Mountain Formation, which rises midway up the quartzite hill of Sheguiandah. At that point the geological record ends, although farther south on Manitoulin Island the end of the Ordovician and part of the later Silurian geological period have been preserved in the Niagara Escarpment, which crosses the island from east to west. These sediments were subsequently removed from Sheguiandah Hill by the same erosion that caused the southward retreat of the Niagara Escarpment to the position it occupies today. No rocks occur on Manitoulin Island dating between late Silurian times, roughly 420 million years ago, and the Ice Age, although some may have formed and subsequently been removed by erosion.

Breaking the Clovis Barrier *continued*

both mastodon and paleo-lama and plant gathering. The best-known plant, at least to us in the modern world, would have been the wild potato.

A surprisingly large range of plants were collected for use not only for food and construction material but also for fuel and even medicine. In fact over a third of the seventy plant taxa exploited were probably used for medicine. Ten of these are today known only for their medicinal properties. Of all the plants used, nearly a quarter are from distant regions: high Andean grasslands 50 kilometres to the east, central Chilean forests 200 kilometres to the north, and the Pacific coast 55 kilometres to the west.

The occupation at Monte Verde II is very well dated from samples of wooden artifacts and wooden objects shaped by humans. The eleven radiocarbon dates range from 12,230 ±140 years BP to 12,780 ±290 years BP, with an average of 12,570 ±230 years BP. There is no question that the artifacts and architectural remains were made by humans and that they are essentially undisturbed in a deposit that was protected by a younger layer of peat. And dates from sterile sediments underlying the occupation episode at Monte Verde II are also consistently older than the archaeological layer. The evidence at Monte Verde II – genuine artifacts in a clearly defined and well-dated stratigraphic context – therefore passes all the tests and must be regarded as

valid. The evidence indicates a human presence in south-central Chile roughly 1,000 years before the earliest dates for Clovis.

If this evidence is accepted by the archaeological community as a whole, the Clovis barrier will have been broken. Clovis still stands out as a remarkably successful culture, one that radiated widely throughout North America and in a different form perhaps through western and southern South America as well. But with evidence of more ancient occupation in South America involving the sophisticated use of wild plants, archaeologists have compelling evidence that peoples outside the Clovis or ancestral Clovis tradition may also have colonized the New World, possibly on numerous occasions. Archaeologists will be reminded once again that they know almost nothing of the original colonizing peoples who crossed Beringia and later the isthmus of Panama. With Clovis as the only early well-documented culture in the New World, archaeologists tended to look to those still obscure Beringian colonizers for evidence of the origins of the Clovis tool kit and the development of a focus on big game hunting. And that search must continue. But with Monte Verde II the story of the earliest period in the occupation of the New World becomes more complex. And archaeologists may discover that their own approaches for thinking about this period of the human record will have to be reinvented.

The accident of this great erosional gap explains why Ice Age hunter-gatherers were attracted to Sheguiandah Hill. The white quartzite toolstone was a Precambrian island in the midst of a "sea" of Ordovician dolostone and other sedimentary rocks that elsewhere on Manitoulin Island cover the deeply buried Precambrian rocks of an earlier eon. The beach of an Ordovician sea that formed around Sheguiandah Hill but survived only around its south and northeast margins may have offered protection to an Ice Age people seeking shelter from an Ice Age lake. This ancient beach, washed over once again by a glacial lake, was to have unforeseen consequences to archaeologists several thousand years later. But we wouldn't begin wondering about this until long after we'd started archaeological excavation and Peter von Bitter dragged us reluctantly away from our work.

Reopening Pandora's Box

We started digging on 27 May, ten days after first carrying our equipment onto the site. Earlier we had walked over the site, getting familiar with the various surface features described by Lee: the Nipissing strandline, a post-glacial beach between approximately 5,500 and 4,000 years old; the Habitation Area; and the Mid-Quarry Ridge. After this we started our search for the boundaries of the site and Thomas Lee's old excavation units. The units were not difficult to find because after backfilling Lee had marked the edges of his trenches and squares with lines of stones.

Our strategy for re-excavation was the same as I had planned in 1975-6: to reopen several of the excavation units to re-examine the stratigraphy that Lee and Sanford had recorded and to obtain fresh samples of sediments for laboratory analysis. This approach had several advantages over digging new excavation units. First, by digging in Lee's units we would be assured of seeing exactly what he did. This was important if we wanted to re-examine the questions raised by his work. Second, we would be digging through Lee's backfill, not previously unexcavated deposits, which meant we would not have to worry about keeping records as we dug downward. This would save time, an important consideration because of our small crew of four to five people and only four weeks in which to do the work. Third, once we exposed Lee's wall profiles, we could excavate from the surface downward a column 20 to 60 cm wide of fresh deposits adjacent to Lee's now re-excavated squares, following his stratigraphic horizons. This would tell us whether we could verify his findings: in essence, a test of his field observations.

On 31 May we finished exposing one of Lee's stratigraphic profiles in the Habitation Area of the site, along the west wall of two adjacent squares labelled Stations 7-8 and 7-9 by Lee. Finally, Pandora's box was fully open and we could see, for the first time and at a single glance, the deposits that had created so much controversy. There, at a depth of between 18 and 61 centimetres, was the deposit that Lee and Sanford thought was till. This was underlain by water-sorted sands and then a boulder layer. Below that, at the base of the site, was a thick layer of sediments that Lee and Sanford thought had been deposited in a lake, along with isolated cobbles and boulders that had been carried and then dropped by melting blocks of ice. What impressed me most was not the supposed till unit but the boulder layer, which was packed nearly solid with cobbles and large boulders. These could only have been moved by great energy, either fast-flowing water or the inexorable power of glacial ice.

Geologist Peter Barnett taking notes on the boulder layer in a trench excavated in 1991 on the Sheguiandah site along the edge of one of Thomas Lee's former excavations in the so-called Habitation Area.

Photograph by Peter Storck.

As we stood back looking at the trench profile we realized that we had encountered all the stratigraphic units described by Lee, and in the same sequence. Later in the lab, however, we saw that we had found a somewhat different pattern of artifact distribution. Over three-quarters of the artifacts we recovered in our new cuts adjacent to Lee's excavation units occurred in the upper ten centimetres of the profile, above the supposed till. Surprisingly, some of these appeared to us to be very similar to those Lee described from the lower part of the profile, Levels IV and V in the supposed till. We found very few artifacts in our excavations at these two crucial levels, and those we did could easily have migrated downward from the upper part of the profile through mechanical disturbance such as root growth or animal burrowing. Below this, in the underlying water-sorted sands and boulder layer, we found only a few flakes, which we thought were probably of natural rather than human origin.

The differences between the artifact distribution pattern we obtained and that described by Lee are difficult to interpret. It's possible that the pattern we observed, concentrated in the very upper part of the site, is an artificial product of our much smaller excavations. Lee didn't provide enough quantitative data in his publications to allow us to compare his results with ours, and it's also possible that, in placing emphasis on the material within and below the supposed till, his presentation masks a distribution pattern basically similar to ours. We don't know, one way or the other. Insofar as the geological profile is concerned we certainly corroborated Lee's and Sanford's work. The controversy, then, derived not from *what* was observed but *how* it was interpreted.

Shortly after we finished exposing Lee's profile, Peter Barnett, our Pleistocene geologist, arrived at the site with his assistants. After introductions to the people on the site, Peter stepped down into the trench and looked carefully at the profile, mumbling things we couldn't quite hear and poking and scraping about with his knife. I asked him for his initial impression and he said that he was surprised, and disappointed, to see that the supposed till was totally within the zone of weathering and that it looked and felt "dirty." This seemed an odd thing to say about something most people would simply regard as dirt. He explained that he thought the sediment had changed since it was initially deposited and that fine material had probably been added by the weathering of small pieces of bedrock and windblown dust, called loess; hence, to him, the dirty feel. For this reason geologists prefer to study Pleistocene sediments below the zone of weathering. The crucial unit at Sheguiandah, the supposed till, was within the weathering zone and had therefore been subtly changed from whatever it once was. This wasn't a good thing if we wanted to determine its origins. Peter looked concerned, and I had a sinking feeling that things weren't going to work out well. After a few moments Peter talked a bit in geology-speak with his assistants, then looked at the other trenches we were reopening. After a short time of this, he left!

He did a very crucial and significant thing. He went off site, driving around the roads in the region looking for exposures of till that had been mapped previously by geologists who worked on Manitoulin Island between the time of Lee's excavations and our own newly started work. He also visited several exposures of postglacial beaches, sampling the sands and gravels deposited by wave action. In his travels he looked for evidence of the direction of ice movement across the eastern end of Manitoulin Island. This he found in drumlins – hills deposited and elongated in the direction of ice flow – and grooves and long striations in the bedrock made by rocks embedded in the bottom of the ice sheet and dragged across the underlying, exposed rock. Some of these striations and other marks of glacial erosion occurred on the bare quartzite ridges of Sheguiandah itself. They indicated that the ice sheet had flowed between 220 and 240 degrees, in a roughly southwesterly direction.

The information on the direction of ice flow, and the sediment samples Peter Barnett collected from the off-site tills and postglacial beach deposits, would be essential in interpreting the lower deposits at Sheguiandah, necessarily suspect to a geologist because they were on an archaeological site, not a good place to observe natural, undisturbed deposits. Because of his thorough training Peter was, in time-honoured fashion, moving carefully from the known (the off-site deposits of known origin) to the unknown (the lowermost deposits at Sheguiandah, of unknown origin).

John Sanford had not done this, although in 1978, long after their work at Sheguiandah, Thomas Lee published the results of some grain-size analyses that Sanford's students had produced from samples of the supposed till from the site. These studies reflect the amount of clay, silt, sand, granules, and pebbles present in a deposit. This type of analysis was a essential step in what today is routine in geological studies of Pleistocene sediments. Sanford had previously conducted grain-size analysis of pulverized Silurian-age bedrock in his own research, but when he extended this approach to Sheguiandah it was done in an ad hoc manner on a single sample of material. Peter Barnett's more systematic approach illustrates the advantage of a later generation of scholars. Each successive generation benefits from the advances and mistakes of the preceding one and from the development of different approaches to research and new, more powerful research tools. Peter Barnett was preparing to bring these new approaches and research tools to bear on the problems at Sheguiandah as the key to resolving the age of the earliest human occupation at the site.

The laboratory analysis of the sediments Peter Barnett collected in the field confirmed what he had suspected: the grain-size distribution of off-site tills differed substantially from that in the unit at Sheguiandah that Sanford and Lee thought was a till. Glacial ice will grind material very fine but will also carry a wide range of coarser particles that, in a true till, will all be deposited in a mix called a diamicton: literally, a mixed deposit. This will produce on a graph plotting the percentages of clay, silt, and sand, a line called a grain-size curve that slopes diagonally across the paper from lower left to upper right, reflecting a significant amount of those substances. As expected, the off-site till produced this characteristic grain-size curve. By contrast, the supposed till deposits at Sheguiandah produced a very different grain-size curve, beginning farther down on the left of the graph and having the appearance of a backward letter L. This "dished" curve, while also recording a mixed deposit, reflected much less clay, silt, and fine sand, indicating that it had been more highly sorted and was much coarser than the off-site till. It looked very much like the grain-size curves that Peter had obtained from postglacial beach deposits in the vicinity of Sheguiandah except that it was somewhat less sorted, containing higher percentages of clay and fine silt.

Evidence from the grain-size distribution thus suggested that the supposed till was, in fact, not a till. This was supported by observations made by Patrick Julig and William Mahaney on individual sand grains from samples of the supposed till that Lee and Sanford had collected during their work. Examined under very high magnification in a scanning electron microscope the grains exhibited the gouges, furrows, and evidence of crushing produced by the grinding action of ice but these tell-tale features had also been weathered and rounded by the action of water. Though the sand grains had at one time been carried in glacial ice, they had therefore more recently been re-deposited in a different environment.

The structure of the deposit, or rather its lack of structure, also supported the interpretation that the supposed till was not a till. Oblong pebbles in a deposit laid down by moving ice will be aligned in the direction of ice flow. The supposed till showed no evidence of any such alignment.

The accumulating evidence was consistent and pointed to a nonglacial origin for the unit Lee and Sanford interpreted as a till. But before making final judgment it was necessary to examine and identify the underlying deposits because no individual unit in a stratigraphic sequence can, or should, be interpreted in isolation.

Below the problematic unit – looking more and more like a poorly sorted beach deposit – was a thin unit of coarse sands deposited by water. Below that was the impressive boulder layer. Seventy percent of the boulders in this layer are exotic to Manitoulin Island, metamorphic rocks derived from the Canadian Shield to the north and clearly moved to this location by glacial ice. They do not appear to form a true boulder pavement, a geological term for a layer of cobbles and boulders deposited at the base of flowing ice and then overridden, scratched, and planed by the movement of particles embedded in the ice. The upper surface of the boulder layer at Sheguiandah is very irregular and therefore not characteristic of a true boulder pavement, and there is no consistent orientation in the facets created by the planing action of glacial ice. On the few boulders that have been scratched, the orientation of the scratches ranges widely from 195 to 348 degrees, not consistently in the direction of ice flow, which would average 230 degrees. These several observations are all consistent and suggest one thing: that the cobbles and boulders have been disturbed since deposition, perhaps by water.

Below the boulder layer, at the very base of the site, is the unit Sanford and Lee regarded as lake sediments. I wouldn't have argued otherwise. Peter Barnett examined the profile carefully, however, probing here and there with his knife and rubbing small pinches of the sediment between his thumb and fingers. After a time he suddenly declared that it was a till. A subglacial till deposited at the base of the ice sheet. He seemed very confident about this. And also somewhat relieved, as if he were in familiar territory again, below the zone of weathering and looking at sediments he understood. The grain-size distribution would later confirm Peter's field interpretation. The lowest unit is, in fact, poorly sorted, and the grain-size curve is very similar to that of the off-site till.

Thus, ironically, there is a till at Sheguiandah, but not where Sanford and Lee thought. The till is at the very base of the site and far below any evidence of human occupation.

The till helps to clarify the origin of the overlying boulder layer. The boulders were probably originally part of the basal till deposit – Peter Barnett's subglacial till – but concentrated in a layer by water erosion after the ice sheet retreated. The water, perhaps wave erosion along the edge of a lake slowly falling to a lower level, removed the finer materials in the till, leaving only the boulders as a residual, or lag, deposit. It's quite possible that a metre or so of material was removed by wave action and in the process the boulders rotated slightly as they fell upon themselves and became concentrated. This would explain the wide divergence in orientation of glacial scratches from the direction of ice flow, as well as the inconsistent orientation of glacial facets on individual boulders and the irregular upper surface of the boulder layer.

The process that created the boulder layer stopped abruptly, and a much reduced flow of water deposited fine sands and gravels among the boulders and in a thin overlying unit. It was after this that Sanford's and Lee's supposed till, actually a poorly sorted beach deposit, was accumulated.

The poor sorting of the beach deposit is probably the result of several different agencies. First, it is partly the after-effect of weathering after the deposits were laid down: the addition of fine particles derived from the breakdown of fragments of shale bedrock, which produces clay, and perhaps from wind-blown dust, or loess. Second, it is partly genetic, or inherent in the way the sediments formed, and related to the fact that beach sediments in the Habitation Area were deposited in a protected environment between the Ordovician-age storm beach of Mystic Ridge and the higher quartzite barrier of Sheguiandah Hill. The 460-million-year-old beach would have prevented thorough washing of the much younger beach sediments behind it. Because the Ordovician beach was a mixed deposit in its own right, composed of a wide range of particle sizes as well as broken, angular fragments of shale and dolostone and water-worn quartzite boulders, it was a ready source of material for re-deposition in the Habitation Area. Peter von Bitter found evidence for this in microfossils recovered from dolomite fragments in Mystic Ridge. They were of a type known as conodonts, tooth-like remains of animals that once lived in Paleozoic seas. The same kinds of conodonts were also obtained from the poorly sorted beach sediments in the Habitation Area behind the ridge. Although Sanford and Lee correctly identified Mystic Ridge as an early Paleozoic beach, they failed to realize its importance as a source of mixed sediment and its effect on the depositional environment in the Habitation Area.

Additional agencies that contributed to the poor sorting of the beach deposits above the boulder layer in the Habitation Area are such things as root growth, tree fall during storms, which tears roots and soil from the ground and produces that hummocky appearance so often seen on forest floors, animal burrowing, and possibly even prehistoric human activities such as trampling and digging. Evidence of mechanical mixing is readily apparent in the distribution of broken artifacts Lee obtained from the supposed till deposits. Fragments of ten of the twenty-four artifacts he refitted together came from different levels, indicating that one or both of the matching pieces of each refit had been moved at least one stratigraphic level up or down after deposition, and in some instance two or three levels. Additional evidence of mixing was provided by a radiocarbon date on wood charcoal Lee collected from the lowest level of another portion of the site. Submitted for dating by Patrick Julig, the sample produced a date of 50 ±70 years BP, essentially recent, or historical. This was a considerable surprise since the sample was obtained from a depth of approximately one metre below the surface.

We believe that all of the data we have been able to gather indicate that the supposed till above the boulder layer is in fact a poorly sorted beach deposit that formed in a protected environment behind an ancient beach and was further altered by postdepositional mechanical mixing and weathering.

If we are correct, what then is the age of the deposit? To date, only one till has been recognized on Manitoulin Island and it is believed to be Late Pleistocene. If the subglacial till at the base of the deposits at Sheguiandah records the same glaciation as the till exposed off site, then all the sediments above that unit are postglacial.

A more precise estimate of the age of these postglacial deposits is provided by radiocarbon dates from the base of Swamp 3, which occurs in a bedrock fissure at the top of Sheguiandah Hill. Lee's single radiocarbon date of 9,160 ±250 years BP is consistent with three dates we obtained, ranging between 9,170 ±80 and 9,440 ±60 years BP. All four dates probably record the first growth of plants following an episode of flooding in the Great Lakes region related to deglaciation in the far west and north. This episode, called the Mattawa phase in early postglacial chronology, began when a huge body of cold meltwater in central Manitoba called Lake Agassiz broke around the continental ice margin and drained suddenly into the Nipigon basin in western Ontario and from there into the Superior and then the Huron basins. The cold meltwater lowered the air temperature adjacent to the lakes and caused a brief reversal of vegetation from warmer pine-dominated to colder spruce-dominated forests. These two pollen zones, the earlier Pine zone and the later Spruce zone, are represented in the core from Swamp 3 at Sheguiandah. Thane Anderson, the paleobotanist who worked with us at Sheguiandah and analyzed this core, was also, by great good fortune, the person most likely to realize its significance. In earlier work he and geologist C.F.M. Lewis were the first to correlate the final stages of glacial Lake Agassiz with a climatic reversal in the mid-continent region, now recorded in nearly forty-five pollen cores from sites in the Great Lakes region and as far as the Canadian maritimes.

Sheguiandah may well have been occupied earlier, before the catastrophic floods of the Mattawa phase. Manitoulin Island probably first
emerged as dry land around 10,500 years ago, shortly after ice retreat and
the draining of glacial Lake Algonquin, which at its highest had risen to a
level roughly 60 metres above Sheguiandah. For the next 500 years lake
levels dropped steadily, exposing much of the Georgian Bay basin as dry
land. It may have been during this period that Sheguiandah was first occupied, by the Late Paleo-Indian people who would leave their distinctive
spear points and other tools in the Habitation Area behind Mystic Ridge.
During those intermittent occupations, and perhaps later after the Late
Paleo-Indian people were forced to abandon Sheguiandah at the onset of
the Mattawa floods, some of these artifacts became mixed with poorly
sorted beach sediments and the underlying boulder layer. Ten thousand
years later, partly because of misinterpretations stemming from fieldwork
done slightly ahead of the development of necessary research tools in
Pleistocene geology, these sediments and the artifacts they contained
would be confused with much earlier geological events and a hypothetical
stage in the human occupation of the New World. Although the late
Thomas Lee and John Sanford might not accept our revisionist interpretation, I'm sure we would all agree that our short lives, and all we do, are part
of the flow of much larger events of which we are mostly unaware. And
because of that, I and my colleagues who worked at Sheguiandah in 1991
realize that our interpretations are likewise vulnerable as long as people
seek knowledge and the fragile records of the past survive to stimulate
wonder and pose questions for future generations.

8 THE SEARCH CHANGES DIRECTION

THE WORK AT SHEGUIANDAH IN 1991, which I anticipated for so many years but was involved with for only a few weeks, proved to be just a short diversion for me. This chapter returns to the main story of my research and of this book: the effort to learn about the Early Paleo-Indian people who lived in southern Ontario during the final phases of the Ice Age.

The threads of the story yet to be told can be traced back as far as November 1979, when my colleague at the ROM, Peter von Bitter, discovered the identity and geological source of a toolstone preferred by some Early Paleo-Indians for making tools: Fossil Hill chert. He found the chert in a bedrock formation of that name near the top of the Niagara Escarpment in the southern Georgian Bay region, and his discovery prompted me to shift my fieldwork from the lowlands of south-central Ontario and the former beaches of glacial Lake Algonquin to the Blue Mountain/Kolapore uplands. This highland region is located on the crest and back-slope of the Niagara cuesta: the inclined surface that slopes gradually west from the top of the Niagara Escarpment toward the Huron basin. In terms of familiar landmarks the highland region is a short distance south of the shoreline of southern Georgian Bay, roughly between the cities of Collingwood in the east and Owen Sound in the west. In making a jump to this region I could say, with only a little exaggeration, that my work shifted from the beaches to the mountains. This shift was significant in two ways, the first having to do with a long-standing and very difficult question and the second with what I might loosely call the big picture.

First, the difficult question: Where does one look for archaeological sites? This is certainly one of the most fundamental problems in archaeology, especially for research in the earlier and therefore more hidden parts of the prehistoric record. It is the archaeologist's version of the question commonly asked by the general public: How do you know where to dig? The problem confronted me in 1969 when I started work in Ontario. I found a temporary solution then and after that a series of other solutions. But the question never really went away and has perplexed me almost continuously over nearly three decades of research.

My most successful work was on fossil beaches, but this could take me only so far because the totality of the landscape used by Early Paleo-Indians almost certainly included much more. While these places were clearly an important focus of occupation, Early Paleo-Indians probably spent only a part of their year in lakeside habitats, perhaps just a few weeks or a couple of months at different times of the year. If so my focus on this one aspect of their land use and, presumably, on one aspect of their seasonal subsistence round as well would give us only a narrow glimpse into their lives, almost like looking through a keyhole into a slice of the large room beyond. To change this, to see the big picture or at least a bigger one, I needed to explore other parts of the landscape and to develop new ways of looking for sites. The most basic question was, and is, how? I couldn't just throw a shovel into the back of a truck, drive out into the countryside, and stop at the first place that looked as if it might have been a good place for Paleo-Indians to camp. No granting agency or academic institution would support that kind of non-oriented work. I needed a sense of direction and a clear vision of the contribution that particular course would make to Paleo-Indian research as a whole, along with a reasonable chance of success. The Ice Age beaches provided that. What else might?

Peter von Bitter's discovery provided at least one answer: Fossil Hill chert. This rock, deposited in warm Paleozoic seas over 400 million years ago, is almost unimaginably distant in time from Early Paleo-Indians and yet it strongly influenced their lives. It was about to change my life as well. The brittle, glass-like rock gave me an opportunity to leave the Ice Age beaches of the central lowlands and search for Paleo-Indian sites in a completely different ecological zone. The upland environment provided the new sense of direction I had been looking for and another keyhole glimpse into Paleo-Indian life.

The Fossil Hill chert also gave me a very specific geographic focus for my search, a narrow band perhaps 90 metres wide at an elevation of roughly 460 metres in the Blue Mountain/Kolapore uplands. This is the elevation at which the chert-bearing portion of the Fossil Hill Formation occurs. It is easily spotted on a map showing contours of the land, marked by a series of parallel lines of equal elevation. It is also relatively simple to walk along an imaginary line of constant elevation and look for fragments of chert that have eroded from bedrock exposures farther upslope. This debris trail was probably walked in places by Early Paleo-Indians. Eleven thousand years later I could follow the same trail, and like the supposed caribou game trails I had been following elsewhere, this less ghostly one should also lead to the places visited by Paleo-Indians. Here should be the places where they camped briefly to pry blocks of chert out of the ground or to gather what the glacier had plucked from the bedrock and later dropped during melting.

Aside from discovering new sites, what exactly did I hope to find out about Paleo-Indians by working in this new region? How would this new direction in fieldwork contribute to our knowledge of Paleo-Indian life? When I first thought about working in the mountains, in 1982, I hoped to find the answers to the questions who and how.

I knew from the Fisher site and other sites in southwestern Ontario that of the three different groups of Early Paleo-Indians in Ontario – Gainey, Parkhill, and Crowfield – the Parkhill people appeared to have the strongest preference for Fossil Hill chert as a toolstone. I thus expected to find sites that these particular people had used. This part of the question was already known, but I wanted to find out more precisely *who* in Parkhill *society* actually obtained the chert. We knew the material had been carried from the source area and discarded as broken tools and flintknapping debris on sites throughout southwestern and central Ontario. The distances ranged from 30 to 180 kilometres in an easterly direction (Fisher, Udora, and sites farther east near Peterborough) and as much as 200 kilometres in a southerly direction (at sites such as Thedford II and Parkhill). The broad range of tool types at many of these sites suggests that they were occupied either by family groups, perhaps part of a small band, as at Thedford II, or by a much larger band or even several bands, as at Fisher and Parkhill. But, and this is where the question *who* re-emerges, which of these social groups visited the chert source area to obtain the toolstone? Was it an extended family? An entire band? Or was the toolstone collected by narrow segments of these social groups, such as hunting parties or special-purpose task groups interested solely in the toolstone?

The several possible answers to the question *who* have different implications for Paleo-Indian land use; that is to say, the social dimensions of land use. If the toolstone were collected by individual families or the band as a whole we could infer that the geological source area was part of the annual geographic range used by the entire social group. If it were collected by hunting parties or special-purpose task groups, we would then have to ask where the rest of the social unit was: the women with children, the adolescents, the elders. Were they at a base camp located outside the region? If so, was the geological source area in the Blue Mountain/Kolapore uplands essentially outside the range of band movements, reached only by a few individuals?

The second question, *how*, as I conceived it in 1982, was concerned really with two issues: the mechanics of chert acquisition, whether by collecting material from the surface of the ground or by digging into bedrock; and how the stone was prepared for transport, whether as finished tools made at the source of the stone or as large blanks from which tools could be made later at far distant sites. This might also, I thought, help tell us *who* obtained the toolstone. If the site had been occupied by family groups or the entire band concerned with replenishing their tool kits at the source of the toolstone, for example, I expected that the excavations would produce evidence for the discard and replacement of a wide range of tool types, reflecting the domestic activities of both sexes. At the opposite extreme, if the site had been occupied by small hunting parties or specialized task groups prepared only for a short-term, maintenance level of subsistence and concerned primarily with acquiring toolstone for transport elsewhere, I expected to recover only a very narrow range of tools, such as broken spear points, butchering tools, and failed tool blanks.

This was the state of my thinking in 1982. During preparations for fieldwork that year I thought I had asked the right questions and knew both where to look for the answers and what to look for. Unknowingly, I still hadn't got it quite right. Even so, I was excited, optimistic, and, I hoped, open-minded because I suspected, unconsciously, that I might find something quite different from what I expected.

The following newsletter describes the first step in my new project, almost three years after Peter von Bitter discovered the source of Fossil Hill chert in November 1979. This delay was caused, in part, by a new project on the eastern shoreline of Lake Algonquin between Udora and Kirkfield and the follow-up excavations at Udora in 1980. It is also explained by the fact that I was a little gun-shy after the problems of the 1980 field season. Why it took another two years, until September 1984, to publish my first important discovery in the mountains puzzles me to this day:

Ice Age Hunters in Ontario:
Finding the Best Way to Find Sites
September 1984

The archaeological sites I excavate in Ontario are remarkable for their "unremarkableness." Except for the thin scatter of broken tools in the upper few centimetres of the soil, they are so inconspicuous as to appear part of the earth itself. This is partly because the Ice Age hunters who lived on these sites were highly mobile and left little behind to mark their passage, but also because of the extreme age of the sites and the 10,000 to 12,000 years of erosion and decomposition that have destroyed everything not made of stone. In addition, because of the tremendous geological, environmental, and cultural changes that have occurred in the last 12,000 years, these sites are no longer on the main thoroughfares of human activity; rather they are hidden on small rises in sprawling hundred-acre cornfields or are tucked away in secluded woodlots, overgrown fencerows, and isolated pastures.

The question I am asked most often by occasional visitors who manage to find me in the field is how on earth I ever found the site. Why did I come to this particular spot? This is a very difficult question to answer and in fact much of my work has been, and continues to be, concerned with finding the best way to find sites. I have tried a number of different approaches with varying degrees of success and have, of course, tended to focus on those that are most productive. What I have found is that these tend to produce the same kinds of information, so that there is always a need to develop new ways of looking in order to find different kinds of things with different kinds of research potential.

A possible new approach to "the search" was suggested by the type of stone (actually chert) which the Ice Age hunters used in tool making. If we could find the geological source of this raw material, survey work could be focused along a particular elevation where the rock outcropped on the surface of the ground. This might lead to the discovery of quarry or manufacturing sites where the chert was prepared for tool making. This approach promised to turn up totally new kinds of information about these early hunting peoples.

The story of the search for the chert source was told in an article in *Rotunda* magazine in the fall of 1981. After two years of fieldwork, Dr Peter von Bitter of the ROM's Department of Invertebrate Paleontology succeeded in tracing the chert to the Fossil Hill Formation that outcrops on the upper part of the Blue Mountain highlands in the southern Georgian Bay region. This discovery provided a new geographic focus for archaeological survey

work and I was eager to reap the fruits of our labours and see how successful our new approach would be.

Every time I go into the field with a new approach for looking for sites I
have to learn how to walk all over again. At first I find myself concentrating
on every step, with the anticipation of finding something at any moment.
Gradually, as reality sets in and I realize how many dozens or even hundreds
of kilometres I may walk before finding anything, I think more and more
about the long-term problem and start preparing myself for a long, hard
pull. This time, however, things happened quite differently.

I decided to start the survey in a ploughed field directly above the best
exposure of chert that had been found. Peter von Bitter and his assistant,
Betty Eley, decided to head off into the bush to try to trace the chert outcrop farther to the east. My assistant, Kathy Mills, and I gathered together
some paper bags and walked onto the field to start work. Almost immediately we started finding the debris of tool manufacture and soon were
busily filling the sample bags. The field was literally paved with chert fragments and it was exhilarating to find so much material – so much, in fact,
that we hardly even looked at it after picking it up because of our eagerness
to pick up the next piece. The two of us did this for a long time, mumbling
happy little sounds, and enjoyed ourselves thoroughly filling many paper
bags, which were stashed at prominent landmarks in the field. Finally,
we stopped to relax for a few minutes and to look around at what we had
been doing. On an impulse, I asked Kathy to make a final pass along the
fencerow on the far side of the field. We were about fifty yards from each
other when she turned and exclaimed laughingly that I owed her a glass
of "bubbly."

In amazement I asked her to repeat what she had said since I had a standing offer with my field crews to buy a bottle of champagne whenever we
found the distinctive "fluted" spear point that was made by Ice Age Early
Paleo-Indian hunters.

Kathy was right! I did indeed owe her a glass of champagne. Although
considerably resharpened and much smaller than it must have been originally, it was clearly a "fluted" point and indicated that Early Paleo-Indian
hunters had visited the chert source and probably used it to replace worn-
out tools and weapons. Considering all of the different styles of tools and
weapons made during the 12,000 years of prehistory in this province, it was
incredible that Kathy had found the very one we had been looking for. Not
only that, but this proved to be the only diagnostic artifact out of the 52 kg
of chert we picked up. This had never happened to me before and I don't
expect it ever to happen again.

Several months after standing in the middle of the field with the "fluted" spear point in my hand, I am still stunned at having found a diagnostic artifact of the culture we were looking for, on a large manufacturing site of the type we had hoped to find, and on the very first day of using a new survey approach. In a matter of hours we had accomplished what I had expected would take weeks, if not years. Next spring, before the trilliums and other spring flowers come up, I intend to visit the site again, and the adjacent chert outcrops, looking for additional workshops and opportunities for excavation. We have already determined that the new survey approach has exciting potential. It will be fun to see just where this will lead us.

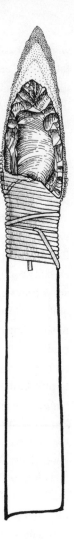

Early Paleo-Indian spear point found on the surface of the Thomson site in 1982. The point is shown as it might have been hafted. The left ear is missing and the basal portion would have been completely covered by the binding, which has been only partially drawn. The point was probably broken and resharpened several times before it was finally discarded, indicated in the drawing by the different types of shading to reflect progressive shortening.
Emil Huston, ROM.

Postscript

Like many letters, the preceding *Archaeological Newsletter* was out of date before it was received by the intended reader. In this case the project it described had died a year earlier, even as it started.

Shortly after our return to the new site in the spring of 1983, and while we were in the act of labelling paper bags of artifact material we had just collected, the landowner walked out into the field and told us that after our work was done that day I could no longer work on his property. Why? It wasn't because of anything I had done. The landowner had changed his mind for reasons that had nothing to do with my work. I sympathized in part but I was also very disappointed. And a bit numb.

In the nearly three decades of my fieldwork, I have seldom had any problem getting permission to work on private land. I'm scrupulous about asking in advance and explaining what I want to do. Most people listen politely though sometimes distractedly, but some become very interested in the work and the potential significance of their land, especially if it contains archaeological sites or ancient landforms such as an Ice Age beach or a hill deposited by glacial ice. Rarely, someone seems not to understand what I'm asking, such as the farmer who asked me how an archaeological site would affect his crops, as if the site might carry the same threat as a disease. More rarely still, someone will refuse permission to work on the land for religious reasons, such as the person who thought there could be nothing on his land dating from the Ice Age because he believed the Bible indicated that humankind was created 7,000 years ago in the Middle East. On another occasion a very successful farmer who had business interests in several farms intentionally discouraged fieldwork by demanding to be paid $50 per day for the time we worked on his land. This sum might have exceeded the daily food costs for my entire crew, an impossible additional financial burden on a shoestring budget and one that wouldn't have been supported by a granting agency. Finally, the saddest and most troubling occasion was the attitude of a young man, ironically also a very successful farmer and one who had benefited enormously from technological advances in farm machinery and agricultural research, who stated bluntly that he didn't "believe in university." Had I asked he probably would have refused permission for excavation.

These refusals stand out in my mind because they were rare experiences. By and large, people were generous as long as you asked first, closed gates, didn't dig without prior arrangement, and occasionally offered to pay a nominal and largely symbolic fee for crop damage if you had to excavate in a corn or grain field. In some instances the farmer willingly left a corner of a field unplanted to make fieldwork easier, or even backfilled the excavations after we finished our work saving me much field time and enabling me to excavate larger areas than I would otherwise. And we were assisted in other ways, by being allowed to use household water from an outside tap or to camp in an orchard or pasture and set up portable toilets over holes in the ground along fencerows or on the edge of a field. Mind you, we helped out in unexpected ways from time to time: by herding wayward cattle back into a field with a broken fence, monitoring the daily water supply of grazing stock, and removing with gloved hands in a sort of bucket brigade an enormous number of bats from the attic of a house we were renting. On one frightening occasion, we even ran to the assistance of a man on a neighbouring farm who shouted for help after he became trapped between his running tractor and the side of a barn. By chance camping on a remote field, we were the only people who might have heard him.

Because of the tremendous amount of co-operation I had received from the public, I was shocked to have a landowner suddenly withdraw permission to work on his land. I returned to the city not knowing what to do.

The Longer Road

I decided to put the new project on hold for a while and turned to other things: a gallery that opened in 1985, the second season's excavation of Udora in 1987, and the interlude at Sheguiandah in 1991.

Nearly a decade passed, during which Peter von Bitter bought a house in the Beaver valley, an area he grew to love during the search for that mysterious toolstone that eventually turned out to be Fossil Hill chert. In due course Peter invited his friends to visit his new house and one of them was so impressed with the area that he too bought a property, an old farm in the shadow of the escarpment. Eventually, this friend, needing to resurface the lane to his house, hired a local contractor to grade the drive and lay new gravel. One day, while the two men were talking casually during a break in the work, Peter von Bitter's name came up. And then mine as well. The contractor paused, surprised at the coincidence, and remarked that he remembered us well since we once worked on his property. Apparently the matter that had caused him to retract permission to work on his land had been resolved because he then said that I was more than welcome to return to his farm and continue my work. Whenever I wanted!

This is how I came to revive a project conceived in 1978 with a commitment to search for the geological source of a white toolstone, made practical in 1979 with Peter's discovery of the identity and source of that toolstone, begun explosively in 1982 with the surprising first-day discovery of an Early Paleo-Indian spear point, and now after an abrupt and premature ending and long hiatus, raised out of the ashes in the fall of 1992.

By 1992, however, I would not be the first to follow up on Peter von Bitter's discovery of Fossil Hill chert. In the intervening years avocational archaeologists Michael and Christine Kirby did extensive and very careful survey work in the Blue Mountain/Kolapore uplands and surrounding area. The Kirbys had immigrated to Canada from England in 1973 and became involved in the Ontario Archaeological Society. There they met Charlie Garrad, the man who turned me in the direction of the Banting site. Charlie, who had a long-standing interest in the Petun branch of the Ontario Iroquois in the Collingwood area, introduced the Kirbys to the Beaver valley area. At the request of a government staff archaeologist the

Kirbys soon initiated their own project in the Beaver valley and nearby Kolapore uplands. Before long they found themselves leaving Toronto every weekend for quiet walks over ploughed fields and down forest trails in search of archaeological sites. In this manner a weekend obsession turned into a long-term commitment and, ultimately, stimulated an exodus from the city to a permanent home at the top of the Beaver valley and in the midst of their research area.

The Kirbys worked hard and systematically for nearly eleven years. By the time I was preparing to begin working in the Blue Mountain/Kolapore uplands in 1992, however, they had largely stopped. This happened in part because they had walked every field that was regularly or intermittently ploughed and all of the hiking trails they knew, at least once. The results of their archaeological work, accumulated slowly over years of weekends and summer holidays at their own expense, remain to guide others. Their meticulous field notes and hand-drawn maps fill two thick volumes, one set on file with the provincial government and the other set with the Kirbys. In addition to field notes and maps this compilation also includes carefully filled out licence report forms with the latitude and longitude and map co-ordinates for each site discovered, a description of the geographic location, the number and types of artifacts collected, and a considerable amount of other documentary information. These records are absolutely superb and could be held up as examples for other avocational and professional archaeologists alike to emulate.

During the eleven years of their work Michael and Christine Kirby discovered sixteen new archaeological sites, in nearly every corner of the chert source area. They also monitored several other sites that had been found previously by other archaeologists. Only one produced a Paleo-Indian artifact. This site, technically designated BcHc-2 following a Canada-wide classification scheme based on latitude and longitude, had been discovered in 1980 by William Fox, the archaeologist who initially encouraged the Kirbys to work in the Kolapore uplands and the Beaver valley and who also gave invaluable help to Peter von Bitter in his search for the geological origins of what ultimately became known as Fossil Hill chert. Fox named BcHc-2 the von Bitter site in honour of Peter's work and showed it to the Kirbys for continued monitoring. One day during a brief visit Christine Kirby found an Early Paleo-Indian fluted point, the only such artifact they had ever found. At the suggestion of another archaeologist, however, she left the artifact in the ploughed field, expecting it would later be found by Peter or me. Considering how very rare this type of artifact is and what a thrill it must have been to find it, leaving it for someone else to discover was a tremendously thoughtful gesture. But although the two of us have searched the field often, the artifact has never been seen since though it is almost surely still there.

Despite the Kirbys' very productive work it clearly didn't answer the two questions I had posed in 1982: who obtained the toolstone, and how was it obtained? The answers were still very much up in the air a decade later when I was finally able to start my own work. The fluted point that the Kirbys discovered on BcHc-2, the von Bitter site, as well as the one discovered by my assistant on the Thomson property less than a city block away, confirmed what we already knew, that Early Paleo-Indians had visited the chert source. But these people were still essentially archaeologically invisible. Perhaps we hadn't looked deeply enough. The Kirbys, after all, had limited themselves to surface collecting, which cannot be relied on to indicate very accurately what an archaeological site contains. I needed to find a productive way to excavate. The question was where? The following *Archaeological Newsletter* picks up the story after the landowner agreed to let us work on his property again and we could return to the site I had discovered in 1982:

SHOULD IT BE THE BEACH OR THE MOUNTAINS THIS YEAR?
JANUARY 1993

Last July I went to the mountains [and a] ... workshop site, called Thomson after the landowner ... The site is adjacent to one of the better exposures of Fossil Hill chert discovered by Peter von Bitter. At first, most of the site appeared to be on high ground above the chert exposure. There, prehistoric flintknappers made use of large blocks of chert that had been plucked out of the bedrock by glacial ice and subsequently deposited "downstream" of the ice flow. The cultivated fields above the exposure were almost paved with chert fragments and the debris of flintknapping.

Despite the overwhelming abundance of the archaeological material, our surface collecting at first produced nothing culturally diagnostic. Then, by a stroke of luck that still astounds me, my field assistant ... [found] ... a diagnostic Early Paleo-Indian spear point ... The downside of this discovery was that the debris from flintknapping was almost continuous across the surface of the site and there seemed no way of segregating the material produced by Early Paleo-Indian peoples from the products of later groups who may also have used the stone.

Before I go any further, let me tell you a horror that is shared by all archaeologists and curators who cope with limited storage space: QUARRY

SITES! The archaeologist immediately sees in his mind tens of thousands, or millions, of broken and rejected artifacts, few of which are culturally diagnostic; the curator envisions an unmanageable storage problem. The challenge is to find a quarry site containing: (1) very few artifacts, just enough to reconstruct how people used the stone; and (2) discrete occupations by the people you wish to learn about ... Both conditions are seemingly contrary to the nature of a quarry site, and unfortunately neither seemed present at the Thomson site ...

[In an attempt to find a way around this problem] ... Peter von Bitter and I ... decided to walk over some fields we had not been on before. To my great delight we chanced upon a scatter of artifacts exposed by the removal of a brush pile, and Peter von Bitter picked up the tip fragment of what I thought at the time was an Early Paleo-Indian spear point. With this artifact in hand I ... returned to the office with all kinds of plans. Full of excitement, I pooled my ROM research funds from two fiscal years, hired a crew of six university students, and in due course started digging. I expected to learn soon and fairly directly about Early Paleo-Indian quarrying techniques and the early stages of tool manufacture.

It's never really simple, whatever you do, is it?

The area I started work in (near the discovery spot of the point tip) began producing the very thing I wanted to avoid: lots of broken artifacts and the discarded flakes and fragments produced by flintknapping. As time passed, it became apparent I probably wouldn't find the anticipated Early Paleo-Indian tools (and, in my dreams, perhaps a heat treatment pit for preparing the chert for knapping, a cache of finished artifacts, and, if we were very, very lucky, maybe even some bone fragments from food remains). Instead, I had an archaeologists's and curator's nightmare: thousands of non-diagnostic artifacts. This unpleasant situation was compounded by the fact the site was proving very difficult to dig (because of unexpected stratigraphy that could only be revealed through the sound and feel of the trowel in the differently compacted layers of the soil). We were forced to spend ever-increasing amounts of time to obtain data we couldn't relate to a specific group of people.

In a mood of, as they say, quiet desperation, I began looking for another place to dig – a place where, in addition to breaking rock, Early Paleo-Indian flintknappers might have built a few cooking fires (thus leaving charcoal for radiocarbon dating) and carried on some domestic chores (which required culturally diagnostic tools).

I discovered a likely area adjacent to an intermittent stream, about ninety metres away. Although I wanted to transfer the crew to the new location immediately, we had some work to finish up first and it took over a week to transfer everybody, leaving two and a half weeks of field time.

It wasn't long before the nightmare returned! We soon had an overabundance of the same non-diagnostic material we recovered from the first area. Meanwhile, a large trench I had excavated in the side of a hill to find the chert in place in bedrock (together with evidence of Paleo-Indian mining) indicated instead that the chert seam had eroded away during some earlier geological epoch. The prehistoric people hadn't mined the chert (at least at that location) but had dug loose blocks of it from the "ghost" horizon within which it formerly occurred.

Finally, near the end of the project, it was apparent I would have to return to the site another field season and try a different approach to discover evidence of Early Paleo-Indian quarrying and flintknapping activity. This new approach may involve a remote sensing technique (such as seismic work to produce a map of the bedrock under the surface, and therefore the depth of the overburden [or overlying sediments]), perhaps drilling (to determine whether chert occurs at depth in the bedrock), and, unquestionably, a hand-excavated test square to obtain samples of artifacts. We'll need to work in an area of the site not affected by bedrock movements or severely eroded by glacial ice, processes that badly disturbed the first area we investigated and to which I had been attracted by that spear point tip I thought was made by an Early Paleo-Indian. I now think the tip was broken by what is termed "end shock" – a force created by thinning a blank for a tool – and that it was not part of an Early Paleo-Indian point. This, of course, is a disappointment but it only means I was looking in the wrong place. The ... [general area] contains the same potential it always had for teaching us about Early Paleo-Indian quarry work. But with the experience I gained during the first field season, it is I who have changed and have greater potential for discovering that evidence.

Postscript

The first season's fieldwork, in 1992, didn't even come close to answering the questions I had about how Early Paleo-Indians used the chert source area. What I did discover was that I hadn't dug in the right places. Instead of being discouraged, though, I was quite optimistic because I thought I knew where to dig next. I would select a small, geologically stable section of hillside where I thought Fossil Hill chert might be found in the bedrock and then dig downward to expose the chert and look for evidence of Paleo-Indian tool making or subsistence activities immediately adjacent to the chert beds. This was a very chancy thing to do, to attempt to find buried archaeological material where the chert outcrop ought to be. But I could spend years digging in the adjacent ploughed field and have no more to show for it than what I had now, so at least I was trying something different. I didn't yet think this new approach was an act of desperation, but it seemed to be my only other option.

I carefully selected a section of the hillside I thought had been geologically stable – I didn't want to dig around bedrock slabs that had become dislodged and moved downslope – and set out a series of three-metre squares over where I thought we might encounter buried chert. Then we started digging with shovel and trowel. After a few days of this, having excavated only a few centimetres, I began to worry that we might not have time to dig deeply enough to uncover bedrock containing chert and any related archaeological material. Over the next few days my worry increased as I began wondering if the squares we were laboriously digging, still less than half a metre deep, were correctly positioned. They might be too far upslope or too far downslope to intersect the chert beds: beds that, after all, I only assumed to exist.

At this point I received some very timely help. I was visited by Bern Feenstra, a Dutch-Canadian geologist who then worked for the Ontario Ministry of Northern Development and Mines. Bern is a Pleistocene geologist and several years earlier had mapped the area in which I was working and a large part of the surrounding region. Before leaving for the field I had asked Bern to visit us at the start of our work, intending to explain what we were doing and also ask about some of his unpublished data on the glacial history of the area. I was especially interested to see a draft of a map he was preparing for publication. I was totally unprepared, however, for the other, much more crucial help he was to offer.

Bern arrived within a week of when we started work and after taking one look at our pathetically small excavations, asked in a perfectly reasonable manner why I didn't use a backhoe to excavate down to bedrock. I looked at him stupidly for a long moment and said, "But I can't, Bern, this is an archaeological site. The backhoe would be destructive." He looked unconvinced and we talked back and forth around this for a very long time. Very slowly I came around to his point of view. I finally accepted that if I continued as I started I probably wouldn't be able to dig enough to learn anything, which would be a waste of time and money. If I used a backhoe to get down to bedrock quickly and find out where and how deeply buried the chert beds were, the information lost in the machine-excavated trench might be more than compensated for by the knowledge I gained and by the time I saved, which I could use to explore that knowledge using archaeological techniques. It was a trade-off, the kind conceivable only because the archaeological site was very large and thus hardly threatened with destruction, and the information sacrificed to the machine excavation was probably duplicated in many places across it. Although I still had considerable misgivings I decided to follow Bern's advice.

I asked the landowner for his permission. He had first agreed to our work using hand-held tools. Now he agreed to an escalation to heavy construction equipment. But he was also willing to become involved in the excavation itself. He offered to dig the trench with his own backhoe.

Ken Thomson was very skilled in the use of a backhoe, and Bern Feenstra knew how to read the rapidly emerging stratigraphy as the trench deepened and from that rapidly changing picture, where next to direct the work. It was a great team. Weeks of hand labour were reduced to mere seconds as the thick veil of slope debris was removed and the trench grew in size. And I have to admit that it was truly exciting, standing there next to the rapidly growing backdirt pile in the midst of the backhoe's noise and swirling exhaust fumes, watching the underlying bedrock being revealed.

Then we saw the first large block of chert, dislodged by the shovel of the backhoe and dragged out onto the top of the backdirt pile. At that moment we knew for certain we had reached the crucial level. Slowly, Bern directed the backhoe shovel back into the trench to clean the area. This exposed a short, nearly flat bench of bedrock. Directing the shovel forward to the front face of the bench, Bern motioned for it to drop downward once again. This exposed another bench of bedrock, and then another after that, and another still, like a series of steps that descended into the earth. When finally the digging was done and we entered the excavation, even before the last small avalanches of earth and rock fragments stopped raining down the sides of the trench, we found we had discovered more than I dared imagine: at least seven distinct beds of chert, four more than we had observed at the best surface outcrop known. For me, this totally unexpected discovery was tempered by the disquieting realization that the uppermost chert bed was nearly three and a half metres below ground surface at the back, or upslope, end of the trench, and the lowermost bed was a metre below that, nearly eleven metres away horizontally, at the front, or downslope, end of the trench. Even with the best of crews we could never have reached that depth, or covered such a distance, in one field season with hand-held excavation tools. Even then we wouldn't have been entirely successful because I saw that nearly half my original excavation units, staked out before Bern's visit at a time when I thought all the excavation would be done by hand tools, were wrongly placed. Clearly, the machine-dug trench worked.

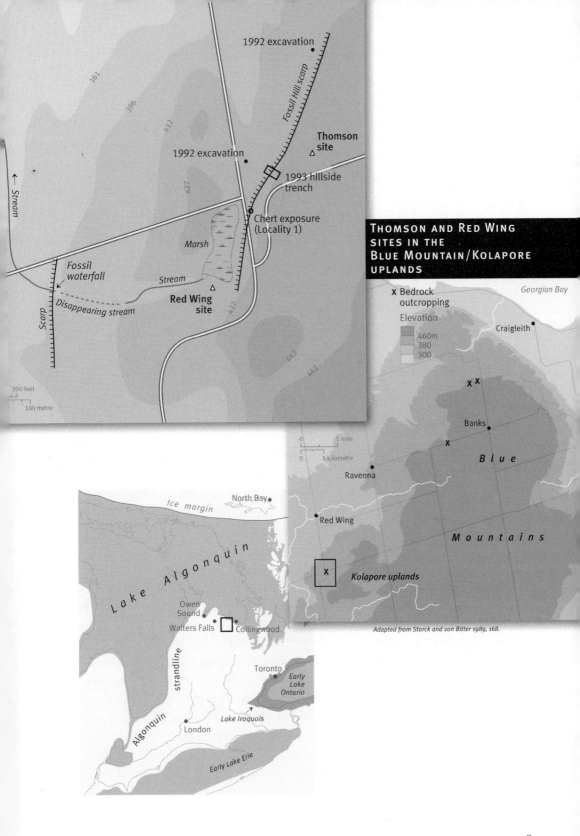

THOMSON AND RED WING SITES IN THE BLUE MOUNTAIN/KOLAPORE UPLANDS

1992 excavation

Fossil Hill scarp

Thomson site

1992 excavation

1993 hillside trench

Chert exposure (Locality 1)

Marsh

Stream

← Stream

Fossil waterfall

Disappearing stream

Scarp

Red Wing site

427

427

442

442

381

396

412

427

200 feet
100 metre

x Bedrock outcropping

Elevation

460m
380
300

Georgian Bay

Craigleith

x x

Banks

x

Blue

Ravenna

Red Wing

Mountains

0   1 mile
0   1 kilometre

x   Kolapore uplands

Adapted from Storck and von Bitter 1989, 168.

Ice margin

North Bay

Lake Algonquin

Owen Sound

Walters Falls   Collingwood

strandline

Toronto

Early Lake Ontario

Lake Iroquois

Algonquin

London

Early Lake Erie

The trench exposed something else. On both the north and south walls it had quite fortuitously sectioned three features: basin-shaped depressions that had been filled with layers of burned rock, ash, and charcoal. These looked to me like prehistoric firepits. I quickly staked out one-metre squares in an expanded excavation grid along the sides of the trench in order to excavate the remaining parts of the features in the archaeologically pre-scribed manner: from the top down to expose the outline first and then downward within the feature itself, carefully saving all the contents for water screening in the laboratory to recover the smallest of plant or animal remains that might be present. I also set out other squares at relevant loca-tions along the sides of the trench to expose larger areas of the step-like beds of chert and search for evidence of prehistoric quarrying or flintknapping.

The backhoe provided wonderful opportunities for highly focused archaeological excavation, and the time to do it. Now it was up to the hand tools, the shovel and the pointed mason's trowel, a humble but vital tool that actually does most of the work in archaeological excavation.

We focused first on the features, as I didn't want them exposed to the elements and possible contamination any longer than necessary. After a few days of work we quickly determined that one of them had been deposited relatively recently since some of the pieces of charcoal con-tained bits of rotten wood. The other two features looked good – no wood adhering to the charcoal fragments – but they contained no tool frag-ments or anything else that I could see. They could therefore be dated only through radiocarbon and this would tell us only the age of the activity that produced the feature, not the cultural identity of the people behind that activity. In the end I decided to date some charcoal from a level below one of the features on the north wall of the trench and another sample from the same profile, both about midway down the stratigraphic column. These were the deepest I could find anything to date. In my excitement, and to make best use of the information in the field, I wanted the radiocar-bon dates yesterday, as the expression goes, so I called IsoTrace, the radio-carbon lab at the University of Toronto, and asked how long the dating would take. Weeks, they said, and possibly longer because they were recal-ibrating the equipment and after that they had a long line of samples to process on a first-come, first-served basis. This reminded me that there are many urgent matters and different agendas in the world, something the self-absorbed and isolated fieldworker often forgets.

We turned next to exploring further the deeply buried chert beds immediately beyond the south wall of the trench. This required excavating down from the surface of the ground, for the most part with trowels, to a depth of over two metres. It was slow going but eventually we got there – or we should have. A portion of chert bed number 5 was missing.

This missing section, about a metre wide, was puzzling. Chert bed number 5 was exposed at the rear and deepest portion of the trench and visible all along its south wall toward the front of the trench, where it suddenly disappeared. A metre or so away from its point of disappearance the chert suddenly reappeared and was visible in the wall of the trench right up to the front of the excavation at the hillside end, where it was buried perhaps a half metre below the ground surface. If it were not for the erosion that created the Beaver valley, this chert bed and the limestone of the Fossil Hill bedrock formation would have extended across the space now occupied by the valley.

Excavations at the Thomson hillside trench in 1993, looking for evidence of prehistoric mining of Fossil Hill chert. Note the upward tilt of bedrock originally deposited horizontally. The bedrock had been shoved out of place by glacial ice as it advanced up the hillside. Left to right: Natalie Rogers, Angela Keenlyside, and Rhan-Ju Song. *Photograph by Peter Storck.*

Clearly the hillside edge of the chert bed had been broken off by gla-cial ice and removed some time during the Ice Age, or perhaps many times, as the ice sheet advanced south through the Beaver valley, deepen-ing the valley and planing its walls into the classic U-shaped valley seen today. The rock that was quarried by the ice sheet was then dropped on top of the Niagara Escarpment when the ice melted. Later the eroded edge of the bedrock along the surface of the valley walls was covered by slope debris and reburied. This eroded surface is what we had exposed at the front of the trench. But deeper into the hillside, just behind this eroded surface, a section of the chert bed not accessible to glacial erosion was missing. What could account for that?

I discovered the answer several days later, or to be more precise, I saw it in the vertical profile of two additional squares we excavated adjacent to the first unit that exposed the missing chert layer. This profile showed that the missing chert had been removed by people. Some person or group of people had dug a vertical shaft down to the chert layer and then removed blocks of the material, perhaps with wooden, bone, or antler levers. The shaft, long since in-filled with rubble, was visible immediately above the missing section of the chert bed, and we could trace it vertically up the profile of our excavation until it was lost in later prehistoric disturbances near the top of the site.

Clearly, someone had dug a deep pit into the hillside to remove stone for flintknapping. This explained in a general sense how the chert had been obtained. I now knew that at least some of the material was obtained by mining, presumably to get the freshest material. (Chert at the surface of the ground will lose some of its moisture and become fractured by the freeze-thaw cycle, reducing its usefulness for knapping or ruining it alto-gether.) But I didn't know *who* had done the mining because we found no culturally diagnostic tools associated with either the hole where the chert should have been or the mine shaft above it.

Nor did we find the answer in the more deeply buried parts of the deposits and lowermost chert beds. Although there were small nests of toolmaking debris at the very base of the site, some beneath large slabs of rock lying against the chert beds, we found no artifacts that would cultur-ally identify the people who left that material. Later, when I received the radiocarbon dates from the two charcoal samples I had removed from the mid-part of the stratigraphic section, I knew that the deepest nests of tool-making debris were probably older than 5,700 to 5,600 years BP, the dates obtained on the charcoal, but how much older I couldn't say.

I was greatly disappointed: all this effort and I still hadn't got very far.

In the fall of 1993, when I wrote my field report for submission to government under the licensing requirements, I thought I had run into the proverbial brick wall. I stated this quite clearly in the final section of my field report, entitled "Recommended Future Work." I wrote, "No future excavations are anticipated at the Thomson site ... since continued fieldwork along the same lines as that conducted in 1992 and 1993 would probably produce similar kinds of data. New approaches need to be formulated and, until they have, continued work would be redundant." I filed the licence report and also requested new licences for the following year, 1994, but I didn't plan to do any major fieldwork that year. Instead, I thought I'd just think about things a bit.

WINDOWS WHERE WALLS ONCE STOOD:
LOOKING FOR NEW INSIGHTS INTO THE PAST
MARCH 1995

Sometimes my greatest challenge as an archaeologist is overcoming my own limitations. I have come to realize that clues to discovering the past are hidden not only in the ground but also in the less familiar places in the mind, just beyond the edges of my previous experience, assumptions, and preconceptions. Thus, like other scientists, or people in sports and many other walks of life, I am in competition with myself. In my work, this means finding new ways of looking at things and new questions to ask, a challenge that often must be met before a new discovery is possible. The road to that discovery is almost never straight or clearly seen, and it may be inadvertently or unconsciously travelled.

This has certainly been true of my recent work on the Blue Mountain uplands in southern Ontario. There, among the apple orchards, pastures, and woodlots of modern-day rural Ontario, I have been looking for traces of a very different, much earlier world and its inhabitants. I have been investigating the spruce parkland and tundra of Ontario during late glacial times and the first people to live in the province after the retreat of the ice sheet – prehistoric hunter-gatherers called Early Paleo-Indians.

I was drawn to the Blue Mountain region over fifteen years ago on a joint project with a geological colleague at the Royal Ontario Museum, Peter von Bitter. We went there (and to other places) looking for the source of the stone preferred by some Early Paleo-Indian groups for tool making. Von Bitter eventually found the source in a small area of the Kolapore uplands on the southeastern rim of the Beaver valley. His discovery was quite important because it indicated that some Early Paleo-Indians in southern Ontario visited the Kolapore uplands, perhaps seasonally, to obtain stone for their tool kits. Hence, contrary to widespread archaeological belief, some Paleo-Indians in North America lived and moved within at least partially defined ranges and were not "free wandering."

The next question was a short step from the first. Now that we knew where the toolstone came from, could that knowledge be used for the purpose of finding Early Paleo-Indian archaeological sites? The answer to that question was, and is, both yes and no. The "yes" part is that almost immediately I found a large workshop where toolstone was tested and shaped into blanks for tool manufacture. By incredibly good luck we also found a single heavily used and discarded spear point, the only culturally diagnostic tool found at the time, and for a long time thereafter. The point indicated that Early Paleo-Indians actually visited the workshop and were responsible for at least some of the vast amount of stone "garbage" (the debris – debitage – from tool making) that littered the site in all directions.

The "no" part of the answer was that, with this essentially continuous sheet of debris, I didn't think I would be able to differentiate material produced by Paleo-Indians from that produced by later peoples. After reflection, I thought perhaps a way around this problem would be to search for isolated clusters of debris containing Paleo-Indian artifacts or, alternatively, to excavate "blindly" at some location above the bedrock source of the toolstone, hoping to come down on buried evidence of Paleo-Indian activity.

For the next two years (1992 and 1993), my excavation crews and I moved a huge amount of earth, most of it with heavily worn trowels not much bigger than serving spoons. In the process we collected hundreds of tool fragments and tens of thousands of pieces of stone debitage in an effort to find a discrete Early Paleo-Indian workshop and a related campsite used for food preparation, tool repair, and other domestic activities. In the course of that work we found several workshops and evidence that some prehistoric people, of as yet unknown age, actually mined the chert. However, we failed to find clear evidence that Early Paleo-Indian peoples actually used the site for living purposes. This negative data suggested that toolstone was obtained not by the band as a whole but by special task groups of a few individuals who visited the chert source area for only short periods and were supported from residential base camps located elsewhere, perhaps outside the region. This hypothesis propelled me into a prominent, ongoing debate in North American archaeology concerning the ways in which prehistoric hunter-gatherers moved about, and exploited, the landscape.

Now that I had a working hypothesis about how toolstone was obtained by Early Paleo-Indians – by special task groups who returned to the source for short periods from year to year – I needed to test it. The question was, how? I had already spent a lot of time digging and had more debitage than I wanted or needed. A new approach was required.

Walking ... and Thinking

In the early spring of 1994 I went back to the chert source area, but this time alone. I wanted to do some slow walking and thinking without the distractions of a field crew. During one of those visits something happened to me that, although trivial at the time, would later unexpectedly alter my way of looking at things. I had been staying at a friend's house adjacent to a millpond in a small village at the top of the Niagara Escarpment. The house was convenient because it is at the western end of the chert source area and just a short drive from where I had been doing most of my fieldwork. One morning while it was still dark, I was pulled out of sleep by the incongruous sound (for 5:00 a.m.) of people in boats. Two and a half hours later, at a more decent hour for me, and over coffee at the only store in the village, I learned that fishing season had just opened. Having discovered the reason for my interrupted sleep, I finished my coffee, put the matter out of my mind and focused once again on my work.

Several weeks later, on a sunny hillside on the edge of a large hollow, I found myself looking down at a small knoll adjacent to a cattail marsh. I had just picked up several hundred pieces of debitage and a diagnostic Early Paleo-Indian tool from the cultivated part of the knoll and was reflecting on the fact that I had not previously excavated in such a location. Raising my eyes, I gazed into the middle distance and then to the horizon and, because there were still very few leaves on the trees, I imagined that I could follow the course of the small stream as it zig-zagged through increasingly larger valleys to a major tributary of the Beaver River several kilometres northwest. At that moment, through some unexplained operation of the mind (often called "lateral" thinking), I remembered the people fishing who had disturbed my sleep. I looked again at the cattail marsh and then at the newly discovered site. This time I saw them connected, and in a vastly different light.

I sat there somewhat stunned, while a rush of questions tumbled around in my head. "Could I have been looking for living sites in the wrong places? What if, during late glacial times, that marsh was actually a pond? Would the pond have held fish? If so, would there have been enough to support people while they were obtaining their yearly supply of toolstone?" And, the most surprising and shocking question of all: "Could Early Paleo-Indians have discovered the toolstone because of their interest in fish, essentially 'backtracking' the fish upstream from the glacial lakes in the surrounding lowlands

to the stream sources in the upland?" Suddenly, I saw tremendous significance in the fact that many streams in the chert source area, including the
one flowing out of the cattail marsh I was looking at, originate from springs
underlying the bedrock layer that contains the toolstone. "Backtracking"
fish upstream would lead directly to the toolstone! To find it, Paleo-Indians
did not need to be geologists, like my colleague, or even explorers, as many
archaeologists supposed.

Thinking these thoughts I remembered something else, a seemingly
small matter from a Paleo-Indian site I had excavated fifteen to twenty years
earlier ... It concerned some artifacts that appeared to have been used for
butchering fish at a site located about twenty-five kilometres east of the chert
source area and on the edge of a former lagoon of a glacial lake. I didn't
make too much of those artifacts at the time, partly because the evidence
was fairly controversial. Now, as I sat on a hillside, looking down at a small
site next to a cattail marsh, those enigmatic artifacts suddenly seemed to be
almost prophetic.

Fossil Rapids
With these thoughts whirling in my head, I lurched down to the marsh and
then unsteadily along the stream to look at my suddenly very different world
from a larger perspective. About a kilometre west of the marsh the modern
stream passed through a cultivated field and then, much to my surprise,
over a small bedrock cliff into another cattail marsh. I stood at the cliff thinking, "I'm looking at a 'fossil' rapids!" This was vivid evidence that the stream
that flowed from the upper marsh and gently past the newly discovered site
on the small knoll was, at some time in the past, very much larger. Thus, the
marsh adjacent to the site may well have contained a lot of water. This geological evidence, still imprecise, offered tentative support for my new way of
thinking and the new questions I was asking.

During the next couple of months I returned several times to the cattail
marsh near the new site and to the "fossil" rapids with many different people – geologists, wildlife ecologists, and specialists in various paleoecological disciplines – to discuss the research potential of the marsh and the
adjacent archaeological site. Gradually I developed a strategy and objectives
for a two-year field project involving extensive archaeological excavation,
cooperative work with several scholars in the geological and natural sciences, and some state-of-the-art technology. By late summer I had the project worked out in detail, and in early September I started preparing a grant
request for federal funding to supplement anticipated ROM funds. I submitted this request in mid-October, five months after I looked through what may

be a new window into the past. Now, as I write this in the grey light of mid-winter, I keenly anticipate spring, when the blossoming flowers, new leaves (and, I hope, grant money) renew life and archaeological endeavours once again, and start a new natural and academic cycle. If I receive the funds I need and find what I hope to find the story I will have for you in the next newsletter will be ... major, major ...

Postscript

This newsletter is full of optimism. Unexpectedly, after two years of hard digging with ambiguous results, I thought I had found a new approach for answering old questions and even some I hadn't thought of before. This turnabout happened because of the new site I had just discovered adjacent to a small marsh in a deep hollow, an environmental situation I had never before investigated. The new site was just across the road from where I had worked in 1992 and 1993, so how, you might ask, could I not have discovered the site earlier? The marsh is screened from the road, and from the field and hillside where I had been working, by a dense growth of cedars and other trees. It is visible only much farther down the road, across a grassy hillside that slopes steeply down to the distant marsh. The roadside edge of the grassy hillside is simply another anonymous place in the landscape, with nothing about it that would cause you to walk over and look at it or stop beside it on the edge of the road and glance beyond.

Besides, I hadn't been looking for another place to work. I thought I'd already found it in the low ridge or scarp that marked the buried face of the Fossil Hill bedrock formation and the chert it contained. Because of the satisfaction I felt when Peter von Bitter finally discovered the geological source of the white chert, its potential for telling us about the lives of Early Paleo-Indians, and the wonderful exposure we found once the source had been discovered and used to quarry material for experimental purposes, I was mesmerized by the white toolstone. When I started my work in the chert source region I therefore chose first to excavate at a location adjacent to the Fossil Hill bedrock scarp and then later on the scarp itself. It was only after these approaches didn't work that I paused, not knowing what to do next, and stood back a bit. Only then was I receptive once again to seeing things around me that I had either not noticed before or to which I had paid little attention in my preoccupation.

Returning to the area alone one early spring day I stood in the road that bordered the field and hillside where I had been working. After a few moments I turned away from the disturbances that marked our earlier excavations and walked along the road as it climbed the steep hill that was the Fossil Hill scarp. Opposite the roadside outcrop of Fossil Hill chert I had become so familiar with I crossed the road, hoping to see a continuation of the outcrop on the other slope of the hill. Seeing nothing in the dense woods I returned to the road and walked along it farther as it climbed to the top of the Fossil Hill scarp. Past the edge of the woods and around a bend I soon reached the top edge of a grass-covered slope that fell away steeply down to a small marsh. Looking at that marsh and then back along the way I had come I suddenly realized that I had unconsciously allowed the road, which cut the marsh off from the Fossil Hill scarp physically and visually, to constrain my thinking. I should have moved easily back and forth intellectually across the narrow asphalt strip on which I was standing, part of the thin veneer of the modern world, but I had allowed my thinking and my work to become circumscribed by both the very recent (the modern road and field system) and the very ancient (the Fossil Hill scarp). I saw at that moment that I needed a much broader perspective to make any more progress in my work.

This other approach to fieldwork, and the new questions I now asked, were stimulated by the marsh. This low-lying area, filled ankle-deep with water and underlain by water-saturated sediments, was an ideal habitat for preserving the plant and animal remains needed to reconstruct climatic and environmental changes over the history of the marsh and any earlier ponds. Being adjacent to an archaeological site, or perhaps overlapping it somewhat if the borders of the marsh and human occupation had fluctuated, these data might also help date the human occupation. The biological record of the marsh or former ponds might also identify food resources used by the people at the site, such as fish, the first thing that sprang to my mind. This idea was novel to me but it also raised a far more significant question, one that I referred to in the newsletter but didn't explain.

My hypothesis that Early Paleo-Indians may have discovered Fossil Hill chert because of an interest in fishing introduced a new, ecological slant to the question of how Ice Age hunter-gatherers integrated the need for toolstone into other aspects of their lives. To explain the significance of this new slant to an old question it is necessary to backtrack a bit. Early Paleo-Indians made some very complex and sophisticated tools, the most prominent being the fluted spear point, which even the best flintknappers today find very difficult to replicate. To make these tools Early Paleo-Indians selected some of the very best stone available and often carried it in the form of blanks and finished artifacts over extremely long distances. Because of this apparent three-way correlation between complex tools, high-quality stone, and long-distance transport, Albert Goodyear, an archaeologist in the southeastern United States, developed the hypothesis that Early Paleo-Indians actually required high-quality stone to support a mobile way of life, the stone providing the potential for tools that demanded a high level of flintknapping control over breakage patterns and also flexibility for resharpening broken tools or reshaping them into other tool types. It is this potential and flexibility, the hypothesis states, that supported mobility on a scale several times larger than used by later hunter-gatherers in the so-called Archaic period, extending from perhaps 9,500 to 3,000 years BP. Considering that Early Paleo-Indians of the Clovis or Clovis-related cultures such as Gainey are the first to appear in the archaeological record in most regions of North America, presumably reflecting migration and the colonization of previously unknown territories, the ability of these Ice Age people to search out the best toolstones is astounding. Especially to geologists and archaeologists such as Peter von Bitter and myself, who, despite the greater resources at their disposal for exploration have sometimes had great difficulty rediscovering Paleo-Indian discoveries.

Archaeologists have come to think of Early Paleo-Indians as something akin to "hunter-gatherer geologists," but few seem to consider how that geological knowledge might have been obtained. Did these people send out small parties of explorers into the unknown to look for sources of toolstone deliberately and then adjust their pattern of movements across the landscape accordingly? Or did Early Paleo-Indians discover toolstone incidentally during the course of learning the seasonal distribution of food resources and then lock in to those types of toolstone that fit their mobility requirements for subsistence? The latter concept provides the ecological slant to the question of toolstone procurement that struck me when I first contemplated the possible significance of the marsh or whatever habitat that predated it. I framed a new question that took its place alongside *who* and *how: Why?* Why did some Early Paleo-Indians prefer Fossil Hill chert over the other types of toolstone available? Why not Onondaga chert along the northeast edge of the Erie basin or Kettle Point chert on the southeast edge of the Huron basin, both in extreme southwestern Ontario?

The answer, I speculated, must have something to do with the seasonal availability of food resources in different parts of the province or, alternatively, with the properties of Fossil Hill chert as a toolstone. Because I was experienced enough in making stone tools to appreciate that Fossil Hill chert wasn't necessarily superior to other types for flintknapping,

I suspected that it might have been preferred out of convenience because Early Paleo-Indians wanted or needed to be in the southern Georgian Bay region at certain times for subsistence purposes.

Years earlier, while excavating at Fisher on the edge of glacial Lake Algonquin along the margin of the Blue Mountain/Kolapore uplands, I had speculated that food resources in a lake-edge environment, possibly caribou and to a lesser extent fish, drew people to the southern Georgian Bay region for part of the year. This seasonal movement also brought them within striking range of the Fossil Hill toolstone in the Blue Mountain/Kolapore uplands. Hence Fisher, I thought, was strategically positioned between the mountains and the inland sea for exploiting both local biological and distant mineral resources. Several years later while working at Udora, also located on Lake Algonquin but in another part of the central Ontario lowlands and with hard evidence for caribou hunting, I wondered again if the seasonal migration of caribou might have drawn people to the geological source of Fossil Hill toolstone.

Now, working in the uplands, I wondered more seriously about fish. I also wondered whether changing patterns in the distribution of food resources at the end of the Ice Age – or in the case of caribou perhaps its disappearance altogether – might also explain why Fossil Hill chert was eventually replaced by other types of toolstone, or at least used much less extensively. After the disappearance of Parkhill peoples from the archaeological record, Fossil Hill chert appears to have been little used by later groups of Early Paleo-Indians (those of the Crowfield complex) and, following them, by Late Paleo-Indians, most of whom preferred Onondaga chert from southern Ontario along the northeastern edge of the Erie basin.

Why Fossil Hill chert was preferred for a time as a toolstone is also related to *how* the chert was obtained. If upland food resources were sufficiently abundant, such as spawning fish or caribou migrating to their spring or summer pastures, they may very well have attracted entire family groups or bands of several families for short periods. If so, it's conceivable that Fossil Hill chert was discovered fortuitously and its use as toolstone embedded in and secondary to the annual subsistence cycle. If, conversely, food resources were sparse and unreliable on the uplands, requiring people to pack their food with them, then the toolstone might have been obtained only by special-purpose task groups supported from base camps located elsewhere. In this case the preference for Fossil Hill chert as a toolstone would reflect a deliberate and costly choice in the sense that it would have taken people temporarily away from food-getting activities in the adjacent lowlands.

These were just ideas, but with the discovery of the new site adjacent to the marsh, I now had a way of exploring them in the field, much like the hypothesis testing other scientists do in what are regarded as the more truly experimental sciences such as physics and chemistry.

I could do this, that is, if I could get the funds. At this point it was once again time to begin that familiar and gruelling process of applying for money. As I've described, the process often requires a month or more, on top of all the exploratory fieldwork and other mental preparations such as I've just outlined. And this preparatory period is followed by several months of waiting.

Finally, I received a letter from the Social Sciences and Humanities Research Council of Canada. My grant request had been approved, and for nearly every dollar I asked. This time, though, the financial implications were much greater than ever before in my experience; I had asked for, and received, a research grant not for just one year but for three. This included funds for two field seasons and a follow-up year for analysis. For an unbelievably long period I didn't have to worry about money, if I could also obtain the necessary supplementary support from the ROM Foundation on an annual basis. But that, too, happened. The peer review panel and senior administrators decided to approve my grant request from the ROM Foundation for 1995 and later for 1996. Thus began, to use an expression from another age in the history of archaeology, my third field campaign in the Blue Mountain/Kolapore uplands.

EVERYWHERE, YET NOWHERE
APRIL 1996

... When I started my fieldwork last summer, I had some ideas about how Early Paleo-Indians exploited toolstone during the course of their annual movements. I intended to explore these ideas through the excavation of a newly discovered site, which I called Red Wing, after a small community nearby located in the Kolapore uplands. The Red Wing site occurs in a topographic setting that had never before been explored: a low-lying area adjacent to a small marsh at the bottom of a deep hollow. I speculated that during the late Ice Age this marsh may have been a small lake and possibly even a source of food (fish) that initially attracted Early Paleo-Indians to the source area of the toolstone and supported them while they exploited the stone. I speculated further that these resources may have been sufficient to support family groups and that, contrary to our previous thinking, the stone source area might have been part of a band range, not an outlying area visited by special task groups from outside the region. If my thinking was correct, I expected to find a whole range of tools on the site such as spear points, knives, scrapers, drills, and all the other tools used by both sexes to meet the needs of daily life.

The fieldwork started out very well. The water table was low, as hoped, allowing us to dig next to the marsh, and we found a large quantity of material over a much, much larger area than I had expected. Then I began to get disturbed. Instead of finding a complete range of tools, which I had expected if the site had been occupied by bands of allied families, I was recovering only broken bifaces. These artifacts had been made to serve as tool blanks for transport from one site to another during the course of the annual subsistence round. During that time they would be used either as a source of raw material for flake tools until they were expended or, alternatively, as "blanks" for formal tools, such as spear points. These tool blanks are exactly what one would expect to find if the stone source area had been visited by special task groups. Thus it looked as if my earlier interpretation, based on my 1992 and 1993 excavations at other sites in the general area, had been right (the toolstone had, in fact, been exploited by special task groups) and that my alternative hypothesis, generated by the unusual topographic setting of the Red Wing site and the biological potential of the former lake, was wrong. The evidence of special task activities was everywhere – yet nowhere was I able to find evidence of a larger tool kit of the kind I thought would reflect the presence of a mixed group of people, and the band. As our excavations expanded, broken tool blanks turned up in every corner of the site, and as they did my sense of disappointment grew deeper and deeper.

Of Fish and Vegetation

While this was happening, the natural scientists (and, vicariously, I through them) were having a great time. Peter Barnett, the Pleistocene geologist working with me on the project, and two other paleoecologists, Stephen Monckton and Denis Delorme, pulled up several cores from the middle of the marsh. These cores indicated very clearly that the marsh had, in fact, been a small lake during late glacial times. The cores also contained sediments that promised good organic preservation, so Stephen would be able to reconstruct the vegetation that surrounded the site and Denis might be able to tell us about the temperature and depth of the water and perhaps even whether fish lived in it. Naturally I was pleased that my hunch about the former environment around the site had been correct. The disquieting thing was, everything seemed to be going well except for the archaeology.

And then I began questioning my disappointment about the archaeology. This questioning started when we began finding pieces of waste stone that had been used as tools, and used so heavily that some of them were worn to a bright polish that glinted through the dust of the excavation. Clearly, these spontaneous tools were used to work something organic, possibly food derived from the former lake or immediate area, or some other raw material. They also provide evidence for something else: in addition to working stone, the Early Paleo-Indians at Red Wing were also involved in a second major activity or group of activities. This raises an important question: Could these two groups of activities – the manufacture of tool blanks and the processing of organic materials – have been conducted simultaneously by members of a small task group, or would they have required a larger and more diverse group of people? As I mentioned earlier, I had expected to find a wide range of formal tools if the site had been occupied by bands of families. But perhaps my expectation was wrong. Maybe I shouldn't have been looking for a broad range of tools. Maybe the simple, spontaneous tools were providing me with the evidence for band occupation I had been seeking. With this surprising thought, the field season ended. And it ended on a high note because I felt that perhaps some aspects of my alternative hypothesis still had some life.

I soon became even more optimistic. Shortly after I returned to the ROM, Stephen Monckton, the paleobotanist, called to say that the longest core provided an excellent record of the vegetation during the life of the lake, the period during which the site was probably visited by Early Paleo-Indians. However, to his complete surprise, there was no record at all for the long period between the time the lake drained, at the end of the Ice Age, and the recent past. Nothing! For 10,000 years! The only explanation he could suggest is that the low-lying area adjacent to the site must have been dry during this period, and so failed to preserve a record of the vegetation. He suggested that the present-day marsh was created at the beginning of the historic period, when forest clearance in connection with agriculture raised the water table. Thus, ironically (and somewhat embarrassingly), the marsh that first attracted me to the site only came into existence a couple of hundred years ago! Be that as it may, the dramatic absence of a vegetation record after the lake drained accentuates the lake itself and gives the environment of the late Ice Age a unique, or at least a distinctive, quality. Because of this, I can't help thinking that something other than the nearby presence of toolstone also attracted Early Paleo-Indians to the Red Wing site. I thought this other something might have been fish. I was in for a rude shock.

Which Way to Turn?

That shock came with a telephone call from Denis Delorme, the paleobiologist on the project. He reported that the lake sediments were essentially sterile!

Not only were there no invertebrate fossils, but he found no evidence of any zooplankton that might have served as food for fish. At that moment, with my hand still on the telephone, my hypothesis that fish may have led Early Paleo-Indians to discover the chert source flew (or swam) right out the window. My only consolation was that it is better to know you're wrong than innocently to follow a false trail. But, I thought, short of digging up the rest of the site and simply hoping for the best, where is the right trail? Which way should I turn next?

Perhaps the answer to this question is to be found on the spontaneous tools themselves: in the minute traces of damage the tools suffered when they were used. Under low-power magnification, it is easy to see that the cutting or scraping edges on these simple tools were rounded, abraded, nicked, and polished. I wondered if this damage might be used to identify the broad classes of materials these tools were used to work and, secondly, if this evidence might be corroborated by plant macrofossils found in the cores we pulled up from the marsh. Fortunately I know an archaeologist who specializes in the study of use-wear damage on stone tools, and I have been impressed and sometimes astonished at what he can read from these barely visible traces. As you read this, he will be just starting his work. As he does, the direction of our combined research will take another sharp turn, one that symbolizes the pathway of all scientific inquiry: never in a straight line, sometimes opportunistic, almost always unexpected. More turns probably lie ahead, but for the moment we are travelling a straight road with a clear objective – down through the tube of a microscope and into the world of the very small.

Postscript

No fish! Or caribou! Or any other evidence of the plants or animals Early Paleo-Indians might have exploited at Red Wing. We hadn't found very many diagnostic Early Paleo-Indian artifacts either, mostly the debris from early stages of flintknapping, which could have been produced by anyone. Not a very auspicious beginning. The wonderful picture we were developing of the late glacial environment around the site would be for nothing if I couldn't answer the questions *who* and *why*.

On a more optimistic note regarding the archaeology we did discover a number of very heavily worn tools. These, I thought, might tell us what people were cutting and scraping, and possibly harvesting, at Red Wing. Who could say where that information might lead?

My second, unstated reason for optimism was that I still had another field season ahead of me. Perhaps I could turn this project around yet. I was determined to pull it off successfully and this meant finding the camp area where the people who worked at Red Wing actually lived. Only a camp area would provide the tools and other information I needed to determine who actually used the site (Early Paleo-Indians, I hoped but had yet to confirm), the make-up of the social groups at the site (whether families or special task groups), and whether they visited for reasons other than acquiring toolstone. This still hypothetical camp had to be some- where. Everyone needs to eat and sleep, and space to do it. The question I had to solve was … where?

Perhaps I had already discovered a hint. During the first season's work we seemed to find a large number of flake tools down by the marsh outlet. These tools hadn't been shaped, just picked up from the discarded flint- knapping debris and used as they were, but they had clearly been very heav- ily employed for plant harvesting, butchering, or making tools from wood, bone, or antler. Many of these spontaneously used tools also appeared to have been heat treated, slowly heated in the ground under a fire to craze the chert microscopically and thus improve its flaking qualities. This sug- gested that the area adjacent to the marsh outlet was used intensively for activities other than rough flintknapping, and being close to water it might also contain some plant and animal remains preserved by burial, charring, or discard in water-saturated sediments. When I finished writing the last sentence of that newsletter just before the second field season, most of my thoughts and hopes were therefore focused on the marsh outlet.

So this is where I started, on 3 June 1996. I hadn't wanted to start that early because the ground doesn't really dry out until late June or mid-July, and August would be even better for excavating down near the marsh. The ROM funds I had received the previous fall, however, had to be accounted for by the end of the 1995-6 fiscal year, 30 June. Some leeway was possible but definitely not, I was pointedly told, beyond mid-July. This was cutting it pretty close for someone who wanted to work beside a marsh. Clearly, the flow of money in our modern world wasn't managed by people who needed to work in wet places.

It was a wet spring. We hit groundwater only a few centimetres below the surface in the first few squares we opened by the marsh outlet. I wasn't prepared for routine excavation in wet ground. So while waiting for the ground to dry out – surely in another week or so, I thought – I transferred the crew to another area of the site that had produced a few Early Paleo- Indian tool fragments the previous year. We found little but flintknapping debris. This filled bag after bag, and then box after box, slowly crowding us out of the makeshift laboratory in the field house we were renting.

From time to time I sent people back to the marsh outlet, only to pull them out again after a few hours because of the wet ground. Back and forth, again and again. Eventually I succeeded in excavating a single short trench on the highest ground near the outlet but the results were a disappointment, and the lower ground seemed as wet as ever.

It soon became apparent that I would never be able to excavate near the marsh outlet as extensively as I wanted. This realization left me in near panic and led to a desperate action. I decided to throw out a series of lines into the unknown, beyond the tested portion of the site, and use a motor-driven auger to search for the camp area I was convinced must be, had to be, there. The auger wouldn't do any damage to the site since I knew from a few probes that the area I would be investigating had been ploughed. The other advantage, considering my 1 July deadline, was that the auger was much faster for testing an unknown area than digging by hand. The only disadvantage was that the auger brought up a lot less soil than was produced by a hand-dug one-metre square. This narrowed slightly our chances of finding something at any particular coring spot, but on the positive side we could dig a far greater number of auger holes than one-metre squares and could place them closely together to ensure adequate sampling. Furthermore, the same technique had detected the Early Paleo-Indian occupation in Area A-East at Udora in 1987. That area, later excavated by hand tools, produced the rich assemblage of artifacts and the calcined animal bone I discussed in Chapter 6. Since the coring at Udora had found something I might not otherwise have discovered, why not again at Red Wing?

Hurriedly, I threw out three auger lines. Then, on 25 June, the auger bit from hole 21 on line 2 in the southeastern portion of the site area brought up two Early Paleo-Indian tools. This was very unusual. Immediately I arranged to transfer a crew member, Susan Tupakka, from the marsh outlet to the line of auger holes. At the start of work the next day she began excavating a one-metre test square centred on auger hole 21. It wasn't long before Susan recovered more artifacts. First the tip of a late-stage tool blank and soon after that a beautifully made and finished preform, obviously intended as a spear point.

I was very impressed by the discovery of four tools in such a small area and hoped this might be prophetic of much more to come. I was also pleased, and very much relieved, to see the nascent spear point because it suggested the answer to the question *who*. Although it was not fluted, possibly because it was regarded as too thin, the artifact looked very much like a Barnes-type point, diagnostic of the Early Paleo-Indian Parkhill culture. Finally, the end of the search seemed to be near at hand. With this artifact and, I hoped, others to follow I could begin to document what we had previously only suspected – that Parkhill people did, in fact, visit the Blue Mountain/Kolapore uplands and had been present at the Red Wing site.

Although I was excited by the artifacts in this newly discovered part of the site, I was also becoming anxious. It was now very late in the field season. We had only nineteen days left, not all of which would be effective field time. An upcoming Monday holiday couldn't be ignored, and we would need several days for backfilling the excavations and closing up the field house. And, of course, I also needed to finish up work in the area of the marsh outlet. Time was short.

I decided to transfer a couple of other people immediately to the new area, which I now called the Southeast grid. This slowed the work at the marsh outlet. In an effort to explore two areas of the site simultaneously I risked overextending myself and thus failing to accomplish either objective. But I needed to have a better idea what else might be found in the Southeast grid before I could make appropriate decisions about where to place people.

On 21 June, our third sunny day in a row and the first period of sunshine that long all month, we discovered the tip fragment of a fluted spear point. That is to say, Luc Bouchet-Bert, one of my crew members, did. I wasn't even on the site at the moment of discovery. In my absence the crew, led by assistant supervisor Heidi Ritscher, decided to spring a surprise. When I returned to the site I saw the crew huddled around a single screen used for sieving earth to recover small artifact fragments and flintknapping debris. I immediately became irritated at the slow pace of work this behaviour implied. As I walked over to the group staring at me with silly smiles and seemingly unembarrassed by their slothfulness, I was doubly irritated when, in a sweet and oddly vacant voice, Heidi asked me to come over and look at the pretty rock they had found. This was a curious and uncharacteristic thing for Heidi to say, one of the best-organized and conscientious supervisors I ever had, and I approached the group with great suspicion. The artifact was handed to me in silence and what a great surprise it was! This moment of celebration marked the discovery of the one thing we wanted to find most of all, a fluted spear point.

It was very small and only fragmentary, about the size of a thumbnail. Its identifying features had been almost obscured by heavy resharpening, and during its last episode of use it had sustained damage from impact fractures, perhaps from contact with bone in the animal it struck. But there was absolutely no doubt what it was. Because of its relatively narrow width I thought it was a Barnes-type fluted point. This was consistent with the point preform found earlier, and it appeared as though we had discovered a discrete activity area used by Parkhill people. Not only that, but the activity area appeared to have been occupied *only* by Parkhill people. There was no evidence that it had been reoccupied by people of different cultures – resulting in intermingled tools that might never be separated – which had been an ever-present worry of mine from the very first moment we started excavating.

0   3 cm

Artifacts from the Red Wing site. Left to right top row: double-edged spokeshave; flake with several graving spurs; reworked tip of exhausted fluted spear point (above); scraper fragment (below); unfluted spear point, possibly unfinished. Left to right bottom row: knife fragment; broken preform; base of broken wood-working adze, with tip removed. *Courtesy ROM.*

As I looked at the fluted point and discussed its identification with the gathered crew, a part of me was also planning the traditional champagne party I threw after the first fluted point was found on a new site. I wasn't sure I'd get to the liquor store before it closed; there was much to do before I could leave the site that afternoon. First it was time to stop doing two things at once. The remaining work in the marsh outlet would just have to wait and perhaps not even get done. I told the crew I was transferring *everyone* to the new area, *immediately.* And while they went off to assemble their equipment from the marsh outlet and cover the unfinished excavation units with plastic tarps, several of us started unwinding measuring tapes, pounding wooden stakes into the ground, and connecting them with taut lines of string for the greatly expanded excavation grid. If necessary, I thought, I would work in the Southeast grid until the end of the project and even beyond with volunteers, borrowed time, borrowed money, and whatever else it took to see this through to the end.

The end finally came at 6:00 p.m. on Friday, 12 July, nearly two weeks after the close of the ROM's fiscal year. But we had done it. By the barest of margins we had completely excavated a small Early Paleo-Indian campsite in the midst of the geological source of Fossil Hill chert. No one had succeeded in this before. The campsite, probably better described as a retooling area – a place where tools already in use, along with their organic components such as handles and shafts, were repaired – covered an area of about 400 square metres. From this small area came a diverse assortment of tools: the spear points described earlier; some late-stage preforms (thin bifaces used as sources of raw material, as tools themselves, or possibly as blanks for spear points); several gravers, small tools with needle-like tips used for piercing holes, shredding fibre, cutting sockets, and incising decorations or making bone buttons or jewellery; end scrapers, for shaving wood and scraping hides; and spokeshaves, for smoothing cylindrical wooden or bone shafts. We also discovered a new tool type. At first I thought they were clumsy attempts at making tool blanks, perhaps by a novice flintknapper. But John Tomenchuk, who had studied some of the Fisher site artifacts and was now working with us on this project, saw microscopic evidence that the so-called novice blanks were actually adzes and had been used to cut wood. The triangular cross sections of the tools that I had interpreted as failed attempts to thin the blanks were instead deliberately shaped to create a stronger tool, able to withstand the stresses of use as an adze. Stone adzes had never before been described from an Early Paleo-Indian site in the Great Lakes region. The only comparable wood-working adzes from an early period are those from a presumably later culture in a distant region: the Late Paleo-Indian Dalton culture in the southeastern United States. If the Red Wing adzes are indeed part of the Early Paleo-Indian Parkhill tool kit in Ontario, they may have been made and used only at sites in the chert source area, possibly for cutting wood used in heat treating chert or for making wooden handles, spear shafts, and other tools.

This small collection of artifacts, from a small corner of the site I might easily never have discovered, contains within it whatever answers I will find to the questions *who* and *why*. What now remains, as I write these words, is to tease every bit of information out of them that we can, by whatever means: comparative morphological analysis, metric analysis, use-wear analysis through the conventional microscope and the scanning electron microscope, and any other kinds of analyses we can think of. I had wanted other kinds of data as well, such as plant and animal remains and charcoal for dating, but what we walked away with on 12 July is all we're going to get, at least for now. Maybe more extensive excavation at Red Wing, in the marsh outlet area or elsewhere, or at new sites in other environments in the chert source area will more fully document the answers to the questions I asked. Alternatively it might correct those answers or raise new questions, but that is for the future and perhaps for another archaeologist.

After three years in the Blue Mountain/Kolapore uplands and nearly two decades in the lowlands of south-central Ontario, looking for the long-abandoned trail of an Ice Age people, it is difficult sometimes not to feel their presence or imagine the environment in which they lived. On occasion I have come close to being transported back to that distant time. Sometimes it happens while I walk slowly across the sand of a fossil beach, far removed in space and time from any water today. Glancing up at the gulls wheeling overhead I wonder if those birds inherited a genetically encoded species-memory of what once was. Not likely, I tell myself. But their screeching cries call that ancient beach into my present and make it almost real. The sand becomes the beach of a glacial lake, washed by waves just beyond my ability to see and hear, and warmed not by the modern sun I feel on my shoulders but by the ancient sun of an Ice Age summer. It is then that I feel the presence of the caribou and the hunter who may not be far behind, and yearn to see into that distant time and experience it directly, emotionally.

I have also come close to that distant past when seeing, from the floor of the Beaver valley, the first storms of winter obscuring the heights of the Blue Mountains. What must the Ice Age storms have been like? How much more severe? Can the rushing clouds of white, driven by winds of silent snow, be anything but a feeble masquerade of the Ice Age winter that drove animals and people alike to the shelter of spruce forests much farther south? And what of the long trek back in the spring of the year? How many human dramas occurred along the way before the ancient pathways climbed once again to the source of the toolstone, renewal, and another season of life?

These are scattered impressions based on the feel of sand beneath the feet and the picture in the mind's eye of a line of hills emerging from beneath the retreating ice sheet, waves lapping against a steep shore bluff or milky white glacial meltwater coursing down a valley that today is empty and silent. This is a parallel world to our own, yet very different; gone, yet still strongly imprinted on the modern landscape.

Unlike the forces of nature, the people who lived in that ancient world left much more ephemeral traces of their passing, just a few fragments of broken tools scattered here and there on the landscape. Yet the tools are silent reminders of those who might otherwise have been forgotten.

Iron-stained quartzite bedrock, fortuitously in the shape of a human figure, near the top of the La Cloche Range. This natural image is evocative of the unknown in the human past and in the human condition.

Photograph by Peter Storck.

These dream-like visions – of a vanished world and a long-dead people – intrude on the disciplined part of the mind, the carefully trained part that uses the methods of science to assemble ever more data, always trying to delay for as long as possible, perhaps indefinitely, the hypotheses and then the conclusions that are continuously forming and threatening to become fixed in the mind. The scholar fights this to remain open minded and guard against bias or error. But the visions spring from emotions, and neither will be denied. From them come images of what may have been.

Approximations
of the Past

THE SMALL GROUP OF HUNTERS and several adolescents arrived just as the frost of early morning was melting. Since midday yesterday, after climbing steep slopes, skirting the edges of rocky cliffs, and finally crossing over onto the edge of the highlands, the group had walked steadily westward. The highland surface was broadly rolling, interrupted occasionally by narrow zones of steep, tightly clustered hills surrounded by deep depressions that had formed during short pauses of the retreating ice sheet. Except for these areas the walking was fairly easy, in part because the exposed terrain was covered with a tundra-like vegetation of herbs and mosses. The only disadvantage of this route was the strong westerly winds that carried a sharp cold, as if from ice itself. Elsewhere on this land – on east-facing slopes warmed by the sun, in small stream valleys, and other protected areas – were groves of spruce. Although dense in the middle the groves thinned toward their exposed outer margins, where trees took the form of small shrubs or distorted dwarves pruned above the winter snow line by particles of ice blown by the wind. As the group travelled farther and farther into the highland interior the lingering cold of the glacial night increased with elevation, and patches of snow grew larger and merged occasionally into unbroken expanses of glaring white. Spring here was much delayed compared to the lowlands on the edge of a great lake where the main camp had been established a week earlier.

To the hunters this lake was larger than the land they knew. It extended from the most distant seasonal camps in the direction of the morning sun to the edge of the lowlands where the band was now camped. From there the lake turned in the direction of the coldest winter winds and then toward the evening sun, making a large loop around the base of the highlands. On the opposite side of the highlands, several days' journey toward the afternoon sun, in the direction the hunters were now walking, the lake expanded to the horizon in three directions: directly ahead toward the place where the sun seemed to fall into the lake itself; to the right in the direction of the winter winds; and to the left toward the sun's lowest seasonal path across the sky, beyond the late fall and winter camps the people occupied in the shelter of the forests. And the people knew that this immense lake washed up against the Ice World itself, in the place of the winter winds, well beyond sight of the youngest eyes or probably even the highest soaring birds. But on the edge of the highlands where they were now walking that world was plainly evident from the countless blocks of ice, some larger than hills, that were seen occasionally, drifting far out from shore.

The group stopped near the base of a limestone cliff near the head of a large valley and dispersed over a gently sloping hillside next to a pond. Some began unpacking their equipment while others prepared to make cooking and warming fires from the dead branches of small spruce that grew around the pond and along the limestone cliff. During the course of this settling in, one or another of the adults would get up and walk a short distance away to the cliff or some other secluded place. There he would say a few words of greeting to the spirit in the rock and leave an offering such as a scrap of caribou meat or a broken fragment of a stone tool retained from the last visit and carried on the year-long journey to be returned to this sacred place.

From the top of the hillside above the pond, and even more so from the limestone cliff above the work party, the entire valley could be seen as it sloped down toward the winter winds, broadening and deepening until the lower portion was flooded by a long arm of the distant lake. The men knew, from stories told by the elders, that a very long time ago this place had been the scene of a tremendous battle. Ice Spirit, who was indifferent to the people, had advanced through the region. It moved up the valley toward the highlands and then over the cliff below which the hunters were now encamped. Earth Spirit, who was protective of the people, became angered at this assault when the people's ancestors first approached this land and started fighting with Ice Spirit. The two spirits struggled furiously and after one horrendous blow Earth knocked Ice to the ground, fell on it heavily and held it down so firmly that parts of it turned to stone.

Ice fought back. But Earth was too strong and Ice had to retreat, leaving fragments of itself where they lay and other parts still buried beneath Earth.

It is this rock the hunters have come to obtain, for it is sharp and good for tools. Betraying its origins the rock of Ice Spirit is white or occasionally bluish white, like the ice floating in the huge lake. Sometimes it is tinged with streaks of yellowish red, reminiscent of blood and a reminder of the battle between two powerful spirits so long ago. Since then the story of battle, preserved in the memory of generation after generation of elders, has led people to this sacred place each spring so that hunters can replenish their nearly exhausted supplies of tools and weapons depleted over the preceding year.

After a brief rest in front of the warming fires, the men began collecting blocks of toolstone in preparation for knapping. Several boys of varying ages helped by carrying the blocks back to the work areas or collected material for their own use. Although some were too young to be of much help, let alone work on their own, their involvement was not discouraged or restrained. By participating in the work they were gradually learning the skills of stone tool making. As was the custom among the people in many things there was little direct teaching in the techniques of flintknapping. Rather the skills were acquired by observing and attempting to duplicate the work of adults and by listening to the comments that accompanied their successes and failures.

In little time a large quantity of toolstone was collected. The men started breaking the blocks open with hammerstones to determine whether they contained any hidden flaws or natural fractures that would cause sudden failure during the knapping process. They worked in small groups for the sake of conversation or simply company and most of the boys, whether only observing or involved in their own work, found a place in the midst of the activity.

One of the older boys, however, decided to work alone. He had already acquired a good deal of experience in knapping and was able to make a wide variety of cutting, scraping, and piercing tools. Today, however, he wanted to make the one tool that still frustrated his abilities: the distinctive hunting point that his people relied on for survival. One of the most significant features of the point was the groove in the middle of each face, produced by a special thinning technique. As a younger boy he had often picked up discarded flakes with fortuitous scars that reminded him of that groove and had chipped the edges to produce the familiar outline of the point. These were only imitations – toys, really – since they had not been made in the proper way. More recently he had made serious attempts to produce the point correctly but had failed time after time. The complex thinning technique used near the end of the manufacturing process to produce the special groove in the middle of the point was very difficult. If the thinning was unsuccessful it almost always broke the point, and there was little margin for error because both faces had to be thinned, sometimes requiring several thinning blows. Even the most skilled knappers in the band broke three or four points, sometimes more, for every ten they tried to make. The thinning was essential, however; it helped in fitting and binding the point solidly to the haft and therefore lessened the possibility of breakage as the spear penetrated the hide of an animal, particularly if it entered at an angle. Properly made and used, the point was a very effective weapon and with it a hunter could kill the largest and most dangerous animals in the land. A well-made point was also something to be proud of; it represented the highest achievement of stone workmanship. A hunter was known among his people by the quality of his tools.

But the distinctive hunting point represented more than this. The boy remembered back to countless evenings around the late night fire when he had listened to the men talk about the hunt and all the things that determined its outcome. These men were very observant and pragmatic in a harsh world and they understood the importance of reliable equipment. They also understood the importance of knowing how an animal would behave under different circumstances.

The men also knew that beyond the purely practical or technical were unseen forces – the forces of life – which could be observed in an infinite variety of physical forms but were so powerful that they could not be contained by these forms. Each life force – the caribou, the bear, the raven – had its own particular characteristics, manifested in its behaviour on earth, but these forms moved freely between the physical and spiritual worlds through the continuous process of birth, death, and rebirth. With their power to alter but not destroy the flow of these forces, the people must ensure that their disruptive activities did not alienate the spiritual world. They must show respect for these forces and prove themselves worthy of their own limited powers, taking care that they were used only in great need and with harmonious intent.

The hunting point was especially important in this regard since it directly altered the flow of life, and its intent must not be misunderstood. In its very complexity of manufacture the hunting point was a spiritual offering, an assurance to the animal spirits that having been made with great care and skill it reflected a reverence for the forces of life. According to the wisdom handed down from generation to generation, the hunting point had been a gift from the spirits. It represented the existence of a special relationship between the ancient ones and the spiritual world. Its inheritance by the band to which the boy belonged meant that a continuity existed between life as it had been and life as it promised to be. The people therefore felt a oneness with the past and with the spiritual world that enabled them to meet the uncertainties of the present. Though this special relationship provided for the needs of the people it was also a responsibility. It must be carefully protected and, as embodied in the hunting point, held in trust for future generations so that they would not be disinherited by the spirits.

The boy was keenly aware of this, and because he had not yet mastered the skills required to make the hunting point, his knowledge of its great significance to the people became a burden that continually reminded him of his own incompleteness. He knew that the men were today preparing to make large blanks that could be made into points and other tools at the main camp and other camps in their travels as needed. They were not planning to make hunting points, but because he had failed so often and wanted so desperately to provide for all of his own needs, he was determined to force his skills – to demand them – to make this special effort: to shape from a block of stone the tool that was so vital to the people and to his own feelings of identity with them.

To accomplish this he would need all his powers of concentration to remember everything that he had heard and all that he had seen about the making of the hunting point. He could not be distracted by the talk of others or by his own self-consciousness at being observed at a critical moment. Consequently, he moved off to one side of where the others were working and cleared a work area near small, stunted spruce trees that had the double advantage of protecting him from the wind and partially screening him from view. The boy shook himself from his earlier thoughts, glanced up at the clear blue sky to clear his head, and then started unpacking his small tool kit.

The boy placed his knapping tools within easy reach on either side of him. These consisted of several hammerstones of different weights, an antler baton for percussion flaking, two antler tines for pressure flaking, and several scraps of caribou hide to protect his hands and legs. With these few simple items he would, in time, be able to make all the tools and weapons he would need as a hunter. Longing to leave his childhood behind, the boy treasured his knapping kit for the promise it held.

The first thing he had to do was make a number of flake blanks. He decided that if he made all of the blanks together and then attempted the crucial thinning, he would not have to alternate the different hand and wrist movements and muscle requirements for each process and it might make his work easier and more accurate.

The boy looked over the supply of chert fragments he had collected and selected one he thought would produce several large flakes for use as blanks. After placing the large fragment carefully against the outside of his left thigh, he adjusted it for the proper angle, took several practice swings with a large hammerstone, then struck it firmly on the inside edge next to his leg to detach a large, flat flake. The blow had a hollow-sounding ring to it and the flake came off badly. Suspecting that the block contained a number of flaws, he tapped it gently several times with his hammerstone and it suddenly fell apart at his feet into a number of useless, angular blocks. Although disappointed he knew that this would probably happen often. For most of the men, in fact, their main purpose at the site today was to test the stone in just this way to avoid carrying flawed pieces the long distance back to the main camp. The boy was less patient, however, for he was testing himself as well as the stone and he hadn't given himself much time.

The boy selected another large chert fragment, which he hoped would produce several large usable flakes. He turned it over several times while carefully noting the angles of the various corners, and mentally planned a sequence of blows, each depending on the other for success. This time he accomplished his goal. The stone had a good solid ring when struck and the boy soon developed a smooth rhythm of flaking that looked effortless but was, in fact, the result of intense concentration – continually planning his blows and making countless small but crucial judgments in their angle and force. In just a few seconds he had removed over a dozen large, thin flakes. The boy selected several other chert fragments and repeated the process, occasionally shattering a fragment that had a hidden flaw or a natural fracture. In a short time he had produced more flakes than he could use. The knapping had gone so smoothly that he found it difficult to stop, and besides, he thought, he needed the extra experience and could take some of the material back to the main camp for later use. He sensed but couldn't admit to himself that with the completion of this first step he was much closer to the thinning process and nervous about having to attempt it.

The boy relaxed for a few moments and then reached down and picked up his antler baton and one of the large flake blanks he had just produced. Now he had to trim the blanks to remove irregularities and turn them into leaf-shaped objects. These would be trimmed further by pressure flaking, using the antler tines in his tool kit until the blanks were symmetrical and shaped like willow leaves. The work went very well. Although a few flakes broke unexpectedly as they neared completion, the boy made a number of leaf-shaped blanks that he considered among the best he had ever made. He felt very good about his work today but when he straightened up to relax for a moment, he realized what a strain it had been. He had been concentrating so intensely on his work that when he lifted his head his side vision seemed to increase suddenly as if he had just emerged from a dark tunnel. His neck and back muscles ached with the strain and tension and he became aware that he had been sweating as if running hard. The effort had been so great that he hesitated to start work again.

Far north of where the boy was preoccupied with his thoughts, a flock of ravens flew high above the recently deglaciated land. Calling to each other and flying about in a confusion of flapping wings, the birds flew south toward the highlands.

The boy selected his best blank and began pressure flaking the base to produce a small projection. This would serve as a striking platform for removing the long, rectangular thinning flake. The boy took considerable care in shaping and grinding the small projection and when he was satisfied that it had been prepared properly, he lashed the blank to a forked stick that served as a hand-held vise. He was now ready. He selected a hammerstone of the proper weight, experimented with a number of body positions until he found one that was comfortable, and took a few practice swings, attempting to estimate the force that would be required to remove the thinning flake. The angle of the blow had to be just right as well or it would shatter the striking platform or break the blank itself.

The boy held his breath, made several small, split-second adjustments, even as the blow was released, and struck the platform. It didn't sound or feel right, and he felt a deepening depression as he sensed the mistake. Quickly unlashing the blank from the vise, he saw with bitter disappointment that the blow had taken off the striking platform and a very short thinning flake. The only thing to do was to try again on the opposite face and then maybe he could recover his mistake on this side. He repeated the process of preparing a striking platform, lashed the blank to the vise, and got into position for striking the blow. He worked hurriedly this time, impatient to prove to himself that he could do it, unhappy at the compromise he would be making if he succeeded because he knew that the point would not be perfect, yet knowing that he would not succeed because of his haste. Even as the blow struck he knew it was wrong and he could tell that the force had travelled too deeply into the stone and shattered the blank. The pieces fell from the vise as he unlashed it and he angrily stamped them into the ground with his heel.

The boy was shocked and embarrassed at what he had just done in anger. Immediately, he tried to force his frustration and anger out of his mind. Even if he was successful he couldn't make a weapon as important as this to his people with such an attitude. If he did his own anger might be carried to the very animal he would try to hunt. This was unthinkable. The animal must feel only the hunter's gratitude and respect or it might avoid him or cause the spear to be turned against him.

As the boy tried to control his angry thoughts the ravens in the distance grew larger as they flew closer toward the cliff where the hunters were working. Most of the birds stayed loosely together but one suddenly turned away and flew generally in the boy's direction.

He sat back against a tree and took several deep breaths to lose some of his nervous excitement and relax his tense muscles. After a few moments, when he felt calmer and thought he had a better attitude, he selected another blank and began preparing a striking platform as before. He remembered thinking earlier that perhaps the first two platforms he had made were too massive, requiring too much force to remove a thinning flake, so he made this platform much smaller and shaped it to project a bit more. He lashed the blank to the vise, manoeuvred himself into position while rehearsing the angle and force of his blow, hesitated a moment, and then started his swing.

The impact of the blow sounded good. Instinctively he felt a thrill of excitement rising in his chest and he quickly unlashed the vise and turned the blank over, dreading the thought that it might actually have broken and would fall apart in his hands. He could hardly believe what he saw. The blow had been perfect and the force carried through almost to the tip, removing a long thinning flake that left a shallow groove in the centre of the blank. The boy trembled with excitement and stared at the blank in disbelief, afraid that it would fall apart at any moment from the fractures that his wishful thinking prevented him from seeing. But it didn't; his thinning blow had worked. The result was frozen in stone, timeless and indestructible.

The boy's awareness of things other than that single, long thinning scar returned slowly. At first he was conscious only of a vague sense of disquiet intruding on his happiness and then he suddenly realized, with a cold shock, that he hadn't finished yet. He still had to thin the opposite face. He had an impulse to save the unfinished weapon as it was and not attempt to thin it further. But no, he would have to risk breaking it and try to thin the other face. Perhaps if he made a mistake it would result in a short thinning scar that would only affect the appearance of the finished point, not ruin it entirely.

As if following a magical formula the boy repeated exactly his method of preparing the preceding striking platform. He took special care in lashing the blank to the vise and in rehearsing the angle and force of his blow. Then, with a fleeting thought of the ancient ones, he struck as accurately as he could.

At that instant the raven that had left the flock earlier was caught in a sudden downdraught high above the copse of trees where the boy worked. As the bird dropped sharply downward it cried out loudly and wheeled swiftly above the boy toward the flock in the distance. Despite his concentration the boy was startled by the bird's call, but his blow had just struck and he resisted the urge to glance upward toward the sound.

This time neither the sound nor the feel of the blow conveyed anything at all to him. With a sense of dread he unlashed the blank from the vise and caught the artifact as it fell into his hand. For a moment he was puzzled because he couldn't tell which face he had just attempted to thin, and then he suddenly realized that he had done it. The thinning blow worked again. He was filled with joy and relief over his success but his feelings were also much more profound.

He realized now that his childhood was over. He had been accepted by the ancient ones and given the skills needed to make the hunting point. He remembered the raven's call now and glanced up to the sky to look for the bird. It was gone as if it had never been and yet the boy knew, as surely as he could see the newly made hunting point before him, that the bird had been a messenger spirit: a spirit that was his own and had come from that other world to give him the gift of the hunting point and serve as his guardian. With this gift he acquired the larger identity of being one of the people. He also became part of the special relationship between the ancient ones and the animals and all the other powers in the world. With this gift he belonged to all that had been, and would be.

THE PERSON IN THE PRECEDING STORY never existed, but someone like him once did. And although his life and that of his people are remembered only imperfectly in the archaeological record he probably had many of the thoughts shared by all human beings, irrespective of time and place. Most likely one of these was the expectation that all he had learned, and expected yet to learn, would guide him throughout his life, much as the same knowledge and wisdom had guided his parents and relatives, the elders in his band, and all who lived before … from the beginning.

But change occurred, no less profoundly then as now in our modern world. Change would have been very apparent to our imaginary person and the Early Paleo-Indians he represents, for they lived at the end of the Ice Age. Within only a few generations, a period short enough to be remembered in stories and passed down from one generation to the next, the whole character of the land changed. This was caused by a switch from a glacial to a non-glacial climate, though it may have occurred long before Early Paleo-Indians appeared in North America, possibly even before the last ice sheet reached the line of farthest advance. Ice flow was determined in part by the physical properties of ice itself, and the mass would respond slowly to a change in climate. In time, however, the gradually warming climate triggered the beginning of glacial retreat and then a long succession of environmental changes: ultimately the end of one geological epoch, the Pleistocene, and the beginning of another, the Holocene. Early Paleo-Indians experienced both the ending of one and the beginning of the next.

The changes during this period, which lasted well into the Holocene, totally reshaped the landscape. The distribution of different plant species shifted as they responded to the non-glacial climate by expanding or contracting their ranges. At first dense forests of spruce replaced the open spruce parkland and then pine replaced spruce, whose range contracted in the south but expanded north. Caribou probably disappeared from southern Ontario, most likely following more open habitats as they expanded north in the wake of the retreating ice. Replacing the caribou and the Ice Age fauna that had become extinct came white-tailed deer, which colonized the emerging hardwood forests in the south, and moose, which somewhat later occupied wetland habitats in the northern conifer forests.

These changes, dramatic as they were, marked only the beginning of the Holocene. Other changes were to come, altering the composition of the vegetation as the warming trend continued into the middle of the Holocene. The warming trend peaked between 8,000 and 4,000 years ago, an interval called the Altithermal or Hypsithermal, when the mean annual temperature in southern Ontario probably reached one or two degrees centigrade warmer than today. Throughout this period the composition of the deciduous forests in southern Ontario changed as various species such as hemlock, oak, elm, maple, and beech competed for dominance. Sometime after 4,000 years ago the general warming trend reversed, and climate underwent a long period of deterioration, oscillating between short warming and cooling trends down to our present time.

The lakes changed as well, paralleling the long history of change on land. In Ontario, shortly before the end of the Pleistocene, the huge "inland sea" of glacial Lake Algonquin found new outlets to the St Lawrence valley and the Atlantic beyond. Shortly thereafter the glacial lake dropped to a lower level and in this way became transformed into the first of a long series of postglacial lakes in the Huron and Georgian Bay basins: lakes with such names as Wyebridge, Penetang, Cedar Point, Payette, Sheguiandah, and Korah, all named after fossil beaches preserved by the rising land that slowly readjusted to preglacial heights after the release of the weight of the ice sheet. These lakes succeeded one another as new outlets were found to the east through northern Ontario in the region of North Bay to the Ottawa River and the St Lawrence beyond, resulting in progressive drops in water level. With this, the lakes retreated downward and inward into the middle of their basins. After little more than 500 years, lake levels retreated to the deepest parts of the Huron and Georgian Bay basins, forming two separate lakes joined by a river. Through that river, water flowed northeast from Lake Stanley in the Huron basin (more than 100 metres lower than present-day Lake Huron) to Lake Hough (roughly the same elevation) in the Georgian Bay basin and then east through a North Bay outlet. Except for that river, dry land stretched continuously across what today is the water of Lucas Channel between the Bruce Peninsula and Manitoulin Island.

And then the process reversed. The rising land, which was still rebounding after the release of the weight of glacial ice, caused a shift in the outlet from the region of North Bay to the southern part of the Huron basin at Port Huron, raising lake levels and causing the waters of the Huron and Georgian Bay basins to merge once again roughly 5,000 years ago, creating a new lake: Lake Nipissing. This lake reoccupied the former beach of glacial Lake Algonquin around the southern part of the Huron basin and inundated parts of the Bruce Peninsula in southern Ontario – still depressed from the earlier weight of glacial ice – as well as the low-lying margins of Georgian Bay. Some time after 4,000 years ago water levels slowly dropped once again as the Port Huron outlet continued to erode downward, forming yet another lake phase, called Algoma, intermediate in level between Lake Nipissing and the modern lakes. Gradually, this lake level dropped to the modern level of Lake Huron and formed the present-day shoreline.

Throughout all these transformations in the land and water changes also occurred in the human landscape. In southern Ontario the descendants of the Early Paleo-Indians who first colonized the region would have found it necessary at the beginning of the Holocene to shift their hunting from animals that had become extinct, or were no longer locally available, to other species. They would have shifted their plant use as well. The shift would have required hunting skills and patterns of land use very different from those of their ancestors several hundred or a thousand years earlier. In this way the Early Paleo-Indians gradually lost one identity and acquired another. The biological continuity between human generations probably remained unbroken, but with the appearance of new tool types and fragments of a different way of life in the archaeological record, the descendants of Early Paleo-Indians become known by another name, Eastern Plano. Sometimes they are given more exclusive and tentative names with western connotations, such as Agate Basin, Hell Gap, and Eden/Scottsbluff, or local names such as Flambeau and Minocqua (in northern Wisconsin), Reservoir Lakes (in northern Minnesota), and Lakehead (in the western Lake Superior region of northern Ontario).

Later cultural transformations between perhaps 9,500 and 3,000 years ago led to the appearance of Early, Middle, and Late Archaic cultures, and then between approximately 3,000 years ago and the time of contact with Europeans in the sixteenth and seventeenth centuries, depending on location, Early, Middle, and Late Woodland and Mississippian cultures. This basic sequence of culture change occurred throughout much of eastern North America. Evidence for a succession of cultures is based in part on changes in tool types and other kinds of artifacts: the replacement of Late Paleo Indian-type projectile points by a long series of stemmed and notched points, culminating in simple or delicately notched triangular arrowheads; the brief appearance of a wide variety of large tools hammered into shape from raw nuggets of naturally occurring copper during the Late Archaic in the Great Lakes region; the appearance of pottery in the Early Woodland that over the remainder of the prehistoric record underwent a long succession of changes in vessel shape, finish, and methods and style of decoration; and earthen mound construction of various kinds such as large conical burial mounds built by Early, Middle, and Late Woodland peoples, effigy burial mounds created in the forms of birds and animals by some Late Woodland peoples, and truncated, pyramidal platform mounds for houses and ceremonial structures built by Mississippian peoples.

In addition to these and other changes in material culture, a wide range of information shows how Archaic, Woodland, and Mississippian people lived.

Plant and animal remains show that subsistence practices covered a broad spectrum. During the Archaic period hunting and gathering were ubiquitous. Beginning possibly in the Late Archaic, however, certainly during the early part of the Early Woodland period, the harvesting of wild and then partially domesticated plants played an increasingly important role in subsistence for many cultures. This trend toward food production continued during the Middle and Late Woodland periods, when a succession of cultures developed ever greater dependence on domesticated plant foods, culminating for some groups in a near total dependence on slash-and-burn horticulture based principally on the "three sisters": corn, beans, and squash. Prominent Late Woodland horticulturalists in the Great lakes region include, for example, the Iroquoians of New York State and Ontario and Mississippian peoples in the upper Midwest.

The archaeological record also shows how people lived together. Evidence of social relationships is derived from grave goods, for example, betraying social status, and from the analysis of house types and other structures as well as their spatial layouts and arrangements within communities. These and other kinds of data show that, like subsistence, the sociopolitical world of prehistoric people covered a vast spectrum. At one end was the band composed of related, extended families, a pattern that continued in various cultures from Early Paleo-Indian times down to the historic period. At the other and more complex end of the spectrum were chiefdoms based on inherited power and social stratification, developed by some Mississippian peoples, and political confederacies of allied tribes, such as the Five Nations Iroquois in New York State, and the Huron, Petun, and Neutral in Ontario.

In addition to broad patterns of subsistence and social organization, the archaeological record also reflects the spiritual life of prehistoric peoples. In the Great Lakes and upper Midwest, for example, the cultural efflorescence of the Early Woodland Adena people, Middle Woodland Hopewellian people, and Mississippian cultures – influenced by the large ceremonial-residential complex of Cahokia in west-central Illinois and adjacent Missouri – are all remarkable expressions of complex intrasocietal relations, strong community leadership, artistic creativity, and widespread trade networks. All stem from or are associated with powerful religious ideas.

The story told in this book, focused on late Ice Age Early Paleo-Indian people in Ontario, is just a small part of the larger picture of human life in eastern North America and the continent as a whole over a period of at least 11,000 years, and possibly very much longer. Yet this smaller story is well worth highlighting. It concerns a very ancient people who lived during a time that to us is very evocative. Many of the millions of North Americans who today live in the same region may be surprised to realize that the Ice Age exists in fragments all around them. From there it is a short step to the strange thought that they live as if permanent residents in a huge museum, as large as life and time itself. This is a transforming thought that often leads to heightened awareness of, and efforts to protect, the surrounding natural and cultural heritage.

From an archaeological perspective the brief glimpse into Early Paleo-Indian life in Ontario helps throw into relief broader North American patterns. This is because Ontario was near the geographic centre of a distinct paleoecological zone during the latter part of the Ice Age. This zone extended from the Lake Superior basin on the west to the St Lawrence valley on the east and may also have included much of New England, excluding the mountains and the marine coastal margins. Early Paleo-Indian life ways that evolved in Ontario and the greater northeast thus provide interesting contrasts with those in other Ice Age paleoecological zones such as the far north, the Pacific coast, the Rocky Mountain cordillera, the North American Plains, the southeastern United States, and the American Southwest, where the first traces of Paleo-Indians were discovered.

The second, and parallel, story in this book goes beyond what was discovered to talk about the essence of archaeology itself – how discoveries are made. I don't mean by this the technical ways in which sites are excavated or data analyzed, although to be sure there is great interest in this. I am referring instead to the decision making that underlies this activity: the thinking that determines where, how, and why the work is done. This is the true behind-the-scenes view of archaeology, or any scientific activity for that matter. For me the strong public interest in the thought processes underlying archaeology is betrayed by the simple question: How do you know where to dig? I have come to hear this question in a more general way: How do you do what you do? I think this intrigues people in part because it is the more human aspect of what archaeologists and scientists generally do.

I've tried to answer that question in this book. I described how it was that I came to work in a particular geographic area or site and the significance of the things I found. Each milestone in the story was achieved by employing all the knowledge and experience I had acquired up to that time. This is what gave me a sense of direction in my work and told me what I had to do next to create new knowledge.

Yet something else was involved as well: asking questions that challenged what was believed to be known or that attempted to reach into the unknown. For questions, and the nature of those questions, largely determine what will be discovered. That which is unquestioned is not likely to change, nor will the unexpected lead to new knowledge unless its potential significance is recognized and used to generate new questions. Questions are primary.

The role of questions in archaeological research is often overshadowed by the artifacts the work uncovers because of their great antiquity or aesthetic appeal. All may touch us deeply. Yet these objects do not automatically tell us about the long-vanished people we wish to know. Without deeper study they reflect only ourselves. The stories behind unusual artifacts and the more commonplace ones that largely constitute the archaeological record can be read only if we ask questions that will ultimately reveal patterns of human behaviour and those of our prehuman ancestors. The idea that the archaeological record is not self-revealing but has to be decoded before it can be read took a very long time to emerge during the growth of archaeology as a scientific discipline, and archaeologists today are still struggling with the implications. To me, this is one of the most important concepts in the development of archaeology, perhaps second only to the concept of *pre*history itself.

Throughout the history of archaeology, changing methods of excavation and new technologies and conceptual approaches to research have provided ever more powerful tools for discovery: stratigraphic excavation, improved methods of artifact classification and analysis, the application of statistical methods of analysis to archaeological material, radiocarbon dating and the development of other methods of absolute dating, advances in archaeological theory, and new avenues of exploration such as blood residue analysis. But these diverse tools are powerless without the sense of direction provided by questions. Discovering that pathway or pathways into the unknown is the fundamental task of archaeologists.

But the questions asked and the code used to read the past are transient, specific to a particular time because they are not only the expression of individuals but also reflect the development of archaeology as a discipline. This is why sites must be preserved and museum collections carefully curated for future study. Only then can future generations re-examine and reshape older questions and raise new, perhaps more penetrating ones as knowledge improves about the complexities of the past and the code that obscures it.

Without questions to unlock the past, both the prehistoric record and the technology to reveal that record will remain mute. The potential for new discoveries dwells within ourselves, for it is within the mind that we are first prepared to see the world, the cosmos, and the countless ages, past and future.

DRIVING INTO ICE AGE ONTARIO AND BEYOND

THIS SELF-GUIDED TOUR IS KEYED to the narrative in this book. The tour, to which you can devote a single, long day or a full holiday, takes you from Toronto north to views of glacial Lake Algonquin and then to the Kolapore uplands in the southern Georgian Bay region. On this first part of the route you see the hill on which the Banting site occurs, the general location of the Fisher site, and the bedrock cliffs that contain the Fossil Hill chert sought after by Early Paleo-Indian peoples.

If you choose to take the rest of the tour you spend the night on the south shore of Georgian Bay. The next day you drive to Tobermory on the tip of the Bruce Peninsula, take the Ontario Northland ferry to South Baymouth on Manitoulin Island, and visit the Little Current-Howland Centennial Museum in the village of Sheguiandah to see the exhibits on the Late Paleo-Indian and alleged pre-Clovis site named after the village. At the end of this day you could either return to Tobermory by ferry or spend another day or two on the road and drive north across the North Channel to the TransCanada Highway and then southeast around the eastern edge of Georgian Bay. On this final segment you drive through the remnants of Precambrian-age mountains, nearly two billion years old.

This tour is regarded as both easy and safe. Road signage and route directions were checked carefully on test drives using the most recent maps available. Because of the inherent risk and unpredictability of any driving venture, however, no responsibility can be assumed for personal injury, property damage, or loss of direction.

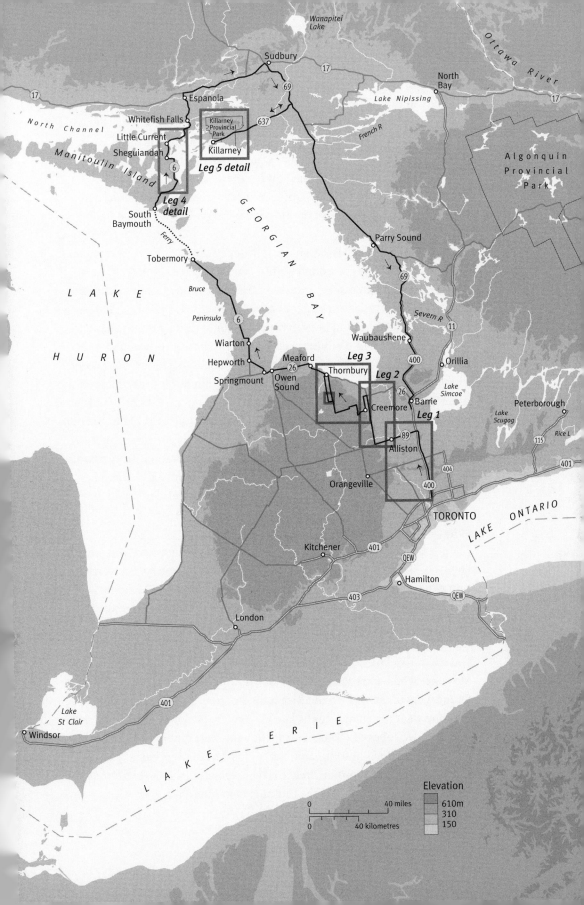

Today these former mountains are startlingly white quartzite hills, which in the bright sun become almost glaringly bright against the deep blue of the sky and the deeper blue and turquoise of the waters of the North Channel. This is certainly some of the most beautiful scenery in the world.

South of Sudbury you could also make a detour to Killarney Provincial Park, which encompasses the eastern end of those ancient Precambrian mountains you saw on northern Manitoulin Island. Archaeologically the park is significant because, as at Sheguiandah on Manitoulin Island, the quartzite ridges were exploited for toolstone by Late Paleo-Indian people.

South of Killarney Park, on the journey back to southern Ontario and Toronto, you will pass through quintessential cottage country of the Canadian north and catch glimpses of the bays, sounds, and inlets in the Thirty Thousand Island region of Georgian Bay, beautiful enough to con-jure up dreams of sailing in even the most confirmed landlubbers.

For assistance in planning your route or to find accommodation in advance write to municipal and regional tourist associations, your auto-mobile or travel association, or visit your local library for travel books and other guides. For the ferry schedule from Tobermory to Manitoulin Island phone or e-mail Ontario Northland. Because this tour is keyed to the nar-rative in this book, many points of interest – local museums and heritage sites, wildlife refuges, places of geological, ecological, and historical inter-est, and so forth – are not mentioned but can be found highlighted in other travel and tourist material. Be alert for opportunities for side trips.

Leg 1: Toronto to Alliston

The starting point of the tour is the intersection of Highways 400 and 401. Highway 401 crosses the northern edge of Toronto in an east-west direc-tion while Highway 400 begins at 401 and heads north.

Take Highway 400 and drive north toward Barrie. Approximately twenty-three kilometres from the starting point at Highway 401, near Interchange 43, you start driving through very rolling terrain with hills and marsh- or lake-filled depressions. This is the Oak Ridges Interlobate Moraine, which extends east-west across southern Ontario from Orangeville in the west to the Rice Lake area south of Peterborough. The moraine was created during the late Ice Age by the deposition of sediments between two lobes of glacial ice, one flowing west down the Ontario basin and the other flowing south and west across the Simcoe basin. The Oak Ridges Moraine is approximately twelve kilometres wide where crossed by Highway 400. You descend the moraine near Interchange 55, where you will see another glacial feature directly ahead through an overpass: a deep valley with flat, intensively cultivated fields of very dark, almost black soil. This is the former basin of glacial Lake Algonquin. The black soil is actually mostly peat, the preserved remains of marsh and bog plants that grew in the lake basin during the Holocene after the glacial lake drained. During the second half of the last century the Holland Marsh was logged and drained, and today the organic-rich soil is used for market gardens to grow vegetables for sale in the Greater Toronto Area.

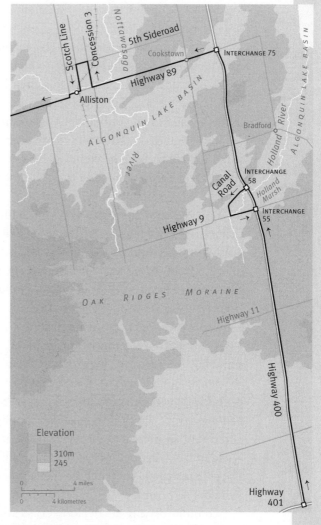

To have a closer look at the market gardens and the former basin of Lake Algonquin, **leave Highway 400 at Interchange 58.** Be cautious because after you turn off the exit the ramp is short. **At the T-junction, turn left (north) and proceed to Canal Road, also known as Simcoe County Road 8. Turn left (west) onto Canal Road.** The road heads in a southwesterly direction between the Holland Canal on the right and the market gardens on the other side of the road. **Follow Canal Road until it intersects Highway 9. Turn left (east) and proceed to Interchange 55. Enter Highway 400 northbound.**

Proceed along Highway 400 approximately seventeen kilometres to Interchange 75. Exit Highway 400 and enter Highway 89 westbound to Cookstown and Alliston. The flat surface you are driving on here and a short distance west is the former lake basin of another arm of glacial Lake Algonquin. This arm is oriented roughly northeast-southwest and terminates a few kilometres northeast. The main body of the arm trends in a southwesterly direction for several kilometres and then opens out into a large embayment.

As you drive west from the highway interchange area you'll leave the Algonquin lake basin and drive up to high ground, passing through Cookstown and beyond it through more rolling terrain. Approximately ten kilometres west of the 89/400 interchange you start descending down a long hill and catch your first glimpse of the Alliston embayment of glacial Lake Algonquin. The water in this embayment filled the lowlands you see stretching far into the western horizon. Once down on the former lake bottom you'll see some hills a short distance north of Highway 89. These were once large islands in the glacial lake.

Proceed west along 89 toward Alliston. Watch for New Tecumseth Concession 3 (3rd Line, or Sir Frederick Banting Road) on the outskirts of Alliston, a short distance west of Simcoe County Road 10. **Turn right (north) onto Concession 3.** The road descends abruptly into the valley of the Nottawasaga River – deeply cut into Algonquin lake sediments during the Holocene – and then climbs up onto the Algonquin lake plain. The utter flatness of the lake plain is quite striking, caused by the planing effect of the bases of waves as they moved across the lake bottom. Today the light, silty, and sandy soils are used for growing potatoes and occasionally asparagus.

North along Concession 3 the first farmhouse you see on the left, counting from the river valley, will be the boyhood home of Frederick Banting, one of the co-discoverers of insulin. This farm is also the location of the Banting site, off to the west on top of a large hill that was once an island in Lake Algonquin. Please don't walk beyond the Banting memorial. The archaeological site itself is either cultivated or held in pasture and therefore not visible.

Continue driving north along Concession 3. After a kilometre or so you will cross railroad tracks. The hill to the left (west) is actually an Algonquin beach. As you drive up out of the lake basin look to the right and you'll be able to see another section of the Algonquin shoreline as it turns north. From that point, 11,000 years ago, the Alliston embayment opened out into a huge expanse of lake that stretched beyond the northern horizon to the edge of the continental ice sheet in northern Ontario.

Continue north to 5th Sideroad and turn left (west). At the next road, Scotch Line, turn left (south). This will take you back down into the Algonquin lake basin, and Highway 89. **Turn right (west) onto Highway 89 and drive through Alliston.** About three kilometres west of Alliston, where the road starts climbing a long, gently sloping hill, you'll leave the Algonquin basin and once again find yourself driving on ground moraine, a continuous sheet of deposits left on the surface of the ground by the retreating ice sheet.

The next stop is the Fisher site on a more northerly stretch of Algonquin beach.

Leg 2: Alliston to Stayner

Leaving Alliston, proceed west along High-way 89. About fourteen kilometres west of Alliston, turn right (north) onto Dufferin County Road 18 (also known and signed as Airport Road). Shortly after the turn-off to Mansfield, a popular downhill ski area, County Road 18 crosses the Pine River, which flows east through the Niagara Escarpment. The broad valley of the Pine River is one of those river cuts I explored during the mid-1970s looking for Early Paleo-Indians who might, I speculated, have followed or intercepted caribou as they moved east-west across the province along corridors through the Niagara Escarpment. Like other prominent gaps through the escarpment I thought the Pine River valley would have provided easy access to the escarpment uplands for both animals and people. I found only traces that early humans passed through these gaps: enough to know people were present, but not enough to tell me anything else about them. Thus, like you in your car, I travelled onward.

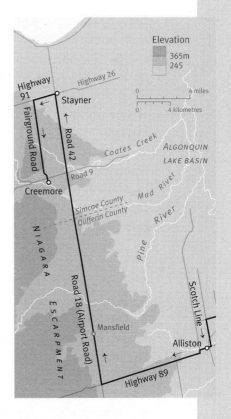

Continue along Dufferin County Road 18, which becomes Simcoe County Road 42, to the town of Stayner. In Stayner, County Road 42 ends at the intersection of Highways 26 and 91. Highway 26 comes from the east and turns north at the intersection; Highway 91 starts at the intersection and runs west. Turn left (west) onto Highway 91. Once again you're driving on the former bottom of glacial Lake Algonquin, which you entered on Simcoe County Road 42 just a few kilometres south of Stayner. Drive west on Highway 91 to the first concession line, Fairground Road, and turn left (south), toward the village of Creemore. The Fisher site is located on one of the farms off to your left, on the mainland side of a former lagoon of Lake Algonquin. Fortunately, the site is intensively cultivated, offering reasonable protection from those who might be tempted to pick up as souvenirs what few bits of artifacts are to be seen. With additional monitoring by concerned landowners the site will survive into the future and be available for continued research either to modify or to expand on my initial work or that of my collaborators.

Leg 3: Stayner to the Kolapore Uplands

Continue driving along Fairground Road to Simcoe County Road 9, just outside Creemore. Straight ahead, the road leads to the business section of Creemore, which has several interesting shops and is also home to a prominent microbrewery. The village will make an interesting stop at the end of the driving day and a refreshing one when the local brew is first opened.

Returning to County Road 9, turn west and drive to the village of Dunedin. You're about to drive through some of the most rugged terrain in southern Ontario. This segment of the tour will take you to the top of the Niagara Escarpment and the geological source of Fossil Hill Formation chert, a stone preferred by some Early Paleo-Indians for making tools.

At Dunedin, turn right (north) onto County Road 62 toward Glen Huron. Glen Huron is a small mill town nestled in the valley of the Mad River. **Continue along County Road 62 to the intersection with Highway 124 just beyond Glen Huron and turn left (west) onto Highway 124 to Singhampton.** Just a short distance north is the highest point on the Niagara Escarpment, a rocky butte at an elevation of 544 metres. This area has numerous recessional moraines, deposited by the ice sheet during temporary halts in its retreat when melting kept pace with ice flow. These moraines were deposited by the Georgian Bay and Simcoe ice lobes flowing from the north. The moraines are named after small hamlets in the area: Singhampton, Gibraltar, and Banks. You will pass over two of these moraines – Singhampton and Gibraltar – identified by very rough terrain formed by steep hills and basins, or kettles, the latter created by ice blocks that persisted long after glacial ice retreated from the area.

Follow Highway 124 south through Singhampton and proceed to the junction with Grey County Road 4. You will pass over the Singhampton moraine on this leg of the journey. **Turn right (west) onto County Road 4 toward Maxwell and proceed just over ten kilometres to Grey County Road 2. Turn right (north) onto County Road 2 toward Feversham.** About eight kilometres north you will drive onto the Gibraltar moraine. After another kilometre or so (approximately nine kilometres from Feversham), at the Osprey-The Blue Mountains Townline, drive onto

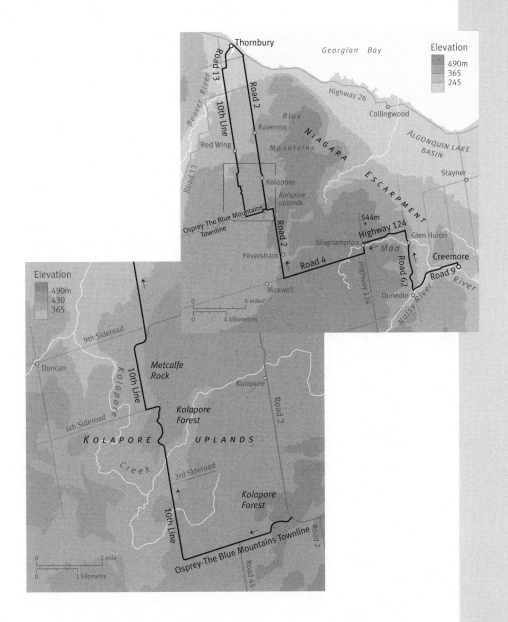

the edge of the road and park for a moment because you have a decision to make. You have just entered the Kolapore Uplands Resource Management Area, a semi-wilderness area of some 12,000 hectares managed by the Ontario Ministry of Natural Resources, Grey Sauble Conservation Authority, and Grey County. The vegetation consists of a mosaic of deciduous forest, swamps of spruce and tamarack (larch), pine plantations, and farm fields. In the western part, the University of Toronto Outing Club maintains approximately sixty kilometres of marked trails for cross-country skiing. In fact you can probably see one of the orientation signs, labelled Kolapore Uplands Demonstration Forest, from where you are now. Maps of the trail system are available in the general store at Ravenna, three kilometres farther north on Grey County Road 2.

Now for your decision. You can continue driving north on County Road 2, along the eastern edge of the Kolapore uplands through the hamlets of Kolapore – actually just a single stone church – and Ravenna to the town of Thornbury on Georgian Bay, one of your options for an overnight stop. Or you can be a bit more adventuresome and drive through the heart of the Kolapore uplands on a gravel road through very rugged country. This is a trip of about nine kilometres. Although narrow the road is well maintained and there is little chance of getting lost although it might not seem that way from time to time. Drive slowly because of blind curves and hidden drives that provide access to the road from private residences.

If you decide to drive through the Kolapore uplands **turn left (west) off Grey County Road 2 onto the Osprey-The Blue Mountains Townline.** Almost immediately you will come to an apparent fork in the road, actually Grey Road 2B. **Stay on the townline and continue west.** At first the road curves a bit and but shortly straightens out. You will soon pass Grey Road 45, which meets the townline on your left. Continue west on the townline. About three kilometres from the starting point at Grey Road 2, the townline meets the 10th Line, which runs north-south. **Turn right on the 10th Line and drive north. You will stay on the 10th Line for the remainder of this segment of the tour.** This narrow road passes though some very beautiful, and dark, forests. After a time the road alternately climbs and falls while simultaneously twisting through narrow valleys and around vertical cliffs of bedrock in the dim light of dense forest. At this point you may ask yourself how you came to this wonderful place and reflect on that question I have often been asked, and ask myself: How do you know where to dig? Eventually, the road will descend gradually down a long hill and come to a T-junction (the T is upside down, and you enter from the lower right). Ahead is 6th Sideroad. To your right (north) is a continuation of the 10th Line. Both are marked on a sign on your left. Turn right, staying on the 10th Line, and proceed north. If you miss the turn you will continue west about 2.4 kilometres to the Blue Mountains-Euphrasia Townline, where it is a simple matter to turn around and retrace your route. Shortly after your turn, you will see, ahead and to your right, a vertical, sixty-metre-high cliff of Amabel dolostone called Metcalfe Rock, a popular place for rock climbing. The Amabel Formation forms the caprock of the Niagara Escarpment. At its base, hidden under the broken rubble of talus slopes, is the upper part of the Fossil Hill Formation and the source of the white chert preferred for toolstone by Early Paleo-Indian peoples of the Parkhill culture. The Red Wing and Thomson archaeological sites are not far from here but since both are vulnerable to unauthorized collecting and one is on private land, the exact locations cannot be disclosed.

Continue north on the 10th Line, through Red Wing, to the intersection with Grey County Road 13, known locally as the Beaver Valley Road. Turn right (north) onto County Road 13 and travel through Clarksburg to Thornbury. This is the end of the first day of the tour. Incidentally, the journey you've just finished – from Lake Algonquin to the Kolapore uplands near Red Wing – took me nearly three decades to travel.

Returning to the present, you will find many inns, bed and breakfasts, and some motels in Clarksburg/Thornbury and, if you're taking the next segment of the tour, also in the community of Meaford farther up Highway 26 to the northwest, the direction of travel tomorrow.

Leg 4: Thornbury-Meaford to Manitoulin Island

To begin the northern section of the tour **drive northwest on Highway 26 from Thornbury to Owen Sound and then on to Springmount. There take Highway 6 (formerly 70) all the way to Tobermory,** approximately sixty kilometres distant at the very tip of the Bruce Peninsula.

The ferry from Tobermory to Manitoulin Island docks in the village of South Baymouth on the southeastern corner of the island. **Take Highway 6 north toward Little Current on the northeast end of the island.** The village of Sheguiandah is about two-thirds of the distance to Little Current. On the way to Sheguiandah there is an interesting stop that will help you to understand the geology underlying the archaeological site there, as well as the wonderful scenery you will be seeing farther north. **Park at Ten Mile Point on Highway 6, approximately seventeen kilometres north of the turn-off to the village of Manitowaning.** Now read ahead to

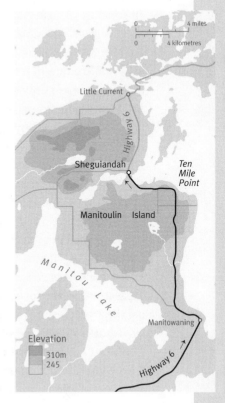

the description of Killarney Provincial Park and then walk over to the lookout to see a panorama of the La Cloche Range roughly twenty-five kilometres to the north and east. These high hills are the remnants of Precambrian-age mountains that are very near the boundary between the Canadian Shield (Precambrian-age rocks dating from the earliest history of the earth to perhaps 600 million years ago) and the younger Paleozoic rocks exposed in southern Ontario (dating between 400 and 600 million years ago). At Ten Mile Point you are standing on Paleozoic rocks. But six kilometres to the north, at Sheguiandah, the underlying Precambrian rocks are exposed at the surface. These rocks are quartzite of the La Cloche Range. This small "island" of Precambrian rock, protruding through the softer Paleozoic rocks that have been eroded away, attracted Late Paleo-Indian people to Sheguiandah about 9,500 years ago because the quartzite was excellent for knapping into tools.

Now continue northwest on Highway 6. After approximately six kilometres you will come to the Sheguiandah First Nation Reserve and, shortly beyond, the village of Sheguiandah. The archaeological site is located on the northern edge of the village. Please do not attempt to walk onto the site because it is extremely vulnerable to disturbance, the land is all privately owned, and no formal trails exist. Remember that it is not only illegal to pick up or remove objects from any archaeological site in Ontario without a licence but to do so is roughly equivalent to tearing a page out of a one-of-a-kind history book owned by a public library. The missing page not only mutilates the book but changes forever what we and future generations might otherwise have learned from the past. I urge you instead to limit your explorations to a visit to the Little Current-Howland Centennial Museum and Park in the village of Sheguiandah. **Shortly after passing the highway sign announcing Sheguiandah, turn right off Highway 6 onto Limit Street.** You can then proceed to the main building of the museum, left through a gate onto museum property and up a curvy gravel road to the top of the hill. The museum was expanded and renovated in 1996 and contains a larger display of artifacts from the archaeological site than any other institution in Canada and the United States. It also has an impressive selection of photographs of Thomas Lee's excavations in the 1950s, showing the crew at work and proudly displaying the artifacts they recovered. Of special interest is a guest book signed by visitors to the site in 1953 and 1954, the last two years of excavation. The fifty-two-page book is filled with the names of people who were deeply impressed with the precision of the excavation, the potential age of the occupations, and the need for site protection. Several prominent archaeologists visited the site during this period: Albert Spaulding, George Quimby, and Emerson Greenman. But perhaps the most arresting signature is that of Lester B. Pearson, who in 1953 described himself as unemployed. This must have been an exaggeration during an election year because before and after he was not only the MP for the riding of Algoma East but also deputy minister and then minister for External Affairs and, in 1952, president of the United Nations General Assembly. In 1957 he was awarded the Nobel Peace Prize for his political efforts to resolve conflicts in the Near East, and in 1963 he became the fourteenth prime minister of Canada.

Leg 5: Sheguiandah, Killarney Park, and Georgian Bay

If you are going to continue the tour north and then around the eastern end of Georgian Bay, **take Highway 6 north from Sheguiandah to Little Current and across the North Channel over Great La Cloche Island to Whitefish Falls. Continue to Espanola and just beyond it turn right (east) onto Highway 17, the TransCanada, and drive toward Sudbury.** A short distance west of Sudbury, before Copper Cliff, the TransCanada dips southeast to become the Southwest Bypass, ringing the southern fringe of Sudbury. Instead of following it to the Southeast Bypass, you **fork south-east at the turnoff for Highway 69, a continuation of the TransCanada. Approximately thirty-five kilometres south, you meet Highway 637 and turn west.** This is the turn-off to Killarney Provincial Park, approximately sixty kilometres to the southwest. A short distance beyond the park is the village and harbour of Killarney at the end of a peninsula on Georgian Bay.

Killarney Provincial Park is a wilderness park encompassing 48,500 hectares on the southern edge of the Canadian Shield, the oldest rocks on the North American continent. The western and southern edges of the park are bordered by Georgian Bay, while the body of the park stretches several kilometres north and east into the interior.

The park contains a well-marked system of land trails (the outer trail, the Silhouette loop, being approximately 100 kilometres long), several dozen established portages connecting at least an equal number of inlets and lakes, and roughly 150 numbered interior campsites (small cleared areas with rock-lined fireplaces). The scenery is beautiful, in part because of the high local relief from valley bottom to ridge top, and the whole area makes for wonderful overland hiking, canoeing, and off-trail ridge hiking. The high quartzite ridges and deep blue lakes of the park inspired several paintings by Canadian artists of the Group of Seven from 1918 into the 1950s. Earlier it prompted one of artists, A.Y. Jackson, to argue successfully for the protection of the area. A small forest reserve was established in 1933, to become the nucleus of the future park in 1964, which was then expanded in 1983.

The white quartzite ridges of the La Cloche Mountains are composed of quartz sand grains deposited during the early Proterozoic Eon, beginning around 2.5 billion years ago. The quartz sand was deposited as thick, nearly horizontal sheets in a shallow sea on the edge of the North American continent, then formed by older rocks of the Canadian Shield to the north. Beginning around 1.9 billion years ago, these sediments were compressed and metamorphosed (heated) into rock. With the underlying rock formations, they were folded and uplifted into mountains during an event called the Penokean Orogeny. These early Proterozoic mountains, known as the Penokean-Killarney Mountains, were probably comparable in height to the present-day Rocky Mountains. Thus, although the ridges of the La Cloche Mountains you see today are very impressive, rising some 210-50 metres above the surrounding lakes, they are little more than eroded mountain roots, exposed like the stump of a tree that has been cut.

The deep valleys between ridges of this ancient mountain range are often underlain by softer, more easily eroded rocks. Some of the rocks contain evidence of continental glaciation, presumably much like that of the Pleistocene, although predating it by nearly two billion years. In fact, three such glacial episodes have been detected, all dating from the early part of the Proterozoic Eon.

Killarney Ridge, the southernmost ridge of the La Cloche Mountains, is visible from the George Lake campground just within the entrance to Killarney Park. Beneath and on the south side of George Lake are the bright pink granites of the Killarney Batholith, a body of once viscous rock that formed deep below the surface of the earth 1.75 to 1.45 billion years ago, was intruded into upper layers, and later exposed by surface weathering. The contrast between the pink rocks of the batholith and the white rocks of the Killarney Ridge is visually striking, but it is not the only contrast. A short distance south of the entrance to Killarney Park is the Grenville Front Boundary Fault. This is the location of a collision during continental drift between the Shield and a piece of the earth's crust, itself a patchwork of other pieces, called the Grenville Province, which underlies southern Ontario. Many years ago, as I sat in a canoe on George Lake, suspended above a great division in the earth's crust and between forces that had thrust up a mountain range to one side of me and brought continents together on the other, I had a sudden feeling of vertigo and felt a vague, imminent danger, as if something powerful beneath me might suddenly be released once again. Such is the feeling for deep geological time and the elemental forces of nature that Killarney Park inspires.

Returning to present, or near present, Killarney Park is interesting in another way because it contains evidence of Late Paleo-Indian occupation roughly contemporaneous with that at Sheguiandah on Manitoulin Island. The evidence was first uncovered in the early 1940s by Emerson Greenman, an archaeologist at the University of Michigan's Museum of Anthropology in Ann Arbor. The discovery was made at two sites Greenman called George Lake 1 and 2. The sites are not located on George Lake itself but in the vicinity of another smaller lake nearby and on an elevated, early postglacial beach high above the present-day lake surface. Although test excavated in the early 1940s, portions of both sites still exist and would be worth investigating again in the future, particularly to restudy their geological settings. Other still undiscovered Late Paleo-Indian sites almost surely occur in the park and surrounding region. And of course the area contains numerous other archaeological sites of varying ages, as well as historical sites.

To return to the tour, **take Highway 637 back out to Highway 69, where you'll turn right (south) toward Parry Sound.** As you drive south you will be moving in the direction of ice advance of the first continental ice sheet at the beginning of the Pleistocene nearly two million years ago, and opposite to the direction of ice retreat at the end of that geological epoch. You will also be driving over the former bed of glacial Lake Algonquin, which flooded the eastern edge of the Georgian Bay basin and ended along beaches and wave-cut terraces many kilometres to the east. All along the drive you will be passing through what to most of the population of southern Ontario is thought of as cottage country: the districts of Parry Sound and Muskoka and the northern part of Simcoe County. Soon after you pass Waubaushene at one entrance to the Trent-Severn Waterway, Georgian Bay is left behind. As the scenery changes to broad fields of agricultural land and traffic interchanges you'll probably become much more conscious of Highway 400, the multi-lane, high-speed throughway you've been travelling on for some time, and will begin thinking ahead to the faster pace of life associated with urban living. Thoughts of the long history of the earth, the cold of the last Ice Age, and the lives of the ancient colonizing people who followed the retreating glaciers will gradually recede and be replaced with concerns for the here and now. But the past remains, scattered about us in small fragments in a vast outdoor museum. With care and enlightened planning, this museum will survive into the future, ready to stimulate again in the minds of future travellers thoughts about other times and places – so distant from the world of our experience, yet so surprisingly near.

SUGGESTED READING

The following contains a list of material for the general reader and a list of scholarly papers and books for those interested in the sources of some of the ideas and supporting documentation alluded to in the text. Neither list is intended to be comprehensive.

General Interest

Adovasio, J.M., with Jake Page. 2002. *The First Americans: In Pursuit of Archaeology's Greatest Mystery.* Toronto and New York: Random House.

Birmingham, Robert A., and Leslie E. Eisenberg. 2000. *Indian Mounds of Wisconsin.* Madison: University of Wisconsin Press.

Chatters, James C. 2001. *Ancient Encounters: Kennewick Man and the First Americans.* New York: Simon and Schuster.

Daniel, Glyn. 1962. *The Idea of Prehistory.* Cleveland and New York: World Publishing Company.

Debicki, R.L. 1982. *Geology and Scenery, Killarney Provincial Park Area, Ontario.* Ontario Geological Survey Guidebook no. 6. Toronto: Ministry of Natural Resources.

Dewar, Elaine. 2001. *Bones: Discovering the First Americans.* Toronto: Vintage Canada.

Dixon, E. James. 1999. *Bones, Boats and Bison: Archaeology and the First Colonization of North America.* Albuquerque: University of New Mexico Press.

Eyles, Nick. 2002. *Ontario Rocks: Three Billion Years of Environmental Change.* Markham, ON, and Allston, MA: Fitzhenry and Whiteside.

Fagan, Brian M. 1987. *The Great Journey: The Peopling of Ancient America.* London: Thames and Hudson.

Guthrie, R. Dale. 1990. *Frozen Fauna of the Mammoth Steppe: The Story of Blue Babe.* Chicago: University of Chicago Press.

Irving, George. 1960. *Indian Life in the Upper Great Lakes: 11,000 B.C. to A.D. 1800.* Chicago: University of Chicago Press.

Killan, Gerald. 1983. *David Boyle: From Artisan to Archaeologist.* Toronto: University of Toronto Press.

Killarney Provincial Park. 1983. Park map. Toronto: Ministry of Natural Resources.

Kolapore Uplands Wilderness Ski Trails. 1997. Trail map, 18th ed. Toronto: University of Toronto Outing Club.

McGhee, Robert. 1991. *Canada Rediscovered*. Ottawa: Canadian Museum of Civilization.

Mason, Ronald J. 1981. *Great Lakes Archaeology*. New York: Academic Press.

Mehringer, P.J. 1989. "Clovis Cache Found: Weapons of Ancient Americans." *National Geographic* 174 (4): 500-3.

Meltzer, David J. 1993. *Search for the First Americans*. Montreal, QC: St. Remy Press; Washington, DC: Smithsonian Institution.

Robertson, J.A., and K.D. Card. 1972. *Geology and Scenery, North Shore of Lake Huron Region*. Ontario Division of Mines Geological Guidebook no. 4. Reprinted 1975. Toronto: Ministry of Natural Resources.

Schick, Kathy D., and Nicholas Toth. 1995. *Making Silent Stones Speak: Human Evolution and the Dawn of Technology*. London: Phoenix.

Stanford, D.J. 1979. "Bison Kill By Ice Age Hunters." *National Geographic* 155: 114-21.

Tattersall, Ian. 1998. *Becoming Human: Evolution and Human Uniqueness*. New York: Harcourt Brace.

Tovell, Walter M. 1992. *Guide to the Geology of the Niagara Escarpment*. Georgetown, ON: Niagara Escarpment Commission.

Whittaker, John C. 1994. *Flintknapping: Making and Understanding Stone Tools*. Austin: University of Texas Press.

Scholarly Works

Barnett, P.J. 1991-2. "Quaternary Geology of Ontario." In *Geology of Ontario*, ed. P.C. Thurston, H.R. Williams, R.H. Sutcliffe, and G.M. Stott, 1011-88. Ontario Geological Survey special volume 4. Toronto: Ministry of Northern Development and Mines.

Begay, Richard M. 1997. "The Role of Archaeology on Indian Lands: The Navajo Nation." In *Native Americans and Archaeologists: Stepping Stones to Common Ground*, ed. Nina Swidler, Kurt E. Dongoske, Roger Anyon, and Alan S. Downer, 161-6. Walnut Creek, CA: AltaMira Press.

Binford, Lewis R. 1978. *Nunamiut Ethnoarchaeology*. New York: Academic Press.

Bonnichsen, Robson, C.W. Bolen, M. Turner, J.C. Turner, and M.T. Beatty. 1992. "Hair from Mammoth Meadow II, Southwestern Montana." *Current Research in the Pleistocene* 9: 75-8.

Boyle, David. 1906. "Notes on Some Specimens: Flints." *18th Annual Archaeological Report, 1905, Being Part of Appendix to the Report of the Minister of Education, Ontario*, 10-12. Toronto: Government of Ontario.

Breitburg, Emanuel, John B. Broster, Arthur L. Ressman, and Richard G. Strearns. 1996. "The Coates-Hines Site: Tennessee's First Paleoindian-Mastodon Association." *Current Research in the Pleistocene* 13: 6-8.

Brush, Nigel, and Forrest Smith. 1994. "The Martins Creek Mastodon: A Paleoindian Butchery Site in Holmes County, Ohio." *Current Research in the Pleistocene* 11: 14-15.

Burwasser, G.J. 1974. *Quaternary Geology of the Collingwood-Nottawasaga Area, Southern Ontario*. Ontario Division of Mines preliminary map P.919. Geology Series.

Chapman, L.J., and D.F. Putnam. 1984. *The Physiography of Southern Ontario*. 3rd ed. Ontario Geological Survey special vol 2. Toronto: Ministry of Natural Resources.

Chappell, John, John Head, and John Magee. 1996. "Beyond the Radiocarbon Limit in Australian Archaeology and Quaternary Research." *Antiquity* 70 (269): 543-52.

Chatters, James C. 2000. "The Recovery and First Analysis of an Early Holocene Human Skeleton from Kennewick, Washington." *American Antiquity* 65 (2): 291-316.

Cinq-Mars, J. 1979. "Bluefish Cave 1: A Late Pleistocene Eastern Beringian Cave Deposit in the Northern Yukon." *Canadian Journal of Archaeology* 3: 1-32.

Clausen, C.J., A.D. Cohen, Cesare Emiliani, J.A. Holman, and J.J. Stipp. 1979. "Little Salt Spring, Florida: A Unique Underwater Site." *Science* 203 (4381): 609-14.

Cleland, Charles E. 1965. "Barren Ground Caribou (*Rangifer arcticus*) from an Early Man Site in Southeastern Michigan." *American Antiquity* 30 (3): 350-1.

Condie, Kent C., and Robert E. Sloan. 1998. *Origin and Evolution of Earth: Principles of Historical Geology*. Upper Saddle River, NJ: Prentice-Hall.

Cook, Harold J. 1927. "New Geological and Paleontological Evidence Bearing on the Antiquity of Mankind in America." *Natural History* 27 (3): 240-7.

Cotter, John Lambert. 1938. "The Occurrence of Flints and Extinct Animals in Fluvial Deposits Near Clovis, New Mexico. Part IV, Report on Excavations at the Gravel Pit, 1936." *Proceedings of the Academy of Natural Sciences of Philadelphia for 1937*, 89: 1-16.

Crabtree, Don E. 1966. "A Stoneworker's Approach to Analyzing and Replicating the Lindenmeier Folsom." *Tebiwa* 9 (1): 3-39.

Curtis, Edward S. 1972. *Portraits from North American Indian Life*. Toronto: McClelland and Stewart.

Dana, E.S., and W.E. Ford. 1932. *A Textbook of Mineralogy*. 4th ed. New York: John Wiley and Sons.

Darwin, Charles. 1859. *On the Origin of Species By Means of Natural Selection, or the Preservation of Favoured Races in the Struggle for Life*. London: Murray.

Davis, Stephen A. 1991. "Two Concentrations of Palaeo-Indian Occupation in the Far Northeast." Instituto Panamericano de Geografía e Historia. *Revista de Arqueología Americana* 3: 31-56.

Deane, R.E. 1950. *Pleistocene Geology of the Lake Simcoe District, Ontario*. Geological Survey of Canada Memoir 256. Ottawa: Department of Mines and Technical Surveys.

Deller, D. Brian. 1988. "The Paleo-Indian Occupation of Southwestern Ontario: Distribution, Technology and Social Organization." PhD diss., McGill University, Montreal.

Deller, D. Brian, and Christopher J. Ellis. 1992. *Thedford II: A Paleo-Indian Site in the Ausable River Watershed of Southwestern Ontario*. Museum of Anthropology Memoirs no. 24. Ann Arbor: University of Michigan.

Dillehay, T.D. 1989. *Monte Verde: A Late Pleistocene Settlement in Chile*. Vol. 1, *Paleoenvironment and Site Context*. Washington, DC: Smithsonian Institution.

–. 1997. *Monte Verde: A Late Pleistocene Settlement in Chile*. Vol. 2, *The Archaeological Context and Interpretation*. Washington, DC: Smithsonian Institution.

Dunbar, James S. 1991. "Resource Orientation of Clovis and Suwannee Age Paleoindian Sites in Florida." In *Clovis: Origins and Adaptations*, ed. Robson Bonnichsen and Karen L. Turnmire, 185-213. Corvallis, OR: Center for the Study of the First Americans and Oregon State University.

Ellis, Chris J., and Neal Ferris. 1990. *The Archaeology of Southern Ontario to A.D. 1650*. Occasional Publication no. 5. London, ON: Ontario Archaeological Society.

Fisher, Daniel. 1987. "Mastodont Procurement By Paleoindians of the Great Lakes Region: Hunting or Scavenging?" In *The Evolution of Human Hunting*, ed. Matthew H. Nitecki and Doris V. Nitecki, 309-421. New York: Plenum Press.

Fisher, Daniel C., Bradley T. Lepper, and Paul E. Hooge. 1991. "Evidence for Butchery of the Burning Tree Mastodon". In *The First Discovery of America: Archaeological Evidence of the Early Inhabitants of the Ohio Area*, ed. William S. Dancey, 43-57. Columbus, OH: Ohio Archaeological Council.

Freeman, E.B., ed. 1979. *Geological Highway Map, Southern Ontario*. Ontario Geological Survey map 2441.

Frison, George C. 1982. "Paleo-Indian Winter Subsistence Strategies on the High Plains." In *Plains Indian Studies: A Collection of Essays in Honor of John C. Ewers and Waldo R. Wedel*, ed. D.H. Ubelaker and H.J. Viola, 193-201. Smithsonian Contributions to Anthropology 30. Washington, DC: Smithsonian Institution.

–. 1989. "Experimental Use of Clovis Weaponry and Tools on African Elephants." *American Antiquity* 54 (4): 766-84.

–. 1993. "North American High Plains Paleo-Indian Hunting Strategies and Weaponry Assemblages." In *From Kostenki to Clovis: Upper Paleolithic – Paleo-Indian Adaptations*, ed. Olga Soffer and N.D. Praslov, 237-49. New York: Plenum Press.

Fulton, Robert J., and Victor K. Prest. 1987. "The Laurentide Ice Sheet and Its Significance." In *The Laurentide Ice Sheet*, ed. Robert J. Fulton and John T. Andrews. *Géographie physique et quaternaire* 41 (2): 181-6.

Funk, R.E., and D.W. Steadman. 1994. *Archaeological and Paleoenvironmental Investigations in the Dutchess Quarry Caves, Orange County, New York.* Monographs in Archaeology. Buffalo, NY: Persimmon Press.

Garrad, C. 1971. "Ontario Fluted Point Survey." *Ontario Archaeology* 16: 3-18.

Graham, Russell W., C. Vance Haynes, Donald Lee Johnson, and Marvin Kay. 1981. "Kimmswick: A Clovis-Mastodon Association in Eastern Missouri." *Science* 213: 1115-17.

Gramly, R.M. 1993. *The Richey Clovis Cache.* Monographs in Archaeology. Buffalo, NY: Persimmon Press.

Grayson, Donald K. 1983. *The Establishment of Human Antiquity.* New York: Academic Press.

Green, Thomas J., Bruce Cochran, Todd W. Fenton, James C. Woods, Gene L. Titmus, Larry Tieszen, Mary Ann Davis, and Susanne J. Miller. 1998. "The Buhl Burial: A Paleoindian Woman from Southern Idaho." *American Antiquity* 63 (3): 437-56.

Greenman, E.F. 1941. "Excavation of a Prehistoric Site in Manitoulin District, Ontario." *Man* 41, Correspondence 56: 67-8.

–. 1942. "Further Excavations in Manitoulin District, Ontario." *Man* 42, Correspondence 69: 119.

–. 1943a. "An Early Industry on a Raised Beach Near Killarney, Ontario." *American Antiquity* 8 (3): 260-5.

–. 1943b. "Further Excavations in Manitoulin District, Ontario: the Chronology." *Man* 43, Correspondence 32: 48.

–. 1955. "Wave Action at George Lake I, Ontario." *American Antiquity* 20 (4): 376-7.

Greenman, E.F., and George M. Stanley. 1943. "The Archaeology and Geology of Two Early Sites Near Killarney, Ontario." *Michigan Academy of Science, Arts and Letters* 28: 505-31.

Grimes, John R. 1979. "A New Look at Bull Brook." *Anthropology* 3 (1 and 2): 109-30.

Grimes, John R., William Eldridge, Beth G. Grimes, Antonio Vaccaro, Frank Vaccaro, Joseph Vaccaro, Nicholas Vaccaro, and Antonio Orsini. 1984. "Bull Brook II." *Archaeology of Eastern North America* 12: 159-83.

Gwyn, Q.H.J., and S. White. 1973. *Quarternary Geology of the Alliston Area, Southern Ontario.* Ontario Division of Mines preliminary map P.835. Geology Series.

Hansel, A.K., D.M. Mickelson, A.F. Schneider, and C.E. Larson. 1985. "Late Wisonsinan and Holocene History of the Lake Michigan Basin." In *Quaternary Evolution of the Great Lakes,* ed. P.F. Karrow and P.E. Calkin, 39-53. Geological Association of Canada special paper 30. St John's, NF: Geological Association of Canada.

Haury, Emil W. 1953. "Artifacts with Mammoth Remains, Naco, Arizona: I. Discovery of the Naco Mammoth and the Associated Projectile Points." *American Antiquity* 19 (1): 1-14.

Haury, Emil W., E.B. Sayles, and William W. Wasley. 1959. "The Lehner Mammoth Site, Southeastern Arizona." *American Antiquity* 25 (1): 2-30.

Haynes Jr., C. Vance. 1964. "Fluted Projectile Points: Their Age and Dispersion." *Science* 145 (3639): 1408-13.

–. 1969. "The Earliest Americans." *Science* 166 (3906): 709-15.

–. 1992. "Contributions of Radiocarbon Dating to the Geochronology of the Peopling of the New World." In *Radiocarbon after Four Decades,* ed. R.E. Taylor, A. Long, and R.S. Kra, 355-74. New York: Springer-Verlag.

Haynes, Gary. 1992. *Mammoth, Mastodonts and Elephants: Biology, Behavior and the Fossil Record.* Cambridge: Cambridge University Press.

Hemmings, C. Andrew. 1998. "Probable Association of Paleoindian Artifacts and Mastodon Remains from Sloth Hole, Aucilla River, North Florida." *Current Research in the Pleistocene* 15: 16-18.

Hester, James J. 1972. *Blackwater Locality No. 1: A Stratified, Early Man Site in Eastern New Mexico.* Ranchos de Taos, NM: Fort Burgwin Research Center and Southern Methodist University.

Hofman, Jack L., and Russell W. Graham. 1998. "The Paleo-Indian Cultures of the Great Plains." In *Archaeology on the Great Plains,* ed. W. Raymond Wood, 87-139. Lawrence, KA: University Press of Kansas.

Hopkins, David M. 1982. "Aspects of the Paleogeography of Beringia during the Late

Pleistocene." In *Paleoecology of Beringia*, ed. David M. Hopkins, John V. Matthews Jr., Charles E. Schweger, and Steven B. Young, 3-28. New York: Academic Press.

Irving, W.N., and C.R. Harington. 1973. "Upper Pleistocene Radiocarbon-Dated Artefacts from the Northern Yukon." *Science* 179 (4071): 335-40.

Jablonski, Nina G., ed. 2002. *The First Americans: The Pleistocene Colonization of the New World.* Memoirs of the California Academy of Sciences number 27. San Francisco: California Academy of Sciences.

Jackson, L.J. 1986. "Figgins and Patterson: The Forgotten Beginning of Ontario Palaeo-Indian Studies." Ontario Archaeological Society, *ARCH NOTES* 86-4: 11-16.

Jackson, Lawrence, J.H. McKillop, and S. Wurtzburg. 1987. "The Forgotten Beginning of Canadian Palaeo-Indian Studies, 1933-1935." *Ontario Archaeology* 47: 5-18.

Jones, Scott, and Robson Bonnichsen. 1994. "The Anzick Clovis Burial." *Current Research in the Pleistocene* 11: 42-4.

Jopling, A.V., W.N. Irving, and B.F. Beebe. 1981. "Stratigraphic, Sedimentological and Faunal Evidence for the Occurrence of Pre-Sangamonian Artefacts in Northern Yukon." *Arctic* 34 (1): 3-33.

Julig, Patrick J., ed. 2002. *The Sheguiandah Site: Archaeological, Geological and Paleobotanical Studies at a Paleoindian Site on Manitoulin Island, Ontario.* Mercury Series, Archaeological Survey of Canada paper 161. Ottawa: Canadian Museum of Civilization.

Karrow, P.F., T.W. Anderson, A.H. Clarke, L.D. Delorme, and M.R. Sreenivasa. 1975. "Stratigraphy, Paleontology, and Age of Lake Algonquin Sediments in Southwestern Ontario, Canada." *Quaternary Research* 5 (1): 49-87.

Karrow, P.F., and P.E. Calkin, eds. 1985. *Quaternary Evolution of the Great Lakes.* Geological Association of Canada special paper 30. St. John's, NF: Department of Earth Sciences, Memorial University of Newfoundland.

Karrow, P.F., and B.G. Warner. 1990. "The Geological and Biological Environment for Human Occupation in Southern Ontario." In *The Archaeology of Southern Ontario to A.D. 1650,* ed. Chris J. Ellis and Neal Ferris, 5-35. Occasional Publication no. 5. London, ON: Ontario Archaeological Society.

Kenyon, W.A. 1977. "Some Bones of Contention: The Neutral Indian Burial Site at Grimsby." *Rotunda* 10 (3): 4-13.

—. 1982. *The Grimsby Site: A Historic Neutral Cemetery.* Toronto: Royal Ontario Museum.

Kidd, Kenneth E. 1951. "Fluted Points in Ontario." *American Antiquity* 16 (3): 260.

Kirkpatrick, M. Jude, and Daniel C. Fisher. 1993. "Preliminary Research on the Moon Mammoth Site." *Current Research in the Pleistocene* 10: 70-1.

Krieger, Alex D. 1964. "Early Man in the New World." In *Prehistoric Man in the New World,* ed. Jesse D. Jennings and Edward Norbeck, 21-81. Rice University Semicentennial Publications. Chicago: University of Chicago Press.

Kurtén, Björn, and Elaine Anderson. 1980. *Pleistocene Mammals of North America.* New York: Columbia University Press.

Lahren, Larry, and Robson Bonnichsen. 1974. "Bone Foreshafts from a Clovis Burial in Southwestern Montana." *Science* 186: 147-50.

Laub, Richard S., Norton G. Miller, and David W. Steadman, eds. 1988. *Late Pleistocene and Early Holocene Paleoecology and Archaeology of the Eastern Great Lakes Region.* Bulletin of the Buffalo Society of Natural Sciences vol. 33. Buffalo, NY: Buffalo Society of Natural Sciences.

Lee, Thomas E. 1954. "The First Sheguiandah Expedition, Manitoulin Island, Ontario." *American Antiquity* 20 (2): 101-11.

—. 1956. "Position and Meaning of a Radiocarbon Sample from the Sheguiandah Site, Ontario." *American Antiquity* 22 (1): 79.

—. 1957. "The Antiquity of the Sheguiandah Site." *Canadian Field-Naturalist* 71: 117-37.

—. 1978. "Sheguiandah and Early Man." In *Geology of the Manitoulin Area,* 87-9. Michigan Basin Geological Society special paper 3. Lansing: Michigan Geological Survey.

MacDonald, George F. 1968. *Debert: A Palaeo-Indian Site in Central Nova Scotia.* Anthropology Papers no. 16. Ottawa: National Museum of Canada.

McGhee, Robert. 1984. "Contact between Native North Americans and the Medieval Norse: A Review of the Evidence." *American Antiquity* 49 (1): 4-26.

Mason, Ronald J. 1962. "The Paleo-Indian Tradition in Eastern North America" and "Comments." *Current Anthropology* 3 (3): 227-78.

Meltzer, David J. 1988. "Late Pleistocene Human Adaptations in Eastern North America." *Journal of World Archaeology* 2 (1): 1-52.

–. 1993. "Is There a Clovis Adaptation?" In *From Kostenki to Clovis: Upper Paleolithic – Paleo-Indian Adaptations*, ed. Olga Soffer and N.D. Praslov, 293-310. New York: Plenum Press.

Meltzer, David J., and Bruce D. Smith. 1986. "Paleoindian and Early Archaic Subsistence Strategies in Eastern North America." In *Foraging, Collecting, and Harvesting: Archaic Period Subsistence and Settlement in the Eastern Woodlands*, ed. Sarah W. Neusius, 3-31. Occasional Paper no. 6. Carbondale, IL: Center for Archaeological Investigations and Southern Illinois University.

Meltzer, David J., Lawrence C. Todd, and Vance T. Holliday. 2002. "The Folsom (Paleoindian) Type Site: Past Investigations, Current Studies." *American Antiquity* 67 (1): 5-36.

Morlan, Richard E. 1986. "Pleistocene Archaeology in Old Crow Basin: A Critical Reappraisal." In *New Evidence for the Pleistocene Peopling of the Americas*, ed. Alan Lyle Bryan, 27-48. Orono, ME: Center for the Study of Early Man and University of Maine.

Morlan, Richard, D.E. Nelson, T.A. Brown, J.S. Vogel, and J.R. Southon. 1990. "Accelerator Mass Spectrometry Dates on Bones from the Old Crow Basin, Northern Yukon Territory." *Canadian Journal of Archaeology* 14: 75-92.

Nelson, D.E., Richard E. Morlan, J.S. Vogel, J.R. Southon, and C.R. Harington. 1986. "New Dates on Northern Yukon Artifacts: Holocene Not Upper Pleistocene." *Science* 232: 749-51.

Nicholas, George P., and Thomas D. Andrews, eds. 1997. *At a Crossroads: Archaeology and First Peoples in Canada*. Department of Archaeology Publication no. 24. Burnaby, BC: Archaeology Press, Simon Fraser University.

Norton, Mark R., John B. Broster, and Emanuel Breitburg. 1998. "The Trull Site (40PY276): A Paleoindian Mastodon Association in Tennessee." *Current Research in the Pleistocene* 15: 50-1

Occhietti, Serge. 1987. "Dynamique de l'Inlandsis Laurentidien du Sangamonien à l'Holocène." In *The Laurentide Ice Sheet*, ed. Robert J. Fulton and John T. Andrews. *Géographie physique et quaternaire* 41 (2): 301-13.

Overstreet, David F. 1996. "Still More on Cultural Contexts of Mammoth and Mastodon in the Southwestern Lake Michigan Basin." *Current Research in the Pleistocene* 13: 36-8.

Overstreet, David F., Daniel J. Joyce, Kurt F. Hallin, and David Wasion. 1993. "Cultural Contexts of Mammoth and Mastodont in the Southwestern Lake Michigan Basin." *Current Research in the Pleistocene* 10: 75-7.

Overstreet, David F., Daniel J. Joyce, and David Wasion. 1995. "More on Cultural Contexts of Mammoth and Mastodon in the Southwestern Lake Michigan Basin." *Current Research in the Pleistocene* 12: 40-2.

Palmer, Harris A., and James B. Stoltman. 1976. "The Boaz Mastodon: A Possible Association of Man and Mastodon in Wisconsin." *Midcontinental Journal of Archaeology* 1 (2): 163-77.

Powers, William R., and John F. Hoffecker. 1989. "Late Pleistocene Settlement in the Nenana Valley, Central Alaska." *American Antiquity* 54 (2): 263-87.

Protsch, Reiner R.R. 1978. *Catalogue of Fossil Hominids of North America*. New York: Gustav Fischer.

Roosa, W.B. 1977. "Great Lakes Paleoindians: The Parkhill Site, Ontario." In *Amerinds and Their Paleoenvironments in Northeastern North America*, ed. Walter S. Newman and Bert Salwen, 349-54. Annals of the New York Academy of Sciences 288. New York: New York Academy of Sciences.

Sanford, John T. 1957. "Geological Observations at the Sheguiandah Site." *Canadian Field-Naturalist* 71: 138-48.

–. 1971. "Sheguiandah Reviewed." *Anthropological Journal of Canada* 9 (1): 2-15.

Saunders, Jeffrey J. 1980. "A Model for Man-Mammoth Relationships in Late Pleistocene North America." *Canadian Journal of Anthropology* 1 (1): 87-98.

–. 1992. "Blackwater Draw: Mammoths and Mammoth Hunters in the Terminal Pleistocene."

In *Proboscidean and Paleoindian Interactions,* ed. John W. Fox, Calvin B. Smith, and Kenneth T. Wilkins, 124-49. Waco, TX: Markham Press Fund of Baylor University Press.

Spiess, Arthur E. 1979. *Reindeer and Caribou Hunters.* New York: Academic Press.

Spiess, Arthur E., Mary Lou Curran, and John R. Grimes. 1985. "Caribou (*Rangifer tarandus* L.) Bones from New England Paleoindian Sites." *North American Archaeologist* 6 (2): 145-59.

Spiess, Arthur E., and Deborah Brush Wilson. 1987. "Michaud: A Paleoindian Site in the New England-Maritimes Region." Occasional Publications in Maine Archaeology, no. 6. Augusta, ME: Maine Historic Preservation Commission and Maine Archaeological Society.

Stafford Jr., Thomas W. 1994. "Accelerator C-14 Dating of Human Fossil Skeletons: Assessing Accuracy and Results on New World Specimens." In *Method and Theory for Investigating the Peopling of the Americas,* ed. Robson Bonnichsen and D. Gentry Steele, 45-55. Corvallis, OR: Center for the Study of the First Americans and Oregon State University.

Stanford, D.J. 1978. "The Jones-Miller Site: An Example of Hell Gap Bison Procurement Strategy." In *Bison Procurement and Utilization: A Symposium,* ed. L.B. Davis and M. Wilson, 90-7. Plains Anthropologist memoir no. 14. Lincoln, NB: Plains Anthropologist.

Stanford, Dennis, Robson Bonnichsen, and Richard E. Morlan. 1981. "The Ginsberg Experiment: Modern and Prehistoric Evidence of a Bone-Flaking Technology." *Science* 212: 438-40.

Stoltman, J.B., and D.A. Baerreis. 1983. "The Evolution of Human Ecosystems in the Eastern United States." In *Late-Quaternary Environments of the United States,* vol. 2, ed. H. Wright, 252-68. Minneapolis: University of Minnesota Press.

Storck, Peter L. 1979. *A Report on the Banting and Hussey Sites: Two Paleo-Indian Campsites in Simcoe County, Southern Ontario.* National Museum of Man Mercury Series, Archaeological Survey of Canada paper no. 93. Ottawa: National Museums of Canada.

Storck, Peter L., with contributions by Betty E. Eley, Q.H.J. Gwyn, J.H. McAndrews, André Nolin, Andrew Stewart, John Tomenchuk, and Peter H. Von Bitter. 1997. *The Fisher Site: Archaeological, Geological and Paleobotanical Studies at an Early Paleo-Indian Site in Southern Ontario, Canada.* Memoir no. 30. Ann Arbor: Museum of Anthropology; Toronto: Royal Ontario Museum.

Storck, Peter L., and Arthur E. Spiess. 1994. "The Significance of New Faunal Identifications Attributed to an Early Paleoindian (Gainey Complex) Occupation at the Udora Site, Ontario, Canada." *American Antiquity* 59 (1): 121-42.

Storck, Peter L., and John Tomenchuk. 1990. "An Early Paleoindian Cache of Informal Tools at the Udora Site, Ontario." In *Early Paleoindian Economies of Eastern North America,* ed. Kenneth B. Tankersley and Barry L. Isaac, 45-93. Research in Economic Anthropology supplement 5. Greenwich, CT, and London: JAI Press.

Storck, Peter L., and Peter von Bitter. 1989 "The Geological Age and Occurrence of Fossil Hill Formation Chert: Implications for Early Paleoindian Settlement Patterns." In *Eastern Paleoindian Lithic Resource Use,* ed. Christopher J. Ellis and Johnathan C. Lothrop, 165-89. Boulder, San Francisco, and London: Westview Press.

Taylor, R.E., C. Vance Haynes Jr., and Minze Stuiver. 1996. "Clovis and Folsom Age Estimates: Stratigraphic Context and Radiocarbon Calibration." *Antiquity* 70 (269): 515-25.

Trigger, Bruce G., ed. 1978. *Handbook of North American Indians.* Vol. 15, Northeast. Washington, DC: Smithsonian Institution.

Webb, S. David, Jerald T. Milanich, Roger Alexon, and James S. Dunbar. 1984. "A *Bison Antiquus* Kill Site, Wacissa River, Jefferson County, Florida." *American Antiquity* 49 (2): 384-92.

West, Frederick Hadleigh, ed. 1996. *American Beginnings: The Prehistory and Palaeoecology of Beringia.* Chicago: University of Chicago Press.

Wilke, Philip J., J. Jeffrey Flenniken, and Terry L. Ozbun. 1991. "Clovis Technology at the Anzick Site, Montana." *Journal of California and Great Basin Anthropology* 13 (2): 242-72.

Wilson, Daniel. 1863. *Prehistoric Annals of Scotland.* 2 vols. 2nd ed. London and Cambridge: Macmillan.

Wormington, H.M. 1957. *Ancient Man in North America.* 4th ed. Popular Series no. 4. Denver, CO: Denver Museum of Natural History.

Wright, Henry T., and William B. Roosa. 1966. "The Barnes Site: A Fluted Point Assemblage from the Great Lakes Region." *American Antiquity* 31 (6): 850-60.

TEXT CREDITS

Newsletter extracts have been reproduced courtesy of the Royal Ontario Museum.

22 "Beachcombing into the Past," *ROM Archeological Newsletter,* New Series no. 63 (August 1970)

38 "Recollections of a Busy Summer," *ROM Archeological Newsletter,* New Series no. 89 (October 1972)

57 "Ancient Beaches and the Trail of Early Man in Ontario," *ROM Archeological Newsletter,* New Series no. 115 (December 1974)

68 "A Summer at the Beach," *ROM Archeological Newsletter,* New Series no. 124 (September 1975)

90 "At the Water's Edge," *ROM Archeological Newsletter,* New Series no. 161 (October 1978)

139 "Beachcombing Again, and then a Short Midsummer's (K)nap," *ROM Archeological Newsletter,* New Series no. 174 (November 1979)

148 "A 'Behind the Scenes' View of Fieldwork, or the Coming of Age of a Research Program," *ROM Archeological Newsletter,* New Series no. 188 (January 1981)

186 "A Question of Time," *ROM Archeological Newsletter,* Series 2 no. 23 (November 1987)

196 "The Other Face of Time" *ROM Archeological Newsletter,* Series 2 no. 38 (May 1990)

270 "Ice Age Hunters in Ontario: Finding the Best Way to Find Sites," *ROM Archeological Newsletter,* Series 2 no. 4 (September 1984)

276 "Should It Be the Beach or the Mountains This Year?" *ROM Archeological Newsletter,* Series 2 no. 50 (January 1993)

285 "Windows Where Walls Once Stood: Looking for New Insights into the Past," *ROM Archeological Newsletter,* Series 2 no. 57 (March 1995)

293 "Everywhere, Yet Nowhere," *ROM Archeological Newsletter,* Series 3 no. 2 (April 1996)

INDEX

Note: "(f)" denotes figure; "(m)" a map; "(p)" a photograph; "(t)" a table; *Newsletter* stands for the *Royal Ontario Museum Archaeological Newsletter*

blood-residue analysis, 220
Debert point, 103
radiocarbon dating, 32, 33
deer, white-tailed, 227, 224, 314
Deller, D. Brian
    background, 66
    dating of Fisher site, 118-19
    finds in Ontario, 146, 155
    Gainey-type spear points, 155-6
    at Parkhill, 77, 95, 97, 116-17, 147
    Thedford II excavation, 74
Delorme, Denis, 294, 295-6
Dent site, 29(m), 32
Department of Lands and Forests
        (Ontario), 16
de Perthes, Boucher, 4
Detroit, Michigan, 219
diamicton, 261
Dibb, Gordon, 136, 153
Dillehay, Thomas, 255
dire wolf (Canis dirus), 225
dolostone bedrock, 255-6
Don Formation, 234
Don Valley Brickyard, 234
Dorset people (Paleo-Eskimos), 49
driving tour of area, 320-34
drumlins, 52, 260
Dummer moraine, 60, 211(m)
Dunbar, Frank, 124-5
Dundalk uplands, 210, 211(m), 213
Dundas Valley, 39, 43(m)
Dunedin, Ontario, 327
Dutchess Quarry Caves site, 29(m), 36, 217,
        218(m), 219

Early Archaic peoples, 64, 81, 316
Early Paleo-Indians
    at Banting and Hussey sites, 59, 64
    colonization of North and South
        America, 8, 33-4, 74, 187
    Crowfield culture, 268, 292
    Eastern Plano descendents, 316
    families/bands/social groupings, 74-6
    at Fisher site (see Fisher site)
    fluted points (see fluted spear points)
    food resources and toolstones, 291-2
    greater northeast adaptive zone, 228
    as "hunter-gatherer geologists," 291-2
    known through stone tools, xviii
    predicting land use from hunting activi-
        ties, 38, 40-2
    regional adaptations, xvii, 147, 223, 226-8
    seasonal movements, 125-6, 291-2
    social dimensions of land use, 268-9
    use of spruce roots, 157
    See also Clovis culture; Folsom culture;

Flint, Richard Foster, 233-4
flintknapping
    "chest crutch," 143-4
    complexity of, 34, 36-7
    fieldschool, 138-9, 141-5
    imaginary account, 307-13
    lithic technology, 137-8, 141
    Newsletter description, 139-43
    replication, 138
    See also fluted spear points
Florida sites, 223, 224-5
fluted spear points
    at Banting site, 52-3, 59, 63
    Barnes-type, 96(p), 97, 100-1, 102-3, 156
    Barnes-type at Red Wing site, 298-300
    at Blackwater Draw, 33, 254
    in Bronte Creek gap, 42, 43(m)
    Clovis-type, 11(f), 32-3, 88, 156, 183
    complexity of manufacture, 36-7, 98,
        169(f)-173(f)
    Crowfield-type, 156
    Cumberland-type, 103
    dating of Fisher site, 119-20
    Debert point, 103
    earliest find in Ontario, 30(f)
    at East Wenatchee, 88
    effectiveness, 32-3, 34, 36-7
    at Fisher site, 70, 90-2, 95-100
    Folsom-type, 11(f), 31, 33, 102-3
    Gainey-type, 155-6, 189-92
    hand drawings showing manufacture,
        169, 169(f)-173(f), 178
    Hell Gap-type, 99
    at Hussey site, 59, 63-4
    imaginary flintknapping tale, 307-13
    isolated fluted point finds (1970s), 28,
        30-1, 32-3, 37-8, 48, 52
    miniature spear points, 99-100
    Newcastle point, 180, 181(p), 182, 184-5
    notched points at Coates Creek site, 81
    ROM collection (early 1970s), 28, 30, 37-8
    at Sheguiandah site, 231, 232(p)
    size differences and hunting patterns,
        119-20
    at Thomson site, 271-2, 276
    toolstones, 34-6
    See also flintknapping
fluting technique, 33
Flying Horse of Kansu, 62
Folsom culture
    bison kills, 8, 32-3, 214-15
    fluting technique, 102-3
    human occupation in Americas, 8, 254
    postdated Clovis culture, 215
    spear point, 11(f), 31
    spear points at Blackwater Draw, 33

type site, 214
Folsom site, 29(m), 30-1
forest tundra, 202-3, 204
Forks of the Credit River, 39, 43(m)
Fossil Hill chert
    acquisition, 269, 284, 286-7
    beds at Thomson site, 278-80, 281(m), 282
    focus in search for sites, 267-8
    location, 72(m), 211(m), 267
    source, 67, 92-4, 122-5, 270
    tools at Mt. Albion West, 45
    tools at Udora, 155, 157-8, 193
    See also Red Wing site; Thomson site
Fossil Hill Formation, 123-5, 158, 268, 270,
    278-80, 282, 329
Fox, William, 123, 275
France, 4, 130, 215
Franklin Park Zoo, 162

Gainey culture
    colonization of Ontario, 189, 191, 268
    Gainey-type spear points, 155-6, 180, 189,
        191-2
    hunting and trapping, 200, 202
    tool cache at Udora, 155-8
    at Udora site, 193
    See also Udora site
Garner, D., 69
Garrad, Charles, 31, 47-8, 52, 274
Geochelone crassiscutata (giant land tortoise),
    223, 225
Geological Survey of Canada, 132, 133
geological time scale, 5(t), 237(t)
George Lake, 332-3
George Lake 1 and 2 sites, 16, 17(m), 18-19,
    21, 23, 333
Georgia (state), 226
Georgian Bay
    and La Cloche Range, 22
    Parkhill culture in south, 147
Georgian Bay basin, 58, 61, 265, 315
Germany, recolonization, 214-15, 217
giant beaver, 108, 221, 222
giant ground sloth (*Glossotherium harlani*),
    224-5
giant land tortoise (*Geochelone crassiscutata*),
    223, 225
Gibraltar moraine, 326
Gilmour, Cary, 247
Ginsberg (elephant), 162, 165
glacial lakes
    Agassiz, Lake, 51(m), 264
    Algonquin, Lake (*see* Algonquin, Lake
        [glacial])
    Chippewa, Lake, 51(m)
    Iroquois, Lake, 5(t), 44, 50(m), 58, 61, 134

Osprey-The Blue Mountains Townline, 327
Ottawa, Ontario, 61
Ottawa people, 49
Ottawa River, 61, 204, 210, 245, 315
Overstreet, David, 222
Owen Sound, Ontario, 266

Paleo-Eskimos (Dorset people), 49
Paleo-Indian period, 6(t), 49
Paleo-Indians. *See* Early Paleo-Indians; Late
    Paleo-Indians
Paleolithic peoples
    American, 31
    Early, 27
    Upper, 213, 215, 217, 229, 231
Paleozoic Era/rocks, 237(t), 330
Parkhill culture
    artifact concentrations, 116-17
    at Banting and Hussey sites, 147
    and Barnes-type points, 77, 95, 100-1,
        102-3, 298-300
    at Fisher site (*see* Fisher site)
    hunting tool kit, 35(f), 37
    at Red Wing site, 299-300
    at Thedford II site, 74, 75(f), 76
    use of Fossil Hill toolstone, 93, 100, 119,
        155, 268
Parry Sound district, 333
Patterson, William J., 31
Payette, Lake (postglacial), 315
Pearson, Lester B., 331
pebble tools, 178
peccaries
    flat-headed (*Platygonus compressus*), 225
    long-nosed (*Mylohyus nasutus*), 224-5
Peel, Lake (glacial), 60
Pembroke, Ontario, 61
Penetang, Lake (postglacial), 315
Pennsylvania sites, 32, 128, 220, 234
Penokean Orogeny, 237(t), 254, 332
Penokean-Killarney Mountain Range, 254-5,
    332
periglacial tundra, 204, 226
Perth, Ontario, 61
Petawawa, Ontario, 61
Peterborough, Ontario, 60, 212
Petun Iroquois, 47, 49, 317
Pine River Valley, 39, 43(m), 325
Pine zone, 264
Plains
    early hunters, 32, 34, 222
    Folsom-type point, 103
    paleoecological zone, xvii, 318
Plano peoples, Eastern, 316
Platygonus compressus (flat-headed peccary),
    225

Pleistocene Epoch (Ice Age)
    Bering land bridge, 9(m), 12-13
    climate change to non-glacial, 314-15
    deglaciation of Ontario, 50(m), 51(m), 60-1
    Early Pleistocene, 5(t), 10
    in geological time scale, 5(t), 237(t)
    glacial advances, 10
    Late Pleistocene, 5(t), 10, 218(m), 233-4, 248
    Middle Pleistocene, 5(t), 10
    Sangamonian interglacial, 5(t), 10, 233-4
    unglaciated areas in Yukon, 161
    Wisconsinan glaciation, 5(t), 10, 233-4,
        248
    See also glacial lakes
polygons, fossil/frost, 203
Polynesians, 12
Pomme de Terre River, 218(m), 224
Port Huron outlet, 315
Port Severn, Ontario, 134
postglacial lakes, 51(m), 252(m), 315
pottery, of Early Woodland culture, 316
pre-Clovis period, 6(t)
    Monte Verde II in Chile, 255-6
    Sheguiandah as possible site, 234-5
    theories, 11, 15, 159-61, 234-5
Precambrian time, 237(t), 254
prehistoric time, 4, 7
prehumans, 7
Pre-Projectile Point stage, 11, 15, 234-5
Prevec, Rosemary, 198
proboscidean. *See* elephants; mammoth
    (*Mammuthus* spp.); mastodon (*Mammut
    americanum*)
productivity paradox, 13
Proterozoic eon, 237(t), 332

quartzite
    of La Cloche Range, 22-3, 303(p), 330, 332-3
    Manitoulin Island and Killarney Park, 16,
        332-3
    at Sheguiandah site, 251, 253, 254-7
Quaternary Period, 5(t), 10, 237(t)
Quebec, 226
Quebec City, Quebec, 15, 235
Quimby, George Irving, 34, 331

radiocarbon dating
    bison kill at Folsom, 214
    "bone dates," 197
    calcined bones, 190-1, 193
    caribou bones, 219
    of Clovis people's existence, 254
    postglacial deposits at Sheguiandah, 264
    radiocarbon vs calendar years, xviii-xix
    tandem accelerator mass spectrometry,
        197, 228

South Baymouth, Ontario, 329
southwest United States. *See under* United
    States
Spanish River, 22
Spaulding, Albert, 331
spear points. *See* fluted spear points
Spiess, Arthur, 198-9, 200, 206
Spirit Cave mummy, 89
Springmount, Ontario, 329
Spruce (*Picea*) zone, 107-8, 204, 264
spruce-parkland habitat, 107-8, 204, 226
Stafford, Tom, 197-8
stag-moose, 222
Stanford, Dennis, 162
Stanley, George, 16, 18-19
Stanley, Lake (postglacial), 51(m), 252(m), 315
Stayner, Ontario, 325
steppe antelope, 12
Stevenson, Ross, 187
Stewart, Andrew, 41, 65, 188, 249
strandlines
    around present-day Lake Simcoe, 133(m),
        134-5, 140
    Coates Creek site, 69, 72(m)
    Fisher site, 72(m), 73, 76, 78, 105-6, 108-11
    maps of, 133-4
    Nipissing strandline, 252(m)
    Parkhill site, 77
    Udora site, 132, 133(m), 135
    See also relic beaches
Stratford, Ontario, 210
stratigraphy
    dating method, 4
    relationship between Clovis and Folsom
        points, 33, 215
    at Sheguiandah site, 238, 257-9
    at Thomson site, 280
    using pollen in drill cores, 108-9
structure of archaeological record. *See*
    archaeological record
Sudbury, Ontario, 331
Superior basin, 264, 318

Taconic Orogeny, 237(t)
taiga. *See* boreal forest
tandem accelerator mass spectrometry
    (TAMS), 197, 228
Tanzania, 7
taphonomy, 216
Taylor, Byron, 187
Telford, Peter, 123
Ten Mile Point, 329-30
Tennessee sites, 224-5
Terra Amata site, 178
Tertiary Period, 237(t)
Thedford II site, 74, 75(f), 76

thinning. *See* flintknapping; fluted spear
    points
Thirty Thousand Island region, 322
Thomson, Ken, 280
Thomson site
    acquisition of chert, 269, 284, 286-7
    chert beds, 278-80, 281(m), 282
    discovery (1982), 270-3
    excavations, 281(m), 283(p)
    features found, 282
    non-diagnostic artifacts, 276-8
Thornbury, Ontario, 69, 327(m), 328, 329
thrush (family *Turdidae*), 247
Thule people (Inuit), 49
Thunder Bay, Ontario, 244
till deposits, 233, 236, 238
Tobermory, Ontario, 41, 43(m), 320, 321(m)
Tobermory ferry, 322, 329
Tomenchuk, John, 115-16, 126-9, 156-7, 301
toolstones
    Bobcaygeon chert, 193
    crystal quartz, 180, 181(p), 182
    flint, 35-6
    food resources and, 291-2
    Fossil Hill chert (*see* Fossil Hill chert)
    geologic sources, 72(m)
    Gull River chert, 193
    Kettle Point chert, 72(m), 119
    Lockport chert, 45
    obsidian, 142
    Onondaga chert, 45, 72(m), 193, 292
    qualities needed, 34-6
    quartzite, 16, 23, 251, 253, 254-7
    sedimentary rocks, 35-6
    source and search for sites, 267-8
    See also flintknapping
Toronto, Ontario, 60, 61
Tou Wan, Princess, burial suit, 62
Tovell, Walter, 133
treeline, 108, 202-3, 204
Trent River system, 134
Trent University, 135, 136
Trenton, Ontario, 134
Trent-Severn Waterway, 58, 134, 333
Trull site, 218(m)
tundra, 202-4, 212, 226
Tupakka, Susan, 209
Tushingham, A.D., 12-13, 84-5
Tweed, Ontario, 60

Udora, Ontario, 44
Udora site
    Area A, 205, 206-7
    Area A-East, 189-90, 206-7
    artifacts, 188-90
    association with Lake Algonquin, 187

Naughty Cakes

Naughty Cakes

Step-by-step recipes for fabulous, fun cakes

DEBBIE BROWN

BARNES & NOBLE

NEW YORK

This edition published by Barnes & Noble, Inc.
by arrangement with New Holland Publishers (U.K.) Ltd

2005 Barnes & Noble Books

M 10 9 8 7 6 5 4 3 2 1

ISBN 0 7607 7494 3

Senior Editor: Clare Sayer
Production: Hazel Kirkman
Design: AG&G Books
Photographer: Ed Allwright
Editorial Direction: Rosemary Wilkinson

Reproduction by Pica Digital, Singapore
Printed in Singapore

This book is dedicated
to all my students,
some of whom have now
become firm friends.
Thank you for all your
enthusiasm, good
company and laughter
during our classes.

Contents

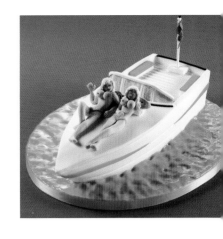

Introduction

 Although this book covers a rather risqué subject, I kept the cake designs fun, looking on the lighter side by injecting them with lots of humour to bring on a few giggles and chuckles when presented to the recipient.

Most of the cakes are relatively simple to make, even for a novice cake decorator. There is nothing that is too complicated, needing specialist skills in baking and sculpture. Some of the designs are a little more involved but if you wish, can be simplified just by leaving out some of the modelled items or figures.

If you find your modelling skills need to be honed, there are projects throughout the book with very simple figures, which can be used instead of the more involved models. For example, it probably wouldn't be noticed if the gorgeous pole dancer (see above left) had simply made hands without intricately cut fingers, especially with her other attributes on show!

Use this book to inspire your own ideas too. Just changing a colour scheme, adding an item from another design or making caricatures of people you know will add a fantastic personal touch to your cake, making it into a real talking point and leaving behind nice memories of the special celebration.

Basic recipes

I would always recommend making your own cake base, as shop-bought versions do not produce the same results. Many specialist cake decorating suppliers will supply ready-made sugarpaste, modelling paste, royal icing and other ingredients, but you will find recipes for making your own in this section. All spoon measures are level unless otherwise stated.

MADEIRA SPONGE CAKE

I prefer to use a Madeira sponge cake recipe for all my cakes as you need a cake which is moist and light, but still suitable for carving and sculpting without crumbling. Shop-bought cake mixes and ready-made cakes will not produce the same results, as they are often too soft and crumbly to withstand sculpting into different shapes. For each of the cakes in this book, refer to the chart on page 11 for specific quantities and baking times, then follow the method given below.

1 Preheat the oven to 150–160°C/ 325°F/Gas 3, then grease and line your baking tin.
2 Sift the self-raising and plain (all-purpose) flours together in a bowl.
3 Soften the butter and place in a food mixer or large mixing bowl with the caster (superfine) sugar and beat until the mixture is pale and fluffy.
4 Add the eggs to the mixture one at a time with a spoonful of the flour, beating well after each addition. Add a few drops of vanilla extract.
5 Using a spatula or large spoon, fold the remaining flour into the mixture.
6 Spoon the mixture into the tin, then make a dip in the top of the mixture using the back of a spoon.
7 Bake in the centre of your oven for the time stated in the cake chart (see page 11), or until a skewer inserted in the centre comes out clean.

8 Leave to cool in the tin for five minutes, then turn out onto a wire rack and leave to cool completely. When cold, store in an airtight container or double wrap in clingfilm (plastic wrap) for at least eight hours, allowing the texture to settle before use.

MADEIRA CAKE VARIATIONS

CHOCOLATE MARBLE CAKE
Before spooning the cake mixture into the tin, fold in 200 g (7 oz) of melted chocolate until marbled. Fold in completely for a light chocolate cake.

CHOCOLATE ORANGE MARBLE CAKE
Follow the instructions for a Chocolate Marble Cake, adding the grated rind and juice of one organic orange.

LEMON CAKE
Add the grated rind and juice of one organic lemon to the cake mixture.

ORANGE AND LEMON CAKE
Add the grated rind of one organic orange and one lemon to the cake mixture and add a squeeze of orange juice.

COFFEE CAKE
Add two tablespoons of coffee essence to the cake mixture.

Madeira sponge cake

ALMOND
Add 1 teaspoon of almond essence and 2–3 tablespoons of ground almonds to the cake mixture.

BUTTERCREAM
Buttercream is very versatile as it is suitable as a cake filling as well as for creating a crumb coat. This seals the cake to stop it from drying out, and provides a good adhesive base for the sugarpaste coating. For intricately sculpted cakes, leave the buttercream crumb coat to set firmly, then add a little more or rework the surface to soften so that the sugarpaste will stick to the cake.

Makes 625 g / 1¼ lb/ 3¾ c

- 175 g /6 oz/ ¾ c unsalted butter, softened
- 2–3 tbsp milk
- 1 tsp vanilla extract
- 450 g /1 lb/ 3 ¼ c icing (confectioners') sugar, sifted

1 Place the softened butter, milk and vanilla extract into a mixer. Add the icing sugar a little at a time, mixing on medium speed, until light, fluffy and pale in colour.
2 Store in an airtight container and use within 10 days. Bring to room temperature and beat again before use.

BUTTERCREAM VARIATIONS

CHOCOLATE
Add 90 g (3 oz) of good-quality melted chocolate, or use 3–4 tablespoons of cocoa powder mixed to a paste with milk.

ORANGE OR LEMON CURD
Add 2–3 tablespoons of orange or lemon curd.

COFFEE
Add 2–3 tablespoons of coffee essence.

RASPBERRY
Add 3–4 tablespoons of seedless raspberry jam.

ALMOND
Add 1 teaspoon almond essence.

SUGARPASTE
Good-quality ready-made sugarpaste is easy to use, produces good results and comes in a range of colours. It is readily available in large supermarkets and through specialist cake decorating outlets – see page 78 for a list of stockists and suppliers. However, if you prefer to make your own sugarpaste, try the following recipe. CMC is an abbreviation of Sodium Carboxymethyl Cellulose, an edible thickener widely used in the food industry. Check that it is food grade C1000P/E466. Gum tragacanth can be used as an alternative.

Makes 625 g /1¼ lb/ 3 ¾ c

- 1 egg white made up from dried egg albumen
- 2 tbsp liquid glucose
- 625 g /1¼ lb/ 3 ¾ c icing (confectioners') sugar
- A little white vegetable fat, if required
- A pinch of CMC or gum tragacanth, if required

1 Put the egg white and liquid glucose into a bowl, using a warm spoon for the liquid glucose.
2 Sift the icing sugar into the bowl, adding a little at a time and stirring until the mixture thickens.
3 Turn out onto a work surface dusted liberally with icing sugar and knead the paste until soft, smooth and pliable. If the paste is dry and cracked, fold in some vegetable fat and knead again. If the paste is soft and sticky, add a little more icing sugar or a pinch of CMC or gum tragacanth to stabilize.
4 Put immediately into a polythene bag and store in an airtight container. Keep at room temperature or refrigerate and use within a week. Bring back to room temperature and knead thoroughly before use. Home-made sugarpaste can be frozen for up to 3 months.

ROYAL ICING
Royal icing is used to pipe details such as hair, fur effect, etc. It is also used to stick items together, as when dry it holds items firmly in place. Ready-made royal icing or powder form (follow instructions on the packet) can be obtained from supermarkets. To make your own, use this recipe.

Makes 75 g (2½ oz)
- 1 tsp egg albumen
- 1 tbsp water

Sugarpaste blocks

- 65–70 g /2¼ oz/ ½ c icing (confectioners') sugar

1 Put the egg albumen into a bowl. Add the water and stir until dissolved. Beat in the icing sugar a little at a time until the icing is firm, glossy and forms peaks if a spoon is pulled out.

2 To stop the icing from forming a crust, place a damp cloth over the top of the bowl until you are ready to use it, or transfer to an airtight container and refrigerate.

SUGAR GLUE

This recipe makes a strong sugar glue which works extremely well. Alternatively, ready-made sugar glue can be purchased from specialist cake decorating outlets.

- ¼ tsp CMC powder or gum tragacanth
- 2 tbsp water

1 Mix the CMC with water and leave to stand until the powder is fully absorbed. The glue should be smooth and have a soft dropping consistency.

2 If the glue thickens after a few days, add a few drops more water. Store in an airtight container in the refrigerator and use within one week.

3 To use, brush a thin coat over the surface of the item you wish to glue, leave for a few moments to become tacky, and then press in place.

MODELLING PASTE

Modelling paste is used for creating figures and other smaller modelled items as it is more flexible. This quick and easy recipe makes a high quality modelling paste, which has been used throughout the book.

- 450 g (1 lb) sugarpaste (see page 9)
- 1 tsp CMC powder or gum tragacanth

1 Knead the CMC into sugarpaste. The sugarpaste starts to thicken as soon as CMC is incorporated so it can be used immediately. More thickening will occur gradually over a period of 24 hours.

2 The amount of CMC can be varied depending on usage; a firmer paste is more suitable for limbs, miniature modelling etc., so a little more can be added. This tends to dry the paste much faster, so modelling should be done quickly. Simpler or larger modelled pieces should need less CMC. It is also dependent on room temperature, atmospheric conditions, etc., so adjust accordingly. Store in an airtight container and use within two weeks for best results.

QUICK PASTILLAGE

Pastillage is a fast-drying paste, suitable for creating the sides of boxes (see page 34) as the paste dries extremely hard and will keep its shape.

Makes 260 g (9 oz) pastillage

- 2 tsp CMC powder or gum tragacanth
- 260 g (9 oz) royal icing

1 Mix the CMC or gum tragacanth into stiff-peaked royal icing. The mixture will thicken immediately. Knead on a work surface sprinkled liberally with icing sugar until the mixture forms a paste and is smooth and crack-free.

2 Keep in an airtight container and store in the refrigerator. Bring back to room temperature before use.

EDIBLE GLITTER

There is a lot of choice available through specialist cake decorating outlets for edible sparkling powders, but the glitters tend to be non-toxic food-safe, which I recommend be removed before serving. If you prefer to use something edible, try this quick and simple glitter recipe.

1 Mix equal parts (¼–½ tsp) gum arabic, water and your chosen edible metallic or sparkle powder food colouring. The mixture should look like thick paint.

2 Place a non-stick ovenproof liner/sheet onto a baking tray and brush the mixture over the surface. The mixture may congeal, so brush it out as thinly as possible. Bake on a very low heat for around ten minutes, until dry and starting to peel away from the liner.

3 Remove from oven and leave to cool. Lift with a palette knife and place into a sieve. Gently push through the sieve to produce small glitter particles. Store in a food-safe container.

SUGAR STICKS

These are used as edible supports, mainly to help hold modelled heads in place, but they can also be used for a variety of other purposes – flagpoles, for example – depending on their size.

Makes around 10–20 sugar sticks

- 1 level tsp stiff peak royal icing
- ¼ tsp CMC or gum tragacanth

1 Knead the CMC or gum tragacanth into the royal icing until the mixture forms a paste. Either roll it out and cut it into different sized strips of various lengths using a plain-bladed knife, or roll individual thin paste sausages. Let dry on a sheet of foam, preferably overnight. When dry, store in an airtight container.

Cake chart

To create the cakes in this book you will need to refer to this cake chart for specific quantities and baking times, then simply follow the appropriate method given on page 8.

- **HUNKY FIREMEN**
- **SEXY BUILDERS**

25cm (10 in) square tin

Unsalted butter, softened . . .400g/14oz/1⅔c
Caster (superfine) sugar .400g/14oz/2c
Large eggs 7
Self-raising flour 400g/14oz/3½c
Plain (all-purpose) flour . .200g/7oz/1⅔c
Baking time . . . . .1¼–1½ hours

- **THONG WATCH**
- **COME AND GET ME**
- **HIPPY FLASHERS**

25 cm (10 in) square tin

Unsalted butter, softened . .340g/12oz/1½c
Caster (superfine) sugar . .340g/12oz)1¾c
Large eggs 6
Self-raising flour 340g/12oz/3c
Plain (all-purpose) flour . .175g/6oz/1½c
Baking time . . . . .1–1¼ hours

- **HULA GIRLS**

18 cm (7 in), 15 cm (6 in) and 10 cm (4 in) round tins

Unsalted butter, softened . . .340g/12oz/1½c
Caster (superfine) sugar . . .340g/12oz/1¾c
Large eggs 6
Self-raising flour 340g/12oz/3c
Plain (all-purpose) flour . .175g/6oz/1½c
Baking time . . . . .1–1¼ hours

- **BEDTIME FUN**
- **NAUGHTY PLAYTIME**

23 cm (9 in) round tin

Unsalted butter, softened . . .340g/12oz/1½c
Caster (superfine) sugar . . .340g/12oz/1¾c
Large eggs 6
Self-raising flour 340g/12oz/3c
Plain (all-purpose) flour . .175g/6oz/1½c
Baking time . . . . .1–1¼ hours

- **ROLY POLY STRIP-O-GRAM**

2 x 15 cm (6 in) square tins and 1 x 12 cm (5 in) round tin

Unsalted butter, softened 340g/12oz/1½c
Caster (superfine) sugar 340g/12oz/1¾c
Large eggs 6
Self-raising flour 340g/12oz/3c
Plain (all-purpose) flour . .175g/6oz/1½c
Baking time . . . . .1–1¼ hours

- **WET T-SHIRT**

2 x 1 l (2 pint) ovenproof bowls or 16 cm (6½ in) spherical tin

Unsalted butter, softened 285g/10oz/1¼c
Caster (superfine) sugar . . .285g/10oz/1½c
Large eggs 5
Self-raising flour 285g/10oz/2½c
Plain (all-purpose) flour . .145g/5oz/1¼c
Baking time . . . . .1¼–1½ hours

- **ALMOST FULL MONTY**
- **TUNNEL OF LOVE**

20 cm (8 in) and 10 cm (4 in) round tins

Unsalted butter, softened 340g/12oz/1½c
Caster (superfine) sugar . . .340g/12oz/1¾c
Large eggs 6
Self-raising flour 340g/12oz/3c
Plain (all-purpose) flour . . .175g/6oz/1½c
Baking time . . . . .1–1¼ hours

- **JACUZZI FUN**

20 cm (8 in) round tin

Unsalted butter, softened 285g/10oz/1¼c
Caster (superfine) sugar 285g/10oz/1½c
Large eggs 5
Self-raising flour 285g/10oz/2½c
Plain (all-purpose) flour . .145g/5oz/1¼c
Baking time . . . . .1–1¼ hours

- **MUD PIT**

23 cm (9 in) ring tin

Unsalted butter, softened . . .225g/8oz/1c
Caster (superfine) sugar . .225g/8oz/1c, 2 tbsp
Large eggs 4
Self-raising flour 225g/8oz/2c
Plain (all-purpose) flour . .115g/4oz/1c
Baking time . . . . .50–60 minutes

- **GREEK GOD**

25 cm (10 in) round or petal-shaped tin

Unsalted butter, softened . . .340g/12oz/1½c
Caster (superfine) sugar 340g/12oz/1½c
Large eggs 6
Self-raising flour 340g/12oz/3c
Plain (all-purpose) flour . .175g/6oz/1½c
Baking time . . . . .1–1¼ hours

- **POLE DANCERS**

3 x 12 cm (5 in) round tins

Unsalted butter, softened . . .340g/12oz/1½c
Caster (superfine) sugar 340g/12oz/1¾c
Large eggs 6
Self-raising flour 175g/12oz/3c
Plain (all-purpose) flour . .175g/6oz/1½c
Baking time . . . . .1–1¼ hours

- **HOTPANTS**

25 cm (10 in) heart shaped tin

Unsalted butter, softened . . .340g/12oz/1½c
Caster (superfine) sugar 340g/12oz/1¾c
Large eggs 6
Self-raising flour 340g/12oz/3c
Plain (all-purpose) flour . .175g/6oz/1½c
Baking time . . . . .1–1¼ hours

- **RACY SPEEDBOAT**

30 x 12 cm (12 x 5 in) oblong tin

Unsalted butter, softened . . .285g/10oz/1¼c
Caster (superfine) sugar 285g/10oz/1½c
Large eggs 5
Self-raising flour 285g/10oz/2½c
Plain (all-purpose) flour . . .145g/5oz/1¼c
Baking time . . . . .1–1¼ hours

Basic techniques

Cake decorating is easier than it looks, although it can seem a little daunting if you are a complete beginner. This section shows you a few simple, basic techniques that will help you achieve great results and professional-looking cakes.

SCULPTING A CAKE

The first rule of cake sculpting is to have a moist but firm sponge cake that will not crumble. I recommend that you follow the recipes and method given in this book for a Madeira sponge cake (see page 8). If you are tempted to buy a cake mix or a ready-baked cake, make sure that it won't crumble away as soon as you start to cut into it. Ready-made cakes are really only suitable for projects involving minimal sculpting and stacking of layers.

Use a serrated knife for cake carving. When trimming away the crust of a cake, keep the cake as level as possible so there are no problems with balance if the cake is being stacked. Use a ruler for straight cuts and be aware of the knife blade, keeping it in the correct position for the cut you need.

ROLLING OUT SUGARPASTE

Sugarpaste can be rolled out successfully on any even food-safe work surface, but I recommend that

Rolling out sugarpaste

you use a large polypropylene board and rolling pin, both of which have tough, smooth surfaces.

Start by dusting your worksurface lightly with icing (confectioners') sugar. Knead the sugarpaste thoroughly, until soft and warm. Sugarpaste can start to dry out when exposed to the air, so roll out as quickly and evenly as possible to a covering thickness of around 3–4 mm (⅛ in), moving the paste around after each roll using a sprinkling of icing (confectioners') sugar. Make sure there isn't a build up of sugarpaste or icing (confectioners') sugar on either your board or your rolling pin, to help keep the sugarpaste perfectly smooth. Sugarpaste can stick to the work surface very quickly. If this happens, re-knead and start again.

COLOURING SUGARPASTE

Some brands of ready-made sugarpaste are available in a range of colours, but I usually prefer to mix my

Sculpting a cake

Colouring sugarpaste

Covering a cake board with sugarpaste

Covering a cake with sugarpaste

own colours. The best food colourings are obtainable as a paste or concentrated liquid. Avoid the watery liquid food colourings and powder colours, unless you want to achieve very pale shades. Powder food colours are usually only used to brush over the surface of dried sugarpaste to enhance certain areas.

The best way to apply food colour paste is with the tip of a knife. Simply dab a block of sugarpaste with the end of a knife (if you are creating a new colour, remember to keep a record of how many "dabs" of paste you use). Add a little at a time until the required shade is achieved. Knead thoroughly after each addition until the colour is even. Bear in mind that the colour will deepen slightly on standing, so be careful not to add too much.

If you wish to colour a large amount of sugarpaste, colour a small ball first, and then knead into the remaining amount to disperse the colour quickly. Wearing plastic gloves or rubbing a little white vegetable fat over your hands can help when colouring deep shades, as this can prevent a lot of mess. Some food colours can temporarily stain your hands.

COVERING A CAKE BOARD WITH SUGARPASTE

Knead the sugarpaste thoroughly until soft and warm. Roll out to roughly the size and shape of the cake board, using a sprinkling of icing

(confectioners') sugar and move around after each roll to prevent sticking.

Place the rolling pin on the centre of the rolled out sugarpaste and lift the back half over the top. Hold both ends of the rolling pin, lift and position the sugarpaste against the cake board and unroll over the top. Roll the rolling pin gently over the surface to stick the sugarpaste firmly to the board. If the sugarpaste is still loose, moisten along the outside edge only, using a little water or sugar glue on a brush.

Rub the surface with a cake smoother for a smooth, dimple-free surface. Lift the cake board and trim away the excess around the outside edge using a plain-bladed knife. Keep the knife straight to gain a neat edge, carefully removing any residue along the blade for a clean cut.

COVERING A CAKE WITH SUGARPASTE

Before applying sugarpaste to the buttercream-covered surface of a cake, make sure the buttercream is soft and sticky by reworking a little using a knife, or by adding a little more. Roll the sugarpaste out approximately 15 cm (6 in) larger than the top of the cake to allow enough icing to cover the sides of the cake. You can lift and position the sugarpaste on the cake as you would to cover a cake board, and then press the sugarpaste gently but firmly in position, smoothing over the

surface using your hands. Rub gently with your hands over any small cracks to blend them in. If you have any gaps, stroke the sugarpaste surface to stretch it slightly. Trim away excess any using a plain-bladed knife.

OBTAINING A GOOD FINISH

You will invariably find that you have occasional bumps on the surface of your cake or trapped air bubbles. A cake smoother is invaluable for obtaining a perfectly smooth finish for your sugarpaste. Rub firmly but gently in a circular motion to remove any small dents or bumps.

Any excess icing (confectioners') sugar can be brushed off dried sugarpaste. With stubborn areas, use a slightly damp large soft bristle pastry brush. The moisture will melt the excess, but take care not to wet the surface or streaks may result.

Obtaining a good finish

General equipment

There is a huge selection of cake decorating tools and equipment available now. Listed below are the basic necessities for cake decorating, some of which you likely already have in your kitchen. I've also added some specialist items that can help achieve great results.

1. WORKBOARD
You can easily work on any washable, even work surface, but for best results use a non-stick polypropylene work board. They are available in various sizes, with non-slip feet on the reverse.

2. ROLLING PINS
Polypropylene rolling pins are available in a variety of lengths, but basic large and small pins are the most useful.

3. SERRATED KNIFE
A medium-sized serrated knife is invaluable when sculpting a cake, as it cuts away neatly when using a slight sawing action.

4. PLAIN-BLADED KNIFE
Small and medium plain-bladed knives are used to cut through paste cleanly and evenly.

5. PALETTE KNIFE
This is used for the smooth spreading of buttercream, and also to help lift modelled pieces easily from a work surface.

6. CAKE SMOOTHER
Smoothes the surface of sugarpaste to remove any bumps or indents by rubbing gently in a circular motion.

7. SUGAR SHAKER
A handy container filled with icing (confectioners') sugar. Used for sprinkling the work surface before rolling out paste.

8. PAINTBRUSHES
Available in various sizes, choose good quality sable paintbrushes for painting details. Use a flat-ended brush for dusting powder food colours over the surface of dried paste.

9. LARGE PASTRY BRUSH
Invaluable for brushing excess icing (confectioners') sugar and crumbs away. When dampened slightly, it will lift any stubborn residue icing (confectioners') sugar from the surface quickly and easily.

10. RULER
Used for approximate measuring during cake and paste cutting and for indenting neat lines in sugarpaste.

11. SCISSORS
Needed for general use of cutting templates, piping bags and some small detailing.

12. PLAIN PIPING TUBES
Not only are these tubes used for piping royal icing, they are also used as cutters and indenters. For finer cuts use good quality metal tubes in preference to plastic ones.

13. PAPER PIPING BAGS
For use with royal icing. Parchment or greaseproof paper piping bags are available ready-made from cake decorating suppliers.

14. COCKTAIL STICKS
Readily available in food-safe wood or plastic form, these are useful for marking any fine detailing in paste.

15. FOAM PIECES
Used to support modelled pieces whilst drying, as the air can circulate all around. When the piece is dry, the foam is easily squeezed smaller for easy removal.

16. CUTTERS
Available in an array of different styles and shapes. Metal cutters usually have finer, cleaner edges but are more expensive. Some small cutters have plungers to remove the cut out shape.

17. TURNTABLE
When working on a cake, placing on a turntable allows you to quickly and easily move the cake around. Some bakers find it invaluable as it lifts the cake to a higher level.

18. FOOD COLOURING
Paste colours are suitable for colouring paste and royal icing, while powder colours add a subtle hue when brushed onto the surface of dried sugarpaste.

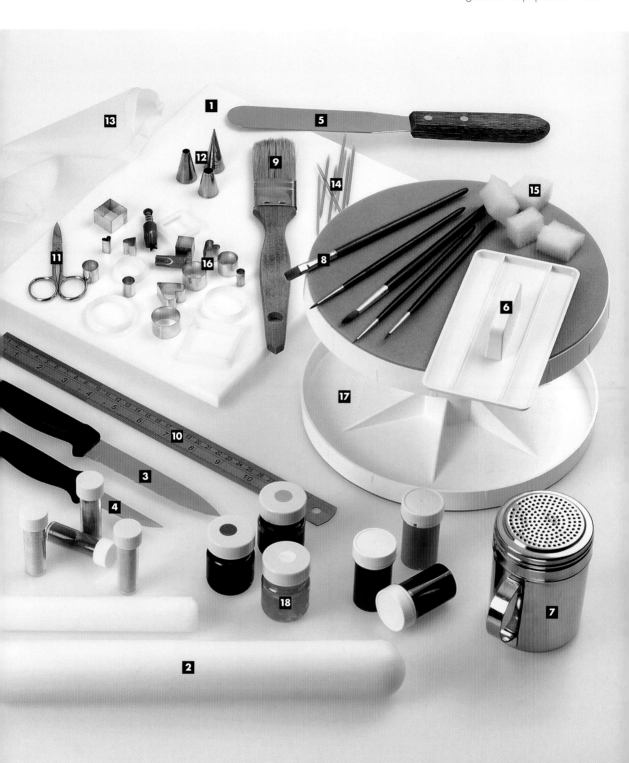

Thong Watch

Here's a typically ordinary and probably familiar looking fellow checking out the gorgeous girls in their sexy thongs whilst investing in his growing beer belly.

YOU WILL NEED

- 25 cm (10 in) square sponge cake (see page 11)
- 35 cm (14 in) square cake board
- Icing (confectioners') sugar in a sugar shaker
- 600 g / 1 lb 5¼ oz/2½ c buttercream (see page 8)

SUGARPASTE *(see page 9)*

- 260 g (9 oz) yellow
- 260 g (9 oz) pale chestnut
- 1.4 kg (3 lb 1½ oz) white
- 125 g (4½ oz) mauve
- 125 g (4½ oz) deep blue
- 125 g (4½ oz) pink
- 30 g (1 oz) bright green
- 30 g (1 oz) bright yellow

MODELLING PASTE *(see page 10)*

- 425 g (14¾ oz) flesh-colour
- 20 g (¾ oz) mauve
- 15 g (½ oz) white
- 5 g (just under ¼ oz) black
- 15 g (½ oz) brown
- 15 g (½ oz) pale yellow

- Sugar stick
- Sugar glue and paintbrush
- Edible silver powder

EQUIPMENT

- Plain-bladed kitchen knife
- Large and small rolling pins
- Cake smoother
- Ruler
- Serrated carving knife
- Palette knife
- Small pieces of foam (for support)
- Small circle cutter (to mark smiles)
- A few cocktail sticks

1 Slightly dampen the cake board with water. For a marbled effect, knead the yellow and pale chestnut sugarpaste together until streaky. Roll out using a sprinkling of icing sugar and move the paste around after each roll to prevent sticking. Lift the sugarpaste by draping over the rolling pin and cover the cake board. Use a cake smoother to smooth and polish the surface, then trim the excess from around the edge. For the tiled effect, mark lines using a ruler. Set aside to dry, preferably overnight.

2 Trim the crust from the cake and level the top. To make the sunbeds, cut the cake into three evenly-sized strips. Cut a layer in each strip and sandwich back together with buttercream using the palette knife, and then spread a thin layer of buttercream over the surface of each cake as a crumb coat.

Covering the sides of a cake

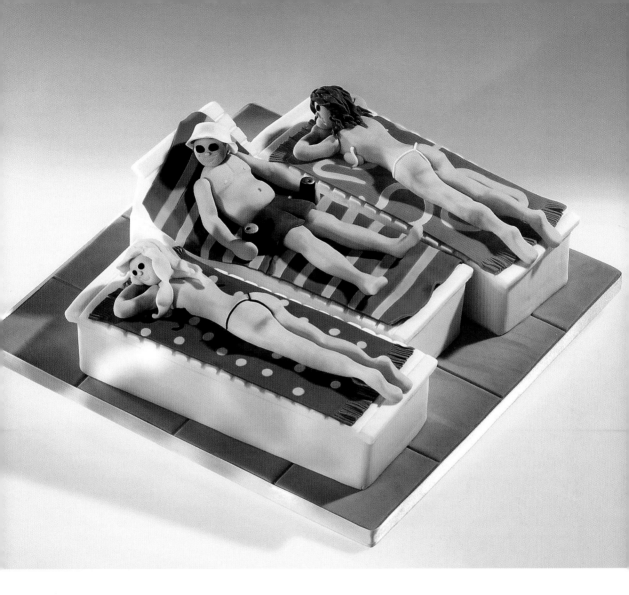

3 To cover the sides of the cake, first measure the depth using a ruler. Roll out 285 g (10 oz) of white sugarpaste and cut a strip to fit, measuring 66 cm (26 in) in length. Dust with icing sugar and roll up. Position against the side of the cake and unroll around it, covering all sides and trimming any excess from the join **(see left)**. To close the join, press it together, sticking it with a little sugar glue, then rub it gently with your fingers. Cover the remaining two cakes in the same way and position all three cakes on the cake board.

4 To build up the height at the back of the central sunbed, cut a wedge of white sugarpaste the size of the sunbed base, roughly 225 g (½ lb), and stick in place using a little sugar glue. For the slatted top of each sunbed, roll out and cut oblong shapes slightly larger than the top using the remaining white sugarpaste. Indent even lines for the slats using a ruler. Position on the top of each cake and rub the surface with a cake smoother.

5 The towels have a simple inlaid effect with coloured sugarpaste. Roll the paste thinly, making sure it is well dusted with icing sugar on the reverse to prevent sticking. Apply the pattern by very thinly rolling out another coloured paste and sticking on with minimal sugar glue, so when rolled to inlay, the glue doesn't ooze out. Make three towels, one mauve with yellow dots cut from the miniature circle cutter, one deep blue with thin bright green strips and the last bright pink with a thin strip of yellow paste winding around in a squiggle pattern.

Roll gently with a rolling pin until the pattern is inlayed. Cut into oblong shaped towels to fit the top of each sunbed. Cut tassels at each end of the mauve and pink towels. Secure on the sunbeds with a little sugar glue.

Modelling the women's bodies

6 Use 125 g (4½ oz) of flesh-coloured modelling paste for each of the women's bodies **(see above)**. To make a body, roll into a long sausage shape and pinch around just above halfway to indent a waist. Press down to flatten slightly and cut the longer half in two to separate legs. Smooth down each cut edge to round off each leg on both sides. Bend at the bottom for the feet and pinch up heels. Pinch around each ankle to narrow and shape the leg. For knees, push in halfway to indent the back. When proportioned, round off the bottom by smoothing with your fingers, pushing

TIP: When modelling the bodies, if the modelling paste starts to dry before you have finished, cover the part you are not modelling with a slightly damp cloth.

up the excess and rounding off. Mark a line in the centre using the knife and, again, smooth to round off.

7 Split 45 g (1 ½ oz) of flesh-coloured sugarpaste in half and use to make the man's legs. First roll into a sausage shape and bend one end for the foot, pinching up gently to shape the heel. Pinch around the ankle to narrow and give shape. Lay the leg down and push in at the back, halfway between the ankle and the top of the leg, pinching at the front to shape the knee.

Modelling the man's shorts

8 To make the shorts **(see above)**, roll the mauve modelling paste into a ball and press down to flatten slightly. Make a small cut to separate the legs and pinch up a rim on each that will sit over the top of each leg. Shape the sides by smoothing straight and pinch a rim around the top for the waistband.

9 Model the man's chest using 45 g (1½ oz) of flesh by shaping into a rounded teardrop, the full end for the top of a body with the narrower end for a waist. Press to flatten slightly and mark the pectorals. Encourage a rounded tummy by pushing up and smoothing in a circular motion. Split

20 g (¾ oz) of flesh-coloured sugarpaste in half and model two arms. To make an arm, roll into a sausage shape and pinch one end gently to round off for a hand. Press down on the hand to flatten it only slightly, without indenting. Lay the arm down and push in halfway, pinching out at the back to shape the elbow.

10 For the women's arms, split 30 g (1 oz) of flesh-coloured sugarpaste into four pieces and follow the instructions in step 9 above. Bend each arm at the elbow and stick in position, raised up with the hands one on top of each other. Split the remaining flesh into three pieces and make the oval-shaped heads and noses, marking smiles with the small circle cutter pressed in at an upward angle. Use a cocktail stick to draw the open smile on the man.

11 Make a sunhat for the man from a 10 g (¼ oz) ball of white modelling paste, pushing into the centre and pinching out a rim. Shape flattened sausages in different sizes in brown and pale yellow to make the women's hair. Stick tiny pieces of brown under the hat for the man's hair.

12 Cut thin strips of black and white paste to make the thongs and bra straps, finishing with a small ball of each shaped into a bra cup. Model six black flattened oval shapes for the sunglasses. Roll the remaining black paste into a sausage shape and cut two cans, shaping gently to remove the harsh cut edge. Indent into the top using a cocktail stick and rub the top of each can with a little edible silver powder.

Naughty Playtime

Pink fluffy handcuffs are guaranteed to raise a smile, so I made this naughty cake using a pretty hot pink colour scheme. If you prefer something a little more serious, red and black would make a much raunchier combination.

YOU WILL NEED

- 23 cm (9 in) round sponge cake (see page 11)
- 35 cm (14 in) round cake board
- 450 g /1 lb/2 c buttercream (see page 8)
- Icing (confectioners') sugar in a sugar shaker

SUGARPASTE (see page 9)

- 680 g (1 lb 8 oz) deep pink
- 315 g (11 oz) pale pink

MODELLING PASTE (see page 10)

- 45 g (1½ oz) grey
- 45 g (1½ oz) pale pink
- 145 g (5 oz) medium pink
- 30 g (1 oz) dark pink

- Sugar glue and paintbrush
- Edible silver powder
- Edible dark pink glitter

EQUIPMENT

- Serrated carving knife
- Palette knife
- Plain-bladed kitchen knife
- Large and small rolling pins
- No. 2 plain piping tube
- 1 cm (½ in), 1.5 cm (just over ½ in) and 2 cm (¾ in) circle cutters
- Foam pieces
- Large and small heart cutters
- A few cocktail sticks

3 Roll out the deep pink sugarpaste using a sprinkling of icing sugar and move the paste around after each roll to prevent sticking. Lift the sugarpaste by draping over the rolling pin and cover the cake, stretching out pleats and smoothing downwards. Trim excess from around the base.

4 Using the paintbrush handle, roll pleats radiating from the centre **(see below)**. With trimmings, shape a circle for the button and roll a long, thin sausage for the piping around the edge of the cushion, sticking both in place with a little sugar glue. Mark more pleats along the edge of the piping using the tip of a knife.

Sculpting the cake centre

1 Trim the cake crust and level the top. To sculpt the cushion, cut away the top and bottom edges so the sides curve, and trim the centre so it slopes gently inwards **(see above)**. Cut a layer in the cake and sandwich back together with buttercream.

2 Spread the centre of the cake board with buttercream so the cake will stick to it and place the cake down onto it. Spread buttercream over the surface of the cake as a crumb coat and to help the sugarpaste stick.

Create pleats

5 To make the handcuff bolts, thickly roll out 30 g (1 oz) of grey modelling paste and cut two oblongs measuring 5 x 4 cm (2 x 1½ in). Cut a curve into the top of each and then mark a line off-centre using the back of a knife. Use the piping tube to cut the keyhole, trimming out a little more and making the key shape with the tip of a knife. From the trimmings, cut four strips for between the fur and the bolt on either side and stick three tiny flattened circles on top of each. Rub edible silver over the surface and assemble on the cake.

6 Split 115 g (4 oz) of medium-pink modelling paste in half and roll two thick sausages, each measuring 15 cm (6 in). Bend and pinch the surface to give a furry, textured effect.

7 Use 15 g (½ oz) of grey modelling paste to make the chain **(see right)**. To make rings, cut circles, then cut smaller circles from the centre of each, making four large and five small rings (keep the circles to one side). Rub edible silver powder over the surface of each ring. Cut open each ring and loop alternate large and small rings together. Stick onto the top of each handcuff with a pea-sized ball to secure.

8 Using six of the smallest circles cut when making the rings, stick together in threes to make the top of each key, cutting a further tiny circle from the centre of each using the piping tube. With grey modelling paste trimmings, roll out and cut thin strips and tiny squares to complete each key. Assemble and apply edible silver as before. Put aside to dry on a flat surface.

9 To make the thong, thinly roll out the pale pink modelling paste and cut a 15 cm (6 in) triangle, placing it directly on the cake and securing with a little sugar glue. Turn up the end and support it with a foam piece until dry. Thinly roll out the remaining pale pink and cut strips for the thong. Use a shorter strip for the centre, attaching it to the bottom of the thong.

10 For the garter, roll out the remaining medium-pink modelling paste and cut a strip measuring 20 x 2.5 cm (8 x 1 in). Press along the edge between your thumb and finger, creating a frilled effect. Loop it around and stick in place on the cake. Roll out deep pink sugarpaste trimmings and cut a thin strip for around the centre.

11 Thinly roll out dark pink modelling paste and cut out one large and one small heart shape. Also cut strips for the thong and to edge the garter. Moisten the surface of each heart with sugar glue and sprinkle on the edible pink glitter.

12 For the fabric effect around the cake board, moisten the cake board with a little sugar glue, then roll out the pale pink sugarpaste thinly and arrange it around the cake, pushing up pleats and tucking the edge underneath. Smooth around the outside edge of the cake board and trim any excess away. When the keys are dry, stick them into position on the cake.

Making the chain

You don't need to hopefully glance at this building site to take advantage of these gorgeous beefcakes. You can stare and admire their muscles –and anything else on show –for as long as you wish!

YOU WILL NEED

- 25 cm (10 in) square sponge cake (see page 11)
- 35 cm (14 in) round cake board
- Icing (confectioners') sugar in a sugar shaker
- 650 g /1 lb 7 oz/2¾ c buttercream (see page 8)

SUGARPASTE *(see page 9)*

- 450 g (1 lb) medium brown
- 945 g (2 lb 1¼ oz) grey
- 400 g (14 oz) white

MODELLING PASTE *(see page 10)*

- 115 g (4 oz) cream/ivory
- 30 g (1 oz) turquoise
- 65 g (2¼ oz) yellow-brown (brown with a touch of yellow)
- 60 g (2 oz) pale navy
- 130 g (4½ oz) pale brown
- 175 g (6 oz) flesh-colour (golden brown/ivory with a touch of pink)
- 20 g (½ oz) yellow

- Sugar glue and paintbrush
- 2 sugar sticks (see page 10)

ROYAL ICING *(see page 9)*

- 20 g (½ oz) dark brown
- Black food colouring paste

EQUIPMENT

- Plain-bladed kitchen knife
- Large rolling pin
- Ruler
- Serrated carving knife
- Palette knife
- New kitchen scourer
- Sheet of kitchen paper
- 1.5 cm (½ in) circle cutter (to mark smiles)
- A few cocktail sticks
- Paper piping bag
- Scissors
- Fine paintbrush

1 Slightly dampen the cake board with water. Roll out the medium-brown sugarpaste using a sprinkling of icing sugar and move the paste around after each roll to prevent sticking. Lift the sugarpaste by draping over the rolling pin and cover the cake board, trimming any excess from around the edge. Press your hands firmly over the surface to mark indents and ridges, then set aside to dry.

2 Make the wood planks to allow for plenty of drying time. Roll out the cream/ivory modelling paste and cut three strips measuring 23 x 2.5 cm (9 x 1 in). Mark lines with a knife for a wood grain effect, then put aside to dry on a completely flat surface.

3 Trim the crust from the cake and level the top. Cut the cake into three equally sized strips. Cut each strip in half and sandwich one on top of the other using buttercream, making three oblong cakes for the building block piles. Using the palette knife spread a thin layer of buttercream over the surface of each cake as a crumb coat.

4 Roll out 315 g (11 oz) of grey sugarpaste and cover each cake completely, stretching out pleats and smoothing down and around the shape. Trim away any excess from around the base. Pinch along each

Indenting to form blocks

edge at the top and down the sides to sharpen. Use a ruler to indent even lines outlining the building blocks, **(see above)**. The top and two opposite longer sides have narrower lines indented, depicting the top and sides of blocks. The two smaller opposite sides have much wider lines for the front face.

5 For the wrapped effect on two block piles, very thinly roll out 200 g (7 oz) of white sugarpaste and cover each block pile, folding over pleats and flattening them level with the cake surface. Indent twice around the centre of each wrapped pile creating, straight lines to hold the retaining ties. Thinly roll out the turquoise paste and cut four thin strips. Stick into position around the covered block piles. Arrange each cake on the cake board.

6 To make the boots, split the yellow-brown modelling paste into four pieces. Model a teardrop shape and bend halfway, pinching out a heel. Make a flat area for the jean leg. Make all the boots and set aside.

7 Put aside 5 g (¼ oz) of navy paste. Make the jeans one pair at a time. Roll into a sausage and press down to flatten. Make a cut to separate legs, leaving 2 cm (¾ in) at the top **(see below)**. Smooth each leg to remove edges. Press the bottom to flatten. Push in at the back centre of each leg and pinch the front to shape knees. Mark pleats and wrinkles.

Boots and jeans

8 Position the sitting builder by bending one leg up and stick securely with one of the boots onto the side of a wrapped block pile. Stick his other boot in place, if necessary using a piece of foam for support until dry. To shape the bottom of the standing builder, lay the jeans down on the front and smooth to push up any excess. Round off a bottom, making a small indent in the centre using a cocktail stick. Stick in position with the boots resting against the block pile.

9 To make the cement sack, shape the pale brown sugarpaste into an oval and press to flatten. Make a cut across the top and open one side further by moving the knife up and down, then stick in place with a little sugar glue. Press kitchen paper onto the surface to give texture.

10 To make the loose blocks, thickly roll out and cut four oblong shapes the same size as the indented blocks using 30 g (1 oz) of grey sugarpaste. Mould the trimmings into the spilt powdered cement, texturing by pressing the kitchen scourer over the surface. Knead the grey and brown sugarpaste trimmings together until slightly streaky, roll out and put aside to dry (this will break into crumbs for mud when dry).

11 To make the builders' chests, split 90 g (3 oz) of flesh-coloured modelling paste in half. Model rounded teardrop shapes, the full end for the top of a body with the narrower end for a waist, and press to flatten slightly **(see above)**. Using the paintbrush handle, mark a line down the centre on both sides, mark pectoral and stomach muscles and stick in place on the trousers. Stick two tiny oval shapes onto each pectoral. With the remaining pale navy

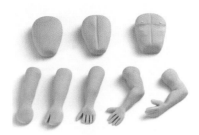

Chests and arms

modelling paste, cut two back pockets for the standing builder and two thin strips for both builders' waistbands.

12 Model each arm using 15 g (½ oz) of flesh colour paste. To make an arm, roll into a sausage shape and pinch one end gently to round off for a hand. Press down on the hand to flatten only slightly, without indenting. Make a cut for the thumb halfway on one side and pull down. Make three more cuts to separate fingers, push together and stroke to lengthen and bend round. To naturally shape the hand, push the thumb towards the palm from the wrist. Lay the arm down and push in halfway, pinching out at the back to shape the elbow. Indent at the top to round off a large muscle.

13 Push a sugar stick into the neck of each builder, leaving half protruding to hold their heads in place. Model their heads, noses and ears using the remaining flesh colour. For the head, flatten the facial area, then press the small circle cutter in at an upward angle to mark a smile, adding dimples using a cocktail stick. To make the ears, shape two small ovals and indent the centres using the end of the paintbrush. Stick in position level with the nose. Press each head down over the sugar sticks, securing at the neck area with sugar glue.

14 Put aside two pea-sized amounts of yellow modelling paste, then split the remainder into two and roll into ball shapes for the main part of each hat. Press into the centre of each and pinch up an edge to hollow out **(see below)**. Press either side at the top to narrow slightly and stick in place on each head. Use the remainder for rims and strips on top of each hat. To make the rims, model a small oval shape, press down to flatten, smoothing until thin and cut in half lengthways making the two hat rims.

Head and hats

15 Colour some modelling paste trimmings black and use to make tiny oval-shaped eyes. Put the brown royal icing into a piping bag and cut a small hole in the tip. Pipe the hair, moustache and beard. For dirt patches, mix a little brown royal icing with water making it runny and brush over the boots, jeans and bodies.

16 When the cake is dry, dilute black food colouring paste with a few drops of water and paint the tattoos using a fine paintbrush. Pile the wood planks one on top of each other, securing with sugar glue. Break the dried, rolled out piece of streaky grey/brown sugarpaste into crumbs and sprinkle around the cake board.

Boobs Everywhere

Make just one pair of these sexy boobs as a special gift for your man, or give him a choice. These individual cakes are perfect for any party celebration or even a stag night. Hopefully there won't be a scramble after favourites!

YOU WILL NEED

- 10 x shop-bought muffins
- 5 x 18 cm (6 in) heart-shaped cake cards
- 300 g /10½ oz/1¼ c buttercream (see page 8)
- Icing (confectioners') sugar in a sugar shaker

SUGARPASTE (see page 9)

- 285 g (10 oz) pale flesh-colour (golden brown/ivory with a touch of pink)
- 550 g (1 lb 3½ oz) medium flesh-colour (golden brown/ivory with a touch of pink)

- 550 g (1 lb 3½ oz) dark flesh-colour (golden brown/ivory)
- 60 g (2 oz) pale pink
- 30 g (1 oz) bright pink
- 60 g (1 oz) turquoise
- 60 g (1 oz) deep purple
- 90 g (3 oz) black

- Sugar glue and paintbrush
- Miniature gold, standard turquoise and large silver dragees
- Edible silver powder colouring

EQUIPMENT

- Plain-bladed kitchen knife
- Large rolling pin
- Cake smoother
- Palette knife
- 4 cm (1½ in) and 2.5 cm (1 in) square cutters
- 5 cm (2 in) circle cutter
- No.2 plain piping tube

1 Put a little buttercream centrally on the cake card and press two muffins down side by side **(see right)**. If the raised tops are uneven, spread with a layer of buttercream to create a smooth surface and help the sugarpaste stick. Spread a little extra buttercream between each muffin and over the cake board, keeping away from the cake board edge.

2 Using a sprinkling of icing sugar to prevent sticking, roll out the different shades of flesh sugarpaste, one at a time, and cover all five pairs of cakes, stretching out pleats and smoothing downwards around each shape. Rub gently around the edge of the cake boards until the sugarpaste becomes thin with a rounded edge and then trim any excess using a knife. With the trimmings, stick a small pea-sized ball on each boob using a little sugar glue.

Covering muffins with buttercream

Creating pleats for the pink tassles

6 BLACK STRAP TOP
Roll out black sugarpaste and cut two strips, sticking one across the side of a boob and secure on the opposite side. Stick the other strip across the top of both boobs. Stick silver dragees into the surface using sugar glue to secure. Roll out black trimmings and cut a square using the large square cutter. Cut a smaller square from the centre making a buckle. Rub edible silver powder over the surface, and then stick in place with a silver dragee.

7 PURPLE BASQUE
Thinly roll out the deep purple sugarpaste and cut a straight line in the top. Cut a small 'V' centrally. Lift and stick in place on the boobs, smoothing around the shape. Trim excess from around the edge and secure in place with a little sugar glue. Thinly roll out the remaining black sugarpaste and cut strips. Cut out circles along each strip using the piping tube and stick in place **(see below)**. Roll out trimmings and cut tiny strips for the laces, crossing them over down the centre.

3 PINK AND GOLD TOP
Roll out the pale pink sugarpaste and cut two strips measuring 15 cm (6 in) in length and 4 cm (1½ in) at the widest central point. Gently roll the paintbrush over the surface to create pleats, and then stick onto each boob. Smooth along each edge to round off. With the trimmings, roll out and cut very thin strips to edge across the bottom, pressing miniature gold dragees into the surface and securing with a little sugar glue.

5 SPARKLY TURQUOISE TOP
Roll out the turquoise sugarpaste, cut two triangles measuring 8 cm (3 in) each and stick onto the cake using a little sugar glue. With the trimmings, roll out and cut the straps. Stick the turquoise dragees over the surface using a little sugar glue.

4 BRIGHT PINK TASSLES
Roll out the bright pink sugarpaste and cut two circles using the circle cutter. Roll the paintbrush handle over the surface creating pleats radiating from the centre, frilling the edge **(see above)**. Stick in place. Thinly roll out the trimmings and cut about 20 very thin strips for the tassles. Pinch into two bunches at the top and stick centrally on each boob.

Decorating the basque with strips of black lace

Racy Speedboat

Sun-worshipping topless girls adorning a speedboat in a jade green tropical sea has to be up there in the top ten of male fantasies, so give him a treat with this gorgeous pair.

YOU WILL NEED

- 30 x 12 cm (12 x 5 in) oblong sponge cake (see page 11)
- 35 cm (14 in) oval-shaped cake board
- Icing (confectioners') sugar in a sugar shaker
- 450 g /1 lb/2 c buttercream (see page 8)

SUGARPASTE (see page 9)

- 800 g (1 lb 12 oz) white
- 100 g (3½ oz) black
- 340 g (12 oz) pale jade green

MODELLING PASTE (see page 10)

- 75 g (2½ oz) white
- 15 g (½ oz) black
- 15 g (½ oz) mauve
- 15 g (½ oz) yellow
- 60 g (2 oz) flesh-colour (golden brown/ivory with a touch of pink)
- 35 g (1¼ oz) pale blue
- 5 g (just under ¼ oz) pink

- Sugar glue and paintbrush
- 3 x sugar sticks,1 x 9cm (3½ in) long (see page 10)
- Black and pink food colouring pastes

ROYAL ICING (see page 10)

- 15 g (½ oz) pale cream
- 3–4 tbsp clear piping gel

EQUIPMENT

- Serrated carving knife
- Template (see page 76)
- Plain-bladed kitchen knife
- Large and small rolling pins
- Palette knife
- Ruler
- Cake smoother
- Small circle cutter
- Small pieces of foam (for support)
- A few cocktail sticks
- Fine paintbrush
- Teaspoon
- Scissors

1 Trim the crust from the cake and level the top. To shape the front of the boat, trim the sides to slope down to halfway, leaving a 5 cm (2 in) edge centrally at the front. Trim to slope inwards down to the base on either side.

2 Using the template (see page 76) as a cutting guide, slice a 1.5 cm (½ in) layer from the top of the cake at the back and trim both sides to slope inwards. Cut a layer in the cake and sandwich back together with buttercream. Place the cake centrally on the cake board, sticking with buttercream. Spread a thin layer of buttercream over the surface of the cake as a crumb coat.

Padding at the front of the boat and black recess covering

3 To shape the pointed front of the boat, roll 100 g (3½ oz) of white sugarpaste into a teardrop and press down to flatten the full end. Stick against the front of the cake and shape into the pointed front of the boat, smoothing down to the base and pressing the join firmly onto the surface of the cake so it is secure **(see bottom left)**. Thinly roll out some black sugarpaste and cut a strip to cover the dashboard, as well as a further piece for the inside recess using the template (see page 76).

4 For the decking, roll out 90 g (3 oz) of white sugarpaste and cut a piece to cover the top of the cake at the back using the template (see page 76). Keeping the paste on the work surface, indent even lines with a ruler, then carefully lift and position, keeping the indented lines straight.

5 To cover the boat's sides, first measure the length and depth. Roll out 185 g (6½ oz) of white sugarpaste and cut a strip to fit. Position against the side and rub with a cake smoother. Repeat for the other side. To close the join at the front, press together, sticking with a bit of sugar glue, then rub gently with your fingers in a circular motion. Using the back of a knife, mark two lines each on either side.

6 Roll out 60 g (2 oz) of white sugarpaste and cut a piece to cover the back of the cake, sticking the join closed on either side with a little sugar glue. Roll out the remaining white sugarpaste and cut a piece to cover the top of the cake at the front, sticking securely around the outside edge. Rub with a cake smoother down the centre and then either side to make it slightly angular.

7 For the windscreen, roll out 30 g (1 oz) of white modelling paste and cut out the shape using the template (see page 76). Indent lines using the ruler **(see below)**. Stand the windscreen up and bend into position. Moisten along the bottom edge and then stick in place on the boat. Using 15 g (½ oz) of white modelling paste, cut strips to edge the top and along the front of the windscreen, and also two strips to edge the sides at the back of the boat.

Making the windscreen

8 Thickly roll out the remaining white modelling paste and cut three oblong shapes, two for benches on either side of the boat and one for the pole support. Use the large sugar stick as a flagpole, pushing it down into the pole support. Using the trimmings, roll a small ball for the top of the pole.

9 Using black modelling paste, thinly roll out and cut strips to edge the front of the windscreen and the top edge at the back of the boat. Roll a tiny ball to top the pole and then, to make the steering wheel, roll the remainder into a ball and press in the centre to indent. Cut out small circles around the edge using the small circle cutter. Stick the steering wheel in place on the dashboard.

10 For the sea, moisten the surface of the cake board with a little sugar glue, roll out pale jade green sugarpaste and press over the surface using your fingers. Push up the excess around the bottom of the boat to create ripples. Trim any excess from the edge of the cake board, then smooth with your hands to round off.

11 For the rolled up towels, which will support the figures, use the mauve and yellow modelling paste. Thinly roll out and cut oblong shapes measuring 10 x 4 cm (4 x 1½ in), fold in half lengthways and roll up. Stick onto the top of the boat near the windscreen.

12 Use 20 g (¾ oz) of flesh-coloured modelling paste for each of the girls' bodies. To make a

TIP: When modelling the bodies, if the modelling paste starts to dry before you have finished, cover the part you are not working on with a slightly dampened cloth.

body, roll the modelling paste into a long sausage shape. To shape the waist, roll between your thumb and finger to indent just above halfway **(see right)**. Press down to flatten slightly and cut the longer half to separate legs. Smooth down each cut edge to round off legs, front and back, twisting gently to lengthen. Bend at the bottom for the feet and pinch out heels. Roll each ankle between your thumb and finger to narrow and shape the leg. To form the knees, push in halfway to indent the back and pinch gently at the front to give shape. Stick the body in its pose using a little sugar glue to secure.

13 Split 5 g (just under ¼ oz) of flesh-coloured modelling paste into four parts and model the arms. The arms modelled here have fully cut hands, but if you prefer to make simple hands, see page 50, step 10. To make an arm, roll a sausage shape and gently pinch one end to round off for a hand. Press down on the hand to flatten slightly, without indenting. Make a cut halfway down on one side for the thumb. Make three cuts along the top to separate fingers and twist gently to lengthen, press together and bend round. To naturally shape the hand, push the thumb towards the palm from the wrist. Lay the arm down and push in halfway, pinching out at the back to shape the elbow. Stick in position as each is made using a little sugar glue.

14 Use 5 g (just under ¼ oz) for the boobs, rolling out four tiny ball shapes and sticking in place with a little sugar glue. Push a sugar stick down through the top of each body, leaving half protruding to help hold their heads in place. Split the remaining flesh-colour in half and make their oval shaped heads and noses. Make a hole in the bottom of each head using a cocktail stick, and then, using a little sugar glue, stick in place over the sugar stick.

15 Thinly roll out 15 g (½ oz) of pale blue modelling paste and cut strips to decorate the sides of the boat. Roll out 10 g (¼ oz) and cut oblong shapes for the cushions on top of each bench. To make the two seats, split 5 g (just under ¼ oz) in half and shape into ovals. Press down to flatten slightly and cut in half, making the seat and back. Trim the seat to take off the rounded edge and assemble on the boat, bending the back to slope down slightly. Use the trimmings for the blue bikini bra top hanging on the flagpole. Press two pea-sized oval shapes flat for the bra cups and stick onto the pole with a thin strip of blue. Make a pink bikini bra top.

16 Make the sunglasses by flattening very small oval shapes using pink and blue trimmings, then thinly roll out and cut strips for the bikini thongs. Dilute pink food colouring with a little water and paint the lips, then add some colour to each boob. Dilute black food colouring and paint a translucent wash over the windscreen for a cloudy effect.

17 To pipe the hair, put the royal icing into the piping bag and cut a small hole in the tip. Pipe straight hair on one girl and curly hair on the other. For the sea's wet effect, spread a thin layer of clear piping gel over the surface using the back of a teaspoon.

Making the bodies

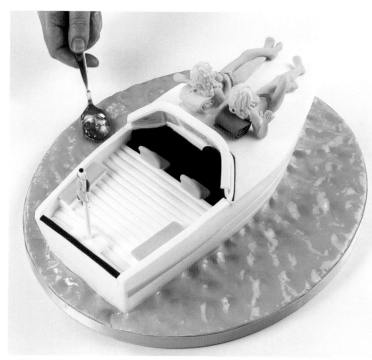

Adding piping gel

Hotpants

If you want to set the scene for a memorable celebration, these skin-tight gold hotpants will be a real treat for that special man in your life.

YOU WILL NEED

- 25 cm (10 in) heart-shaped sponge cake (see page 11)
- 25 cm (10 in) heart-shaped cake board
- 400 g /14 oz/1¾ c buttercream (see page 8)

SUGARPASTE *(see page 9)*

- 820 g (1 lb 13 oz) flesh-colour (golden brown/ivory with a touch of pink)
- 315 g (11 oz) golden brown/deep ivory

- Icing (confectioners') sugar in a sugar shaker
- Sugar glue and paintbrush
- Edible gold powder
- A little white vegetable fat (optional)

EQUIPMENT

- Plain-bladed kitchen knife
- Palette knife
- Large rolling pin
- Serrated carving knife
- Cake smoother
- Ruler

1 Place the cake on the cake board, sticking with a little buttercream. Cut down at an angle from the top of the cake, one-third from the point of the heart, cutting right down to the base. Use some of these cake trimmings to build up the top of each cheek, then trim to round off and take off the top edges of the heart shape, rounding it completely.

2 Make a cut in the centre to separate the cheeks and trim again until well rounded. Trim around the base of the cake so it curves in slightly, leaving a 3–4 mm (⅛ in) gap between the cake and the cake board edge for the sugarpaste covering.

3 When the cake is sculpted into an even, well proportioned shape, skim over the surface using a knife to make sure the surface is as smooth as possible. If there are uneven areas, these can be easily levelled using a spread of buttercream. Sandwich layers together with buttercream using the palette knife, and then spread a layer over the surface of the cake as a crumb coat **(see top right)**.

4 Roll out the flesh-coloured sugarpaste, using a sprinkling of icing sugar to prevent sticking. Lift using the rolling pin and cover the cake completely. Smooth around the shape, stretch out any pleats and

Spreading buttercream

smooth downward. Keep smoothing carefully around the base with your hands until the sugarpaste becomes thin and starts to break. Level the paste with the cake board edge, then trim to neaten. Rub a cake smoother over the surface of the cake to obtain a smooth, even finish.

5 To make the hotpants, thinly roll out the golden brown/deep ivory sugarpaste and cut a strip measuring at least 35 x 20 cm (14 x 8 in). Lift using the rolling pin and use to cover the bottom of the cake. Smooth around the shape and trim either side level with the edge of the cake board, securing with a little sugar glue.

Cutting hotpants

6 Trim around the bottom of each cheek so they peek out, and cut a dip at the top of the hot pants to shape the waistband area **(see above)**. By now, the sugarpaste should have stuck to the flesh-coloured sugarpaste without any extra sugar glue, but if it seems to slip, then add a little just underneath around the outside edge. Mark fabric-effect pleats using the paintbrush handle. Roll out the trimmings and cut thin strips to edge either side, securing with sugar glue.

7 Sprinkle the edible gold powder over the hotpants and rub the surface gently with your fingers **(see right)**. The powder will stick to the damp sugarpaste. If the sugarpaste has become dry, rub a little white vegetable fat over the surface and then rub on the gold powder.

Applying gold powder

Roly Poly Strip-o-gram

This fun adaptation of a sexy strip-o-gram would look fantastic centre-stage on a birthday party table, and is bound to make the guests collapse with laughter.

YOU WILL NEED

- 2 x 15 cm (6 in) square sponge cakes and 1 x 12 cm (5 in) round sponge cake (see page 11)
- 30 cm (12 in) round cake board
- Icing (confectioners') sugar in a sugar shaker
- 650 g / 1 lb 7 oz/2¾ c buttercream (see page 8)

SUGARPASTE (see page 9)

- 710 g (1 lb 9 oz) black
- 1.25 kg (2 lb 12 oz) white
- 750 g (1 lb 10½ oz) flesh-colour (golden brown/ivory with a touch of pink)
- 30 g (1 oz) red

ROYAL ICING (see page 9)

- 45 g (1½ oz) white

- Sugar glue and paintbrush
- 260 g (9 oz) pastillage (see page 10) or a large sheet of white rice paper
- Black food colouring paste
- Red powder colour

EQUIPMENT

- Plain-bladed kitchen knife
- Large and small rolling pins
- Cake smoother
- Serrated carving knife
- Palette knife
- Ruler
- Sheet of card
- Foam pieces
- A few cocktail sticks
- Small heart cutter
- No. 4 plain piping tube
- Fine paintbrush
- Paper piping bag
- Scissors

1 Slightly dampen the cake board with water. Roll out 400 g (14 oz) of black sugarpaste using a sprinkling of icing (confectioners') sugar, moving the paste around after each roll to prevent sticking. Lift the sugarpaste by draping over the rolling pin and cover the cake board, trimming any excess from around the edge. Rub gently with a cake smoother and set aside to dry.

2 Trim to level the top of each cake and turn over to use the base of the cake as the top. Trim off the top edge from the round cake, making the rounded body. Cut a layer in the two square cakes and sandwich back together, one on top of the other, using buttercream. Spread a little buttercream onto the cake board where the cake will sit and place the cake centrally on the cake board. Spread a layer of buttercream over the surface of each cake.

3 Using 595 g (1lb 5 oz) of white sugarpaste, roll out and cut pieces to cover all four sides of the square cake, cutting level with the top. Rub the surface with a cake smoother to obtain a smooth, level finish. Roll out 145 g (5 oz) of black sugarpaste and use it to cover the top of the cake, trimming any excess from around the edge.

Making the body

4 To make the body, first pad out the shape using flesh-coloured sugarpaste. Use 175 g (6 oz) to roll an oval and stick onto the top of the body, slightly towards the back, to help shape the chest and neck area. Split 100 g (3½ oz) in half and roll two ball shapes, sticking these in front to pad out the boobs **(see above)**.

5 Moisten the sugarpaste on the body with sugar glue and rework the buttercream if set, or add a little more. Roll out 260 g (9 oz) of flesh-coloured sugarpaste and cover the body completely, smoothing out any pleats and trimming any excess from around the base. Accentuate the cleavage by smoothing with your fingers. Stick a ball of paste on the front of each boob using trimmings.

6 Moisten the sides of the cake with sugar glue. Measure the box sides and add 4 cm (1½ in) to the height. Thinly roll out the remaining white sugarpaste and cut pieces to cover the four sides. To place the sides against the cake without disturbing their neatly cut edges, push the sheet of card underneath and lift, using the card to help position against the cake **(see right)**. Close each join by smoothing along the edge with a little icing sugar on your fingers. Smooth the surface using a cake smoother.

7 Cut the four box flaps using the pastillage, each with a 7 cm (3 in) depth. Cut one at a time as the pastillage dries extremely quickly. Turn the corners slightly and place on a flat surface to dry, preferably overnight, flipping over after a few hours for the reverse to dry also. Alternatively, use a sheet of white rice paper cut to size.

8 To make the arms, split 90 g (3 oz) of flesh-coloured sugarpaste in half. Roll one into a fat sausage shape and pinch one end to round off a hand. Press down on the hand to flatten only slightly, without indenting. Make a cut for the thumb, cutting down halfway on one side and pull down. Make three more cuts to separate fingers, stroking each to lengthen. To naturally shape the hand, push the thumb towards the palm from the wrist, and then open again. Push gently into the palm to indent. Lay the arm down and push in halfway,

pinching out at the back to shape the elbow. Press against the body in the pose to flatten the arm so that it sits neatly in position, then remove and put aside to set. Make the second arm in the same way.

Making the head

9 For the head **(see above)**, roll a 125 g (4 ½ oz) of flesh-coloured sugarpaste into a rounded teardrop shape and place on the work

Applying the box sides

surface with the point up. Press down on the point to flatten slightly. Split 5 g (just under ¼ oz) of flesh-coloured sugarpaste into three. Use one piece to make the chin, rolling into a sausage and taper the ends to points. Moisten with sugar glue and press onto the bottom of the face, smoothing the points level with the surface and blending the join in at the top. To remove the join completely, smooth a little icing (confectioners') sugar over the surface using your fingers.

10 Roll the two remaining pieces into oval shapes for cheeks and stick in place, smoothing the join closed at the bottom of each by rolling the paintbrush handle underneath. Using trimmings, roll a pea-sized oval for the nose and stick centrally on the face. Roll another pea-sized amount into an oval, press into the centre to indent, cut in half and use for the ears. For eyes, split a pea-sized amount of white trimmings and roll into oval shapes. Press flat and stick onto the face, slightly turned in at the top.

11 Using a pea-sized amount of black sugarpaste, model two oval-shaped pupils, two tiny strips for eyelashes and stick a flattened oval onto the face for the shadow of the mouth. Now take about 45 g (1½ oz) of the black paste and roll into small, different sized ball shapes and build up over the head to make the hair. Shape 5 g (just under ¼ oz) of red sugarpaste into a small sausage shape and pinch around both ends to widen, then stick on top of the head for the hair band. Model two teardrop shapes and press flat for the top lip; roll a tapering sausage for the bottom lip. To make earrings, roll long, tapering sausages and loop round. Build up more hair for the bun using 15 g (½ oz) of black sugarpaste.

Forming the basque

12 Thinly roll out the remaining black sugarpaste and wrap around the back of the body, joining at the front and securing with sugar glue. Trim away any excess at the front, leaving a gap at the join, and trim a neat line across the chest and down the back **(see above)**. Cut laces from the trimmings and criss-cross down the front of the basque.

13 Position the body on the cake with a dab of butter-cream. Stick the arms and head in position, making sure they are well balanced as they dry. Use pieces of foam sponge for support if needed. Cut strips of red sugarpaste and pinch to frill along the top edge, sticking in place for straps and to edge the basque. For the necklace, roll tiny ball beads and stick in place around the neck.

14 Thinly roll out the remaining red paste and cut out hearts and circles, sticking hearts over the box and circles on the flaps. Roll out the remaining white trimmings and cut four strips for ribbon, gathering them up and sticking at the base of the box.

When the cake is dry, dilute some black food colouring with a few water drops and paint kisses on the box using the fine paintbrush.

15 Put the royal icing into the piping bag and cut a hole in the tip. Pipe a thick line of royal icing along the top edge of the box cake and stick on a box flap, holding for a few moments to secure. Use pieces of foam sponge to support until dry. Repeat for the remaining three sides. Rub a little red powder colour over the top of each cheek using your fingers.

TIP: If the cake needs to travel, use food-safe plastic dowels to support the head and arms in position. Don't be tempted to use cocktail sticks, as these are very sharp and could cause an injury.

Mud Pit

A playful mud pit can be set anywhere: in a barn, in a castle, wherever you wish! I decided on a simple concrete-effect floor and a bright blue plastic liner for the pit, but you can easily let your imagination take you elsewhere...

YOU WILL NEED

- Chocolate marble ring cake (see pages 8 and 11) or 2–3 shop-bought chocolate swiss rolls
- 35 cm (14 in) square cake board
- Icing (confectioners') sugar in a sugar shaker

SUGARPASTE *(see page 9)*

- 500 g (1 lb 1¾ oz) stone (a touch each of black and ivory food colouring)
- 500 g (1 lb 1¾ oz) turquoise

MODELLING PASTE *(see page 10)*

- 30 g (1 oz) bright green
- 180 g (6¼ oz) flesh-colour (golden brown/ivory food colouring with a touch of pink)

- Black food colouring paste
- Sugar glue and paintbrush
- 225 g (½ lb) luxury milk cooking chocolate

EQUIPMENT

- Serrated carving knife
- Palette knife
- Plain bladed kitchen knife
- Large and small rolling pins
- Long ruler or straight edge
- Small circle cutter
- A few cocktail sticks
- Heat resistant bowl
- No. 4 paintbrush

1 Slightly dampen the cake board with water. Roll out the stone sugarpaste using a sprinkling of icing (confectioners') sugar. Move the paste around after each roll to prevent sticking. Lift the paste by draping over the rolling pin and cover the cake board, trimming excess from around the edge. For a concrete effect, indent four slabs using a ruler. Press diagonal and horizontal lines on two slabs each using the small rolling pin. Set aside to dry overnight.

2 Trim the crust from the cake and turn over, using the bottom of the cake as the top. Position the cake centrally on the cake board. If using swiss rolls, gently bend each one and

position on the cake board in a ring. Melt half the chocolate in a heatproof bowl by placing over a pan of gently simmering water. Allow to cool, then spread over the cake as a crumb coat using the palette knife. For the mud liner, roll out turquoise sugarpaste and cut a square measuring 30 cm (12 in). Lift carefully using the rolling pin and drape over the cake, creating pleats, and push gently into the centre. Don't worry if the paste cracks – it will be covered later. Split the bright green modelling paste into three equal pieces. To make the mud bowls, roll into ball shapes and press in the centres to indent, pinching around the top to create edges. Set aside to dry.

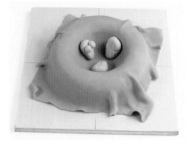

Chests in the pit

3 For the mud wrestlers, assemble in position as each piece is made and secure with sugar glue **(see above)**. Make three chests using 50 g (1¾ oz) of flesh-coloured modelling paste, two male and one female. For the males, model rounded

teardrop shapes, the full end for a body top and the narrower for a waist. Press to flatten. Using the brush handle, mark a line down the centre on both sides, marking pectoral and stomach muscles. For the female, model two ball-shaped boobs and use the rest to shape a smaller chest.

4 Use 60 g (2 oz) to model five legs. To make a leg, roll into a sausage and bend one end for the foot, pinching up to shape the heel and pinching around the ankle. Push in at the back of the leg halfway between the ankle and the top. Pinch at the front to shape the knee.

5 Model several arms and hands, each with outstretched fingers using 30 g (1 oz) **(see right)**. To make an arm, roll into a sausage and pinch one end to round off for a hand.

Press down to flatten the hand slightly. Make a cut for the thumb halfway on one side and pull down. Make three more cuts to separate fingers and stroke to lengthen. To shape the hand, push the thumb towards the palm from the wrist. Lay the arm down and push in halfway, pinching out at the back to shape the elbow. Indent at the top to round off a muscle on the male arms.

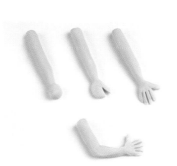

Modelling the arms

6 Make one bum by rolling a ball with the remaining flesh-coloured modelling paste and mark a line down the centre. Make three oval-shaped heads with oval-shaped noses using 30 g (1 oz), marking smiles by indenting the circle cutter in at an angle. Use a cocktail stick to draw open smiles. Colour some trimmings with black and model eyes, sticking in place with a little sugar glue.

7 Melt the remaining chocolate as before. Pour over the wrestlers and dribble little pools around the top edge. Using the paintbrush, brush some melted chocolate over the bodies, allowing some flesh to show through. Encourage little drips from their fingers and toes. Pour chocolate into the bowls and stick in position with a dab of chocolate.

Jacuzzi Fun

Make a fabulous birthday party centrepiece with this fun idea, perhaps filling it with depictions of your friends. Even your favourite celebrities could be splashing about!

YOU WILL NEED

- 20 cm (8 in) round sponge cake (see page 11)
- 35 cm (14 in) round cake board
- Icing (confectioners') sugar in a sugar shaker
- 450 g / 1 lb/2 c buttercream (see page 8)

SUGARPASTE *(see page 9)*

- 1.4 kg (3 lb 1½ oz) grey
- 60 g (2 oz) terracotta
- 30 g (1 oz) white
- 60 g (2 oz) blue

MODELLING PASTE *(see page 10)*

- 110 g (3¾ oz) flesh-colour
- 40 g (just over 1¼ oz) golden brown
- 35 g (1¼ oz) dark brown
- 10 g (¼ oz) bottle green

- 10 g (¼ oz) lime green
- 15 g (½ oz) purple
- 5 g (just under ¼ oz) deep purple
- 10 g (¼ oz) black
- 20 g (¾ oz) white
- 5 g (just under ¼ oz) bright yellow

ROYAL ICING *(see page 11)*

- 5 g (just under ¼ oz) cream
- 10 g (¼ oz) golden brown
- 10 g (¼ oz) pale brown
- 15 g (¼ oz) dark brown

- Sugar glue and paintbrush
- 5 x sugar sticks (see page 10)
- Black food colouring paste
- Bright yellow powder colour
- Clear piping gel

EQUIPMENT

- Serrated carving knife
- Palette knife
- Plain-bladed kitchen knife
- Large and small rolling pins
- Textured kitchen paper
- Cake smoother
- Small circle cutter (to mark smiles)
- Small pieces of foam (for support)
- A few cocktail sticks
- 2.5 cm (1 in) and 1 cm (½ in) square cutters
- 4 x paper piping bags
- Fine paintbrush
- Dusting brush

1 Slightly dampen the board with water. Roll out 450 g (1 lb) of grey sugarpaste using a sprinkling of icing (confectioners') sugar and move the paste around after each roll to prevent sticking. Lift the paste by draping over the rolling pin. Cover the cake board, trimming excess from around the edge. To texture the surface, place a sheet of kitchen paper onto the surface and rub with a cake smoother. Set aside to dry.

2 Trim to level the top of the cake and turn over to use the base of the cake as the top. Slice two layers equally through the depth. Cut a circle from the centre, cutting at an inward angle and leaving a 2.5 cm (1 in) edge. Remove the centre and discard. Sandwich all layers together with buttercream and centre on the cake board. Spread a layer of buttercream as a crumb coat **(see right)**.

3 Roll out 800 g (1 lb 12 oz) of grey sugarpaste and cover the cake completely, smoothing around the shape, stretching out pleats around the edge and smoothing downwards. Trim excess from around the base. Pinch around the top outside edge to sharpen, and texture around the sides and top edge of the cake board surface.

Covering with buttercream

4 For the front steps, thickly roll out the remaining grey sugarpaste and cut two strips, one for the bottom step measuring 5 x 13 cm (2 x 5 in) and for the top step measuring 2.5 x 13 cm (1 x 5 in). Stick one step on top of the other, curving at the front of the cake, and texture the surface as before.

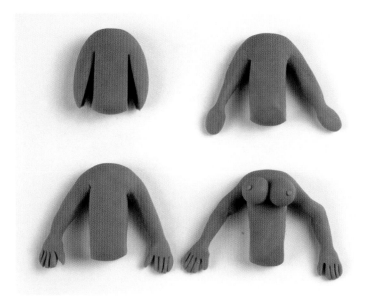

Modelling chests and arms

hand. Push in halfway along each arm, pinching out at the back to shape elbows. Indent at the top of each arm to round off shoulder muscles. Stick in position in the tub using foam for support if necessary. Mark a line down the centre and mark curves and pectorals. Using a cocktail stick, mark a small hole on each pectoral.

8 The female figures use the same amount of modelling paste, but their bodies are smaller, without muscular shoulders. Use the extra paste to make boobs with a tiny ball on each. Using a little sugar glue to secure, push a sugar stick down through each body leaving half protruding to hold the heads in place.

5 For the tiles, thinly roll out the terracotta sugarpaste and cut out squares using the 2.5 cm (1 in) square cutter. Stick around the top edge of the cake and along each step, texturing as before. Thinly roll out white sugarpaste and cut a strip to edge the inside of the Jacuzzi tub, rubbing the join closed with your fingers.

6 The male and female figures are made by modelling the chests and arms in one go **(see above)**. To make a male chest and arms, roll 30 g (1 oz) of flesh-coloured modelling paste into an oval and press down to flatten slightly. Make two cuts for arms either side, keeping enough in the centre for the chest, and smooth down to soften the cut on both sides. Gently twist each arm to lengthen, and roll between your thumb and finger at the end of each arm to round off hands, pressing down on the hand to flatten slightly, but without indenting. Note that some of the figures' hands will be "under water", and so will not need to be modelled.

7 For the hands, make a cut for the thumb, cutting halfway down. Make three more slightly shorter cuts across the top to separate fingers and stroke to lengthen. To naturally shape the hand, push the thumb towards the palm from the wrist. Cut the opposite

9 Thinly roll out the purple modelling paste and cut a small square to use for the bathing costume. With pea-sized amounts of black and all the deep purple modelling paste, make the bikini tops by shaping semi-circles and sticking in place with a

Making water for the tub

little sugar glue. Put aside a pea-sized amount of black and, using the remainder, shape the trunks, sticking them into the blonde man's hand.

10 Knead the white sugarpaste trimmings into 45 g (1½ oz) of blue sugarpaste until streaky. Roll out and place in the tub. Using your fingers to mark an uneven surface, push excess up and around each body **(see bottom left)**. Roll out just over half of the white modelling paste and put aside to dry (this will be crumbled to make the foam).

11 Put aside two pea-sized amounts of golden brown modelling paste. Using the remainder, along with the remaining flesh-colour and dark brown, make their heads, noses and ears. To make a head, shape an oval, flatten the facial area and then press the small circle cutter in at an upward angle to mark smiles, indenting dimples at the corners and marking a curved line to complete the open mouth using a cocktail stick. To make the girl's open mouth, push in the end of a paintbrush and gently move up and down. To make the ears, indent into the centre of the small oval shapes using the end of the paintbrush and stick in position level with each nose. Press the heads down over the sugar sticks, securing at the neck area with sugar glue. Roll tiny oval-shaped eyes with the remaining black.

12 Using the coloured royal icing and the piping bags with small holes cut into the tips, pipe the hair **(see right)**. Curly hair is piped by waving the bag gently. For spiked hair, squeeze out the royal icing from the tip level with the top of the head, then pull straight up.

13 For the small edging tiles, thinly roll out the remaining blue sugarpaste and cut squares using the 1 cm (½ in) square cutter. Stick around the base of the cake, texturing with kitchen paper. To make the candles, roll the remaining white modelling paste into a sausage and cut into various lengths, reshaping to remove the harsh cut edge and pressing down to make some a little fuller. Indent into the top of each to make room for the flame. Model bright yellow teardrop shaped flames and stick on top of each candle.

14 Each bottle is made by rolling bottle green modelling paste into a sausage and pinching round at the top to narrow the neck. Make four bottles, indenting into the top of each using a cocktail stick, and then stick an oval-shaped label on each using lime green. Knead the remaining lime green with a pea-sized amount of purple together until streaky, and roll to create a beach ball.

15 Knead the remaining purple with blue trimmings until streaky. Roll out and cut an oblong-shaped towel, gathering it up and placing it by the steps. For the flip-flops, shape the remaining golden brown paste into the soles. For the strap, stick on a ball of purple, then roll tiny sausages of paste, attaching to the top and down the sides.

16 For the bubbles, break up the dried white modelling paste, sprinkling it centrally into the tub. For a wet effect, spoon a little clear piping gel over the water and spread over the surface. Drip some gel near the bottles on the cake and cake board.

17 When the cake is dry, brush a little yellow dusting powder over it, concentrating more around the candles to make candlelight. Dilute a tiny amount of black paste with a few drops of water and paint the eyebrows using the fine paintbrush.

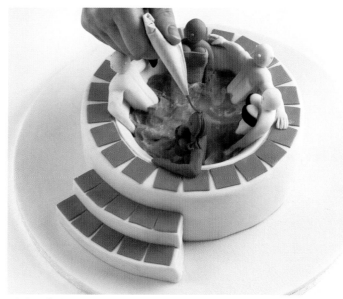

Piping hair

Hunky Firemen

I'm sure most girls would agree it would be very interesting to watch our firemen heroes showing off their fit bodies whilst giving their engine a good wash down.

YOU WILL NEED

- 25 cm (10 in) square sponge cake (see page 11)
- 35 cm (14 in) square cake board
- Icing (confectioners') sugar in a sugar shaker
- 600 g /1 lb 5¼ oz/2½ c buttercream (see page 8)

SUGARPASTE *(see page 9)*

- 820 g (1 lb 13 oz) grey
- 45 g (1½ oz) black
- 650 g (1 lb 7 oz) red

MODELLING PASTE *(see page 10)*

- 65 g (2¼ oz) grey
- 135 g (4¾ oz) black
- 25 g (just over ¾ oz) red
- 20 g (¾ oz) deep blue
- 75 g (2 ½ oz) yellow
- 35 g (1 ¼ oz) flesh-colour (golden brown/ivory with a touch of pink food colouring)
- 20 g (¾ oz) brown

- Sugar glue and paintbrush
- Black food colouring paste
- Edible silver powder
- Clear alcohol
- 3 x sugar sticks (see page 10)
- Clear piping gel

EQUIPMENT

- Plain-bladed kitchen knife
- Large and small rolling pins
- Cake smoother
- Small ruler
- Serrated carving knife
- Palette knife
- 5 cm (2 in) and 2 cm (¾ in) circle cutters
- 2 cm (¾ in) square cutter
- 3 cm (1¼ in) square cutter
- Small pieces of foam (for support)
- Small circle cutter (to mark smiles)
- A few cocktail sticks
- Fine paintbrush
- Teaspoon

1 Slightly dampen the cake board with water. Roll out 500 g (1 lb 1¾ oz) of grey sugarpaste using a sprinkling of icing (confectioners') sugar and move the paste around after each roll to prevent sticking. Lift the sugarpaste by draping over the rolling pin and cover the cake board. Use a cake smoother to smooth and polish the surface, then trim excess from around the edge. Gently press the rolling pin over the surface to mark ridges and then set aside to dry, preferably overnight.

2 Make the ladders first to allow plenty of drying time. Roll out 45 g (1½ oz) of grey modelling paste and cut eight squares in a line using the 2 cm (¾ in) square cutter, leaving a little space in between for each step. Cut down both sides, leaving an edge, and cut across the top and bottom to open. With the trimmings, make a second ladder one square shorter, and put both aside to dry on a flat surface.

3 Trim the crust from the cake and level the top. Cut the cake exactly in half and sandwich one half on top of the other using buttercream, then position on the cake board. Using the palette knife, spread a thin layer of buttercream over the surface of the cake as a crumb coat.

4 Roll out the black sugarpaste and cut a strip to fit around the base of the cake, about 2.5 cm (1 in) in depth. Dust with icing sugar to prevent sticking and roll up. Place against the base of the cake and unroll **(see right)**. Trim excess from join. Moisten with sugar glue and rub the join gently to close completely. Thinly roll out trimmings and cut two circles using the 5 cm (2 in) circle cutter. Cut each in half and stick above the black strip where the wheels will be positioned.

Adding a strip to the base

5 To cover part of the top and down the back of the engine, roll out 175 g (6 oz) of grey sugarpaste and cut an oblong shape to fit the width of the cake measuring 23 cm (9 in) in length. Mark lines across one end up to 7 cm (2¾ in) for the back of the engine. Lift carefully and stick in place, applying to the back of the engine first and smoothing up and over the top, covering about two-thirds. The paste will stretch and may need trimming at the top to straighten.

6 Split 20 g (¾ oz) of red in half, then roll four sausages and use to pad out the engine above each wheel. Roll out 200 g (7 oz) of red and cut an oblong shape to cover one side of the engine, allowing the black strip at the base to show and leaving a proud edge around the grey top and down the back, trimming to curve around on the top corner. Trim to straighten edges, or press the length of a ruler along each edge. Trim around the wheels, smoothing around the shape. Repeat for the opposite side.

Applying the engine sides

7 Cut out two cabin windows and the central storage compartment using the 3 cm (1¼ in) square cutter **(see above)**. Cut out two more storage compartments on either side using this cutter, but then cut down from the square, removing the red sugarpaste to make longer compartments. Using a knife, indent lines into the red covering for each cabin door and step. Press gently with your finger to indent the handle area and model a tiny red sausage-shaped door handle. Cut windows and compartments from the opposite side as before.

8 Roll out 90 g (3 oz) of red and cut a piece to cover the front of the engine. Cut out the windscreen using the 3 cm (1¼ in) square cutter by

cutting out two squares at each end, then cutting out the central part using a knife. Roll out 30 g (1 oz) of red and cut an oblong shape the width of the front up to the windscreen. Mark two even lines using a ruler, indenting three strips. Indent a grille on the central strip using a knife. Stick this strip in place, smoothing at either end to round off. For the red bumper, cut a further strip using trimmings, and then cut a thin strip to edge above the windscreen.

9 Thickly roll out the remaining red sugarpaste and cut an oblong shape slightly larger than the top of the cabin. Stick in place and rub gently around the top edge to round off. Thinly roll out 45 g (1½ oz) of grey sugarpaste and cut pieces to fill all the windows. Using the remaining grey, make all the compartment doors, marking lines using a ruler. Roll thin sausages of paste for long handles at the base of each compartment door and model flattened circles for headlights.

Making the wheels

10 To make the wheels, split 60 g (2 oz) of black modelling paste into four pieces, roll into ball shapes and press down to flatten slightly **(see above)**. Indent the centre of each using the 2 cm (¾ in) circle cutter. Indent the centre of each

again using the small circle cutter and mark small holes around the edge using the end of a paintbrush. Mix the edible silver powder with a few drops of clear alcohol and paint the centres. Using sugar glue, stick each wheel in place, holding for a few moments to secure.

11 Mix a little black food colouring paste with a few drops of clear alcohol until well diluted and translucent. Paint a wash over the windows. Put a little silver powder on the brush and apply in a stippling motion for a cloudy effect. With red trimmings, model two long tapering sausage shapes for the windscreen wipers. To make the blue strip light for the top of the engine, roll a sausage of deep blue modelling paste and cut at an angle on each side and at both ends. Stick in place with sugar glue. Thinly roll out trimmings and cut small squares for the blue lights at the front of the engine and for each door.

12 Thinly roll out 30 g (1 oz) of yellow and cut strips to decorate the engine on each side, including the doors, the front and the top of the blue strip light. To complete the ladder, roll 20 g (¾ oz) of grey modelling paste into a fat sausage and cut angled sides as the blue strip light. Model two tiny flattened ball shapes for bolts on either side and then stick this piece onto the top of the engine, stacking the ladders in place with the longer ladder underneath. Paint silver as before.

13 For the firemens' boots, split 15 g (½ oz) of black modelling paste into six pieces and model teardrop shapes. Press firmly onto each point to round off a heel, then set aside. For the trousers, split the remaining black modelling paste into three pieces. Roll one into a sausage and flatten slightly. Make a cut to separate two legs, three-quarters from the top. Smooth each leg on both sides to remove edges. Press at the bottom of each leg to flatten. Lay down on the front and smooth to round off a bottom, making a small indent in the centre using a cocktail stick. With sugar glue, stick the boots in place with the feet slightly turned out. Lay the two standing firemen's trousers and boots down flat to set. For the sitting fireman, bend each leg halfway and pinch out knees, and then position on the engine.

14 The water hydrant is made using a total of 10 g (¼ oz) red modelling paste. Using just under half, shape a circle for the base. With the remainder, model a smaller, flattened circle and stick on top of the base. Make an oval and cut one end straight, sticking this cut end upright on top of the base. Finish with three flattened circles to decorate the top, making one larger for the hose to attach to. Indent the one at the back by pressing a cocktail stick around the outside edge. Stick the hydrant on the cake board. Roll a 15 g (½ oz) sausage of yellow modelling paste for the hose and stick one end to the hydrant. Position a pair of fireman's trousers over the other end of the hose and secure with glue between his legs, using a foam support if necessary.

15 To make the firemen's chests, use 10 g (¼ oz) of flesh-colour and brown modelling paste for each chest. Model rounded teardrop shapes, the full end for the top of a body with the narrower end for a waist, and press to flatten slightly. Using the paintbrush handle, mark a line down the centre on both sides, marking pectoral and stomach muscles. Stick the remaining fireman in

position against the front of the engine using sugar glue. Using grey trimmings, flatten an uneven circle for the cloth and stick against the side of the engine. Shape a tapered sausage for the hose end, indenting a small hole at the end with a cocktail stick.

16 Use 5 g (just under ¼ oz) of flesh-colour and brown paste for each pair of arms, sticking into position as they are made. To make an arm, roll into a sausage shape and pinch gently one end to round off for a hand. Press down on the hand to flatten only slightly, without indenting. Make a cut for the thumb halfway on one side and pull down. Make three more cuts to separate fingers, push together and stroke to lengthen and bend round. To naturally shape the hand, push the thumb towards the palm from the wrist. Lay the arm down and push in halfway, pinching out at the back to shape the elbow. Indent at the top to round off a large muscle.

17 Push a sugar stick into the neck area of each fireman, leaving half protruding to hold their heads in place. Model their ball-shaped heads, oval-shaped noses and ears using the remaining flesh-colour and brown, indenting into the centre of each ear using a paintbrush. Press the small circle cutter in to mark smiles, completing each open mouth using a cocktail stick.

18 To make the bucket, shape 10 g (¼ oz) of red modelling paste into a rounded teardrop and push down into the full end, pinching up an edge. Roll the sides on the work surface and press down on the base to flatten. Using the remaining red, model a bucket handle and roll out and cut strips for the firemen's braces. Cut thin yellow strips for trouser legs.

19 Split the remaining yellow into three for the firemen's hats. To make a hat, split one piece in half. To make the main part, shape one half into a ball, press into the centre and pinch up an edge. Press either side at the top to narrow slightly. With the remaining half, shape a tiny teardrop and stick to the top of the hat, with the rounded end at the front pressed flat. Roll the remainder into an oval shape for the rim and press down, smoothing until thin, especially around the outer edge. Cut out the centre using the small circle cutter and then stick the rim on top of his head. The bare head will show, so cover this with the main part of the hat, smoothing down until the two pieces meet and the join closes.

20 Make tiny oval-shaped eyes using black trimmings. For the smiling eyes and eyebrows, dilute black food colouring with a tiny drop of clear alcohol and paint using the fine paintbrush. Spoon the clear piping gel into the bucket and add a drip to the end of the hose and drips around the cake and figures. Spread some gel over the cake board using the back of a spoon.

The rear view of the cake

Tunnel of Love

A fun and cheeky idea that has couples going into the tunnel fully dressed and losing all their clothes on the way out!

YOU WILL NEED

- 20 cm (8 in) and 10 cm (4 in) round sponge cakes (see page 11)
- 35 cm (14 in) round cake board
- 450g /1lb/2 c buttercream (see page 8)
- icing (confectioners') sugar in a sugar shaker

SUGARPASTE *(see page 9)*

- 650 g (1 lb 7 oz) red
- 1 kg (2 lb 3¼ oz) pink
- 90 g (3 oz) black
- 175 g (6 oz) deep blue

MODELLING PASTE *(see page 10)*

- 15 g (½ oz) pink
- 15 g (½ oz) mauve
- 15 g (½ oz) orange
- 15 g (½ oz) blue
- 35 g (1¼ oz) flesh-colour
- 10 g (¼ oz) cream
- 10 g (¼ oz) pale brown
- 10 g (¼ oz) mid brown

- Sugar glue and paintbrush
- 6 x sugar sticks (see page 10)
- Clear piping gel or confectioner's varnish
- Black food colouring paste

EQUIPMENT

- Serrated carving knife
- Palette knife
- Plain-bladed kitchen knife
- Large and small rolling pins
- Cake smoother
- Small circle cutter (to mark smile)
- A few cocktail sticks
- Fine and medium paintbrushes

1 Trim the top of each cake level and turn over to use the base as the top. Slice two layers equally through the depth of both cakes and sandwich back together with buttercream. Place the largest cake centrally on the cake board using a dab of buttercream to secure. Spread a layer of buttercream over the surface of both cakes.

2 To cover the top of the large cake, roll out 260 g (9 oz) of red sugarpaste and place on top, trimming excess around the edge. Rub the surface with a cake smoother. To cover the sides, roll out 595 g (1 lb 5 oz) of pink sugarpaste and cut a strip measuring 61 x 10 cm (24 x 4 in) **(see below)**. Sprinkle with icing sugar to prevent sticking and roll up. Lift and position against the side of the cake and unroll around the sides, trimming away any excess from the join. To remove the join, moisten with sugar glue and smooth with a little icing sugar on your fingers.

Covering the sides with pink

3 To make the roof, shape a teardrop of pink sugarpaste using 125 g (4½ oz). Pinch around the wide end, stretching to fit the cake top, then smooth. Cover the small cake sides using 175 g (6 oz) of pink. Cut out hearts using the heart cutter, then cut heart-shaped doorways on the large cake using the template on page 77. Thinly roll out black paste and cut hearts to fill all spaces.

4 To cover the roof, check that the template on page 76 fits around the roof eight times and adjust as needed. Thinly roll out 75 g (2½ oz) of red and pink sugarpaste and cut four roof pieces of each colour using the template, sticking down alternate colours on the roof and smoothing the joins closed **(see right)**.

Making the pointed roof

5 Roll out 20 g (½ oz) of red and cut thin strips to edge both doorways. Cut a large heart for the top of the roof using the trimmings. Roll out 75 g (2½ oz) of red and the remaining pink sugarpaste and cut hearts to edge around the base of the cake and for the fence around the cake board. Stick in place with sugar glue.

6 For the water effect, roll out the blue sugarpaste and cut a strip to fit between the cake and the fence, pressing down with your fingers to indent ripples. Push up against the cake and fence so there are no gaps and stick with sugar glue.

Heart-shaped boats

7 To make the heart-shaped boats, split the remaining red sugarpaste into three equally sized pieces. To make a boat, model a teardrop shape and flatten slightly. Push into the centre to make room for two figures. Cut a small 'V' out of the full end. Trim either side at the front if misshapen and smooth around the shape to remove hard edges. Make two more boats and set aside **(see above)**.

8 Use 10 g (¼ oz) of pink, mauve, orange and blue modelling paste for each of the tops. Make the men a little fuller on the shoulder and push up

excess at the front on the women for their chests. To make a top, shape the modelling paste into an oval and press down to flatten slightly. Make two cuts on either side to separate arms and twist each down gently. Press to flatten the end of each sleeve and then push in the end of a paintbrush to make a small hole for the hands to slot in. Smooth down the sides at the front and back to remove ridges and stick into position in a boat, wrapping the arms around each other.

9 Push a sugar stick down into each top leaving half protruding to hold the heads in place. Model pea-sized teardrops of flesh-coloured modelling paste for hands and slot into the end of each sleeve, sticking with a little sugar glue.

10 For the bare male chest, shape 10 g (¼ oz) of flesh-colour into an oval and cut down either side as before. Pinch gently at the end of each arm to shape wrists and round off hands. Pinch around the top of each arm to accentuate muscles and push in halfway, pinching out at the back to shape elbows. Smooth the front and back as before. Mark a line down the centre of the body and mark curves for pectorals. Stick in position in the boat. Indent a little hole on each pectoral using a cocktail stick.

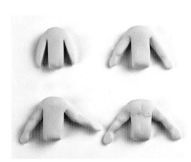

Modelling figures

11 Model two ball-shaped boobs. Use 5 g (just under ¼ oz) to make the female body as before, but make it less muscular at the shoulders. Stick into the boat and stick on the boobs, wrapping the arms across them and securing with sugar glue. Model two tiny ball shapes and stick onto each boob. Push a sugar stick into each body as before.

12 Split 15 g (½ oz) into six pieces and model their oval-shaped heads and ball noses. Model oval-shaped ears for the men only, indenting in the centre of each using the end of a paintbrush. Indent the wide grin using the small circle cutter pressed in at an upward angle. Dimple the cheeks using a cocktail stick. Complete the smile by drawing a curved line across the top holding the cocktail stick flat against the surface.

13 Make the naked woman's open mouth by pushing in the end of a paintbrush and moving up and down. Turn the heads of the kissing couples toward each other and stick together. With the pale cream, pale brown and mid brown modelling paste, make their hair by pinching and shaping flattened pieces over their heads and securing with sugar glue.

14 To make the lights, model small balls with all the coloured modelling paste and stick in place, edging around the doorway and at the bottom of each join on the roof. Using the medium paintbrush, paint a thin coat of clear piping gel or confectioner's varnish over the water to give a shine. Put the boats in position on the cake. When the cake is dry, dilute a little black food colouring paste with a few drops of water and paint the eyes and eyebrows using the fine paintbrush.

Greek God

Bring a smile to any girl's face with this ethereal hunk. I have elevated him onto a cloud-shaped cake, but he would look just as good languishing handsomely on top of a simple round or square cake.

YOU WILL NEED

- 25 cm (10 in) round or petal-shaped sponge cake (see page 11)
- 35 cm (14 in) round cake board
- icing (confectioners') sugar in a sugar shaker
- 600 g /1 lb 5¼ oz/2½ c buttercream (see page 8)

SUGARPASTE (see page 9)

- 225 g (½ lb) pale blue
- 1 kg (2 lb) white

MODELLING PASTE (see page 10)

- 300 g (10½ oz) flesh-colour
- 60 g (2 oz) pale blue

ROYAL ICING (see page 11)

- 30 g (1 oz) dark brown

- Sugar glue and paintbrush
- Large sugar stick (see page 10)
- Black and dark brown food colouring paste

- Edible gold powder
- A few drops of clear alcohol

EQUIPMENT

- Large and small rolling pins
- Cake smoother
- Plain-bladed kitchen knife
- Serrated carving knife
- Palette knife
- Small pieces of foam (for support)
- Small circle cutter (to mark smile)
- A few cocktail sticks
- Small leaf veiner
- Miniature star cutter
- Parchment paper piping bag
- Scissors
- Dusting brush for gold powder

Sculpting the cake

3 Cut two layers in the cake and sandwich back together with buttercream. Position the cake centrally on the cake board and then spread a thin layer of buttercream over the surface of the cake as a crumb coat using the palette knife.

4 Roll out the remaining white sugarpaste. Lift using the rolling pin and cover the cake completely, stretching out pleats and smoothing down and around the shape. Carefully trim away the excess from around the base or smooth underneath tucking under using the knife blade.

5 The figure is assembled by positioning each piece as it is made and securing with a little sugar glue. Use pieces of foam sponge for support whilst drying. First shape his chest using 110 g (3¾ oz) of flesh-coloured modelling paste. Model a rounded teardrop shape, using the full end for the top of his body with the narrower end for his waist. Press to flatten slightly and mark a line down the centre on both sides using the paintbrush handle. For his pectorals, split 5 g (just under ¼ oz) in half and shape flattened circles, sticking in place on the top of his chest. Smooth around each circle and rub gently with a little icing sugar on your hands to blend in the join at the top. Stick in position using a foam support.

1 Slightly dampen the cake board with water. For a sky effect, knead the pale blue sugarpaste and 225 g (½ lb) of white together until marbled. Roll out using a sprinkling of icing sugar and move the paste around after each roll to prevent sticking. Lift the sugarpaste by draping over the rolling pin and cover the cake board. Use a cake smoother to smooth and polish the surface, then trim excess from around the edge. Set aside to dry, preferably overnight.

2 Trim the crust from the cake. If using a round cake, cut small wedges around the cake by first cutting opposite sides, then cut two more wedges from each section, making a total of six. They do not have to be evenly spaced. Trim the cake to round off the top and bottom edge from the round or petal-shaped cake and then cut a dip across the top in which the figure will sit **(see above)**.

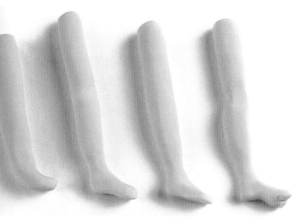

Modelling the legs

6 Add two ball shapes on each pectoral. Model a 20 g (¾ oz) ball and stick in place to shape his bottom. Split 75 g (2½ oz) in half and use to model two legs **(see above)**. To make a leg, roll one half into a sausage and bend one end for the foot, pinching up gently to shape the heel. Pinch around the ankle. Cut toes, pinching up the large toe and stroke down the other toes so they curve underneath. Lay the leg down and push in at the back halfway between the ankle and the top of the leg, pinching the front to shape the knee.

7 Put aside 20 g (¾ oz) of flesh-colour for the head, then split the remainder in half and make two muscular arms. To make an arm, roll into a sausage and pinch one end to round off for a hand. Press down on the hand to flatten. Make a cut for the thumb halfway on one side and pull down. Make three more cuts for fingers, push together and stroke to lengthen and bend around. To shape the hand, push the thumb towards the palm from the wrist. Lay the arm down and push in halfway, pinching out at the back to shape the elbow. Indent at the top to round off a muscle. Push a sugar stick into the neck, leaving half protruding to hold his head in place.

Draping the tunic

8 Thinly roll out the blue modelling paste and cut into strips measuring around 5 x 18 cm (2 x 7 in). Roll the dusting brush handle over the surface to thin and frill, and then pinch together to form pleats. Drape over his body in folds to form his tunic **(see above)**.

9 Model the head, nose and ears using the remaining flesh-colour, marking his smile by indenting the circle cutter in at an angle and use a cocktail stick to draw an open smile. The head is an oval shape with a long teardrop-shaped nose. The ears are small oval shapes pressed in the centre using the end of a paintbrush. For his eyes, first flatten a tiny ball of white trimmings and then cut in half. The straight edge on each half forms the base of each eye. Colour a tiny amount of trimmings brown and black. Model two tiny brown eyebrows and then shape two flattened circles for an iris on each eye. Using black, model two flattened smaller circles for pupils.

10 For the hair, cut a small hole in the tip of the piping bag and fill with the dark brown royal icing. Pipe curls for a fringe across his forehead and pipe long, straight

sideburns and then wavy lengths of hair down his back. When the royal icing dries it will secure his head.

11 To make the crown, shape eight tiny teardrop shapes using trimmings and press each one into the veiner to indent **(see below)**. Arrange the leaves on his head, gently pushing into the royal icing to secure. Mix the gold powder with a little clear alcohol to make a thick paste and paint over each leaf.

Making the leaf crown

12 Thinly roll out trimmings and cut eight stars, sticking them randomly over the cake board. Paint them gold as before. For a golden shimmer, dust gold powder over the figure and cake board.

Pole Dancers

No less than three gorgeous pole dancers to choose from here, although choosing your favourite and placing just one of these stunners on a larger stage would still be a big hit.

YOU WILL NEED

- 3 x 12 cm (5 in) round sponge cakes (see page 11)
- 35 cm (14 in) round cake board
- Icing (confectioners') sugar in a sugar shaker
- Sugar glue and paintbrush
- Edible silver powder
- 550 g /1 lb 3½ oz/2¾ c buttercream (see page 8)

SUGARPASTE (see page 9)

- 945 g (2 lb 1¼ oz) white
- 770 g (1 lb 11 oz) black

MODELLING PASTE (see page 10)

- 45 g (1½ oz) grey
- 60 g (2 oz) pale pink
- 60 g (2 oz) deep pink
- 115 g (4 oz) black
- 60 g (2 oz) flesh-colour (golden brown/ivory with a touch of pink)
- 30 g (1 oz) brown

ROYAL ICING (see page 9)

- 10 g ¼ oz) pale cream
- 10 g (¼ oz) golden brown
- 10 g (¼ oz) dark brown

- 3 x sugar sticks (see page 10)
- Pink and black food colouring pastes

EQUIPMENT

- 3 x 28 cm (11 in) food-safe dowel
- Plain-bladed kitchen knife
- Large and small rolling pins
- Cake smoother
- Serrated carving knife
- Palette knife
- Ruler
- Small pieces of foam (for support)
- A few cocktail sticks
- 3 x paper piping bags
- Scissors
- 2 cm (¾ in) square cutter
- Fine paintbrush

1 Cover the dowel first to allow for plenty of drying time. Roll the grey modelling paste into long sausages the length of each dowel, moisten with sugar glue and press the dowel down into the paste. Wrap the paste around, pinching the join closed. Rub the joins to remove completely and then roll gently over the work surface to obtain a smooth finish. Rub a little edible silver powder over each one and then put aside to dry.

Modelling the skirts

2 Each skirt is made using 45 g (1½ oz) of pale pink, deep pink and black modelling paste for each. To make a long skirt, roll into a sausage shape and indent pleats by rolling a paintbrush handle over the surface. Pinch gently to widen at the bottom to give the skirt support whilst standing **(see above)**. Indent deeply into the top and pinch up an edge, making room for the body on each. Push down at the back so the bottom will peep out

on the pale pink skirt and push down at the front for the deep pink skirt to show the stomach, marking a line with a knife for a wrap-over effect. Push down either side on the black skirt to show hips, indenting at the front also to make room for the leg. Put aside to dry.

3 Slightly dampen the cake board with water. For a marbled effect, knead 600 g (1 lb 5¼ oz) of white sugarpaste and 50 g (1¾ oz) of black sugarpaste together until streaky. Put aside 150 g (5¼ oz) for steps, then roll out the remainder using a sprinkling of icing sugar and move the paste around after each roll to prevent sticking. Lift the sugarpaste by draping over the rolling pin and cover the cake board. Use a cake smoother to smooth and polish the surface, then trim the excess from around the edge. Set aside to dry.

4 Trim the crust from each cake and level the top. Cut a layer in each cake and sandwich back together with buttercream, making sure the cakes are all exactly the same height. Spread a thin layer over the surface of each cake as a crumb coat.

5 To make the stages, first cover the sides of the cakes. Use a ruler to measure the depth. Roll out 240 g (8½ oz) of black sugarpaste and cut a strip measuring 41 cm (16 in) in length by the depth measurement. Sprinkle with icing sugar to prevent sticking and roll up. Place against a cake and unroll the black sugarpaste around it, trimming excess from the join **(see above)**. Smooth the join closed by rubbing gently with your fingers. Cover the two remaining cakes.

Covering the sides with black sugarpaste

6 Roll out 115 g (4 oz) of white sugarpaste and place a cake down onto it. Cut around, and then place the cake upright and in position on the cake board. Use a cake smoother to obtain a smooth finish. Cover the top of the two remaining cakes. Thickly roll out the remaining marbled sugarpaste and cut the oblong-shaped steps for each stage, sticking together and in place using a little sugar glue.

7 Measure the depth of each cake and cut away the modelling paste covering on the dowel using this measurement. Moisten the centre of each cake with a little sugar glue and push the dowel down through the centre of each cake until it reaches the cake board.

8 Each body is made using 15 g (½ oz) of flesh-coloured or brown modelling paste. First model into a sausage and roll between your thumb

and finger to indent the waist halfway, rounding off the bottom **(see below)**. Roll the opposite end to lengthen the chest area. To shape the bottom, mark a line using a knife and rub gently to round off. Stroke the stomach area to flatten and mark a ridge on either side to mark hips. Indent the belly button using the end of a paintbrush. Stick the bodies in place on the skirts as each is made, smoothing them down into the recess of each skirt.

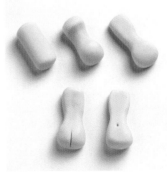

Modelling the bodies

9 Split 10 g (¼ oz) of flesh-colour into four pieces and 5 g (just under ¼ oz) of brown in half and use to make arms, sticking in position as each is made. The arms here have been modelled with fully cut hands, but you can save time by modelling simple hands (see page 50, step 10). To make an arm, roll into a sausage shape and pinch gently one end to round off for a hand. Press down on the hand to flatten only slightly, without indenting. Make a cut halfway down on one side for the thumb. Make three cuts along the top to separate fingers and twist gently to lengthen, press together and bend around. To naturally shape the hand, push the thumb towards the palm from the wrist. Lay the arm down and push in halfway, pinching out at the back to shape the elbow.

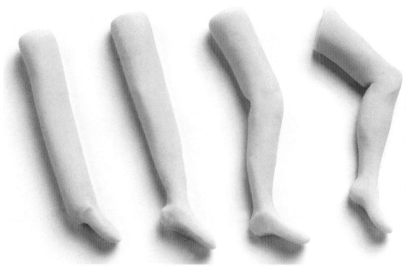

Modelling the legs

TIP: You can make the arms and hands separately, covering the join with bracelet cuffs made from strips of modelling paste.

10 Roll flesh-colour and brown ball-shaped boobs, sticking in place with a little sugar glue. Push a sugar stick down through the top of each body, leaving half protruding to help hold their heads in place. Make their oval-shaped heads and noses using 5 g (just under ¼ oz) for each. Make a hole in the bottom of each head using a cocktail stick, and then using a little sugar glue, stick in place over the sugar stick.

11 To make a leg, roll the remaining flesh-coloured modelling paste into a sausage **(see above)**. Pinch down one end to make the pointed foot. Roll the ankle area between your thumb and finger to indent and shape the leg. Push in halfway at the back and gently pinch at the front to shape the knee. Stroke the shin to straighten, pushing out excess at the back to shape the calf muscle. Using sugar glue, stick the leg in position using foam pieces for support if necessary.

12 Using the remaining pale pink, deep pink and 10 g (¼ oz) of black modelling paste, roll out and cut different sized strips to add to the skirts, rolling a paintbrush handle over the surface to make pleats. Stick in place creating a wrapover effect. Model a little teardrop-shaped tie for the black skirt at the top. Roll out and cut little strips for bracelet cuffs and make bra tops. The tassels are made from small, flattened circles of paste with tiny strips of paste grouped together on the centre of each. Cut a

tiny pale pink triangle for the thong and stick in place, marking the straps by indenting with a cocktail stick.

13 To pipe the hair, put the cream, brown and golden brown royal icing into piping bags and cut small holes in the tips. Pipe straight blonde hair, flicking up the ends; long brown locks and long golden brown waves onto the girls.

14 Stick a flattened pea-sized amount of black modelling paste on top of each pole. Thinly roll out the remainder and cut squares using the square cutter. Cut each square in half and rub edible silver over the surface with your finger. Using sugar glue, stick around the top edge of each cake, leaving a space at the steps. When the cake is dry, dilute pink and black food colouring pastes with a few drops of water and paint the eyes and lips using the fine paintbrush.

Who could resist these gorgeous hula girls saucily wearing only grass skirts and flower garlands, dancing around a bar on a beautiful tropical beach? There couldn't possibly be anything else a man would wish for!

YOU WILL NEED

- 18 cm (7 in), 15 cm (6 in) and 10 cm (4 in) round sponge cakes (see page 11)
- 30 cm (12 in) round cake board
- 15 cm (6 in) cake card
- Icing (confectioners') sugar in a sugar shaker
- 550 g /1 lb 3½ oz/2¾ c buttercream (see page 8)

SUGARPASTE (see page 9)

- 450 g (1 lb) pale cream
- 285 g (10 oz) black
- 260 g (9 oz) mid brown
- 450 g (1 lb) deep cream

MODELLING PASTE (see page 10)

- 10 g (¼ oz) bottle green
- 110 g (3¾ oz) pale cream
- 110 g (3¾ oz) deep cream
- 100 g (3½ oz) pale brown
- 110 g (3¾ oz) flesh-colour (golden brown/ivory)
- 10 g (¼ oz) mauve
- 10 g (¼ oz) pink
- 10 g (¼ oz) orange

- 10 g (¼ oz) yellow
- 10 g (¼ oz) white

ROYAL ICING (see page 9)

- 10 g (¼ oz) deep cream
- 20 g (½ oz) dark brown

- Sugar glue and paintbrush
- 3 x sugar sticks (see page 10)
- Black food colouring paste
- Edible gold powder

EQUIPMENT

- Plain-bladed kitchen knife
- Large and small rolling pins
- Cake smoother
- Serrated carving knife
- Palette knife
- Small pieces of foam (for support)
- A few cocktail sticks
- Small blossom plunger cutter
- Paper piping bag
- Scissors
- Fine paintbrush

1 Slightly dampen the cake board with water. Thickly roll out the pale cream sugarpaste using a sprinkling of icing sugar and use to cover the cake board. Press the rolling pin over the surface to create a rippled effect, and then set aside to dry.

2 Trim the crust from each cake and level the top. With a dab of buttercream, stick the 15 cm (6 in) cake onto the cake card. To shape the pointed roof, cut down centrally from the top towards the base all around the cake, creating the sloping sides. Cut two even layers in the largest cake only and sandwich back together with buttercream. Spread a thin layer of buttercream over the surface of all cakes as a crumb coat (**see below**). Position the large cake centrally on the cake board.

3 Roll out 145 g (5 oz) of black sugarpaste and place on top of

Spreading the buttercream

the largest cake. Trim around the outside edge. Measure the depth of the smallest cake using the ruler. Roll out the remaining black sugarpaste and cut a 30 cm (12 in) strip using this depth measurement. Dust with icing sugar to prevent sticking, roll up and position against the side of the cake. Unroll around the cake, trimming the excess at the join and smooth closed with your fingers using a little sugar glue to secure. Spread the bottom of the cake with buttercream and then place centrally on top of the large cake.

4 Thinly roll out 100 g (3½ oz) of mid brown sugarpaste and cover the roof cake completely, smoothing the sugarpaste level to the edge of the cake card and then set aside. To cover the bamboo effect sides of the largest cake, measure the depth and then thickly roll out the deep cream sugarpaste. Cut a strip the depth measurement that is 46 cm (18 in) in length. Make sure the sugarpaste is

loose from the work surface. Using the ruler, indent slightly uneven lines across the surface, taking care not to cut right through the sugarpaste. Cut into three or four pieces, lift and position around the sides of the cake, butting up the joins **(see below)**. Rub the cake smoother over the surface.

5 Thickly roll out the remaining mid brown sugarpaste and cut a long strip for the bar shelf 2.5 cm (1 in) wide. Rub along the cut edges to round off completely and then stick in position on the cake leaving a slight lip. Trim the excess from the join and stick together with a little sugar glue. To remove the join, smooth gently with a little icing sugar on your fingers.

6 Roll out mid brown trimmings into a long sausage and cut six shelf supports. Scratch the surface of each using a cocktail stick to give a wood effect and stick around the central

cake in groups of two 6 cm (2½ in) apart. Roll out 10 g (¼ oz) of deep cream sugarpaste and cut three 6 cm (2½ in) strips for the shelves, sticking in place between the supports. Using the bottle green modelling paste, model six bottles by shaping into sausages and pinching around one end to narrow the neck. Make two more bottles each using the pale cream and pale brown modelling paste. Stick in position along the shelves.

Making the grass

7 Moisten along the top edge of the central cake with sugar glue and position the roof on top. Using 90 g (3 oz) each of pale cream, deep cream and pale brown modelling paste, thinly roll out and cut uneven strips for the grass **(see above)**, building up the roof covering as each strip is made.

8 Each body is built up flat, then when dry, stood upright against the cake and stuck firmly in position with a dab of royal icing. Split 35 g (1¼ oz) of flesh-coloured modelling paste into three and shape into sausages **(see opposite)**. Roll between your thumb and finger to indent the waist halfway, rounding off the bottom. Roll the opposite end to lengthen the chest area.

Covering the sides with "bamboo"

9 To make the legs, split 35 g (1¼ oz) of flesh into six equally sized pieces. To make a leg, roll into a sausage. Bend one end round to make a foot, pinching gently to shape a heel. Roll the ankle area between your thumb and finger to indent and shape the leg. Push in halfway at the back and gently pinch at the front to shape the knee. Stroke the shin to straighten, pushing out excess at the back to shape the calf muscle. Stick the legs in dancing positions as each is made.

10 Make the grass skirts as the roof, using the remaining pale and dark cream and pale brown modelling paste, following the shape of the girl's hips and tucking some strips around the back. Keep some trimmings to replace any strips that break when the figures are positioned.

11 Split 20 g (¾ oz) of flesh-colour paste into six and use to make arms, sticking in position as each is made. I modelled arms with fully cut hands, but if you are short of time, simple hands (see page 50, step 10) are quicker and easier. To make an arm, roll into a sausage shape and pinch gently at one end to round off for a hand. Press down on the hand to flatten only slightly, without indenting. Make a cut halfway down on one side for the thumb. Make three cuts along the top to separate fingers and twist gently to lengthen, then press together and bend round. To naturally shape the hand, push the thumb towards the palm from the wrist. Lay the arm down and push in halfway, pinching out at the back to shape the elbow. Stick onto the body in a dancing position.

12 Split 5 g (just under ¼ oz) of flesh-colour into six and roll ball shaped boobs, sticking in place with a little sugar glue. Push a sugar stick down through the top of each body, leaving half protruding to hold their heads in place. Make their oval-shaped heads and noses using the remaining flesh-colour. Mark smiles using the small circle cutter pressed in at an upward angle, dimple each corner by pressing in with the tip of a cocktail stick and complete the smile by drawing across the top with the cocktail stick flat against the surface **(see below)**. Make a hole in the bottom of each head using a cocktail stick, and then using a little sugar glue, stick each head in place over the sugar stick.

13 Leave the figures to dry completely, preferably overnight. Stick in position with a dab of the deep cream royal icing. To pipe the girls' hair, put the brown royal icing into a piping bag and cut a small hole in the tip. Pipe long, wavy hair, flicking up the ends with a central parting.

14 To make the coloured garlands, shape long sausages, pinching along each length, and decorate each with tiny flowers cut with the blossom plunger cutter. Stick flowers around the heads and on the feet. With the remaining coloured modelling paste, shape little drinking cups from teardrop shapes indented in the centre and roll tiny sausage-shaped straws.

15 Dust the cake and cake board with a little edible gold powder. Dilute black food colouring paste with a few drops of water and paint the smiling eyes using the fine paintbrush.

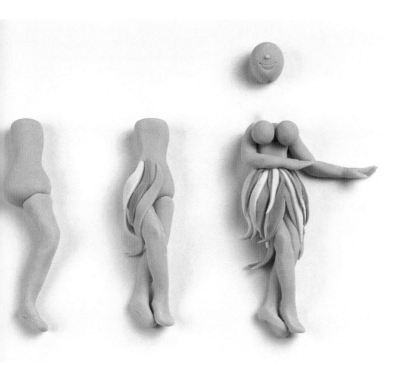

Modelling a body

Hippy Flashers

You'll set the whole room giggling and bring a little 1960s nostalgia back when this Hippy's favourite drives in with a pair of bums hanging out of the window.

YOU WILL NEED

- 25 cm (10 in) square sponge cake (see page 11)
- 35 cm (14 in) oval cake board
- Icing (confectioners') sugar in a sugar shaker
- 550 g / 1 lb 3½ oz/2¾ c buttercream (see page 8)

SUGARPASTE (see page 9)

- 450 g (1 lb) purple
- 115 g (4 oz) black
- 820 g (1 lb 13 oz) lime green

MODELLING PASTE (see page 10)

- 115 g (4 oz) black
- 2 pea-sized amounts of red
- 5 g (just under ¼ oz) pale pink
- 5 g (just under ¼ oz) pale yellow
- 15 g (½ oz) grey
- 65 g (¼ oz) flesh-colour (golden brown/ivory food colouring with a touch of pink)
- 5 g (just under ¼ oz) blue
- 5 g (just under ¼ oz) pale purple

- Sugar glue and paintbrush
- Black food colouring paste
- Edible silver powder
- A few drops of clear alcohol (e.g. vodka, gin)

EQUIPMENT

- Plain-bladed kitchen knife
- Serrated carving knife
- Large and small rolling pins
- Ruler
- Cake smoother
- Palette knife
- 2 cm (¾ in) and 2.5 cm (1 in) circle cutters
- Small pieces of foam (for support)
- A few cocktail sticks
- Fine paintbrush

1 Slightly dampen the cake board with water. Roll out the purple paste using a sprinkling of icing sugar and cover the cake board, trimming excess from around the edge. Press the rolling pin into the surface to make ripples. Set aside to dry.

2 Trim the crust from the cake and level the top. Cut a 5 cm (2 in) strip from one side and discard. Cut the cake in half lengthways and place one half on top of the other. At the top of the cake, measure 7 cm (3 in) from the front. Place the carving knife at this measurement and cut down at an angle to shape the windscreen. Cut down to almost the base of the top layer, then turn the knife outwards and cut the curved bonnet, sloping down to the front and cutting off the top edge of the second layer **(see below)**.

3 To shape the back of the cake, measure 7 cm (3 in) from the back of the cake. Place the carving knife at this measurement and cut

Sculpting the cake

down to the base to shape the curved back of the car. Trim the sides, making them narrower at the window level. Sandwich the layer together with buttercream. Place centrally on the cake board and spread a layer of buttercream over the cake surface as a crumb coat and to help the paste stick.

4 Thinly roll out 90 g (3 oz) of black sugarpaste and cut a strip 2.5 cm (1 in) deep to go around the base of the cake. Dust with icing sugar to prevent sticking, roll up and position against the base. Unroll the strip around the cake and smooth the join closed with your fingers.

5 To cover the car, roll out 550 g (1 lb 3½ oz) of lime green sugarpaste and cover the cake completely, stretching out pleats and smoothing down and around the shape. Trim around the base to reveal the black strip underneath **(see**

Trimming around the base

below). Using templates for the windows (see page 77), mark the outlines using the back of a knife. Cut out the two side windows completely on one side, and cut a little strip on the other side to make the window look slightly open.

6 Smooth either side of the bonnet with your fingers to indent the long ovals, pushing up a slight ridge, and indent small ovals for the door handles to slot into. Push in the tip of a knife to cut little slits under the front and back windscreens. Thinly roll out the remaining black sugarpaste and cut pieces to fill each open window.

7 For the boot, roll out 45 g (1½ oz) of lime green sugarpaste and, using the template on page 77, cut out the boot door, indenting down the sides by smoothing gently with your finger. With trimmings, roll a sausage-shaped handle. Using 45 g (1½ oz) of lime green sugarpaste, cut strips to hold the bumpers at the front and back of the car, making them slightly thicker in the centre. Stick in place. For bumpers, split 30 g (1 oz) of black modelling paste in half and roll two sausages measuring 12 cm (5 in), flattening each slightly using a cake smoother.

8 For wheels, split 60 g (2 oz) of black modelling paste into four, roll into ball shapes and press down to flatten slightly. Press the large circle cutter into the centre of each to indent the hubcaps. Push the end of a paintbrush into the centre and repeatedly around the edge of each hubcap. Stick each wheel in place.

9 Put aside two pea-sized amounts of lime green, and then split the remainder into four. To make the wheel arches, model teardrop shapes, flatten slightly by pressing the cake smoother down onto them and stick over each wheel, smoothing against the car and securing with sugar glue **(see below)**. Stick the two pea-sized amounts onto the back wheel arches for backlights with a little red on each.

10 Using the remaining black, model two long teardrops for door handles and two thin sausages for wipers. Model two flattened circles for headlights, indenting a circle in the centres using the smaller circle cutter and mark a criss-cross pattern in the centre. Roll out and cut two thin strips measuring 10 cm (4 in) in length and stick in place as running boards.

11 Dilute black food colouring with a little clear alcohol and paint a wash over the windows and windscreens. To give a glass effect, sprinkle a little edible silver onto the brush and stipple over the windows. Mix a few drops of clear alcohol with the silver and paint a thin coat over the chrome-effect areas.

12 To make the flowers for the car decoration, roll ten small and five large pink teardrop shapes for petals, pressing each completely flat. Stick the larger petals on the roof and the smaller petals on the doors. Press the cake smoother down onto them all to inlay into the lime green covering. Stick two tiny flattened circles of yellow into the centre of each flower. Make two small yellow flowers in the same way for each door, with pink centres. For the exhaust fumes, split the grey modelling paste into three different sized pieces and roll into oval shapes. Press to flatten slightly and push the back of a knife around the edges.

13 To make the bums, put aside 15 g (½ oz) of flesh-colour, then split the remainder in half and roll into oval shapes **(see above)**. Mark the centre line on each by rolling the knife blade over the surface, keeping it slightly angled to create a curve in the cheek, and repeat for the other cheek. Smoothe with a little icing sugar and your fingers.

14 Thinly roll out blue and purple modelling paste and gather up to create pleats, sticking onto the bottom of each bum for the trousers. Thinly roll out yellow and cut a strip to edge the top of one bum. Stick both bums in position, holding for a few moments to secure. If required, use a piece of foam support until dry.

Making the bums

15 For the hands, split the remaining flesh-colour into three pieces. For the 'thumbs up' hand, roll one piece into a sausage shape and pinch gently one end to round off for a hand. Press down on the hand to flatten slightly. Make a cut for the thumb halfway on one side and pull down. Make three more cuts to separate fingers and stroke to lengthen. Bend the fingers down towards the palm, keeping them close together and pinch up the thumb, rounding it at the top by pressing it down gently. Stick in position using foam supports if necessary.

16 Model two more hands as before, but only bend round the two smallest fingers. Bend the thumb also and secure across the smallest fingers with a little sugar glue. Open the index and middle fingers wide and stick in position on either side of a bum. Stick in place with the palms facing forward.

Forming the wheel arches

Almost Full Monty

Most of us females have a penchant for men in uniform, so bring a chuckle to any girlie celebration with this fun striptease.

YOU WILL NEED

- 2 round sponge cakes, 20 cm (8 in) and 10 cm (4 in) (see page 11)
- 35 cm (14 in) round cake board
- Icing (confectioners') sugar in a sugar shaker
- 600 g /1 lb 5¼ oz/2½ c buttercream (see page 8)

SUGARPASTE *(see page 9)*

- 500 g (1 lb 1¾ oz) navy blue
- 1 kg (2 lb 3¼ oz) white

MODELLING PASTE *(see page 10)*

- 45 g (1½ oz) white

- 25 g (just over ¾ oz) black
- 160 g (5½ oz) flesh-colour (golden brown/ivory with a touch of pink)
- 25 g (just over ¾ oz) navy blue
- 5 g (just under ¼ oz) dark brown
- 5 g (just under ¼ oz) brown
- 5 g (just under ¼ oz) dark ivory
- 5 g (just under ¼ oz) ivory

- Sugar glue and paintbrush
- Miniature and standard gold dragees (balls)
- Edible or food-safe gold glitter (see page 10)
- 5 sugar sticks (see page 10)
- Black food colouring paste

EQUIPMENT

- Plain-bladed kitchen knife
- Large and small rolling pins
- Cake smoother
- Serrated carving knife
- Palette knife
- Small bowl
- Small pieces of foam (for support)
- Small circle cutter (to mark smiles)
- A few cocktail sticks
- Plain piping tubes, nos. 2 and 3
- Fine paintbrush

1 Slightly dampen the cake board with water. Roll out the navy blue sugarpaste using a sprinkling of icing sugar and use to cover the cake board. Use a cake smoother to smooth and polish the surface, then trim excess from around the edge. Set aside to dry, preferably overnight.

Covering the cake with sugarpaste

2 Trim the crust from each cake and level the top. Cut two layers in each cake and sandwich back together using buttercream. Position the large cake centrally on the cake board. Spread both cakes with a layer of buttercream for a crumb coat.

3 Roll out 750 g (1 lb 10½ oz) of white sugarpaste and cover the large cake completely, stretching out any pleats and smoothing downwards **(see left)**. Trim the excess from around the base and then polish with a cake smoother to obtain a smooth finish. Cover the small cake using the remaining white, then position centrally on top of the larger cake.

4 Moisten around the base of each cake with a little sugar glue and sprinkle with miniature dragees. Stick

larger dragees around the outside edge. Put aside a pea-sized amount of white modelling paste, then model the remainder into a large heart shape, slightly flattening the point at the bottom so it will stand upright. Sprinkle gold glitter into a small bowl, moisten the heart with sugar glue and place it into the bowl, covering the heart completely with glitter. Set aside to dry.

NOTE: If using food-safe gold glitter, make sure to remove it before serving.

Modelling the boots

5 To make all the boots, split 15 g (½ oz) of black modelling paste into ten equally sized pieces. To make a boot, roll a ball and then pinch halfway to round off one end **(see above)**. Bend this end around for the foot and press down to flatten slightly, squeezing either side to lengthen. Cut open the boot at the top and roll the paintbrush handle inside to open up a space for the leg. Roll tiny sausages for laces. Make ten boots in total and put each aside to dry.

6 To make the caps, split 10 g (¼ oz) of navy blue modelling paste into five pieces and shape five flattened circles for the base of each hat. Split the remaining navy blue into five and shape into thicker circles, pinching up one side for the top of each hat. Stick onto the bases and then put aside to dry.

7 Each figure is modelled flat and left to dry completely before positioning on the cake **(see right)**. Split 100 g (3½ oz) of flesh-coloured modelling paste into five pieces, some very slightly larger than others to allow for different builds. Roll one into a sausage shape around 6 cm (2½ in) in length and flatten slightly. Make a

2.5 cm (1 in) cut to separate legs and smooth on both sides to remove the hard cut edge. Gently twist each leg to lengthen and pinch halfway down to shape a knee. Indent down the front of the chest using the paintbrush handle and make two curved lines to shape each pectoral. Use a cocktail stick to indent a small hole in each. Stick on the boots.

8 For arms, split 35 g (1¼ oz) of flesh-coloured modelling paste into ten equally sized pieces. To make an arm, roll into a sausage shape and pinch gently at one end to round off for a hand. Press down on the hand to flatten slightly, without indenting. Make a cut for the thumb halfway on one side and pull down. Make three more cuts to separate fingers, push together and stroke to lengthen and bend around. To naturally shape the hand into position, push the thumb towards the palm from the wrist. Lay the arm down and push in halfway, pinching out at the back to shape the elbow. Indent at the top to round off a large muscle. Make all the arms and stick in position as each is made: raised arms with hands bent back from the wrists, and lower arms holding onto the caps.

9 Put aside a pea-sized amount of black modelling paste and use the remainder for each necktie. Model pea-sized flattened circles and stick on top of each body. Roll long sausages, press flat and stick onto the front of each chest and make small, flattened ball shaped knots. Push a sugar stick into the top of each figure, leaving half protruding to help hold the heads in place.

10 Split the remaining flesh-coloured modelling paste into five pieces and use to make the oval-shaped heads, noses and ears,

indenting into the centre of each ear using the end of a paintbrush. Mark each smile by indenting with the small circle cutter, joining across the top with a line marked with a cocktail stick. Push a cocktail stick in underneath to make a hole for the sugar stick.

11 To make eyes, very thinly roll out white modelling paste and cut ten circles using the no. 3 plain piping tube. For each iris, very thinly roll out black modelling paste and cut out ten circles using the no. 2 plain piping tube. Using the dark brown, brown, dark ivory and ivory modelling paste, make the hair by tearing off small pieces, stretching out and sticking over each head, building up little by little.

12 When the figures are completely dry, stick in position against the cake. Moisten the neck area with a little sugar glue, then stick each head in place. Dilute a little black food colouring with a few drops of water and paint eyelashes and eyebrows using the fine paintbrush.

Modelling the figures

Bedtime Fun

This saucy scene will bring a bit of 'spice' to the life of anyone lucky enough to be given a slice of the action going on here.

YOU WILL NEED

- 23 cm (9 in) round sponge cake (see page 11)
- 35 cm (14 in) round cake board
- Icing (confectioners') sugar in a sugar shaker
- 450 g /1 lb/2 c buttercream (see page 8)

SUGARPASTE (see page 9)

- 650 g (1 lb 7 oz) deep cream
- 800 g (1 lb 12 oz) light cream
- 285 g (10 oz) black

MODELLING PASTE (see page 10)

- 60 g (2 oz) flesh-colour (golden brown/ivory food colouring with a touch of pink)
- 10 g (¼ oz) red
- 10 g (¼ oz) black
- 10 g (¼ oz) mauve
- 10 g (¼ oz) white

- Sugar glue and paintbrush
- Black, egg yellow and red food colouring pastes

EQUIPMENT

- Palette knife
- Plain-bladed kitchen knife
- Large and small rolling pins
- Cake smoother
- Serrated carving knife
- Foam pieces (for support)
- A few cocktail sticks
- Fine paintbrush

1 Slightly dampen the cake board with water. Roll out 450 g (1 lb) of deep cream sugarpaste using a sprinkling of icing sugar and move the paste around after each roll to prevent sticking. Lift the sugarpaste by draping over the rolling pin and cover the cake board, trimming excess from around the edge. Rub gently with a cake smoother and set aside to dry.

2 Trim to level the top of the cake and turn over to use the base of the cake as the top. Cut a layer in the cake and sandwich back together with buttercream. Place centrally on the cake board and then spread a layer of buttercream over the surface of the cake as a crumb coat.

3 Roll out 800 g (1 lb 12 oz) of pale cream sugarpaste and cover the cake completely, smoothing around the shape, stretching out pleats around the edge and smoothing downwards. Trim excess from around the base. Smooth from the edge towards the centre creating indents and mark pleats around the base using a knife **(see right)**.

Marking pleats around the base

4 To make the pillows, split the black sugarpaste into four and shape into ovals. Press down to flatten slightly and then pinch four corners on each, sticking three pillows in position on the bed with one on the floor.

5 For legs and feet, split 30 g (1 oz) of flesh-colour into four equally sized pieces. To make a leg, roll into a sausage shape and bend one end for the foot, pinching up gently to shape the heel. Pinch around the ankle by rolling gently between your finger and thumb to narrow and give shape. Cut toes, pinching up the large toe and stroke down the other toes so they curve underneath. Pinch the leg at the front to shape the knee. Model three more legs and stick in position on the cake.

6 For the arms and hands, split 20 g (½ oz) of flesh-colour into

Modelling the arms and hands

three pieces. To make an arm, roll into a sausage shape and pinch gently at one end to round off for a hand **(see above)**. Press down on the hand to flatten only slightly, without indenting. Make a cut for the thumb halfway on one side and pull down. Make three more cuts to separate fingers, stroke to lengthen and bend round. To naturally shape the hand, push the thumb towards the palm from the wrist, then open again. Lay the arm down and push in halfway, pinching out at the back to shape the elbow. Make two more arms and stick in position on the cake.

7 Split the remaining flesh-colour into two pieces, one slightly larger than the other. Use them to make an elbow and a knee by rolling into sausage shapes, pushing in gently halfway and pinching at the front. Stick in position on the cake.

8 Thinly roll out the remaining dark cream sugarpaste and cut a 20 cm (8 in) square for the cover. Lift and position centrally on the cake, pushing up pleats and arranging around all the limbs.

9 Make the underwear using red, black, mauve and white modelling paste. To make bra tops, model flattened teardrops for cups, indent into the centre of each and stick together point to point. Thinly roll out and cut strips, looping them around and securing with sugar glue.

10 To make the white and black thongs, roll out and cut small triangles and thin strips, assembling in position with sugar glue **(see below)**. Loop a black thong over a big toe. For the boxers, model flattened squares and make a small cut at the bottom to

separate legs. Pinch gently into each leg to indent and mark lines for the fly and waistband using a knife.

11 For the ties, cut long thin strips slightly wider at one end, cutting into a point, and stick one over a leg and the other draped on a pillow. With coloured trimmings, shape a tiny red heart for the white thong and stick tiny flattened balls onto the mauve boxers for polka dots.

12 For the socks, roll small sausages from white and red modelling paste, bend halfway and press down. Pinch to open the top of the sock and smooth to round off the opposite end. Push in at the bottom to shape the arch of the foot and stick in place with a little sugar glue.

13 When the cake is dry, dilute a little red food colouring paste with a few drops of water and paint the lips on the white boxers using the fine paintbrush. Dilute egg yellow and black with a little water and paint the animal print on the bedcover. Paint yellow dots in different sizes first and allow to dry, then paint black blotches in a dabbing motion around each.

Making a thong

Come and Get Me

A gorgeous bloke keenly waiting to be unwrapped in his shag pile-carpeted love den. What more could a girl possibly want? Apart from a slice of cake, of course!

YOU WILL NEED

- 25 cm (10 in) square sponge cake (see page 11)
- 35 cm (14 in) square cake board
- 450 g /1 lb/2 c buttercream (see page 8)
- Icing (confectioners') sugar in a sugar shaker

MODELLING PASTE (SEE PAGE

- 225 g (8 oz) white
- 280 g (9¾ oz) flesh-colour (golden brown/ivory food colouring with a touch of pink)
- 115 g (4 oz) red

SUGARPASTE (SEE PAGE 9)

- 595 g (1 lb 5 oz) black
- 175 g (6 oz) red
- 450 g (1 lb) white

- Sugar stick (see page 10)
- Sugar glue and paintbrush

ROYAL ICING (SEE PAGE 9)

- 45 g (1½ oz) white
- 175 g (6 oz) red
- 10 g (½ oz) pale cream/ivory

EQUIPMENT

- Plain-bladed kitchen knife
- Large and small rolling pins
- Ruler
- Serrated carving knife
- Palette knife
- Small heart cutter
- Small circle cutter (to mark smile)
- Small pieces of foam (for support)
- A few cocktail sticks
- Paper piping bag
- Scissors

TIP: To make a large king size bed for more servings, don't trim the cake.

1 To allow plenty of drying time, first make the headboard. Roll out the white modelling paste and cut an oblong shape measuring 15 cm (6 in) by the width of the bed. Trim the top two corners to curve around. Put the headboard aside to dry on a completely flat surface.

2 Trim the crust from the cake and slice a 5 cm (2 in) strip from one side of the cake, making the oblong-shaped bed. Cut a layer in the cake and sandwich back together with buttercream. Position the cake centrally on the cake board, then using the palette knife, spread a thin layer of buttercream over the surface of the cake as a crumb coat.

3 Roll out 145 g (5 oz) of black sugarpaste and cut a 2 cm (¾ in) strip to cover around the base of the cake. Dust with icing sugar and roll up into a spiral. Position against the base of the cake and unroll around it, smoothing the join closed. For the sheet, roll out the white sugarpaste, lift using the large rolling pin and cover the cake completely, stretching out pleats and smoothing down and around the shape. Carefully trim the excess level with the top of the black strip, pushing in along the edge to curves inwards. Mark little pleats with the tip of a knife **(see right)**.

4 Split 175 g (6 oz) of black sugarpaste and all the red sugarpaste in half and make two red and two black pillows. To make a pillow, shape into an oval, press down

Marking pleats

to flatten slightly and pinch up the four corners. Arrange on the bed using a little sugar glue to secure, making sure that they do not overlap the back of the bed when the headboard is positioned. Very thinly roll out red modelling paste and cut hearts to decorate the black pillows.

5 The figure model is made up in pieces and arranged on the bed. Make the chest area first by shaping a

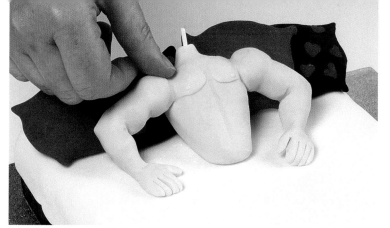

the paintbrush handle across the length, indenting pleats. Turn over, fold over the two ends creating two loops and stick onto the centre. Pinch to shape the bow. Stick in place on the bed; use foam to support inside each loop. Using trimmings, stick a strip on the centre for the knot.

Making the chest and arms

rounded teardrop with 75 g (2½ oz) of flesh-coloured modelling paste, using the full end for the top of his body and the narrower end for his waist. Press down to flatten slightly. Pinch up a neck at the full end. Mark a line down the centre and lines across the stomach using the paintbrush handle. Stick in position on the bed. For pectorals, flatten two large pea-sized amounts of flesh-colour into circles. Stick onto his chest, smoothing up at the tops to blend using icing sugar **(see above)**. Add two tiny oval shapes onto each, using a touch of sugar glue to secure. Push a sugar stick through his neck, leaving half protruding to help hold his head in place.

6 For the arms, split 60 g (2 oz) of flesh-coloured modelling paste in half. To make an arm, roll into a sausage shape and pinch gently one end to round off a hand, and again to narrow the wrist. Press down on the hand to flatten slightly, without indenting. Make a cut for the thumb halfway on one side and pull down. Make three more cuts to separate fingers, push together and stroke to lengthen and bend around. To shape the hand, push the thumb towards the palm from the wrist. Lay the arm down and push in halfway, pinching out at the back to shape the elbow. Indent at the top for a large muscle. Stick in place resting on the pillow and blend in the join. Make the second arm.

7 Make the legs using 115 g (4 oz) of flesh-coloured modelling paste split into two. To make a leg, roll one half into a sausage shape and bend one end for the foot, pinching up gently to shape the heel. Pinch around the ankle to narrow and round off the heel and calf muscle. Cut toes, pinching up the large toe and stroking down the other toes so they curve underneath. Stick onto the bed and press into the arch of the foot to give shape. Make the second leg.

8 Model the head, nose and ears using the remaining flesh-colour. His head is an oval shape, with the face flattened slightly. Model an oval-shaped nose and stick in place lengthways on the centre of his face. The ears are small oval shapes pressed in the centre using the end of a paintbrush. Mark his smile by indenting the circle cutter in at an angle and dimple the corners of his mouth with the tip of a cocktail stick. For eyes, shape two tiny black ovals.

9 To make the bow, first roll out 45 g (1½ oz) of red modelling paste and cut two strips for the two ends measuring 12 x 4 cm (5 x 1½ in) **(see right)**. Indent pleats using the paintbrush handle and arrange across the centre of his body. For the tie, roll out 45 g (1½ oz) and cut a strip 18 x 5 cm (7 x 2 in). Roll

10 For the black bedcover, thinly roll out the remaining black sugarpaste and cut an oblong measuring at least 20 cm (8 in) square. Fold into pleats and arrange over his legs, draping it over the bed and onto the cake board. Thinly roll out the remaining red modelling paste and decorate with heart shapes.

11 Spread the white royal icing over the headboard and stipple using the palette knife. For the carpet, spread the red royal icing over the cake board and stipple as before, taking care that the excess doesn't spill over the edge of the cake board. When the headboard is dry, stick in place using white royal icing.

12 For eyebrows and hair, cut a small hole in the tip of the piping bag and fill with the pale cream/ivory royal icing. Pipe the eyebrows first, but don't make them too heavy. Cut a slightly larger hole in the bag and pipe hair, flicking up a spiked effect on top.

Making the bow

Wet T-shirt

This saucy stunner is perfect for any red-blooded man and an obvious first choice as a quick and easy cake for a last minute celebration. For a bigger party, just make more wet t-shirts and line them up for a competition!

YOU WILL NEED

- 2 x 1 litre (2 pint) bowl-shaped sponge cakes (see page 11)
- 30 x 35 cm (12 x 14 in) oblong cake board
- 450 g /1 lb/2 c buttercream (see page 8)
- Icing (confectioners') sugar in a sugar shaker

SUGARPASTE *(see page 9)*

- 1.25 kg (2 lb 12 oz) flesh-colour (golden brown/ivory with a touch of pink)
- 650 g (1 lb 7 oz) white

- Sugar glue and paintbrush
- Golden brown/ivory food colouring

EQUIPMENT

- Plain-bladed kitchen knife
- Large rolling pin
- Cake smoother
- Serrated carving knife
- Palette knife
- Medium paintbrush

1 Trim the crust from each cake, levelling the tops. Cut a layer in each cake and sandwich back together with buttercream, and then spread a thin layer over the surface as a crumb coat using the palette knife.

2 To shape the chest and stomach area, press a 200 g (7 oz) ball of flesh-coloured sugarpaste onto the centre of the cake board and roll out using the rolling pin so the edges are level with the surface of the cake board, leaving the centre slightly dome-shaped. Spread the underside of each cake with buttercream. Position on the cake board **(see below)**.

Buttercreamed cakes

3 Using a sprinkling of icing sugar, roll out the remaining flesh-coloured sugarpaste, moving the paste around after each roll to prevent sticking. Cover the cake and board completely, smoothing around the shape and stretching out pleats. Trim the excess from around the edge of the

cake board. Using trimmings, stick two pea-sized amounts onto each boob using a little sugar glue.

4 To make the t-shirt, thinly roll out the white sugarpaste and cover the cake up to the top of each boob, smoothing and stretching out pleats as before. Deeply score the white sugarpaste and pull gently away. If required, stick the t-shirt to the flesh sugarpaste using a little sugar glue. Trim excess from the cake board edge and smooth with your fingers.

Cutting the neckline

5 Using your hands, smooth fabric effect pleats onto the stomach area. Roll out trimmings and cut thin strips to edge the neckline and to make straps. To give the t-shirt a wet look, dilute a little golden brown colouring with a few drops of water until translucent. Using the paintbrush, paint a little colour, highlighting areas and along each fabric effect pleat.

Templates

All templates are 100% actual size.

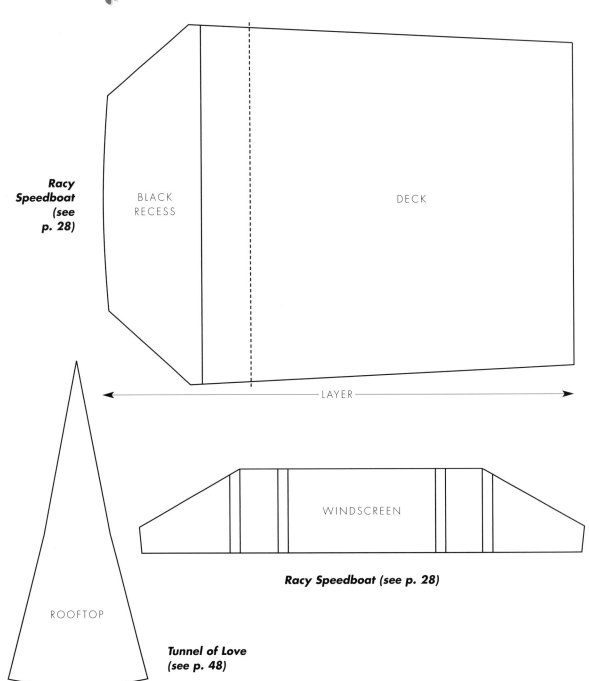

Racy Speedboat (see p. 28)

BLACK RECESS

DECK

LAYER

WINDSCREEN

Racy Speedboat (see p. 28)

ROOFTOP

Tunnel of Love (see p. 48)

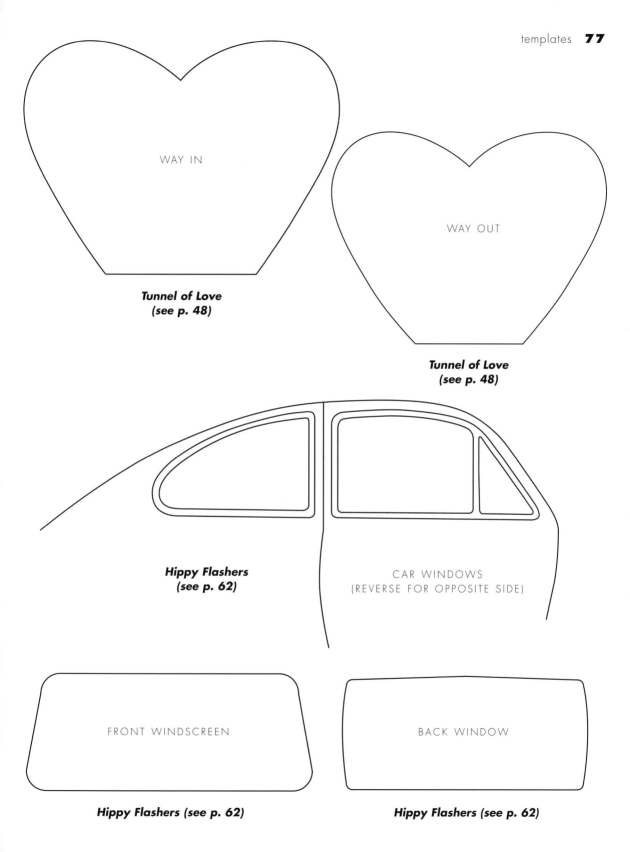

WAY IN

WAY OUT

Tunnel of Love
(see p. 48)

Tunnel of Love
(see p. 48)

Hippy Flashers
(see p. 62)

CAR WINDOWS
(REVERSE FOR OPPOSITE SIDE)

FRONT WINDSCREEN

BACK WINDOW

Hippy Flashers (see p. 62)

Hippy Flashers (see p. 62)

Suppliers and useful addresses

UK

The British Sugarcraft Guild
Wellington House
Messeter Place
London SE9 5DP
Tel: 020 8859 6943

The Cake Makers Depot
57 The Tything
Worcester WR1 1JT
Tel: 01905 25468

Confectionery Supplies
29-31 Lower Cathedral Road
Cardiff CF1 6LU
Tel: 029 2037 2161
Also outlets in Bristol, Hereford and Swansea

Culpitt Ltd
Jubilee Industrial Estate
Ashington NE63 8UB
Tel: 01670 814545
Website: www.culpitt.com
Freephone enquiry line:
0845 601 0574
Distributor of cake decorations, telephone for your nearest retail outlet

Jane Asher Party Cakes
24 Cale Street
London SW3 3QU
Tel: 020 7584 6177
Fax: 020 7584 6179
Website: www.jane-asher.co.uk

Kit Box
1 Fernlea Gardens
Easton in Gordano
Bristol BS20 0JF
Tel/Fax: 01275 374557

London Sugarart Centre
12 Selkirk Road
London SW17 0ES
Tel: 020 8767 8558
Fax: 020 8767 9939

Orchard Products
51 Hallyburton Road
Hove
East Sussex BN3 7GP
Tel: 01273 419418
Fax: 01273 412512

Pipedreams
2 Bell Lane
Eton Wick
Berkshire
Tel: 01753 865682

Renshaw Scott Ltd
229 Crown Street
Liverpool L8 7RF
Tel: 0151 706 8200
Websites: www.renshawscott.co.uk
or www.supercook.co.uk

Squire's Kitchen
Squire's House
3 Waverley Lane
Farnham
Surrey GU9 8BB
Tel: 01252 711749
Fax: 01252 714714
Website: www.squires-group.co.uk
Courses in cake decoration and sugarcraft
Online shop for specialist sugarcraft
products: www.squires-shop.com

Sugar Daddy's
No. 1 Fisher's Yard
Market Square
St. Neot's
Cambridgeshire PE19 2AF

NEW ZEALAND

Chocolate Boutique
3/27 Mokoia Road
Birkenhead
Auckland
Tel: (09) 419 2450

Decor Cakes Ltd
Victoria Arcade
435 Great South Road
Otahuhu
Auckland
Tel: (09) 276 6676

Golden Bridge Marketing Wholesale Ltd
8 Te Kea Place
Albany
Auckland
Tel: (09) 415 8777
www.goldenbridge.co.nz

Innovations Specialty Cookware & Gifts
52 Mokoia Road
Birkenhead
Auckland
Tel: (09) 480 8885

Milly's Kitchen Shop
273 Ponsonby Road
Ponsonby
Auckland
Tel: (09) 376 1550
www.millyskitchen.co.nz

Spotlight
(branches throughout New Zealand)
Wairau Park, 19 Link Drive
Glenfield
Auckland
Tel: (09) 444 0220
www.spotlightonline.co.nz

SOUTH AFRICA

The Baking Tin
52 Belvedere Road
Claremont
7700
Cape Town
Tel: (021) 671 6434

South Bakels
55 Section Street
Paarden Eiland
7420
Cape Town
Tel: (021) 511 1381

Confectionery Extravaganza
Shop 48, Flora Centre
Ontdekkers Road
Florida, West Rand
1724
Johannesburg
Tel: (011) 672 4766

South Bakels
235 Main Road
Martindale
2092
Johannesburg
Tel: (011) 673 2100

Party's, Crafts and Cake Decor
Shop 4, East Rand Mall
Rietfontein Road
Boksburg
1459
Johannesburg
Tel: (011) 823 1988

Chocolate Den
Shop 35, Glendower Shopping Centre
99 Linksfield Road
Glendower
Edenvale
1609
Johannesburg
Tel: (011) 453 8160

Jem Cutters
128 Crompton Street
Pinetown
3610
Durban
Tel: (031) 701 1431
Fax: (031) 701 0559

South Bakels
19 Henry van Rooijen Street
Bloemfontein 9301
Tel: (051) 432 8446

AUSTRALIA

Cake Art Supplies
Kiora Mall
Shop 26 Kiora Rd
MIRANDA
NSW 2228
Tel: (02) 9540 3483

Hollywood Cake Decorations
52 Beach St
KOGARAH
NSW 2217
Tel: (02) 9587 1533

Susie Q
Shop 4/372
Keilor Rd
NIDDRIE
VIC 3042
Tel:(03) 9379 2275

Cake and Icing Centre
651 Samford Rd
MITCHELTON
QLD 4053
Tel: (07) 3355 3443

Petersen's Cake Decorations
370 Cnr South St and Stockdale Rd
OCONNOR
WA 6163
Tel: (08) 9337 9636

Gum Nut Cake and Craft Supplies
SORELL
TAS 7172
Tel: (03) 6265 1463

THE NETHERLANDS

Planet Cake
Dordtselaan 67-69
3081 BG
Rotterdam
Tel: (010) 290 9130

SOUTH AMERICA

Planet Cake
Boloarte Comercio Importacao Ltda
Rue Haddock Lobo
130 - Tijuca
Rio de Janeiro
Brazil
CEP 20260-132
Tel: (55-21) 2273-1922

NORTH AMERICA

Maid of Scandinavia
3244 Raleigh Avenue
Minneapolis
MN 55416

Wilton Enterprises Inc.
2240 West 75th Street
Woodridge
IL 60517

Home Cake Artistry Inc.
1002 North Central
Suite 511
Richardson
TX 75080

Creative Tools Ltd.
3 Tannery Court
Richmond Hill
Ontario L4C 7V5
Canada

Index

The Author and Publisher would like to thank Renshaw Scott Ltd for supplying the Regalice sugarpaste used throughout the book.

For details of sugarcraft tuition, see www.debbiebrownscakes.co.uk